WILL ROGERS

WILL ROGERS

A Political Life

RICHARD D. WHITE, JR.

TEXAS TECH UNIVERSITY PRESS

This book is typeset in Monotype Walbaum. The paper used in this book meets the minimum requirements of ANSI/NISO Z39.48–1992 (R1997). ∞

FRONTISPIECE: *Will Rogers*, a painting by Leon Gordon

Library of Congress Cataloging-in-Publication Data
White, Richard D. (Richard Downing), 1945–
   Will Rogers : a political life / Richard D. White, Jr.
       p. cm.
   Includes bibliographical references and index.
   Summary: "A political biography of Will Rogers; argues that not only
was Rogers the nation's most popular humorist, he was also his era's foremost political critic.
Presents Rogers in a previously unexplored light: that of a true political insider with the
power to shape public opinion and ultimately alter public policy"—Provided by publisher.
   ISBN 978-0-89672-676-5 (hardcover : alk. paper)
   1. Rogers, Will, 1879–1935. 2. Rogers, Will, 1879–1935—Political activity.
3. Entertainers—United States—Biography. 4. Humorists, American—Biography. I. Title.
   PN2287.R74W45 2011
   792.702'8092—dc22
   [B]   2010044608

Printed in the United States of America
11 12 13 14 15 16 17 18 19 / 9 8 7 6 5 4 3 2

Texas Tech University Press | Box 41037 | Lubbock, Texas 79409–1037 USA
800.832.4042 | ttup@ttu.edu | www.ttupress.org

Jesters do oft prove prophets.
King Lear, V, iii, l. 73

CONTENTS

Contents

Illustrations

Abbreviations

BG   Boston Globe

CA   *Convention Articles of Will Rogers.* Ed. Joseph A. Stout, Jr., and Peter C. Rollins. Stillwater: Oklahoma State University Press, 1976.

Chron   Unpublished chronology, Will Rogers Memorial Museum, Claremore, Oklahoma.

DAB   *Dictionary of American Biography.* New York: Charles Scribner's Sons, 1995.

DO   Daily Oklahoman, Oklahoma City

DT 1   *Will Rogers' Daily Telegrams.* Vol. 1, *The Coolidge Years: 1926–1929.* Ed. James M. Smallwood and Steven K. Gragert. Stillwater: Oklahoma State University Press, 1978.

DT 2   *Will Rogers' Daily Telegrams.* Vol. 2, *The Hoover Years: 1929–1931.* Ed. James M. Smallwood and Steven K. Gragert. Stillwater: Oklahoma State University Press, 1978.

DT 3   *Will Rogers' Daily Telegrams.* Vol. 3, *The Hoover Years: 1931–1933.* Ed. James M. Smallwood and Steven K. Gragert. Stillwater: Oklahoma State University Press, 1979.

DT 4   *Will Rogers' Daily Telegrams.* Vol. 4, *The Roosevelt Years: 1933–1935.* Ed. James M. Smallwood and Steven K. Gragert. Stillwater: Oklahoma State University Press, 1978.

EMJR   *Ether and Me or "Just Relax."* Will Rogers. 1929. Reprint, New York: G. P. Putnam's Sons, 1930.

EWB   *Encyclopedia of World Biography.* 17 vols. Detroit: Gale Research, 1998.

HCTR   *"He Chews to Run": Will Rogers' Life Magazine Articles, 1928.* Ed. Steven K. Gragert. Stillwater: Oklahoma State University Press, 1982.

HTBF   *"How to Be Funny" and Other Writings of Will Rogers.* Ed. Steven K. Gragert. Stillwater: Oklahoma State University Press, 1983.

ID   *The Illiterate Digest.* Will Rogers. New York: A. L. Burt Company, 1924.

LAT   *Los Angeles Times*

LSMD   *Letters of a Self-Made Diplomat to His President.* Will Rogers. 1926. Reprint. Ed. Joseph A. Stout, Jr., et al. Stillwater: Oklahoma State University Press, 1977.

ML   *More Letters of a Self-Made Diplomat.* Will Rogers. Ed. Steven K. Gragert. Stillwater: Oklahoma State University Press, 1982.

NYA   *New York American*

NYH   *New York Herald*

NYS   *New York Sun*

NYT   *New York Times*

OCT   *Oklahoma City Times*

PWR 1   *The Papers of Will Rogers.* Vol. 1, *The Early Years: November 1879– April 1904.* Ed. Arthur Frank Wertheim and Barbara Bair. Norman: University of Oklahoma Press, 1996.

PWR 2   *The Papers of Will Rogers.* Vol. 2, *Wild West to Vaudeville: April 1904– September 1908.* Ed. Arthur Frank Wertheim and Barbara Bair. Norman: University of Oklahoma Press, 2000.

PWR 3   *The Papers of Will Rogers.* Vol. 3, *From Vaudeville to Broadway: September 1908–August 1915.* Ed. Arthur Frank Wertheim and Barbara Bair. Norman: University of Oklahoma Press, 2001.

PWR 4   *The Papers of Will Rogers.* Vol. 4, *From the Broadway Stage to the National Stage: September 1915–July 1928.* Ed. Steven K. Gragert and M. Jane Johansson. Norman: University of Oklahoma Press, 2005.

PWR 5   *The Papers of Will Rogers.* Vol. 5, *The Final Years: August 1928–August 1935.* Ed. Steven K. Gragert and M. Jane Johansson. Norman: University of Oklahoma Press, 2006.

RB   *Radio Broadcasts of Will Rogers.* Ed. Steven K. Gragert. Stillwater: Oklahoma State University Press, 1983.

SEP   *Saturday Evening Post*

TNBSR   *There's Not a Bathing Suit in Russia and Other Bare Facts.* Will Rogers. 1927. Reprint. Ed. Joseph A. Stout, Jr. Stillwater: Oklahoma State University Press, 1973.

TDW   *Tulsa Daily World*

WA 1   *Will Rogers' Weekly Articles.* Vol. 1, *The Harding/Coolidge Years: 1922–1925.* Ed. James M. Smallwood and Steven K. Gragert. Stillwater: Oklahoma State University Press, 1980.

WA 2   *Will Rogers' Weekly Articles.* Vol. 2, *The Coolidge Years: 1925–1927.* Ed. James M. Smallwood and Steven K. Gragert. Stillwater: Oklahoma State University Press, 1980.

WA 3   *Will Rogers' Weekly Articles.* Vol. 3, *The Coolidge Years: 1927–1929.* Ed. James M. Smallwood and Steven K. Gragert. Stillwater: Oklahoma State University Press, 1981.

WA 4   *Will Rogers' Weekly Articles.* Vol. 4, *The Hoover Years: 1929–1931.* Ed. James M. Smallwood and Steven K. Gragert. Stillwater: Oklahoma State University Press, 1981.

WA 5   *Will Rogers' Weekly Articles.* Vol. 5, *The Hoover Years: 1931–1933.* Ed. James M. Smallwood and Steven K. Gragert. Stillwater: Oklahoma State University Press, 1982.

WA 6   *Will Rogers' Weekly Articles.* Vol. 6, *The Roosevelt Years: 1933–1935.* Ed. James M. Smallwood and Steven K. Gragert. Stillwater: Oklahoma State University Press, 1982.

WP   *Washington Post*

WRM   Will Rogers Memorial Museum, Claremore, Oklahoma.

INTRODUCTION

A Voice of Political Stability

———

WHEN WILL ROGERS stepped off the train in Mukden, Manchuria, in December 1931, the temperature was thirty below zero, so frighteningly cold and painful that he gasped for a moment, struggling to breathe.[1] Trembling before an arctic wind that sliced through his thin overcoat, Rogers glanced around the station, noticing dozens of Japanese soldiers standing guard, bayoneted rifles slung over their shoulders. The brutal weather, the hostile-looking soldiers, and the gray-drab landscape created a dreary scene for Rogers, who, carrying only a small red suitcase in one hand and a portable typewriter in the other, was lonely, homesick, and six thousand miles away from sunny California where his family was spending Christmas without him.

Rogers had come to a foreboding and dangerous place. Just a few weeks before, twenty thousand Japanese troops had suddenly stormed across the Korean border into Manchuria, captured the city of Mukden, and routed the defending Chinese army. With the rest of the world, Rogers feared the conflict would erupt into a major war, for the Far East was filled with quarreling nations, each trying to dominate the region. American policy makers believed the Japanese had other hostile intentions besides invading Manchuria and might expand their aggression to new areas, particularly the vulnerable U.S.-held Philippines. In the long run the fears proved true. The

Manchurian attack was a harbinger of World War II, with fighting in the region continuing to rage back and forth until the Japanese surrendered to the Allies in 1945.

By the time Rogers arrived in Mukden the Chinese army had fled the city, but some fighting still took place. The Japanese military ordered martial law throughout city, commandeering government offices, railways, telegraphs, banks, and major industries and plundering the homes of wealthy Chinese. Traveling about the city, Rogers could not ignore the military efficiency and hardened discipline of the Japanese troops. "Don't you let anyone tell you these little Japanese are not soldiers," he wrote at the time. "They fight, and will be hard to lick."[2]

What was Will Rogers doing in Mukden? Then fifty-two years old, he was America's most popular entertainer, but in remote northeast China he was just another foreigner, recognized only by American war correspondents trying to stay warm in a crowded Chinese hotel. There were no vaudeville audiences he could entertain or radio stations from which to broadcast his folksy humor, and even if there had been, there was nothing funny for him to talk about in Manchuria in 1931.

Why had the American humorist traveled thousands of miles to one of the most remote parts of Asia in the dead of winter and in the middle of a war zone? Was he traveling to Manchuria as a newspaper columnist to give his readers a firsthand view of a little-known part of the world and to cover a bitter conflict that few back in America truly understood? Or did his visit have a more official and serious purpose, one sanctioned by top-level American policy makers who drafted him to act as an "ambassador without portfolio" whose mission was to observe the crisis personally and report back to them? If Rogers was indeed traveling at the request of U.S. government officials, then his visit to the Manchurian war zone suggests he may have played a larger, more influential role in the American political arena. If so, it is a role that many historians and biographers have ignored or overlooked but nevertheless deserves recognition and deeper study.

Rogers never revealed the exact reason he made the harrowing winter trip to Manchuria. A few weeks before he departed, however, Secretary of War Patrick Hurley had visited him at his California ranch. Hurley, a close friend of Rogers, was returning from the Philippines and also was concerned about

Rogers with performers at the Kabuki Theatre, Tokyo, Japan, December 1931

Japanese intentions in the Far East. Soon after the two men met, Rogers decided to head there. Many who learned of his trip, including the Japanese, believed he traveled to Manchuria for more serious business than entertaining people. He heightened suspicions when he met with the Japanese minister of war in Tokyo, then traveled across the front lines of the war zone to meet with Japanese and Chinese military commanders, including a Manchurian warlord. Suspicions about Rogers's true purpose continued after he returned to the United States and went immediately to Washington DC, where he met in private for several hours with President Hoover and Secretary Hurley.

———

WHEN WILL ROGERS arrived in Manchuria during the winter of 1931, he was one of America's best-known public figures and the nation's foremost political commentator and social critic. From just before World War I, through the Jazz Age, Prohibition, the Great Depression, and up until his tragic death in 1935, his humor captivated the nation and the world. Millions of Americans looked upon him as one of their most loved and trusted friends, and to many he was regarded as family. His popularity was unbounded. During the last two years of his life he was the top male box-office attraction at the movies, one of the most widely read newspaper columnists, and a radio commentator with an audience of over sixty million.[3] For over a decade, he produced a remarkable outpouring of commentary—666 weekly newspaper columns, 2,817 daily newspaper articles, 69 radio broadcasts, 71 movies, and six books.[4] (His grammar and spelling are reproduced in this book's quotations.) Every morning in drugstores and barbershops across the nation, men reading their papers glanced up at their friends and asked, "Did you read what Will had to say today?"

Rogers had an amazing entertainment career, but he was much more than just a talented humorist. He was the most incisive political commentator of his era who, beneath his humor, provided his countrymen a critically honest appraisal of American politics and world affairs. Few men touched the American moral and political conscience more deeply than Rogers. His astute observations, his ability to go straight to the heart of the matter and then put that into words that resonated with his listeners, propelled him to a level of influence unequaled in American history. When the witty one-liners are stripped away from Rogers's message, a sobering and powerful view of his political clout appears. A closer look at whom he met, where he traveled, and the subjects of his writings and speeches reveals not so much a comedian but a true political insider with the power to shape public opinion and ultimately influence public policy.

Rogers's insights are as pertinent today as when he made them. His biting critiques of political corruption, crime, international disputes, economic hardship, and other challenges to society remain timeless. Indeed, his

Rogers pounds out his daily column

reportage seems clearer, more direct, and closer to the truth than today's news coverage, for he did not worry about being politically correct nor did he attempt to give his audience a "fair and balanced" analysis. In one of his first newspaper articles, he promised his readers only the truth, pledging to "lay my chips a little different. . . . I am going to take a shot at the whole works myself, and I want it to go as she lays."[5]

Unfortunately, history has done a disservice to Will Rogers by frequently painting him in caricature as a hayseed cowboy comedian. Scholars and biographers rarely recognize his impact upon the political scene, discounting his influence because of his humorous routine, bucolic and innocent demeanor, lack of formal education, and Native American heritage. But some truly exceptional men such as Will Durant, George Bernard Shaw, H. L. Mencken, Bernard Baruch, and Carl Sandburg saw through Rogers's homespun façade, each recognizing his true brilliance and power to influence public opinion and policy, each recognizing Rogers as a savvy commentator, well read, and the possessor of a keen knowledge of human nature. Like others who knew him well, they saw a streak of genius behind his beguiling grin.

Rogers was always on the go, whether making whistle-stops across the country on his popular lecture tours or trekking his way across Asia or South America. He circled the globe three times and was on his fourth circumnavigation when he died. He seemed to perform everywhere, from a one-horse saloon stage in Butte, Montana, to New York's Carnegie Hall, to Berlin's Wintergarten. As he traveled the world, he stopped everywhere to talk with people, from poor dirt farmers to millionaire tycoons to heads of state, entertaining kings and queens and befriending every president from Theodore Roosevelt, whose family delighted at his rope tricks on the White House lawn, to Franklin Roosevelt, whom he openly supported. He toured the country with cabinet officers, lunched with senators in the Capitol dining room, ate chili with migrant workers in dirt-floor cantinas, and struggled with chopsticks when eating with a Chinese warlord. He spent a week touring Mexico with that country's president, argued politics with Italian dictator Benito Mussolini, and was received by Pope Pius XI. His huge and diverse circle of friends included William Jennings Bryan, John Nance Garner, Charles Lindbergh, the Prince of Wales, Samuel Gompers, Lady Astor, Al Smith, Thomas Edison, Huey Long, and General Billy Mitchell. His humor tickled everyone. Millionaire John D. Rockefeller delighted when Rogers poked fun at him, while the poor and downtrodden, including inmates at New York's Sing Sing prison, welcomed his penchant for defending the underdog and attacking social injustice.

Rogers loved his fellow man, and when he said he never met a man he didn't like, he meant it. But he also mistrusted mankind and the modern monoliths of government, bureaucracy, and large corporations. He defended democracy but put little faith in the political or economic systems of his day to actually improve the lot of the common man. He thought politicians were the lowest of life forms, yet he befriended almost every politician he met. He decried corruption yet expressed sympathy for individuals found guilty of it. He feared extremist organizations, from the Ku Klux Klan to the Communist Party, yet he could share a cup of coffee with their members.

Rogers on one of his
many visits to
Washington DC

Immensely popular and trusted by millions, Rogers gained the public's permission to poke fun in unprecedented ways at the president, Congress, and American governance. Early in his stage career and just before America entered World War I, he stood in front of Woodrow Wilson and jokingly criticized the president for his naïve pacifism and reluctance to arm the nation. At the time, it was unheard of—indeed, unpatriotic—for a comedian to make fun of a president, question his official policy, or broach touchy political subjects. But to Rogers's relief, Wilson laughed heartily and took the barbs in stride. By successfully criticizing a president face-to-face, Rogers paved the way for not only his own unique brand of seriocomedy, but also for dozens of political satirists who continue to follow in his footsteps.

Using comic exaggeration and ludicrous comparisons, Rogers dissected the democratic process, defending it staunchly but exposing flaws when he found them. He admitted that American democracy was not perfect, but added, "that as bad as we sometimes think our government is run, it's the best run one I ever saw."[6] He used poignant comic devices to unmask political rhetoric, reveal hypocrisy, and thrash out controversial subjects that otherwise would have offended his audiences. Overall, he convinced America that performing political humor was not merely good entertainment but served an essential public service and, in the long run, actually strengthened democracy.[7]

Rogers offered the American people a refreshing appraisal of current events and public policy. It was through him that millions formed their opinion of President Wilson's quest for a League of Nations, debated freedom of speech and religion during the Scopes Monkey Trial, questioned the success of several disarmament conferences, took pity upon the sufferers of the Great Flood of 1927, and tried to grasp the awful reality of the Great Depression. Rogers was remarkably prescient, concluding years before the stock market crash of 1929 that the American people were living beyond their means. He condemned the free spending, licentiousness, and Babbittry of the Roaring Twenties, fearing that overspeculation would eventually breed economic havoc. Seven years before the Japanese attack that thrust America into World War II, he traveled to Hawaii where he warned of the vulnerability of American forces. He was one of the first to recognize the rise of fascist and Nazi threats in Italy and Germany. An isolationist at heart but not a pacifist, he demanded the country rearm and modernize its military.

During the turbulent Depression years, Rogers was a voice of political stability when radicals from both sides of the political spectrum vied for power. He distrusted political extremes, including the right-wing tirades of Father Charles Coughlin, the left-wing panaceas of Huey Long and Upton Sinclair, and even the naïve idealism of Wilsonian Democrats. Herbert Hoover, acknowledging the valuable role Rogers played during the Depression, told a radio audience that Rogers's humorous political observations "provided a safety valve for public anger and fear" and that he had "a great understanding of the background of public events." Franklin Roosevelt agreed, saying, "above all things, in a time grown too solemn and sober, he brought his countrymen back to a sense of proportion."[8]

As Rogers's popularity rose during the 1920s and into the 1930s, so did his political influence. With his huge audience, he possessed an immense power to arouse and shape public opinion. "It is claimed his satirical shafts could accomplish any object aimed at," the *Toledo Times* concluded in 1923.[9] If Rogers told the American people to write their congressman about certain legislation, thousands of letters flooded the Capitol. Senators and congressmen sought his support on pending legislation, for they knew a few positive words in his newspaper column or on his Sunday radio show could be life or death to a bill. By March 1925 five of his weekly columns had been read into the *Congressional Record.* He visited Washington frequently to attend congressional sessions, testify at hearings, meet with cabinet officers, attend official receptions, and speak at the exclusive Gridiron and Alfalfa clubs. His open access to the Oval Office, the Senate cloak room, and other inner sancta of national power was unmatched for someone not holding public office.

Rogers did not back away from controversy, taking firm stands on the critical issues of his day. He fought for religious tolerance and freedom of speech, supported government subsidies to boost aviation, struggled to abolish child labor, sympathized with the World War I veterans who marched on Washington demanding a bonus, and argued that the U.S. grant the Philippines independence. While he generally supported every president he encountered, he did not hesitate to speak up when he opposed their policies. He openly disagreed with Coolidge on farm relief and a veterans' bonus, with Harding on the protective tariff and disarmament, and with Franklin Roosevelt on U.S. participation in the World Court, intervention in Cuba, and New Deal policies that drifted toward a welfare state.

Rogers's impact upon public policy was usually subtle and disguised in humor, but he could be devastatingly direct when angered at injustice, often stepping into the political fray to argue for change. Although he seldom drank, he believed Prohibition was not only a hypocritical joke but a disastrous mistake, and his persistent hammering at the Volstead Act played no small part in convincing the American people to favor repeal in 1933. After helping to deliver aid to refugees from the Great Flood of 1927, he appeared before a congressional committee to lobby for more effective flood control measures. By refusing to endorse Upton Sinclair for governor of California, he may have caused the socialist writer to lose a close election. His harsh opposition to U.S. involvement in the World Court helped spur the U.S.

Will Rogers (1879–1935)

Senate to deny membership in that body. An expert on world aviation who flew often and crusaded for aviation progress, he lobbied for safer planes, more trained pilots, and the latest navigation equipment, and, with the exceptions of Charles Lindbergh and Billy Mitchell, did more than any other American to promote civilian aviation as a safe, reliable, and efficient mode of transportation and argue that a modern, large military air force would be essential in future wars.

Presidents Theodore Roosevelt, Woodrow Wilson, Calvin Coolidge, Herbert Hoover, and Franklin Roosevelt all recognized Rogers's ability to sway public opinion and, each in his own way, turned to him to help their cause. Rogers was certainly not a spy and there are no mentions of him as a source of foreign intelligence, but as an unofficial ambassador he provided another set of sharp eyes and keen ears for the U.S. government.[10] The Coolidge administration asked him to travel to Mexico to help mend diplomatic relations with that country. During Hoover's tenure and just seven months before his trip to the Manchurian war zone, he traveled to Nicaragua to help after an earthquake devastated that country. When Hoover made a nationwide radio broadcast calling for public support to combat the Depression, he asked only one other person to join him on the radio—Will Rogers.

By the early 1930s, as the Great Depression dragged on and Franklin Roosevelt entered the White House, Rogers's influence was most profound. In dozens of newspaper columns, radio broadcasts, and lectures, he endorsed the president's monetary policies, relief programs, regulation of big business, high income taxes on the rich, large-scale deficit spending, and efforts to provide jobs through public works. As Rogers became increasingly prominent in public affairs, congressmen complained he influenced lawmaking and a false rumor spread that he wrote some of Roosevelt's speeches. When the president began his Sunday evening fireside chats on nationwide radio in 1933, several of the broadcasts were immediately preceded by Rogers's live radio show, on which he previewed what the president was going to say and urged the public to support him. Other than Franklin Roosevelt himself, Rogers possibly did more than any other American to convince the public to accept the overall New Deal.

THERE HAS NEVER BEEN an American entertainer, before or since, who has wielded more serious political influence than Will Rogers. So, the question remains: How could a part-Cherokee who dropped out of tenth grade become the foremost political critic of his era? It was a very unlikely journey for him to rise to the pinnacle of entertainment and journalism and indeed, to become a political force himself. That amazing journey began modestly a half century before, thousands of miles from Manchuria, on a dusty ranch in the Indian Territory of the American West.

WILL ROGERS

ONE

———•━•••━———

A Funny Man Turns Serious

WILL ROGERS liked to brag that he was born on Tuesday, November 4, 1879, Election Day. For the next fifty-five years, politics would be an ever-increasing part of his life. Rogers was raised on his family ranch four miles from where the small town of Oologah would be settled a few years later in the Cherokee Nation, a vast tract of Indian Territory that became part of the new state of Oklahoma in 1907. When Rogers was a boy, Oologah's one dusty street was lined with a train depot, a two-story frame hotel, a livery stable, a lone church that served as the school, a few clapboard buildings with rickety plank sidewalks in front, and reeking stock pens. There was not a tree in sight.[1]

The rolling prairie surrounding Oologah was an unlikely place to produce one of the country's most penetrating political wits, but politics came naturally to Rogers. He inherited much of his savvy from his father, Clement Vann Rogers, a blustery and loud former Confederate cavalry officer. One of the most influential men in the Indian Territory, Clem served on various boards and commissions, became a district judge in 1877, and two years later was elected senator of the Cherokee Nation.[2] A Jeffersonian Democrat who backed William Jennings Bryan for president in 1896, Clem advocated many

Clem Rogers (father)   *Mary America Rogers (mother)*

Progressive reforms such as initiative and referendum, a popularly elected railroad commission, and state control of primary elections, but opposed women's suffrage. As a former slave owner he defended racial segregation.

Over the years, Clem became a wealthy man by buying cattle in neighboring states, fattening them up on the lush, belly-deep bluestem grasses growing wild near the Verdigris River, and selling them for a fair profit in the Kansas City and St. Louis markets.[3] Prospering, he built a big two-story house from heavy walnut logs cut from the nearby river bottom, with a whitewashed portico covering the front entrance and two wide stone chimneys standing at each end of the house. It was in this house that Will Rogers was born.[4]

Will always took pride that his father and mother, Mary America Schrimsher Rogers, were about one-fourth Cherokee Indian.[5] Mary, a tall, thin woman with dark hair, sparkling black eyes, and a "tongue quick as a jaybird's wing," grew up in a well-off family and studied music at a Cherokee female seminary.[6] Will inherited his mother's gay spirits and her love of jokes, singing, dancing, and meeting with kinfolk. The family valued educa-

Cadet Rogers at military school

tion, and the parents encouraged their children to read. Clem was one of a few residents of the Territory who subscribed to the *New York Times.*[7]

Young Will was a funny, homely little boy with mischievous blue-gray eyes, a big smile always on his mug, and a lock of brown hair forever flopping down into his face. When he turned seven, Clem sent him to a one-room school near Chelsea, about twelve miles from home. He attended several schools over the next few years, earning mediocre grades and rebelling against his piano lessons.

In January 1897, Clem enrolled Will in the Kemper Military School in Boonville, Missouri. The boy could not have been more out of place when he arrived, his schoolmates wearing neat gray military cadet uniforms while Will walked into the barracks wearing his Stetson hat, a flaming red flannel shirt, red bandanna knotted at the throat, and high-heeled red-topped boots with jingling spurs.[8] From the first day, he refused to adapt to the military regime, piling up demerits for being late to formation, wearing an unkempt uniform, and spouting wisecracks at upperclassmen. His grades were barely passable, although he showed an interest in political economy and received a perfect 100 in American history.[9]

Fed up with school, Rogers ran away from Kemper in the spring of 1898, heading to Texas's northeast panhandle to work as a cowhand on a thirteen-thousand-acre ranch. The ranch owner, Perry Ewing, was a great reader and kept up with politics. Rogers shared his interest and devoured the owner's *Kansas City Star* and *Wichita Eagle* each day. When Rogers read that the Spanish-American War had erupted, he rode eighty miles to Amarillo and tried to enlist in the Rough Riders but, only eighteen, was turned down for being too young.[10] After making one long cattle drive, he moved back to Oologah to manage his father's ranch and raise his own herd of steers.

Rogers quickly tired of running the ranch. Managing a small herd of cattle, a few hogs, and farming fields of wheat, corn, and oats did not satisfy his desire for more money or his need to explore the wide-open plains. He occasionally left the ranch to deliver cattle to market or to compete in roping contests, but these diversions neither cured his wanderlust nor filled his empty pockets.

In March 1902 Rogers announced he was going to South America to enter the cattle business. He had heard stories that Argentina was a cattle rancher's paradise, with endless, wide-open pampas of fertile grasslands, and was determined to go there and try his luck. He sold his cattle and all the feed to his father for three thousand dollars and a few days later caught the train out of Oologah, headed for New Orleans, and took a steamer to New York City.[11] Unable to book passage to South America from New York, he sailed to England where departures were more frequent. After arriving in Southampton, he toured London, visiting Parliament, Buckingham Palace, and Westminster Abbey—never dreaming he someday would return there as a celebrity and entertain English heads of state. After ten days in England, he boarded a Royal Mail steamer for South America. Following stops in France, Spain, Portugal, the Cape Verde Islands, and Brazil, he arrived in Buenos Aires on May 5.[12] He had been gone from Oologah for two months.

To find work on a ranch, Rogers traveled five hundred miles into the Argentine interior. He found it to be a "beautiful country with a fine climate," but his hopes of building his own cattle empire soon were dashed. Wages for gaucho cowhands were pitiful, about five dollars a month, and his inability to speak Spanish made finding a job more difficult. "I'm trying to learn," he wrote home. "I think I can say 6 words, did know 7 and forgot one."[13]

Rogers left Argentina, signing on a tramp steamer as a stockherder tending the ship's cargo of cattle, mules, and sheep. After three weeks of seasickness, he landed in Durban, South Africa, around September 1.[14] He worked on a ranch for two months, then took a job driving a herd of mules 250 miles to the town of Ladysmith. When he arrived he saw a poster advertising Texas Jack's Wild West Show and wandered over to look for a job as a cowhand. When he met Texas Jack, the circus owner asked him if he knew how to throw the "big whirl" by spinning an eighty-foot loop of rope in a huge circle. When Rogers said he could, Texas Jack hired him for twenty dollars a week to do rope tricks and ride bucking horses.[15]

Dubbed the "Cherokee Kid," Rogers toured South Africa with the show, each week improving his act to where he could throw two ropes at once, one in each hand, and catch a horse and rider simultaneously. According to the circus program, he became so skilled with his lariat that he could "lasso the tail off a blowfly."[16]

In August 1903 Rogers quit Texas Jack's show and headed for Australia to join a circus touring the coastal cities and outback and later the towns of New Zealand. Dressed in an outrageous tight-fitting, red-velvet, gold-trimmed Mexican cowboy outfit, the "Cherokee Kid" became an instant hit with the Aussies and Kiwis. But eight months down under was enough for the homesick Rogers. By the time the New Zealand tour ended, he had saved enough money for third-class passage from Auckland to San Francisco. Arriving so broke that he was wearing "overalls instead of underpants," he hopped an east-bound freight train, sharing a car with a load of live chickens.[17] When he arrived in Oklahoma in April 1904, he "smelled mightily fowl."[18]

For Rogers, his two-year, fifty-thousand-mile trip around the world provided much more than an extended tour. It was an eye-opening education, a chance to absorb knowledge and form impressions of distant places and people. Everywhere he went he soaked up the culture. He tramped Bourbon Street in New Orleans, was dazzled by the lights of New York's Broadway, visited the sights of London, and roamed the vast ranges of Argentina. During

The Cherokee Kid

his journeys to Australia and New Zealand he discovered his unique talent for entertaining people. A changed young man returned to Oologah, Indian Territory, much worldlier than his rural upbringing suggested. When he returned home he displayed more confidence and was, according to a cousin, a different person, who had "gotten a kind of surefootedness . . . that comes to a fellow who has learned to paddle his own canoe."[19]

After circling the globe for the first time, Rogers could no longer sit still, travel becoming to him as necessary as breathing. He had always had a wanderlust to roam unfettered on horseback across the unfenced prairies of the southern Plains, but now his wanderlust was unbounded, for the entire world had become his prairie and for the rest of his life he would roam it and meet its people.

Rogers's cowpunching days were over. Soon after returning from his first round-the-world trip, the "Cherokee Kid" took his act on the road and within two years was spinning ropes and yarns before the footlights of Broadway.

IT WAS WELL after midnight in December 1915 when Will Rogers ambled onto the stage, standing silent for a few moments and chewing his gum, scratching his head and jamming a hand in and out of his pocket, then lowering his head while raising his eyebrows and shifting his glance quickly between the floor and the audience and back again. Fidgeting restlessly, he appeared nervous at first, but his air of easy confidence and wise innocence put the audience at ease. There was something they liked about the lone cowboy who stood before them. With a twinkling in his eyes he peered at the packed house and gave them the widest grin in the world. Even before he spoke, he looked like he was going to say something darn funny. He fumbled with a coil of rope he carried, at first tying a small loop and slowly spinning it by his side and then, all of a sudden, with a careless flick of one hand he shook the end of the rope magically into a loose but complicated knot.[20] "Swinging a rope is all right as long as your neck ain't in it," he cracked.[21]

Then thirty-six years old, Will Rogers was ruggedly handsome, with a face that had the leathered texture of a well-used saddle, bronzed and weathered from the prairie sun and starting to wrinkle and furrow from earlier days of hard riding. He wore a red flannel shirt, leather chaps, boots, and jingling spurs, and beneath his softly battered hat his hair poked out and unveiled a couple of tousled gray strands. Not quite six-foot tall, angular and hard-boned, he stood on thin bandy legs that looked like they were twisted together from strands of barbed wire.

On that cold December night Rogers was performing in the *Midnight Frolic*, a Florenz Ziegfeld variety show playing the rooftop cabaret of New York's New Amsterdam Theater.[22] As Rogers continued to twirl his rope nonchalantly, he talked about politics and poked fun at Congress, presidents, and bumbling politicians. His main topic for the night was World War I. A week before, automobile tycoon Henry Ford had spent a half-million dollars to send a Scandinavian liner, the *Oskar II*, on a peace mission across the Atlantic to negotiate an end to the war then raging in Europe.[23] "See where Henry Ford's peace ship has landed in Holland. Got all them pacifists on board,"

Rogers began, punctuating his remark with a spin of the rope. "Holland's welcome to them, they ain't much good to us." Another spin while the audience chuckled. "Ford's all wrong, instead of taking a lot of them high-powered fellows on his ship, he should have hired away all these Ziegfeld pippins." Another spin. "He'd not only got the boys out of the trenches by Christmas but he'd have Kaiser Bill and Lloyd George and Clemenceau shooting craps to see which one would head the line at the stage door."[24] As the audience laughed, he launched into the song, "The Thousand Squirrels Have Starved to Death since the Peace Ship Sailed Away."[25]

Rogers's humorous routine tickled the crowd of the New Amsterdam cabaret that night, but his underlying message was dead serious, for nothing could be more serious than a world at war. By saying that chorus girls had a better chance of negotiating peace than Henry Ford, Rogers was resonating with those in his audience who felt the millionaire automaker's mission to end World War I was foolish. It was a ludicrous comparison, yet it penetrated a more serious issue. Beneath his comedy Rogers really was telling the audience that Ford's pacifist mission unfortunately had no chance of succeeding. Rogers was witty, but he also was a realist, suggesting the true targets of his humor and underlying seriousness were "Kaiser Bill" and Lloyd George and Clemenceau, the men who had the real power to end the war. Ford's peace mission, as Rogers had forecasted, failed within a month, and the tycoon returned dejected to the United States.

By the time Rogers poked serious fun at Henry Ford in 1915, he was a seasoned Broadway entertainer. He first stepped onto the New York stage ten years before and had been performing almost nonstop ever since. When he began, vaudeville was the nation's most popular form of entertainment, with audiences in the thousands swelling theaters across the country. In New York City alone, forty theaters offered lavish variety shows of music and dancing, comedy acts, magic shows, barbershop quartets, and all other sorts of amusement. Rogers also arrived during a period when Americans were captivated by the myth of the West as popularized by historian Frederick Jackson Turner, artists Charles Russell and Frederic Remington, Buffalo Bill's Wild West Show, and the cowboy-president Theodore Roosevelt. A best-selling Western novel of the time was Owen Wister's *The Virginian*, the source of the often misquoted line, "When you call me that, *smile*." Dressed like he had just ridden in from a cattle drive, Will Rogers provided the idealized version of the American prairie that his audiences expected to see. He could not have timed better his entrance into vaudeville.

Opening in early 1915, the *Midnight Frolic* was the forerunner of the modern-day nightclub. Lasting almost until dawn, the floor show featured dancing to a live orchestra, glamorous showgirls, delicious food, and buckets of iced champagne. When Rogers opened a few months later, the show high-lighted the Balloon Girls, a flock of beauties who covered their scanty cos-tumes with balloons. As they moved among the tables, men popped the bal-loons with their lit cigars. "I'm just out here while the girls are changing from nothing to nothing," Rogers quipped.[26] For the next six years, until Pro-hibition forced its closure in 1921, the *Frolic* was the place where powerful politicians, Wall Street tycoons, movie stars, and gangland mobsters rubbed elbows with wide-eyed tourists.[27]

Shortly after joining the *Frolic*, Rogers told Ziegfeld's right-hand man, Gene Buck, that he had a new idea for his act. Rogers had married in 1908, and his wife, Betty, knew he had much more talent than as just a wisecrack-ing rope twirler. "My wife says I ought to talk about what I read in the papers," he told Buck. "She says I'm always reading the papers, so why not pass along what I read."[28] Buck, who had originally recruited Rogers for the *Frolic*, liked the idea. To prepare for the late-night show, Rogers sat at his breakfast table for hours devouring the morning newspapers and building a repertory of wisecracks about almost any subject, from the latest fads to gang-land murders to politics and world affairs.[29] No subject was taboo, no person immune from his biting humor. When Buck witnessed Rogers's first political monologue poking fun at Henry Ford's peace mission, he knew immediately the new routine was a hit. He told Rogers to keep adding political humor to his act.

Another of Rogers's early political targets on the *Frolic* stage was the fire-breathing presidential candidate William Jennings Bryan.[30] Rogers's father had been a die-hard supporter of Bryan, but over the years Will became dis-illusioned with the three-time Democratic presidential nominee. Rogers remarked that Bryan was "one of our greatest minds and in most of his the-ories he has been just too far ahead of the mob," but he mistrusted Bryan's extreme fundamentalism, majoritarianism, and socialistic leanings.[31] In 1906

Rogers and cast of Ziegfeld Follies of 1925

he wrote his father from Detroit saying he had heard Bryan speak at a rally of five thousand Democrats. In the speech Bryan denied that he was advocating socialist positions but argued that the rights of working people must be upheld at the expense of corporate wealth. The great orator surely made an impression upon young Rogers as he defended the rights of workers to arbitrate their grievances against companies, opposed the formation of large industrial monopolies, and favored an eight-hour workday and universal education for workers. Bryan soon became one of Rogers's most vulnerable foils, as the orator was known for his long-winded, sermonlike speeches. "Bryan's speeches were used 900 years before he started using them," Will remarked, "and he has been hanging on to them fifty years."[32] Rogers admitted later that Bryan "has been my meal ticket for years."[33]

During his *Frolic* period, Rogers's political commentary was mostly humorous and benign. He did not criticize the nation's leaders or call for dramatic changes in public policy. Such an influential role would evolve over the next few years. During the period surrounding World War I, Rogers and other entertainers were careful what they wrote and said because they were performing during one of the most oppressive periods in American history. It began in 1915, the same year Rogers started at the *Frolic*, when President Wilson launched an attack on citizens whose loyalty was suspect. Then between 1919 and 1921 a wave of repression and xenophobia swept the country, resulting in the notorious Palmer raids that carried out widespread deportations of radicals and Communists. In his stage act, Rogers never mentioned the controversial raids.

ON A RAINY TUESDAY at the end of May 1916, Will Rogers took the train from New York to Baltimore, where he performed at a benefit called the *Friars' Frolic*. George M. Cohan produced the show, which featured an all-star cast of musicians, dancers, and comedians. Just before the opening, the cast learned that President Woodrow Wilson and his wife had driven from Washington DC to attend the performance. Always nervous before a show, Rogers was even more petrified. Just before the president arrived, Cohan noticed Rogers getting drenched in the rain as he paced anxiously back and forth outside the theater's rear door. "He's just a human being," Cohan told him to bolster his confidence. "Go on out and do your stuff."[34] But Rogers remained jittery, for his act contained material that poked fun at the president and he was worried about how Wilson would react. When he saw the president's bodyguards, he got even more panicky. "How was I to know but what one of them might not take a shot at me if I said anything about him personally?"[35] The president, who had a reputation for being cold and humorless, was then busy preparing for his reelection campaign, battling William Jennings Bryan for control of the Democratic Party and involved in diplomatic negotiations trying to stop German submarines from attacking British shipping.[36] Rogers knew that he was treading on dangerous grounds if he were to joke at Wilson.

"I'm kinda nervous here tonight," were his first words as he walked onto the stage and stared down bashfully at his cowboy boots. "I shouldn't be nervous," he added, "for this is really my second presidential appearance. The first time was when Bryan spoke in our town once, and I was to follow his speech and do my little Roping Act." Glancing at the presidential box and seeing Wilson smile, he took a breath and went on. "As I say, I was to follow him, but he spoke so long that it was so dark when he finished they couldn't see my roping." After a pause he asked, "I wonder what ever became of him."[37]

Next came a few jokes about the Mexican bandit Pancho Villa, who had turned against the United States when President Wilson recognized a rival revolutionary as head of the Mexican government. After Villa crossed the border in March 1916 and raided a New Mexico town, killing seventeen Americans, Wilson sent a punitive expedition into Mexico under General John Pershing. Rogers ridiculed the unsuccessful attempts to chase down the elusive bandit, at one point mocking the U.S. Army for hemming Villa "in between the Atlantic and the Pacific." The day before the Baltimore performance, American soldiers had uncovered the first cache of arms belonging to Villa since the troops crossed the border. "I see where they have captured Villa," Rogers announced. "Yes, they got him in the morning editions and the afternoon ones let him get away." He added that the Republicans "are kicking on our Mexican policies. They claim we are paying for a war and not getting it."[38]

Rogers then complained about the country's lack of military preparedness, a thorny subject with the president and the target of intense criticism by the press and by Wilson's most vocal opponent, Theodore Roosevelt. "There is some talk of getting a machine gun if we can borrow one," Rogers began. "The one we have now they are using to train our army with in Plattsburg. If we go to war we will just about have to go to the trouble of getting another gun." Glancing up, Rogers saw the president was leading the laughter. Relieved, he added pointed remarks about the exchange of diplomatic notes between the United States and Germany. "President Wilson is getting along fine now to what he was a few months ago. Do you realize, people, that at one time in our negotiations with Germany that he was five notes behind."[39]

At intermission the president came backstage to shake hands with the cast and invited Rogers to his box after the performance. When Cohan later

*Rogers during early
vaudeville career*

thanked the president for coming to Baltimore, Wilson replied, "I'd travel ten times that distance to listen to a man as wise as Will Rogers."[40] Wilson, who told friends that the joke about diplomatic notes was the best he'd heard during the entire war, would see Rogers's act at least four more times.

Rogers's performance before President Wilson was a turning point in his future calling as an influential political commentator. Rogers walked a fine line between innocent humor and a personal insult whenever he took jabs at important people, especially when he joked at the nation's president and during a time when the country stood on the brink of war. He knew he was taking a gamble. "How was I to know but what the audience would rise up in mass and resent it," he wrote later. "I had never heard, and I don't think any one else had ever heard of a president being joked personally in a public theater about the policies of his administration."[41] Rogers was careful with those first remarks in front of Wilson, writing, "I gave a great deal of time and thought to an act for him, most of which would never be used again, and had

never been used before."[42] On the day before Rogers made his first performance before Wilson, U.S. Marines invaded the Dominican Republic. Rogers
strongly opposed any U.S. intervention into other countries' affairs, but he did
not vent his anger in front of the president. He also refrained from using
more biting material from previous acts, such as a story he told of seeing a
soldier on the street carrying a typewriter under his arm and asking him
what it was. "Oh, just a Wilson machine gun," the soldier answered. Rogers
felt the typewriter remark mocking the president's reluctance to arm the
nation was too personal, and never used the line in Wilson's presence.

Fortunately for Rogers, Wilson's good nature and open-mindedness provided him with the approval he needed to continue to walk the tightrope
between humor and insult. If Wilson had been a stuffed shirt and taken
offense at the remarks, it would have been much more difficult for Rogers to
criticize future presidents and dignitaries. To the ever-nervous Rogers's relief,
the president gave him a much-needed boost of confidence, later writing that
the performances before Wilson were "the happiest moments of my entire
career on the stage."[43] He always was grateful to Wilson for being a good
sport. "You can always tell a big man from a little one," he said. "The big ones
don't get sore when you joke about them."[44]

Two months after his appearance before President Wilson, Will Rogers
joined the *Ziegfeld Follies of 1916*, America's premier vaudeville extrava-
ganza.[45] He was then a star, well paid for the times, and for much of the next
ten years he headlined the *Follies* while continuing his late-night routine at
the *Frolic*. In his acts he poked fun at the famous people who frequently
attended the performance, joking at celebrities such as William Randolph
Hearst, Jay Gould, Cornelius Vanderbilt, and Ethel Barrymore, sometimes
startling them by roping the champagne bottle sitting on their front-row
table. Diamond Jim Brady, the oversize and wealthy financier, was a frequent
guest and a favorite target. "We've got Diamond Jim Brady here tonight," he
cracked, "and if anybody tries to steal one of his diamonds and starts to run
away with them, I'll rope him."[46] Rogers would flick his rope into the audience and drag a dignitary onto the stage. On one night he might lasso Charlie Chaplin, on another it was the visiting governor of Kansas, and on yet
another, Al Smith, soon after his reelection as governor of New York. It
became a badge of honor for the famous and powerful to be hog-tied by

Rogers. As the novelist John O'Hara wrote, "A big shot, a major industrialist type, was not a confirmed tycoon until he had been kidded by Will Rogers, and there was a great deal of snob value to a Rogers rib, like owning a private Pullman car and having your daughter presented to the court of St. James, and belonging to the Links Club."[47]

FIFTEEN YEARS earlier, near the end of 1899, young Will Rogers had walked into the train station in Oologah to pick up a banjo he had ordered from Kansas City.[48] While in the station he met a new girl who had arrived in town from Arkansas to visit her sister.[49] She was twenty, the same age as Will, had brown hair and blue eyes, and was to him "pretty as a picture."[50] Her name was Betty Blake, and over the next few weeks they struck up a close friendship. Both had a sharp-edged sense of humor, playing practical jokes on each other, and shared a love for music. Betty was a talented pianist and Will loved to sing the popular songs of the day. Despite his shyness, he could also be quite charming. According to a boyhood friend, he was "the greatest ladies man you ever saw."[51] Betty returned to Arkansas before Christmas, but several months later she saw him in Springfield, Missouri, where he competed in a steer-roping contest. For seven years, they kept loosely in touch and maintained an on-again, off-again relationship.

In August 1906 Rogers took the train to Betty's home in Arkansas and asked her to marry him. She turned him down, likely sharing the common belief that show business was not respectable, as most vaudevillians were poorly paid, frequently unemployed, and had well-earned reputations as alcoholics and philanderers.[52] Dejected, Rogers headed to Detroit to join the vaudeville circuit.

But he did not give up, aggressively courting Betty over the next two years. In November 1908 he again headed to Arkansas where, soon after arriving unannounced, he abruptly told her he was taking her back to New York. His boldness worked, and two weeks later they married at her mother's home. The couple honeymooned at the Planters Hotel in St. Louis, where they attended a Thanksgiving football game between St. Louis University and the Carlisle Indian School. Rogers enjoyed the game, as the Indians, then coached by Pop Warner and led by All-American Jim Thorpe, won, 17–0.

With Betty tagging happily along, Rogers spent 1909 on the vaudeville tour. His wife played an important part in his early career, for she recognized better than he that his true talent was not so much in his rope twirling but more in his charismatic personality and natural ability to amuse audiences. With Betty's prodding, he soon talked almost continuously, sometimes to the audience, sometimes to himself, and sometimes to no one in particular. One of his earliest one-liners cropped up by accident during a rope trick that involved jumping with both feet inside a spinning loop. The trick was not particularly difficult, but once he happened to miss the trick when he tripped on the loop. Gathering his rope, he hung his head down and drawled an apology, "Well, got all my feet through but one." The line brought down the house. After that he always managed to miss the trick on the first try.[53]

Betty helped Will sharpen his natural bent for politics, and her keen insights often found their way into his material. He once admitted she was the only one allowed to edit his articles before they were printed. After the national elections in November 1910, Betty revealed her strong political convictions when she wrote Clem, saying how delighted she was after the Democrats won control of the House of Representatives, the New York governorship, and both state houses. "What did you think of the election?" she asked. "We were so pleased over it all. Excitement in New York was very great."[54]

During this period Rogers had not yet decided to make show business his lifelong career. He still talked about returning to Oklahoma and raising cattle, using his savings to buy property back home. But he became more serious about his future as an entertainer and his family responsibilities on October 20, 1911, when Betty gave birth to their first child, William Van Rogers, in their New York apartment. In early 1913, Rogers left on a grueling cross-country vaudeville tour. For a year he traveled alone while Betty, pregnant again, lived with her family in Arkansas. On May 18, 1913, Mary Amelia Rogers was born while he was playing the Majestic Theater in Houston.[55]

A YEAR AFTER his daughter was born, Will Rogers embarked on another European tour, this time as an established humorist and this time accompanied by his wife. In May 1914 Betty left their children with her family in Arkansas just as Rogers finished a six-month vaudeville road circuit in the Midwest, the couple then meeting in New York where they boarded the Ger-

Happy parents, around 1912

man liner *Vaterland* and headed to England. In London, Rogers appeared at the Empire Theater in the monthlong variety show *Merry-Go-Round*, starring the American singer Nora Bayes.[56] His act was popular with the Londoners, one reviewer describing him as "a genius at rope throwing and as laughable a patterer as we have seen."[57] Their tour lasted only two months. After Austrian Archduke Franz Ferdinand was assassinated in June 1914, European nations armed themselves and prepared for full-scale war. Not wanting to be stuck in Europe, Rogers quit the London stage early and headed home. On the ship were Theodore Roosevelt's son Kermit and daughter Alice Longworth,[58] both beginning a lasting friendship with the Rogerses. Will and Betty arrived in New York just before World War I broke out in August.

Soon after returning that summer, Rogers was on the road for another tour that lasted until the winter. Betty, pregnant again, headed to her parents' home in Arkansas. He returned to the New York stage in February 1915 and performed in several revues, including the musical *Hands Up* at the Palace Theater on Broadway. Opened only two years before, the posh Palace was already the country's preeminent vaudeville theater. For entertainers, "playing the Palace" would mark the pinnacle of success for decades to come.

Betty joined him in New York, where on July 25, 1915, their second son, James Blake Rogers, was born in their rented house in Amityville, Long Island.[59] For the first time they were settled in their own home, leading as close to a normal family life as a vaudeville entertainer could wish for. They lived across the street from his best friend and fellow Broadway star Fred Stone, and were able to buy their first automobile, a popular and low-priced Overland touring car.[60]

Meanwhile, Rogers's career continued to boom, and he added more and more politics to his routine. During his act he often targeted his favorite president and the person he most admired, Theodore Roosevelt. In 1931, Rogers recalled that Roosevelt "was my best bet in those days. He was the best known public man that ever lived, and [the public] kept up with everything that he did, so when you started in talking about something that he had just said or done, you didn't have to stop to tell what it was before going ahead with your comment. Our public men nowadays haven't got near as much color as the ones then had."[61]

Rogers first met Roosevelt in July 1900 when he was roping steers in a Wild West show performing at a reunion of Spanish-American War Rough Riders. Roosevelt, then governor of New York, was running for vice president on the Republican ticket with William McKinley. Later, while touring in a Wild West show in April 1905, Rogers gave a roping exhibition on the White House grounds before Roosevelt's family.[62]

Like Woodrow Wilson, Roosevelt enjoyed Rogers's humor and never appeared offended by even the sharpest jabs. "Don't be afraid you will hurt my feelings," Roosevelt once told him. "When you can use my name to advantage, go the limit."[63] Roosevelt was impressed enough to forecast the humorist's powerful influence, telling a friend, "This fellow, Will Rogers, has such a keen insight into our American panorama and the thinking of our American people, that I have a feeling that he is bound in the course of time to be a most potent factor in the political life of our country."[64]

Roosevelt was especially pleased after Rogers congratulated him for his staunch patriotism and for sending his four sons to fight in World War I. In July 1918 Roosevelt's youngest son, Quentin, died in an aerial duel over the Marne battlefield in France. Three weeks later, Rogers received a letter from the former president, thanking him for his "kind and friendly allusion to my boys and incidentally to me."[65] Roosevelt wrote the note from Dark Harbor, Maine, where he sought refuge after Quentin's death.

In October of that year, Roosevelt invited Rogers to hear him give the last major speech of his political career.[66] Roosevelt, who turned sixty the day before, stood before a packed house at Carnegie Hall where he attacked his political enemy, Woodrow Wilson. Three months later, he took ill and died.

"We lost Roosevelt," Rogers wrote, "a tough blow."[67]

Two

Battling Suffragettes and Bootleggers

FEELING LIKE he had lost a good friend, Will Rogers mourned terribly after Theodore Roosevelt died. Rogers met every president during his adult life and befriended each of them, but he seemed to resonate most closely with the former Rough Rider. Without fail he agreed with what Roosevelt said and did, especially supporting his overall progressive philosophy as well as his efforts to build a strong military and "carry a big stick." Also like the former president, Rogers was not sure whether women should be allowed to vote, summing up his feelings on suffrage by wishing for "a return of old Jeffersonian democracy, when men chewed tobacco and women could bake real biscuits."[1]

Like Prohibition, the suffrage movement was a longstanding crusade and a major issue debated during the Progressive Era. During the years surrounding World War I, the move to allow women to vote exerted increasing political pressure, culminating on August 18, 1920, when Tennessee became the last state needed to ratify the Nineteenth Amendment. Rogers later told a radio audience that "we're not quite sure if we didn't make as big a mistake [with suffrage] as we did with the Prohibition Amendment."[2]

Using comic exaggeration to mask a more serious criticism, Rogers proposed that suffrage be expanded beyond women. "We have done it for the

wife," he wrote. "Let's do it for the kiddies. Children have the same qualifi-
cation for office the grown-ups have, they are out of work."[3] In another article he continued to exaggerate:

> To us fellows that are not in Politics we are tickled to death, to see the
> Women folks dealing such misery to the Politicians. And in the long run it's
> good for humanity. Every job a Woman can grab off it just drives another
> Politician to either work or the poor house. . . . But this Nineteenth Amend-
> ment is worrying more people in the country than the Eighteenth. It's not
> only caused millions of men to go hungry, (by their wives being away at a
> rally) but it is causing a lot of them to go Jobless, all because the whole thing
> was misunderstanding. The men give 'em the vote, and never meant for
> them to take it seriously. But being Women they took the wrong meaning
> and did."[4]

Rogers not only opposed women voting, he was against them serving in
politics. "I don't think a woman belongs in there [Congress]. Not a nice
woman anyhow."[5] He believed women were too fragile to compete in the
rough-and-tumble male political arena, writing: "The women, poor souls . . .
have paid more attention to the material in the dress than they have to the
material in the speech. They mean well and act awful sincere. But the Girls
just ain't there. It gets 'em out and gives 'em a chance to get away from home,
and wear badges. But it just seems like they havent added anything constructive to the art of politics."[6]

One of the few exceptions Rogers made was for his friend Alice Longworth, the outspoken daughter of Theodore Roosevelt whose political influence as Washington's grand dame spanned the presidencies from William
McKinley to John F. Kennedy. "Of all the *she* political minds I have ever
met," Rogers wrote, "Alice has forgot more than most of the others know put
together. When you meet up with a mind like hers, it gives you a little encouragement for the Nineteenth Amendment."[7]

WHEN WILL ROGERS traveled to Washington DC in March 1917, dozens
of suffragettes marched along Pennsylvania Avenue, picketing the White
House, lighting bonfires, and defying the local police to arrest them. Led by
the militant Alice Paul and her National Women's Party, the suffragettes

handed out leaflets accusing President Wilson of being a hypocrite, saying he championed democracy throughout the world but thwarted it at home by denying the vote to women. At the time, Rogers was in the nation's capital to perform in Ziegfeld's *Follies*, and again Wilson attended the performance. The president laughed loudly when Rogers joked about the suffragettes who had been demonstrating since New Year's Day—on one evening they burnt an effigy of the president. "The more you see of civilization," Rogers remarked later, "the more you feel that those old cavemen about had the right dope."[8]

Rogers was less humorous when, still in front of Wilson, he criticized the administration for its lack of military preparedness, the shape of the war in Europe, and the national debate over involvement. Rogers was an isolationist who, like the president, opposed American participation in the war, but he was also a realist who knew there may be a time when there was no choice but to fight. "Either make it official and go in a shooting, or stay out!" he argued.[9]

On April 6, 1917, Rogers was appearing at the New Amsterdam Theater with the *Frolic* when the United States declared war on Germany. Once the United States entered the conflict, he dropped his isolationist tone and firmly supported the war effort. Thirty-seven at the time, too old for the draft, and with a wife and three children, Rogers knew he could not join the fight but nevertheless felt deeply he should make a sacrifice. He wrote the president of the American Red Cross in May 1917 to say he had tried to estimate what he could contribute. "While not a wealthy man, I earn a very good salary," he wrote, pledging 10 percent of his next year's income, or $5,200, to the organization.[10] When the First Division embarked for France that June, he began donating part of his salary each week to a wartime fund for the Red Cross. Throughout the conflict Rogers performed dozens of benefits for wartime charities, such as serving as an auctioneer to raise money for the Red Cross at New York's Liberty Theater. After the war, President Wilson presented him with a "Certificate of Honor" for his volunteer service.[11] Rogers's Red Cross charity work marked the beginning of a lifelong philanthropy in which he generated hundreds of thousands of dollars to orphanages, hospitals, maternity homes, newsboy homes, churches of all denominations, and other needy causes.

At first Rogers feared joking about such a serious matter as the war, but soon he realized that laughter was essential during wartime both as a morale booster and to reduce tension. He said often that the war was started by a joke—the Kaiser himself.[12] Soon after the United States entered the hostilities, Rogers showed up at a recruiting office on Chambers Street where he gave a spur-of-the-moment monologue poking fun at his two favorite targets. "Bryan says that he will go to war if they want him," he told a crowd of recruits, "but Roosevelt says he will go whether they want him or not."[13] When a newspaper reported that German submarines could not operate in the warm Gulf Stream, he suggested, "If we can only heat the ocean we will have them licked."[14]

Just before the end of the war, Rogers appeared before Wilson at the Metropolitan Opera House in a program honoring Enrico Caruso. At the time the president was secretly negotiating to end the war and drafting his Fourteen Points, a foundation for international peace. Rogers, who had little faith in diplomacy and took frequent shots at peace and disarmament conferences, doubted the president would have much success. "I have always claimed that any International Conference does more harm than good, for they engender more hate than good will," Rogers wrote later. "It's hatreds formed at Conferences that causes the next war."[15]

Beginning in 1917, Rogers became intrigued with Russia, closely following the tumultuous events there after Czar Nicholas II abdicated and a bloody revolution erupted. "Pick up the morning paper and look for Russian news and have a fear of reading the worst," he wrote in the *Chicago Examiner*. "You won't be disappointed."[16] He criticized Elihu Root's futile attempt to convince Russia to keep fighting in World War I. Rogers remarked during a *Follies* show that, "If the United States had sent [Theodore] Roosevelt to Russia instead of Root, you can bet your bottom dollar the Russians would be fighting somebody now!"[17] On December 15, 1917, less than a month after the communists took power, the Bolshevik government signed an armistice with Germany and pulled out of the war.

Rogers was on the road with the *Follies* in Philadelphia on November 11, 1918, when early that morning sirens, whistles, and bells erupted across the city and the rest of country, announcing that World War I had finally ended. A few days later, Wilson attended the road show when it performed in

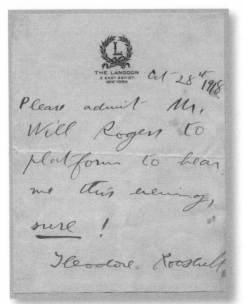

*A note from Rogers's favorite
president, Theodore
Roosevelt*

Washington. "We played to the President last Night," Rogers wrote his sister
Maud. "I joked all about [Wilson's] Peace Ship going to Europe. [H]e sure
enjoyed it."[18] Wilson departed for the European peace conference the following week. Rogers remained pessimistic that Wilson, or anyone else for that
matter, could negotiate a lasting peace, writing later, "It seems we may have
to have two more wars to find out who won the last one."[19]

On October 3, 1919, Wilson, exhausted from his futile and idealistic efforts
to get the United States to ratify the Treaty of Versailles and support the
League of Nations, suffered a debilitating stroke that left him partially paralyzed. For the seventeen months remaining in his term of office, the president could not carry out his normal duties, at times unable to sign documents
awaiting his signature. Rogers, who claimed that he "never joked about a
man who was down," followed the decorum of the day and never mentioned
the human tragedy taking place in the White House and the vulnerability of
a leaderless administration.[20] When Wilson died in February 1924, Rogers
wrote that he lost "the most distinguished person who ever laughed at my little nonsensical jokes." He had great respect for Wilson's attempts at world
peace but questioned the former president's naïve moral idealism. Rogers had
watched with skepticism as Wilson traveled to Paris in 1919 to try to establish

the League of Nations. He thought the president failed to understand that the nations of Europe were not committed to the noble ideals embodied in his Fourteen Points, but instead were more swayed by fear, hate, and narrow nationalism. "It's hard to stamp out selfishness and greed," Rogers wrote after Wilson died. "For after all, nations are nothing but individuals, and you can't stop even brothers from fighting sometimes. But [Wilson] helped it along a lot."[21]

ROGERS AND HIS FAMILY were busy as ever during the years surrounding World War I. On July 15, 1918, Betty gave birth to their third son, Fred Stone Rogers, at their home in Amityville, New York.[22] Besides performing in the *Follies, Frolic,* and other vaudeville productions, Rogers freelanced newspaper and magazine articles to make a few extra dollars. As early as 1916, the *New York American* asked him to write a special article based on his stage act. At the time he was unsure of his own talent but accepted the offer, promising his readers something different from that of the current writers and columnists: "I am going to lay my chips a little different from what they say those birds do. I am not only going to sign my name, but I am going to take a shot at the whole works myself, and I want it to go as she lays, even if the guy that has to set up the type has to get drunk to do it."[23]

Rogers covered a range of political topics in his early articles, from crime in Chicago, to the festering Russian Revolution, and "every subject that had been in the papers since Bryan last got a hair cut."[24] In one article he discussed the upcoming presidential contest between Wilson and Charles Evans Hughes. "Hughes said: 'I'm for America first,'" Rogers wrote. "After the way America has kept him in office all his life, we didn't expect he'd come out for Venezuela!" Mexico continued to be a favorite target during the Pancho Villa disturbance, with Rogers writing:

They say the Mexican soldiers fight without making any trenches. That's right. Unless the Mexicans have a [*sic*] changed a lot since I knew them, they'd rather be shot than go to work and dig a trench. The Mexican soldiers get 10 cents a day for serving in the army. And the only day they earn it is the day they try to collect it. The Mexicans eat so much chili pepper that when they're killed the coyotes can't eat their bodies. But if Uncle Sam ever has to pepper them with his machine guns there won't be a big enough piece left to burn a buzzard's mouth.[25]

During the summer of 1918 Rogers starred in his first motion picture. Written by his friend Rex Beach, the silent comedy *Laughing Bill Hyde* was filmed at Samuel Goldfish's studio in Fort Lee, New Jersey.[26] Rogers plays a hapless thief who laughs constantly whenever he is in danger. His enemies assume that his laughter is proof of his courage, but in fact it is a nervous reaction to mortal terror. Rogers was natural for the part. When the film opened the following September, the *New York Times* greeted it enthusiastically: "Those inclined to believe that all of the magnetic Rogers personality is in his conversation will realize their mistake if they see this picture. The real Will Rogers is on the reels. Whether Rogers can act or whether he can do anything before the camera except be himself, is not the question."[27]

After Sam Goldfish, who soon changed his name to Goldwyn, saw the picture, he signed Rogers to a one-year contract.

"A BREAKFAST don't taste good to me without a good paper," Will Rogers wrote.[28] After he arose each morning—late, almost until 6:30—he began his day by drinking "about a dozen saucers of coffee" and poring through a pile of the daily papers to find fresh material for his act.[29] Sometimes he liked what he read and sometimes he didn't. When he picked up the papers on a gloomy and cold November 22, 1918, Rogers was living in New York and performing his late-night *Frolic* routine. For a change, most of the news was good. Eleven days before, the German army had surrendered and ended the dreadful trench warfare of World War I. The morning's headlines reported the capitulation of the German High Seas Fleet, and President Wilson announced he would go to Europe to attend the peace conference. After nineteenth months of war, the country was overjoyed.

Some of the news that morning, however, was sad. The *New York Times* reported that more than 86,000 American soldiers had died in the war and printed page after page listing recent casualties.[30] As Rogers waded through the news, one item at the bottom of the front page especially irritated him. The *Times* reported that Wilson had signed an agricultural appropriation bill containing a rider banning the sale of liquor. Although the war had already ended, Congress passed the bill as an emergency war measure. The new law effectively banned alcohol sales even though some states were still debating ratification of the proposed Eighteenth Amendment. Wilson's action infuriated those opposing Prohibition, including Rogers. The *New York Times* also objected, calling the new law "dishonest, hypocritical, and superfluous."[31]

Rogers was upset but not surprised to see Prohibition enacted, for all of his life he had heard cries to banish the neighborhood saloon. The Prohibition movement did not happen overnight but was a longstanding social and political crusade that slowly but inexorably gained momentum. In 1851, Maine became the first state to ban liquor; in 1867 the Prohibition Party was formed, followed in 1874 by the Woman's Christian Temperance Union, and in 1895 by the Anti-Saloon League.[32] By the time Rogers joined the *Follies* in 1915, fifteen states had passed their own prohibition laws and a national ban on alcohol appeared inevitable. On January 16, 1919, Prohibition became part of the U.S. Constitution when Nebraska became the thirty-sixth state to ratify the Eighteenth Amendment.[33] A year later, at midnight, America officially went dry, prompting the ardently dry evangelist Billy Sunday to joyfully proclaim: "The rain of tears is over. The slums will soon be a memory; we will turn our prisons into factories, our jails into storehouses and corn cribs, our men will walk upright. Now women will smile, children will laugh, hell will be for rent."[34]

Will Rogers did not share Billy Sunday's cockeyed optimism. As Prohibition became law, Rogers watched with unease as bootleggers, smugglers, and speakeasies thrived while many ordinary citizens resorted to brewing beer and distilling spirits in their home. By 1928 more than two thousand Americans died each year from drinking rotgut. In his stage acts, after-dinner speeches, and newspaper articles, Rogers called Prohibition a national disaster, a hypocritical joke, a purely political issue, and an invasion of government into people's lives with no relevance to morality or the public good. A defender of individual rights, he argued that government should not decide when a man could, or could not, take a drink.[35] "Is Prohibition an issue or a drink?" he asked his audience.[36]

For the next thirteen years Prohibition was the butt of Rogers's gags and a perfect target for his comic exaggeration. "Look at these towns and people after Prohibition has hit them," he joked. "Everybody looks like they had just had a puncture and no extra tire."[37] After his good friend and General Motors president William Durant offered $25,000 for the best suggestion to enforce Prohibition, Rogers devised his own plan. "Have the governments pass a law making it compulsory for everybody to drink," he wrote. "People would rebel against it so that they would stop drinking. That's a funny thing about American people, tell 'em they have to do anything, and they will die twice or do it."[38]

Rogers's jokes, however, could not hide his serious concern for the country. Prohibition began because many believed alcohol caused crime and abuse, but he argued the opposite was true. "Prohibitionists are the originators of Camouflage," he wrote. "They made drinking look worse than it is."[39] He believed Prohibition actually increased crime and corruption, remarking half seriously that "streets that used to be lighted up at nights and thousands of people on them are now used for robbing purposes only."[40] He also believed Prohibition never could be enforced. The Volstead Act,[41] which imposed the ban on alcohol, was especially irksome to him, as Congress overrode President Wilson's veto in October 1919 before the Eighteenth Amendment was ratified and at a time when two million young men were still overseas in the army and unable to vote.

Rogers argued that Prohibition was an economic, not moral, issue, and a waste of taxpayer dollars, writing that:

> You often hear it said that bootlegging is the biggest industry. Well, that is not quite correct, but prohibition is the biggest—that is, taking both sides, money spent for and against it, not only the bootlegging and enforcement end of it, but when you speak of an industry you must consider the by-products. For instance, there's the doctors, the undertakers and the coroners. . . . Figure up the time consumed by the United States senate and congress and different state legislatures. Figure it up at their wages and you will see what a big by-product just speaking about it has been. If all the time had been used in this country on study that has been used up arguing prohibition, we would be the smartest nation in the world.[42]

To Rogers, Prohibition was not the will of the people but instead resulted from pressure exerted by powerful business interests who felt sober workers were more efficient and productive. Giving a lecture in Montclair, New Jersey, Rogers lost his composure, ignored his prepared comic routine, and turned serious and a bit angry. Aiming his comments at businessmen in the audience, he told them Prohibition was a matter of simple economics: "That's why we've got dozens of men in this house tonight who own factories or business concerns where they engage men—and you are for Prohibition. Why? Because your men will produce more dollars. You who are paying them know that they'll be there on Monday morning and give you more for your money than otherwise. . . . You're going to vote for the country being dry, that's what you are going to do."[43]

Like many Americans, Rogers wearied of the endless Prohibition debate. "Eighty percent of America wish the wets would get so drunk they would be speechless for the rest of their lives. And the drys get so perfect that the Lord would call 'em away from this earth up into heaven. . . . This argument is just like a war. It's the innocent that are not in it that suffer."[44]

Rogers was relentless. After he began his weekly column in 1922, he attacked Prohibition in no less than three hundred separate newspaper articles, as well as in countless lectures, speeches, and radio broadcasts. His constant hammering at Prohibition made an impact, as roughly six hundred newspapers across the country carried his articles by the end of 1927. Rogers, more than any other columnist of the day, resonated most closely with the millions of middle-class and poorer-educated Americans, and these would be same people who would eventually vote for repeal in 1933.

BY THE EARLY 1920s, Will Rogers had fine-tuned his act into a well-practiced routine, making him one of the more popular and better-paid entertainers on the vaudeville circuit. His transition from an act mostly of rope spinning and one-liners to one containing more sophisticated political comedy was not difficult, as he was surer of himself, confident that he had the talent not only to entertain people but to give them some thought-provoking and somewhat serious political commentary.

In choosing his nightly topics, he believed there were several keys to the success of a political joke. First, the joke must be brief enough so that it did not lose the audience's attention, which meant usually getting the joke across in a sentence or two. Next, the joke should appear to be spontaneous, for comedy thrives on freshness and surprise. His jokes seemed to be off-the-cuff but were actually the result of painstaking preparation. Early in his career, he recognized the value of always missing that first rope trick, surprising the audience and making them feel they were seeing something different. Likewise, in his later career he delivered his political jokes as if he were shooting from the hip. Next, Rogers believed a joke must be based on fact and have at least enough truth to give the gag some credibility. And lastly, the joke must be recent enough for the audience to understand the event.[45] He realized people laughed more readily at something that had just happened than at a supposedly hilarious joke written by a gag writer. "So I started to reading about Congress," he said, "and believe me, I found they are funnier three hundred and sixty-five days a year than anything I ever heard of."[46]

Rogers was very serious about being humorous. He recognized early that political jokes had more impact than the stock vaudeville gags and slapstick comedy then popular. He was breaking new ground for comedy as he poked fun at individual politicians, especially presidents, and made light of sober issues such as war. He preferred that his audiences consider the meaning of his jokes rather than laugh unthinkingly. Over time, his jokes contained increasingly serious messages embedded within his comic routine, often employing the art of comic exaggeration to mix the funny with the somber. For example, whenever he took shots at Theodore Roosevelt he asked: "You remember when Teddy Roosevelt came back from a long tour of the West? Or can't you remember that? You must remember Roosevelt, don't you? Well, Teddy was a pretty good fellow, when he had it. I wonder what has become of him?"[47]

For years Rogers repeated that same question and the line always got laughs. Asking what became of Roosevelt provides an excellent example of comic exaggeration, for it was a ludicrous question, as everyone in the audience knew what had become of Roosevelt: that he lost the 1912 presidential election to Woodrow Wilson, and thus became one of the president's harshest critics. Despite his joking tone, Rogers was reminding his audience of more serious issues, namely Roosevelt's past accomplishments as president, his status as a living political icon, and his present role as an opponent of the Wilson administration. Besides Roosevelt, Congress, and Henry Ford, there would always be plenty of other fascinating people and happenings for Rogers to stimulate his more serious messages.

Rogers had an instinctive understanding of political comedy and recognized early that it not only made people laugh but also could be diagnostic and therapeutic for a healthy democracy.[48] To him, making fun of politics and politicians was not being nasty—it was necessary. Well before transparency in government became vogue, he placed political leaders and bureaucrats under closer scrutiny, criticizing them when necessary and prodding them to correct their mistakes, and ultimately, making democracy work better.

WILL AND BETTY'S FAMILY had grown during the years living in New York, and by the summer of 1919 there were six of them. Will, Jr., was almost eight; Mary Amelia had just turned six; James Blake was four; and baby Fred, eleven months. In June of that year, as diplomats gathered in Versailles, France, to sign the peace treaty ending World War I, the Rogerses headed west to a new home in southern California where Samuel Goldwyn had moved his studio. Rogers would make thirteen silent movies for Goldwyn until his contract ended in 1921, followed by fourteen comedies produced by up-and-coming movie mogul Hal Roach.

While Rogers was in California making films, Harper Brothers published the first two of six books containing his political humor. In October 1919, a month before his fortieth birthday, *The Cowboy Philosopher on Prohibition* was released. Soon after, a similar political parody, *The Cowboy Philosopher on the Peace Conference,* followed with humor aimed at international diplomacy.

Rogers became a pioneer in the movie industry, eventually starring in fifty silent comedies. In 1921 he produced, directed, and starred in the memorable *Ropin' Fool,* a two-reeler capturing his skills as a roper, writer, and slow-motion cinema innovator. With a rope painted white to show up against his black horse Dopey, Rogers repeated for the camera his roping tricks from the *Follies.*

Politics was a frequent topic of Rogers's silent films, and he wrote much of his own dialogue. In *Water, Water Everywhere* he satirizes Prohibition. Ladies of the local temperance society pressure a saloon to close down and a soda shop opens up instead. But local men get their revenge by hiring the prettiest young women they can find to work there. In 1924 he completed a trio of silent political comedies: *Going to Congress, Our Congressman,* and *A Truthful Liar.* In all three films Rogers plays a shiftless but lovable oaf named Alfalfa Doolittle. Selected by local political bosses to run for Congress,

A growing family, around 1920

Doolittle wins the election by promising rain for his constituents. Made at the height of the Teapot Dome scandal, the trilogy pokes fun at political corruption, Russians, golf, William Jennings Bryan, and a bomb-throwing bearded anarchist named "Ivan."[49]

Soon after he starting filming in California, Rogers noticed the financial success of the independent films of Mary Pickford, Charlie Chaplin, and Douglas Fairbanks and tried making his own pictures. Producing films proved to be a big mistake, for by the end of 1921 he had nearly bankrupted himself and lost all of his $45,000 in savings—roughly a half million in today's dollars. To pay off his debts, he left his family in California and returned to New York to star again in the *Follies*. Rogers did not return to the Hollywood screen until he appeared in the "talkies" in 1929.

"Laws framed in pants like them would be unconstitutional!"

Hal Roach *presents* WILL ROGERS Pathecomedy "OUR CONGRESSMAN"

Rogers in an early silent movie

After returning to New York, Rogers began to make extra money by giving humorous political speeches at conventions and banquets. He was still
edgy before these engagements and, over the years, never completely over-
came his nervousness. According to one reporter, "although the gray is rather
thick in his hair that won't stay combed, Mr. Rogers says he has never reached
the point where he doesn't have stage fright."[50] His usual fee of $1,000 per
speech, however, helped calm his nerves.

Meanwhile, Rogers never seemed able to turn down requests to do charity
benefits. He frequently appeared free of charge to raise money for needy
causes, including hospitals across the country as well as benevolent organizations such as the Actors Fund, Blind Relief War Fund, Hebrew Infant Asylum, New York newsboys, and the Red Cross. Whenever he came across a
down-and-out rodeo cowboy from his past, the soft-hearted Rogers forked
over whatever cash he carried. When tuberculosis struck a chorus girl, he

canceled his *Follies* appearance to do a benefit for the girl at New York's Casino Theater. In May 1919, Rogers made his earliest documented appearance for the Salvation Army at the Hippodrome in New York. The Salvation Army became one of his favorite causes and the recipient of his philanthropy through the years. The last of his many Salvation Army benefits took place less than two months before his death in 1935.[51]

Increasingly popular from his films, books, and after-dinner speeches, Rogers filled his schedule with bookings. In one seven-month period he spoke at least sixty-one times. "I have spoken at so many Banquets during the year," he wrote, "that when I get home I will feel disappointed if my wife or one of the children don't get up at dinner and say, 'We have with us this evening a man who, I am sure, needs no introduction.'"[52] He talked before a wide assortment of audiences, from police chiefs to underwear manufacturers to varnish salesmen. During a stop at the U.S. Military Academy, he told the cadets that "West Point was situated on a bluff and run on the same plan."[53] At Sing Sing prison he confessed to the inmates that he "knew everybody up there."[54] In February 1925 he spoke before the Jewish Theatrical Guild of America at a banquet honoring Eddie Cantor and, to everyone's surprise, gave his ten-minute speech in Yiddish.[55] In all of his talks, he needled his audiences, calling shoe manufacturers a bunch of "pasteboard highbinders"[56] and car dealers "old time horse-trading gyps with white collars on."[57] He labeled advertising men as the "Robbing Hoods of America" and told the Association of Wool Manufacturers to stay indoors in case of rain or there would be "about 500 men choked to death by their own suits." When he lectured at a convention of surgeons, he titled his speech, "'Odds and Ends Left inside after Operations,' or 'Mistakes Doctors have made and covered up.'"[58] When representatives of the U.S. Chambers of Commerce met in New York in May 1923, he called them the modern male equivalent of the old ladies' sewing circles who "knew everybody's business and were into everything."[59] In another speech, he thanked the corset manufacturers for their great contribution to society. "You gentlemen shape the world," he said. "Just think if flesh were allowed to wander around there is no telling where it would wind up."[60]

Sometimes Rogers's humor seemed to go too far and take on a more abrasive tone, especially when the audience belonged to a profession he did not admire. "So, goodbye, paupers," he admonished a meeting of astonished bankers in 1923. "You're the finest bunch of shylocks that ever foreclosed a mortgage on a widow's home." He told the bankers that borrowing money on easy terms was a one-way ticket to the poorhouse. "If you think it ain't a sucker game," he asked, "why is the banker the richest man in town?" He added: "I don't care what you do. Go to work, if there is any job any of you could earn a living at. Banking and after-dinner speaking are two of the most non-essential industries we have in this country. I am ready to reform if you are."[61]

By 1920, newspaper editors across the country recognized that Rogers's brand of humor had national appeal, that he was especially trenchant when he wrote about political events and politicians. In the summer of that year he got the opportunity to test his humor on the American public when a newspaper syndicate hired him to report on his first political convention.

THREE

——•——

A Political Critic Emerges

I N JUNE 1920 the Newspaper Enterprise Association hired Will Rogers to cover the Republican National Convention in Chicago, but he was in California filming a silent Western comedy, *Cupid the Cowpuncher*.[1] During breaks on the movie set he gathered the latest convention news from the morning papers and typed up his daily articles. "I am being paid to write something funny about this Republican convention," he wrote in his first piece. "That's funny."[2]

Rogers saw nothing unusual about covering the convention from over two thousand miles away:

> I've heard a lot about "absent treatments" and that is what I'm giving this convention. You don't have to hear somebody say a thing to know it. Why, I'll bet any typewriter—I'm referring to the machine and not the blonde who runs it—which had lived through a convention or two, could just automatically run off the speeches, including the "applause" and "wild cheering for twenty minutes." Whether anybody but the guy who makes the speech ever reads it is a matter I've thought about a lot. Probably his wife reads it and, of course, if he has a doting old maid aunt, she cuts it out and puts it in the family Bible.

But why make a fuss about my not going to the convention? I've known a bunch of newspaper men in my time and I always noticed that the way they "covered" their assignments was to stand with one foot on a brass rail and then call up the office every now and then.[3]

In order to appear to be in the midst of the political action, Rogers pretended to be in Philadelphia with powerful Republican senator Boies Penrose, the three-hundred-pound Pennsylvania political boss noted for his huge appetite in wine, women, and food.[4] By creating an imaginary dialogue with the colorful and corrupt Penrose, Rogers appeared to have the inside dope on the Republican campaign strategy.

When the political conventions began that summer, there were no obvious candidates from either party. Theodore Roosevelt had died the year before and Woodrow Wilson had suffered a serious stroke, leaving both the Republicans and Democrats without a strong standard-bearer. The Republican convention soon gridlocked with three front-runners: General Leonard Wood, Illinois governor Frank Lowden, and California senator Hiram Johnson. "A week ago the Republicans thought they could win with anybody," Rogers reported. "Now they can't find anybody they think they can win with."[5] When no candidate emerged, Republican wheel horses met secretly in the Blackstone Hotel to select a compromise. Rogers, who grumbled that "more men have been elected between sundown and sunup than ever were elected between sunup and sundown," deplored the backroom political deals and suggested crookedness.[6] "How can you tell who bought delegates?" he asked Penrose in a mock conversation. "That's easy," Penrose replied. "The ones who didn't buy any are the ones who haven't got any."[7]

On the tenth ballot, after Republican leaders finished making their backroom deals, the party nominated a dark-horse senator from Ohio, fifty-four-year-old Warren Harding.[8] Tall, handsome, with lusty black eyebrows, steel-gray hair, and bronzed complexion, Harding looked like perfect presidential material. But he was a lackluster legislator who showed no leadership ability, a man who surrounded himself with corrupt scoundrels and preferred to spend his time playing cards and pursuing peccadilloes.[9] H. L. Mencken called Harding "a downright moron."[10] For vice president, the delegates chose Calvin Coolidge, the laconic, staunchly conservative governor of Massachusetts who, nine months before, became an overnight hero when he broke up the Boston Police Strike, declaring there was "no right to strike against the public safety by anybody, anywhere, anytime."[11]

While the Republican convention met, tragedy struck the Rogers family. The baby, Fred Stone Rogers, became ill with a sore throat, and doctors at first thought he had tonsillitis. But after the other children became ill, they changed the diagnosis to diphtheria. The older children survived, but the baby died on June 17, 1920. Rogers drove all night from location shooting near San Francisco but arrived too late. The baby was twenty months old.[12]

Two weeks later, the Democratic National Convention opened in San Francisco. Still writing for the newspaper syndicate, Rogers reported on the convention but stayed in Los Angeles because of his infant son's death. Again, he pretended to report from afar, this time from Washington DC, where he carried on a fictitious conversation with President Wilson. Rogers's columns on the two conventions were not as sharp, humorous, or penetrating as his later work, and his technique of inventing a conversation from afar was not very effective. He also was distraught over his baby's death. He wrote his first article on the Democratic convention only a few hours after his son died, and the typing, punctuation, and spelling of the original manuscript were worse than his usual careless style.

In San Francisco, the Democrats were in greater disarray than the Republicans had been. With his popularity waning and health ailing, Wilson was noncommittal about running for a third time. Democratic leaders felt he could not win reelection. At first, the front-runner was former treasury secretary William McAdoo,[13] a popular Georgian who embodied all the virtues of small-town Protestant America. Supported by Democratic liberals, labor unions, the Anti-Saloon League, and southerners, McAdoo had the most votes on the first ballot. However, he was married to Wilson's daughter and reluctant to announce his candidacy while the president still might run again. "But, President," Rogers stated in a mock White House conversation, "the boy [McAdoo] says he's not a candidate." Wilson replied, "Well, of course, if he don't feel like taking it, I suppose I will have to be inspired for another four years."[14]

After the president's ambivalence killed McAdoo's chances, the conventioneers turned to dark horses and favorite sons. Attorney General A. Mitchell Palmer, notorious for his raids on communists and radicals, threw

*At work writing
his column*

his hat into the ring, as did Virginia senator Carter Glass. Perennial presidential candidate William Jennings Bryan offered to lead the party and had the support of the drys, isolationists, and populists. As usual, the long-winded Bryan provided an easy target for Rogers's humor. "You know Bryan's speeches are interrupted every four years by elections and then he goes on again," Rogers wrote during the convention.[15] "And yet [Bryan] wonders why he never could be elected President."[16]

In his mock conversation with Wilson, Rogers ridiculed the Democratic platform. "But what about the platform?" he asked the president. "Oh, we don't need much of one," Wilson answered. "All we do is point with pride and let the Republicans view with alarm." When Rogers asked the president where he stood on the liquor question, Wilson responded that the Democrats must act "just like the Republicans do on all questions—straddle."[17]

None of the candidates gathered much support, and, on the forty-fourth ballot, the Democrats abandoned McAdoo and nominated moderate Ohio governor James M. Cox for president and Assistant Secretary of the Navy Franklin Roosevelt for vice president. They adopted a platform that supported both the League of Nations and women's suffrage. The outcome of the convention angered Rogers, who liked McAdoo and thought him the most qualified for the presidency. "If our Government is by the people," he wrote, "how is it that the Candidate with the most votes by the people going into a Presidential Convention never got nominated?"[18]

Cox proved to be a weak candidate who could not overcome the unpopularity of Wilson and the Democrats. In November, Warren Harding won the presidency in a landslide on the campaign promise to return the country to "normalcy." The word was not in the dictionary, one newspaper editor observed, "but it was what Americans wanted."[19]

DURING THE EARLY 1920s Will Rogers watched as tensions rose in the Far East between the United States and Japan. Each morning when he picked up his newspaper there seemed to be yet another international incident that flared between the two countries. The United States protested when the Japanese occupied Shantung, intervened in Siberia, and made hostile gestures toward a large-scale invasion of China. "China wants the open door and it looks like Japan will give it to her," Rogers remarked at the time.[20] Relations deteriorated further after the United States denied racial equality for Japanese by severely restricting immigration. By 1921, tensions had risen enough to spur the United States, Britain, and Japan to begin an expensive arms race, each nation trying to outdo the others by building bigger and bigger battleships.

To lessen the threat of a war in the Far East, Idaho senator William Borah and other isolationists in Congress convinced Harding to propose an international conference. In the summer of 1921, the president invited Great Britain, Italy, France, and Japan to send representatives to Washington for the International Conference on Naval Limitation. Russia was not invited.

A week before the conference convened, Will Rogers arrived in Washington as a paid correspondent for Universal News Service, a news bureau the Hearst organization had established in 1917. Rogers spent his free time wandering the corridors of the U.S. Senate, meeting its members and sharing a joke or a juicy piece of political gossip. Over the next fourteen years he seldom visited the nation's capital without dropping by the Senate, knowing that the country's most powerful circle of politicians supplied him much more valuable information than simply "what I read in the papers." He wasted no time capitalizing on firsthand inside political intelligence. "I went up to the Senate today," he wrote after his visit, "and I want to tell you they got the best show in town. Jim Reed[21] has got the funniest act he has had in years."[22] Always a source of amusement, the Senate became Rogers's favorite playground: "You know I like to make little jokes and kid about the Senators. They are a kind of never-ending amusement, amazement, and Discouragement. But the Rascals, when you meet 'em face to face to face and know 'em, they are mighty nice fellows. It must be something in the office that makes 'em so ornery sometimes. When you see what they do officially you want to shoot 'em, but when one looks at you and grins so innocently, why you kinder want to kiss him."[23]

Hired to write daily newspaper articles on disarmament, Rogers filled his reports with his usual humor as well as serious skepticism of diplomatic negotiations. "Well, here I am in Washington to write you all about this Number 2 Peace Conference," he wrote. "This is really the third attempt a[t] international peace. [Henry] Ford conducte[d] the first one. The only mistake he made was in bringing his troop back to this country."[24]

Beneath his humor, Rogers revealed an increasing understanding of foreign relations and geopolitics. The more he observed, the more he learned, and often, the more cynical he became. "Disarmament can't hurt this country," he wrote. "We were disarmed when we entered the last war and got away with it. Maybe we can do it again."[25] He had little faith that the world powers would cooperate with each other, joking that "France and England think just as much of each other as two rival bands of Chicago bootleggers."[26] He sharply criticized U.S. negotiating efforts, writing that Secretary of State Charles Evans Hughes "had such good luck with his proposals that every jerkwater nation in the world is horning in with a set of proposals."[27] Rogers quipped that disarmament had as much chance of success as he would have by going on stage and "tackling Hamlet in tights."[28] He recognized naval armament limitations were really a waste of time, arguing on several occasions that the next war would be fought primarily by aviation and that costly battleships would be useless.

During the conference Rogers revealed a building mistrust of the Japanese. "I arrived direct with the Japanese delegation," he wrote. "If the conference had been put off two years they wouldn't have to send them from Japan. They could send them from California."[29] Living on the West Coast, Rogers was aware of the controversial influx of Japanese immigrants. In 1920 the

Japanese population in California reached 72,000, an increase of 80 percent in ten years. Large-scale Japanese immigration continued despite the Alien Land Law of 1913, a state law aimed at the Japanese by forbidding land ownership by aliens. The growth of the Japanese population disturbed Rogers, writing they were "multiplying something terrible."[30]

Mistrusting Japanese imperialism in the Far East, Rogers accused the Tokyo regime of having "accumulated more territory in the last few years with less effort than any other nation on earth."[31] He called for the United States to take a hard stand when negotiating with the Japanese: "If you think preparedness don't give you prestige, look at Japan. We are afraid to look at them cross-eyed now for fear we will hurt their 'honor.' Before they got a navy, neither them nor us knew they had any honor. It ain't your honor that is respected among nations, it's your strength."[32]

On February 10, 1922, Rogers watched from the Senate press gallery as President Harding presented the seven separate disarmament treaties negotiated at the conference. Rogers was not pleased with the outcome, aware that while the arms limitation precluded a buildup of naval forces in the Pacific, the Four-Power Treaty effectively conceded Japanese dominance in the region. In the fall of 1921 the Harding administration had expressed a commitment to defend the Philippines, but the new treaty restricted the U.S. ability to fortify the islands and left them more vulnerable to attack. Rogers concluded that the conference failed to lessen the chance of war and "the only things scrapped so far have been friendships."[33] His displeasure with the treaties was clear when he wrote:

> President Harding went slumming and took in the Senate late yesterday. He carried his bale of treaties along. They were all bundled up in wrapping paper so you couldn't tell whether he was a President or a bootlegger. . . . Harding made quite a speech. . . . One treaty says there is to be no war and another tells how many submarines you can have in case there is a war. Japan did pretty well. She used to have a treaty that she wouldn't go to war without England. Now she has one she won't go to war without England, America and France.[34]

Rogers was still furious in 1924 when he wrote a column on, ironically, December 7, describing how the U.S. Navy intentionally sank its newest battleship, the $35 million USS *Washington*, to comply with the treaty. The navy towed the 32,600-ton dreadnought to a secret location off the Virginia capes where another U.S. battleship pummeled it with shells. The *Washington*, the world's most modern and heavily armored warship, stubbornly stayed afloat for five days.[35] Meanwhile, Britain and Japan did not destroy any battleships but fulfilled their treaty terms by tearing up the blueprints of future warships. "Who signed such a fool treaty?" Rogers asked. "If it's against the treaty which some bonehead signed for us, for the Lord's sake let us quit making treaties."[36] On the floor of the House of Representatives, Congressman David Kincheloe of Kentucky had Rogers's column titled "Sinking Battleships" entered into the Congressional Record.[37] "Now they are talking of having another Naval Disarmament Conference," Rogers wrote. "We can only stand one more. If they ever have a second one we will have to borrow a boat to go to it."[38]

The sinking of the *Washington* was the final insane step of diplomatic relations gone awry. Rogers did not need comic exaggeration to describe the absurd events: "Here is the funny part about the Disarmament Treaty. It says there is to be no more war, so we must sink our boats, but we are allowed to practice shooting at them as they go down, in case there is another war and we need the marksmanship. If they are trying to outlaw war, why don't they quit practicing shooting?" Rogers ended the column with an exasperated tone. "But I should be the last one to kick. They furnish me with material to make a good living."[39]

IN OCTOBER 1922, Rogers gave a speech at New York City's Town Hall supporting Ogden Mills, then running for Congress.[40] Rogers rarely campaigned for a single candidate, especially a Republican, but at the time he succumbed to one of Mills's backers, Theodore Roosevelt's son Kermit. Rogers began the speech by telling the audience that he had never entered politics because he wanted to live an honest life. "A great many think I was sent here by Mr. Mills's opponent, but this is not the case," Rogers joked. "I don't know him. But he must also be a scoundrel. From what I have read of politics every opponent is. He must be a tool of the interests."[41]

An editorial writer for the *New York Times* was in the audience and the next morning criticized Rogers for participating in Mills's campaign:

It is impossible to predict in which direction the quips of a humorist will fly. Mr. Rogers was characteristically amusing in his speech in behalf of Mr. Mills, but laughs are not votes, and whether the candidate whom Mr. Rogers was ostensibly supporting gained more by the performance than did his opponent it would be hard to say. Probably the professional engagements of Mr. Rogers will prevent his further entertaining excursions into the political field. Undoubtedly he would prove a great attraction at any political meeting, but that he would attract votes for his man is by no means certain.[42]

A month later, Mills barely won reelection. He was lucky, as many Republicans lost their seats, including Andrew Volstead, the congressman from Minnesota who authored the infamous Prohibition enforcement act. In the election, Democrat Al Smith won back the New York governorship that he had lost two years before. "Al's a mighty good man," Rogers wrote, "and is kinder figuring on the White House in a couple of years. That is, in case they are going to make a change."[43]

Soon after the election, Rogers again stepped into the political arena, this time speaking at a meeting of the Molly Pitcher Club, the most active anti-Prohibition women's group. In earlier appearances, Rogers refrained from interjecting himself into partisan issues, but Prohibition was too serious to avoid. "I don't drink myself," he told a packed house at the Thirty-ninth Street Theater, "but I do like to play to an audience that has had a few nips, because they seem to catch the point quicker and have enough intelligence to applaud." He then endorsed a proposal to legalize light wine and beer, but confessed it would not happen. "It's impossible. The prohibitionists after three years of hard liquor are not going to be content to go back to a beverage that is so light it has to have a prop to hold it up."[44]

IN DECEMBER 1922 the McNaught newspaper syndicate, recognizing Rogers's increasing popularity and his ability to humorously describe politics and world events, hired him to write a weekly column to be sold to newspapers across the country.

On Christmas Eve, while Rogers performed in the *Follies*, the *New York Times* published his first weekly article, titled "Battling for Lloyd George" and discussing the latest events in Europe. A week later McNaught distrib-

Will, Jimmy, Mary, Bill, and Betty on Long Island

uted the column nationwide, expanding to more than a hundred newspapers within two years and to some four hundred by the 1930s. Each Sunday Rogers tackled almost every public issue, humorously dissecting international conflicts, presidential elections, natural disasters, the Depression, Prohibition, and women's suffrage. Across America in big cities, small towns, and on the farm, his features not only entertained but gave the news a sharper focus and helped unravel complex events, soon becoming an eagerly read ritual. Over the next thirteen years and up until his death, Rogers rarely missed a weekly edition, eventually publishing 666 columns.

In his writings and talks, Rogers served as a keen observer of the Roaring Twenties and the Jazz Age, a decade encompassing unprecedented economic prosperity, the emergence of modern womanhood, and enormous technological breakthroughs like the mass-produced radio, Model T Fords, and sleek new aircraft that soared at incredible speeds to dizzying heights. He chronicled the progress of a country where in 1912 only 16 percent of American households had electricity but where by the mid-1920s more than 63 percent could light their homes with the flick of a switch. Rogers not only covered the

big events and the great men and women of the era but also the more hum-
drum aspects of American life. He chronicled the fads that came and went
during the twenties, when everyone played Mah-Jongg, a game imported
from China and played with decorated tiles, then switched to the biggest
craze of the decade, crossword puzzles. In 1924 a stuntman named "Shipwreck"
Kelly sat on top of a flagpole in Los Angeles for thirteen hours and set off a
rage to set pole-sitting records. Marathon dancing swept the country, with a
Cleveland couple dragging themselves around a dance floor for ninety hours.
"There is a magnificent sport!" Rogers wrote. "What a proud feeling it must
be for a fond mother to point out her young hopeful daughter as 'the longest-
winded dancer in the United States.'"[45]

Rogers reported on the latest color of Mary Pickford's hair, told about
Americans who were on a dieting craze of eating only grapefruit and lettuce,
and complained about the traffic jams on the nation's roadways. He suggested
the government "pass a law that only paid-for cars are allowed to use the
highways. That would make traffic so scarce that we could use our Boulevards
for children's playgrounds."[46] He wrote that every boy and girl should play
baseball, a sport he loved, and he wrote about golf, which he loathed. "Corruption and golf is two things we just as well make up our minds to take up,
for they are both going to be with us."[47]

As the popularity of his weekly column quickly rose, Rogers gained the
power to influence public opinion. When he joked that the worst thing Henry
Ford did was make Tin Lizzies, more Fords were sold. When he wrote about
eating leftover fish in the White House with Calvin Coolidge, he made the
stoic president seem more human—and thus more popular to the American
people.[48]

Rogers began writing his weekly column during journalism's golden age,
years before prime-time television and in a time when most Americans
learned about political events from a group of talented and colorful newspaper writers. At the top of the profession were the syndicated national columnists, each with captivating flair and most quite wealthy. Almost overnight,
Rogers joined this elite fraternity. Whenever he reported on a political convention, he shared the press box with writers who were not only legendary
but his good friends. These included Arthur Brisbane, the Hearst syndicate's
top writer, whose column "Today" appeared in more than fourteen hundred

newspapers; Heywood Broun, the widely read but disheveled columnist for the *New York World*, who was "an old tried and trusted friend of mine;"[49] Walter Lippmann, "You all read him. If you don't you ought to;"[50] O. O. McIntyre, whose column "New York Day by Day" appeared in more than five hundred papers; William Allen White, whose *Emporia* (Kansas) *Gazette* was "edited by one of the greatest and best known newspaper men in the business";[51] and Damon Runyon, whose legendary short stories celebrated the colorful underworld of prizefights, speakeasies, and gamblers. Most eccentric of them all was H. L. Mencken, the Baltimore writer whose columns were noted for their inventive vocabulary and relentless iconoclasm.

Often rambling, repetitious, and overfilled with colloquialisms, Rogers's early articles in 1923 were singularly humorous and contained little political controversy or analysis. The first columns provided mostly an amusing sketch of the events of the time, avoiding the more trenchant political commentary he produced a few years later. The best of his earlier columns were not the humorous political ones but the more serious articles coming from his heart and talking about people he cared for. An article he wrote after his sister Maud Rogers Lane passed away was one of those, written when he was deeply distraught. Maud was one of his two older sisters who raised him after his mother died, and he loved them both dearly. The following passage from his long eulogy sums up his deep feelings for Maud:

> She has passed away. But she had lived such a life that it was a privilege to pass away. Death didn't scare her. It was only an episode in her life. If you live right, death is a joke to you as far as fear is concerned. . . . [I]t was the proudest moment of my life that I was her brother. And all the honors that I could ever in my wildest dreams hope to reach, would never equal the honor paid on a little western prairie hilltop, among her people, to Maud Lane. If they will love me like that at the finish, my life will not have been in vain.[52]

After the column's first six months, Rogers began to write articles containing not only his homespun humor but also more strident and serious political commentary. Increasingly he would call for political and social change. His writing style improved considerably and the articles packed more punch. If he was truly serious about a subject, he quickly replaced his cowboy grammar and atrocious spelling with near-perfect, polished syntax.

Nevertheless, he understood the appeal of his Okie dialect. "When I first started out to write and misspelled a few words, people said I was plain ignorant," he explained. "But when I got all the words wrong, they declared I was a humorist."[53]

Over time, Rogers's repertoire expanded into a penetrating satirization of the entire political process. "You know the more you read and observe about this Politic thing You got to admit that each Party is worse than the other. The one that's out always looks the best. . . . I tell you Folks, all Politics is Apple Sauce."[54] He was not an iconoclast, however. When he ridiculed American politics and politicians, he was not necessarily attacking democracy, but rather the ways in which self-interested party politics distorted democracy. He defended democracy faithfully, but any time he saw flaws in the process or its participants, he pounced. Finding gaps between the stated purposes and actual workings of party politics, he often turned to comic exaggeration to reveal the incongruities he observed and expose the duplicity that was at their root. He referred to congressmen as joke makers who themselves did not take their own laws seriously, such as those who hypocritically hid a bottle of illegal booze under their desk on the legislature floor while they voted for Prohibition. In one early article he remarked: "Senator Curtis proposed a bill this week to stop Bootlegging in the Senate, making it unlawful for any member to be caught selling to another member while on Government property. While the bill was being read, a Government employe fell just outside the Senate door and broke a Bottle of Pre-War stuff (made just before last week's Turkish War). Now they are carpeting all the halls with a heavy material so in case of a fall there will be no serious loss."[55]

Rogers's exposure of duplicity in politics found a receptive audience in the American public. In one article he compared Congress to a movie studio, churning out laws that, like movies, could be interpreted as either comedies or tragedies. He dubbed congressmen who attached irrelevant amendments to the laws as "gag men," similar to the stunt directors who introduced superfluous slapstick to their films.[56] In another article he humorlessly described the true nature of a self-serving Congress:

> Every time a bill comes up they have a million things to decide that have nothing to do with the merit of the bill. They first must consider is, or was, it introduced by a member of the opposite Political Party. It if is, why then

something is wrong with it from the start. . . . Then the principal thing is of course, "what will this do for me personally back home?" . . . Politics and self-preservation must come first, never mind the majority of the people. . . . A man's thoughts are naturally on his next term, more than on his country.[57]

In February 1922 Rogers used another mass medium as a platform for his commentary when he made his first broadcast on pioneer radio station KDKA. Radio was still a novelty, as KDKA had aired its first broadcasts from Pittsburgh only three years before. Rogers was a hit on the airwaves, although he never would be as comfortable in a radio studio as he was in front of a live audience. A year later he made a recording of his comedy material for Victor Records. For many Americans, the recording offered the first opportunity to hear his voice. Rogers used the first record to make a more serious call for the British to grant Irish independence. "I'm off Ireland for home rule from now on," he remarked. "I read an Irish paper the other day and it says liquor is eighteen cents a quart. Can you imagine a nation wanting more freedom than that?"[58]

Over the next decade Rogers proved to be as much of a hit on the radio and the phonograph as he was on the stage, screen, and in the newspapers. His career was skyrocketing. With his audience now numbering in the millions, he gave his readers and listeners a surprisingly sophisticated and penetrating analysis of the prevailing issues of the day. Amid this serious business, he also made them laugh.

ON SEVERAL OCCASIONS Will Rogers argued that entertainers should stay out of politics. "We are paid by an audience to entertain them, not to instruct them politically," he wrote. "Then if you want to, as a citizen, go hire you a hall and tell them what you want to. You are a citizen not an actor then."[59] Rogers, however, did not follow his own advice and often used his entertainment career to take firm, serious stands on political issues. Such was the case in May 1923 when he lost his temper at the Harding administration. He learned of a plan to use U.S. Navy warships to intercept bootlegger boats off the coast. Freighters loaded with liquor loitered just outside the three-mile limit and did a thriving business, with rumrunners speeding from U.S. ports to pick up their illegal cargo. The illegal liquor traffic was almost impossible to stop, prompting the Anti-Saloon League to call for the use of the navy to stop the bootleggers. Henry Ford, rumored to be a presidential candidate, also proposed that the military enter the smuggling fray.[60] Rogers disagreed: "Now I think that would be a terrible thing. I am not in favor of [rumrunners] being there, but I am certainly opposed to use such a fine body as the American Navy to chase them with. . . . Just imagine this slogan to get boys in: 'Join the Navy and go out three miles.'"[61]

Rogers opposed using the military to enforce domestic laws. He knew that Prohibition spawned widespread corruption, even among federal agents, and feared it would spread into the military. "The principal reason I am against using them against bootleggers is that UP TO NOW THE AMERICAN ARMY OR NAVY HAS NEVER BEEN BOUGHT OFF."[62]

As he took on more controversial issues, such as protesting the use of the military to enforce Prohibition, Rogers was becoming a political voice. His protests over the use of the military may not have had a significant impact on policy makers, but nevertheless the government dropped the plan.

DURING THE Washington Disarmament Conference, Will Rogers paid a call on Warren Harding in the White House, getting along fine with the president. "I felt just like I was shaking hands with some old cow man from Oklahoma," the humorist wrote afterward. When Rogers told Harding that he wanted to tell him the latest political jokes, Harding interrupted, supposedly saying, "I know them, I appointed most of them."[63] Rogers's friend Postmaster General Will Hays[64] was with them during the visit, remarking afterward that Rogers and the president "hit it off like a couple of collie pups."[65] At times, Rogers praised Harding, writing during the summer of 1923: "Our public men are speaking every day on something but they ain't saying a thing. But when Mr. Harding said that, in case of another war that capital would be drafted the same as men, he put over a thought that, if carried out, would do more to stop Wars than all the International Courts and Leagues of Nations in the world."[66]

But Rogers could not ignore the corruption that surrounded Warren Harding, nor could he approve of some of the president's conservative policies. He criticized Harding for signing the Fordney-McCumber tariff bill in September 1922. After taking control of Congress in 1920, Republicans had rushed the bill through the legislature, but Wilson vetoed it. As soon as Hard-

*Warren Harding, sensitive
to Rogers's jokes.*
Courtesy of the Library of
Congress, LC-USZ62-91485

ing took office, Congress again passed the bill and thus established the highest duties so far in American history, with increases ranging from 60 to 400
percent on some products. Rogers strongly opposed the high tariff, believing
it inflated prices for the average consumer, hurt American farmers' ability to
compete in the world market, and inhibited international trade. He described
the tariff as a protector of privilege, "an instrument invented for the benefit
of those who make to be used against those who buy. As there is more buys
than there is makes, it is a document of the minority. But what a minority."[67]

Rogers also was disappointed with the president's sensitivity. While
Theodore Roosevelt and Woodrow Wilson enjoyed Rogers poking fun at
them from the stage, Harding turned out to be quite sensitive to jokes and
criticism. Rogers was surprised at the president's thin skin, for Harding had a
reputation as being the friendliest man to occupy the White House, a president known for greeting reporters and visitors with a warm handshake and
genial words, his Airedale terrier Laddie Boy faithfully tagging along. The
ruckus started while Rogers was on the road with the *Follies* in early 1922. He

made a number of light-hearted cracks at Harding, including some aimed at the president's taste for golf. "Hello, Mr. Harding," he said into an invisible telephone. "You lost by two holes? Well, you can't win every day."[68] When the *Follies* played in Washington DC in February, he received a visit from a White House aide who asked him to drop the Harding jokes. Rogers was devastated that somehow he had offended the president.

Rogers dropped the Harding jokes and also sent tickets to the president to attend his next Friday performance. Harding did not show up but instead attended someone else's show. Rogers had an easygoing demeanor, but he also was easily upset and took Harding's absence as a personal insult. On the next night he put some Harding jokes back in his act. At first he praised the president for a recent speech on foreign affairs to the Senate, but added that it "sounded like one of the best speeches Hughes ever wrote." Rogers was harsher when he remarked about a recent fire in the Treasury building: "The fire started on the roof and burned down and down until it got to the place where the money ought to be and there it stopped. The Harding administration had beat the fire to it. A fire in the Treasury building is nothing to get excited about during a Republican administration."[69]

After his act, Rogers stepped back on stage for a curtain call to speak about his squabble with the president. Sitting on the edge of the stage he talked with the audience as if they were his family, unloading his troubles:

> You folks know I never mean anything by the cracks I make here on politics. I generally hit the fellow that's on top because it isn't fair to hit a fellow that's down. I played here five times during the Wilson administration and every time Mr. Wilson came and laughed at the cracks I made at him more than he did at those I made against the other fellow. It makes a fellow feel good and sort of at home to find a man like that. If a big man laughs at jokes on him, he's all right.[70]

After suggesting to the audience that Harding was not such a "big man," Rogers continued to make cutting remarks about the president. In April he wrote an open letter addressed facetiously to the president at the Chevy Chase Golf Club. A month later he referred to the president as a man "from the front porch of Ohio, Warren Gamaliel something, I forgot the other." He admitted that "humorous relations between the White House and myself [were] rather strained."[71]

DURING THE SUMMER of 1923, Harding left Washington for a grueling speechmaking tour of the country. Even Rogers, himself a tireless traveler and speechmaker, felt the president was overextending himself by scheduling several speeches a day in the oppressive summer heat. "He has got a rough trip ahead of him," Rogers wrote when Harding left. "He is hitting that stubble field and roastin' ear country right in the hottest weather, when wheat is only half a crop, oats is cheap, and babies are teething. Its going to take an awful lot of perspiring."[72] Rogers's concern was well founded, for on August 2, 1923, Harding unexpectedly died of a heart attack in San Francisco in the midst of the tour.

In his next newspaper column, Rogers recanted any serious disagreements with Harding:

> You may have read in the papers last year that the diplomatic relations were strained between President Harding and some of my jokes on the administration. Now, I want to say nothing was further from the truth. That was simply newspaper stuff. It was reported that he couldn't stand jokes about the administration. Why, he had a great sense of humor and could stand all the jokes ever told about him or his policies. . . . No, I don't think I hurt any man's feelings by my little gags. I know I never willfully did it. When I have to do that to make a living I will quit.[73]

After the president's death, Rogers criticized the Harding administration for the Teapot Dome scandal and other corruption, writing that "back to normalcy consisted of the most cuckoo years of spending and carousing and graft we ever had."[74] But he never again personally criticized Harding. Dropping any hard feelings, he paid a final tribute to the dead president. "If he had weakness, it was in trusting his friends."[75]

FOUR

———

Rooting Out Political Corruption

WILL ROGERS, always mistrustful of politicians, knew the death of Warren Harding did not end the widespread political corruption of the early 1920s. Few people irritated Rogers more than crooked politicians, and plenty of them still remained for him to root out and ridicule. He attacked corruption in all of its forms, lashing out at politicians on the take, businessmen fleecing the public, philanderers leading morally decrepit lives, and mountebanks selling empty promises and false hopes. "Why, even if you talk about the church now you are just as apt to be discussing some of their scandals," he wrote.[1] Never much of an investigative reporter or one to dig up new facts or reveal a breaking scandal, Rogers instead relied on others to unearth political skullduggery. When a scandal broke in the news, however, he was among the first and most vocal to attack any wrongdoers.

One of Rogers's earlier targets was Truman Newberry, a railway, steel, and banking magnate from Detroit who barely defeated Henry Ford in 1920 for the U.S. Senate in Michigan. A year after the election, a court found Newberry guilty of accepting illegal campaign contributions, but the Supreme Court dismissed the case. Despite the Senate censuring Newberry for spending an extravagant $195,000 on his campaign, his colleagues allowed him to be seated. He resigned soon after owing to the public outrage.[2] "You know it just kinder makes you lose confidence in everything when you read and hear all those scandals on everything," Rogers wrote. "I tell you, about the only game we have left that is really on the level is craps."[3]

The Senate later refused to confirm Charles Beecher Warren as attorney general when Warren was found to have violated antitrust laws while serving as president of the Michigan Sugar Company. "Anyhow, the Senate couldn't see hiring a man who had got more money than they had," Rogers wrote. "Mr. Coolidge offered to endorse Warren's check but the Senate turned down the Signature. They are going to pick the President's hired help. They will be selecting his Neckties next."[4] When a scandal erupted at the Veterans Bureau in 1924 that revealed millions in graft and waste, an exasperated Rogers wrote: "We are just in such shape that we can't take care of but one scandal at a time. If any other small affairs come up during the coming week that look like they might develop into a scandal I will let you know."[5]

In Rogers's home state of Oklahoma the state legislature impeached Governor Jack Walton for illegal campaign funds, padding the public payroll, suspension of habeas corpus, excessive use of the pardon power, and general incompetence.[6] Rogers lambasted Walton, who served ten months in prison, for "mistaking a package of pardons for picture post cards and mailing them to all his friends in jail, and before he had discovered his mistake somebody moved his flannel nightgown right out of the Governor's mansion."[7]

None of these shameful affairs matched Teapot Dome, an infamous scandal that shook the very foundation of the Harding administration, a scandal so rotten and egregious that, for the next half century, the term Teapot Dome would symbolize high-level government corruption until replaced by another notorious scandal, Watergate. Taking its name from a massive, teapot-shaped boulder overlooking a remote field in Wyoming, the Teapot Dome oil field had been set aside by the U.S. Navy for national emergencies, the reserves to be tapped only when regular oil supplies diminished. Some politicians and private oil interests, wanting to open the oil fields to private drilling, opposed the limits, claiming the reserves were unnecessary and that American oil companies could provide for the navy.[8]

One of those calling for the oil fields to be opened to drillers was Republican Senator Albert Fall, an ex-prospector and self-taught lawyer who became New Mexico's first U.S. senator in 1912. With a drooping mustache, snakelike eyes, and wide-brimmed black hat, he looked like the crooked sheriff in a Western movie.[9] In March 1921, Harding's political allies and powerful businessmen convinced the president to appoint Fall as secretary of the interior. Harding had said earlier that "we want less government in business and more business in government," which he achieved by pandering to political cronies and corporate bosses.[10]

At the time Harding appointed Fall, Secretary of the Navy Edwin Denby controlled the naval oil reserves, but Fall soon convinced Denby to transfer jurisdiction to him at the Interior Department. Fall then leased the Teapot Dome oil rights to Harry Sinclair without competitive bidding. Fall also leased the oil reserves at Elk Hills, California, to his old prospecting partner, Edward Doheny of Pan American Petroleum, in exchange for hefty personal loans at no interest. Overall, Fall received cash and livestock from the oilmen totaling about $404,000. After the *Wall Street Journal* exposed the shady transactions, the U.S. Senate began an investigation lasting two years, taking testimony from so many witnesses that Will Rogers volunteered to testify himself, as long as he was given "transportation both ways and a room at the Willard [Hotel]."[11]

As the investigation and later trials dragged on, Rogers parodied the proceedings in dialogue. Taking some of his funniest lines verbatim from the hearings, he revealed evasive testimony, irrelevant interruptions, and constant objections over the use of anyone's name, including the president's, as no one involved in the scandal wanted to implicate their cronies. Rogers exposed both the ludicrousness and tragedy of a corrupt government that sacrificed truth and honesty for greed and political ambition, proposing half seriously to start a school of public testimony to teach politicians how to tell the truth. "If I can change that and get them to make their testimonys as smart as the men really are, why then I will have performed a Public service."[12]

In 1927 the Supreme Court ruled the oil men obtained the oil leases illegally. A lower court found Albert Fall guilty of bribery, sentencing him to one year in jail, and making him the first presidential cabinet member to go to prison. Harry Sinclair, who refused to cooperate with the government, was found guilty of contempt and received a short sentence for tampering with the jury.

Overall, Rogers soundly condemned the corruption surrounding the scandal:

> Tea started one war we had, but nobody ever thought that a Tea Pot would boil over enough to scald some of our most honorable financiers. . . . Our history honors no man who betrayed, or attempted to have betrayed a government trust. I don't want the patriotism of my children endangered, by driving around in a car that is propelled by gasoline manufactured from profits derived from tampering with the integrity of those noble officials whom we trust with not only our lives but our oil.[13]

While Rogers deplored the crookedness of Teapot Dome, he felt sympathy for the individuals involved. He had met Harry Sinclair years before after a *Frolic* performance, and the two "hit it off pretty good," Sinclair afterward sending the three Rogers children a share of his oil stock. Later, during the height of the scandal in 1924, Rogers wrote an article describing Sinclair as "an awful nice fellow."[14] He also supported Denby. "Personally and Editorially, I don't think that Mr. Denby is guilty at all of any wrong-doing that he knew of," he wrote. "But somebody has got to go in this thing."[15] When the courts sent Fall to prison, Rogers suggested he was a scapegoat, writing that he did not see much reason in "sending old man Fall to the pen. He got the $100,000, but he evidently did not put up oil lands for security, for he has lost the ranch to Doheny for the same $100,000. Course everything wasn't exactly on the up and up, but that is one case that was tried entirely by politics."[16]

Counter to most editorial opinion of the time, Rogers sympathized with the plight of Edward Doheny, charged with bribing Fall.[17] After a jury acquitted Doheny in December 1926, Rogers was elated. He met Doheny in late 1924 at a Los Angeles dinner party and liked the oil man, writing that Doheny

> is the most pleasant man you ever talked to, and very soft spoken. . . . It would be a terrible bad thing if we got so every time somebody got something from the Government, we would think there was something crooked about it. I like to tell bum jokes about all our great and public men, but I got a lot of confidence in every one of them. . . . That's what has made our government, is our faith in it. Let us keep cussing 'em and joking about 'em, but by golly if somebody is going to call one of them a crook why lets climb his hide.[18]

Doheny again went on trial for bribery four years later and once more Rogers came to his defense:

> Capone goes free to take up his useful life's work, and on the same front page Doheny, who developed a great industry and has given high wages to thousands for years, is called a "menace to society." We who lived neighbors to him know that if he is convicted of "staking" all old mining days friends, he will serve 2,000 years. I joke about our prominent men, but at heart I believe in 'em. I do think there is times when traces of "dumbness" crop up in official life, but not crookedness.[19]

Rogers appears inconsistent when he decries corruption on one hand, while on the other he sympathizes with those accused of it. However, his sense of morality helps explain his behavior, as he deeply loved his fellow man as an individual, but mistrusted the evils inherent in huge corporations, big government, and modern, complex society. He was overly sympathetic to the wrongdoers because he always wanted to be liked and felt he could befriend any man he met—no matter that man's past. He probably never read Rousseau, yet his homespun philosophy also looked upon man as a "noble savage" who, when freed from the corrupt influences of modern society, is unspoiled, naturally good, and happy. Rogers explained his thoughts to his friend philosopher Will Durant: "Any man that thinks that civilization has advanced is an egotist," he wrote. "Indians and primitive races were the highest civilized, because they were more satisfied, and they depended less on each other, and took less from each other."[20] He implied both his faith in his fellow man and his distrust in mankind when he wrote a final conclusion about the Teapot Dome crowd. "Father don't blame them, they know not what they are doing."[21]

IN JUNE 1924 Rogers attended the Republican National Convention in Cleveland. As a syndicated writer he planned to write a column each day describing the excitement of the presidential nominating process and giving the American people a front-row report of democracy in action. But he was sorely disappointed, as he found the convention to be a very tame affair. Incumbent President Calvin Coolidge "could have been nominated by post card," and the only excitement occurred when a delegate lost his hotel room key.[22] Rogers knew the Republican Convention was little more than a rubber stamp of Coolidge's reelection bid. As expected, delegates unanimously nominated Coolidge on the first ballot. They briefly interrupted the boredom when they nominated dark horse Charles Dawes for vice president on the third ballot.

For Rogers, the real excitement in Cleveland was meeting William Jennings Bryan, also attending the convention as a syndicated writer. Rogers described his lunch with the famous orator and presidential candidate as "the thrill of my entire life." According to Rogers, when the two men first met in the press box, they were "the only two aliens [Democrats] in the entire hall."[23] Rogers was a little nervous at first, for Bryan was one of his favorite targets. "Now take the case of W. J. Bryan," he'd once written. "He would make an ideal Sunday President. But would be an absolute liability on week days."[24] Bryan, however, took the barbs in stride, and the two men enjoyed bantering in the press box. During one conversation Bryan turned to Rogers and said, "You write a humorous column, don't you!" Rogers looked around to see if anybody was listening, then said, "Yes, sir." Bryan replied, "Well I write a serious article, and if I think of anything of a comical or funny nature, I will give it to you." Rogers thanked Bryan and told him, "If I happen to think of anything of a serious nature I will give it to you." Later Rogers wrote that, "when he said he wrote seriously and I said I wrote humorously I thought afterward, we both may be wrong."[25]

Bryan's wit surprised Rogers. As they sat in the press box, a long-winded speaker on the convention floor muffed a gag in the middle of a particularly bad speech. Bryan, then the nation's most zealous religious fundamentalist and the leading defender of public morality, turned to Rogers and said that "the speaker suffered from a premature climax." Taken aback at Bryan's earthiness, Rogers admitted, "I will have to give him a couple of good serious ones to make up for that one."[26]

After the Republicans nominated Coolidge, Rogers left Cleveland early and headed to Atlantic City for rehearsal, then to New York City for the opening of Ziegfeld's *Follies of 1924* at the New Amsterdam Theater. The *Follies* began on June 24, the same day as the beginning of the Democratic National Convention at Madison Square Garden. Rogers again covered the event as a correspondent. Staying at the Astor Hotel, he spent each day at the convention and then hustled to Broadway each night to perform in the *Follies*. His *Follies* act was a breeze, for the Democrats, unlike the stuffy Republicans two weeks before, provided him with plenty of hilarious material.

Stuffed in a sweaty convention hall for three long, gruelingly hot weeks in June and July, Rogers watched as the Democratic Party tore itself apart trying to nominate a presidential candidate. The convention proved to be the longest in U.S. history, a marathon of endless speeches, balloting, and dealmaking, and degenerating into a destructive struggle between the northern and southern, urban and rural, wet and dry, and Catholic and Protestant factions of the party.[27] Rogers soon was disgusted at the proceedings. "I saw something yesterday that for stupidity, lack of judgment, nonsensicality, unexcitement, uselessness and childishness has anything I've ever seen beaten. It was the Democratic National Convention."[28]

After the Democrats failed to take a stance on Prohibition, Rogers decried the plank as a farce, looking as if it was "wet on week days and dry on Sundays."[29] The Democrats could not agree on whether to condemn the Ku Klux Klan, at the time numbering five million members nationwide and such a powerful political force that some referred to the convention as the "Klanbake." After the Democrats refused to denounce the Klan, Rogers was appalled. "Saturday will always remain burned in my memory as long as I live as being the day when I heard the most religion preached, and the least practiced, of any day in the world's history."[30]

As the convention crawled along with little hope of ending, Rogers shared his exasperation:

> As I pen you these few lines, the Democratic National Convention is still going on; going on to where, nobody knows. But it has to end sometime for even a delegate can only stand just so much oratory. Perhaps by the time you read this they will have nominated a man for president, but I doubt it very much. . . . There was so many being nominated that some of the men making the nominating speeches had never even met the men they were nominating. I know they had not from the way they talked about them.[31]

In another column, Rogers pretended the convention was still going far into the future, a time when "Japan has owned California for years" and the Philippines were Japan's naval base. He signed the article with his eldest son's name, who claimed that his father had aged so much since the beginning of the convention that the job had to be handed over to the next generation.[32]

On July 5, two Arizona delegates broke the tension when they cast their votes for Will Rogers, at the time dozing off in the press box. After he woke, he said he had never heard of the two delegates before but "had, by the way, heard of Arizona."[33]

Unlike the Republican Convention, where he attended solely as a correspondent, Rogers participated more actively at the Democratic gathering. On the third night of the convention, William Randolph Hearst gave a lavish private party for the Democrats at the Ritz-Carlton. Starting at midnight, Rogers highlighted the entertainment with a humorous attack on the Republicans. The audience included Franklin Roosevelt, William Jennings Bryan, Bernard Baruch, Senator Joe Robinson, and other Democratic notables.[34] During the convention, Rogers lobbied hard for the two front-running candidates, Al Smith and William McAdoo. On July 3, 1924, as the floor fight raged on, Rogers sent a telegram to William Jennings Bryan transmitting a note of urgency. "We want Al Smith and no more hot air."[35] Smith entered the convention as the front-runner with strong support in key states, but opposition to his Catholicism and his "wringing wetness" crippled his chances. At one point Rogers suggested Smith change his religion to Protestant. He admired Smith, writing that the New York governor was "the most sentimental prominent man I ever met. He glories in the past."[36] After it became clear that Smith would not get the nomination, Rogers shifted his loyalty and spoke at a campaign rally supporting McAdoo. He again displayed an inconsistency between how he behaved and what he wrote, openly helping Smith and McAdoo during the convention but four months later writing that a stage performer should not "carry any Campaign Propaganda into his stage work, either for or against any candidate. He has no right to use his privilege as an actor to drive home his Political Beliefs. . . . We are paid by an audience to entertain them, not to instruct them politically."[37]

After 103 ballots, the Democrats "pulled a bonehead" and abandoned Smith and McAdoo.[38] They compromised on dark horse John W. Davis, a successful attorney and former ambassador to Great Britain. For vice president they chose Charles W. Bryan, younger brother of William Jennings, to appease the conservatives. The Democrats assured their own downfall with the weak candidates, for in November the incumbent Coolidge defeated Davis handily and won all states outside of the South except Wisconsin. After the election, columnist Heywood Broun suggested the Democrats could have chosen a much more viable candidate. "The Convention went on to choose John W. Davis, and, meaning no disrespect to Mr. Davis, I insist that Will Rogers could have given the Democratic voters a better run for their ballots."[39]

Rogers took the defeat of both Al Smith and William McAdoo personally. He liked both men and felt both were well qualified to be president and more electable than Davis. On the day the convention ended, he telegraphed Smith his humorous condolences as well as his serious disappointment:

> *Didnt I predict from the first that you would be the lucky one. . . . Personally I am glad you was not nominated, it would have taken two years to have cleaned the paper off the streets here. Had many a pleasant chat with your wife at her box during the three weeks readings of states insanity statistics. Personally I believe she is glad you are beaten, what smart woman would want to leave New York to go to Washington. Remember 1928 is a different year[,] we will make a joint campaign. I am glad you followed my example and withdrew.*[40]

On the same day Rogers sent a telegram to McAdoo as well:

> *Condolence to a fellow defeated candidate, I too know what it is to suffer. Lack of whiskey, and harmony, is all that beat us. But just think what we have to be grateful for. We can return to California while these other poor devils have to stay either here or in Washington. You are too good a fellow WG to be spoiled by being a mere politician. Hell is full of political candidates, but it will be several years before they have a WG McAdoo. . . . When you get to England find out who John W Davis is for and cable particulars.*[41]

The Democratic Convention of 1924, the most bitter and longest continuously running convention in U.S. history, was an important milestone in the political indoctrination of Rogers. He worked the floor, met political bosses from across the country, poked his head into smoke-filled rooms, and learned the political ropes from savvy ward heelers and courthouse gangs. He watched democracy work, albeit not very well, while still admiring most of its participants. Using comic exaggeration, he described a flawed and often foolish convention that was so tangled up that the only way to resolve the bitter stalemate between two strong front-runners was to select a lesser known and politically weaker candidate. Appalled at the widespread hypocrisy and dishonesty, he found little true democracy being practiced. In one of his convention articles, he observed:

> Well, they have been balloting all day at the Democratic side show at the Garden, for that is what some misguided people think is the nominating place.
>
> The real nomination is taking place in a room at some hotel with less than six men present.
>
> And when it is known it will be as big a surprise to those delegates as it will be to you out in Arizona, and you will have just as much to do with it as they will have had.[42]

Rogers was exasperated but also hooked on politics. From this period on he took a more active interest, even at times participating, in political events. The chaotic convention not only infuriated him but hardened his political leanings. "I don't belong to any organized political faith," he admitted. "I am a Democrat."[43]

"WELL, SEE by the papers where the Prince of Wales over in England fell off his horse again today," Will Rogers wrote in April 1923. "That's got so it is not news any more. If he stayed on it would be news. . . . I should suggest they have men follow along on foot with a net and catch him each time as he falls."[44] Rogers could not resist making fun of the prince's frequent riding accidents, but as a fellow horseman who took his own share of spills he also respected the prince's recklessness in the steeplechase and on the polo field. He also took an early liking to the future king of England. "There is a young man that has got away above the average intelligence of most Kings, and a whole lot of Commoners," he wrote.[45] "This Prince seems to be a mighty fine kind of guy and it is a shame he should have been handicapped by birth, for there is a boy who would have made something out of himself."[46]

At the time of Rogers's article, the Prince of Wales, actually christened

Edward Albert Christian George Andrew Patrick David, was the heir apparent to the British throne.[47] A thirty-year-old bachelor whose womanizing spawned juicy newspaper gossip, he was the most pursued, talked-about, and photographed man in the world. During the summer of 1924 when the prince visited New York, the city rolled out the red carpet to fete him in a whirlwind of lavish balls and parties, photographers snapping every move he made, his full-page portrait splashed across the rotogravures.

Appearing nightly in the *Follies* during the prince's visit, Rogers was visited in his dressing room after an evening performance by an aide to the prince, who invited the humorist to entertain His Royal Highness. On September 3, Rogers finished his *Follies* show early and headed to the exclusive Piping Rock Country Club on Long Island. He was the only entertainment and spoke for twenty minutes, a great hit according to the *New York Times*. His "drolleries evidently had charmed the royal visitor."[48] On the next day Rogers played polo and lunched with the prince, who was perfectly dressed in the customary white polo breeches, a tan sweater, and an Indian pith helmet, while Rogers appeared in ordinary riding clothes and his weather-beaten leather jacket.

Two days later the prince invited Rogers to attend the International Polo Tournament at the Meadow Brook Club. That night they attended the lavish dinner that the prince gave at Piping Rock. All of the others at the dinner were attired in strict formal white ties and tails, but Rogers arrived at the club wearing his worn blue serge suit. Two weeks later, the prince put seven of his polo ponies on the auction block at East Williston, Long Island. Rogers showed up and paid $2,100 for a chestnut Welsh gelding named Jacinto, which he later gave to Florenz Ziegfeld's daughter Patricia.[49]

The friendship between the part-Cherokee Oklahoman and the future king of England at first seems odd, for Rogers was not a member of the American diplomatic corps or the wealthy elite and had nothing in common with British royalty. However, each man was interested in the other and they treated each other as equals. The prince owned a ranch in Canada and liked to discuss raising cattle with Rogers. Both loved horses, played polo recklessly, and had an independence of thought. Another reason for their bonding may have been that neither man wanted or needed anything from the other.[50]

The two men rekindled their friendship two years later when Rogers traveled to Europe in May 1926. They met in London at the prince's St. James

Palace, spending several hours bantering about horsemanship, polo, travel, Prohibition, and a general labor strike then paralyzing Britain.[51] During his visit, Rogers detected a reluctance in the prince to become king. "Just between you and I, Calvin," Rogers wrote in an open letter to President Coolidge afterward, "he don't care any more about being King than you would going back to Vice President again."[52] Rogers was right. In 1936, the prince was crowned Edward VIII but, in one of the most stunning events of the century, abdicated his throne the same year to marry an American divorcee.

ON APRIL 23, 1925, Rogers visited Calvin Coolidge in the White House. He liked Coolidge, a meager-looking New Englander with a hatchet face, sandy hair, and tight lips who was as silent as a cake of ice. Alice Longworth said that the dour Coolidge looked like he had "been weaned on a pickle."[53] Rogers, however, found the president to be warm and funny and "as agreeable as an Insurance Agent."[54] He cracked up the usually impassive Coolidge by introducing himself and asking, "Pardon me, I didn't catch the name."[55] After his visit Rogers rejoined Coolidge in the evening when they both spoke at the annual Gridiron Club Dinner honoring General John Pershing.[56] Rogers was upset that the government forced the general to retire on half pay:

> Here is a man that absolutely won the war for us, and all he got was a medal. He had to pay his own taxicab fare to the place where they gave it to him. . . . My Lord! Can't our government do something for a man who is not a politician?
>
> He is not a politician. He was born a soldier and he will die a soldier, so why didn't they give him his rank for life? . . . He not only won the last war, but he has done more than any other man to keep us from losing the next one.[57]

In the Gridiron audience was Broadway producer Gene Buck, sitting next to the famous army pilot General Billy Mitchell. After the dinner, Buck introduced Rogers to Mitchell, who invited him to take a flight over Washington. The flight with Mitchell was not Rogers's first time aloft; he had taken his first flight ten years before when he and Betty spent a day at Atlantic City. A pilot had moored his Curtiss flying boat just off the boardwalk and offered rides in the seaplane for five dollars. Rogers was nervous at first, as he never liked heights, but he built up the courage to take a flight.[58]

Rogers was thrilled by his Atlantic City ride and for years after he would actively promote aviation progress. But it was the flight he made with Billy Mitchell after the Gridiron dinner that turned Rogers into an aggressive lobbyist for aviation. Strikingly handsome in his expensively tailored uniforms and polished knee-high cavalry boots, a championship polo player who spoke flawless French, Mitchell was then America's most vocal advocate for military aviation. In World War I he was a fearless combat pilot and the first American airman to fly over enemy lines.

Mitchell was one of the few military officers who fully appreciated the destructive potential of aircraft. In July 1921 he demonstrated the power of massed bombers when he led a small formation attacking the captured German battleship *Ostfriesland* off the Virginia capes. Using six 2,000-pound bombs, Mitchell's aircraft sent the battleship quickly to the bottom. His demonstration of aerial attacks proved that bombers were a formidable weapon, but also alienated him from the military brass, then not yet ready to embrace the strategic value of air power.

Besides being a famed aviator, Mitchell was a shrewd political insider who knew the power of the press. Well aware of Rogers's popularity and comments supporting military aviation, Mitchell knew the humorist Rogers could be a valuable, influential ally in promoting air power. Eighteen months before, Rogers had criticized Congress for not building a credible air force. "Has Congress heeded what the Airship is doing?" he wrote. "No, they go ahead building battleships which will be as useless as a shipping board."[59]

On the morning after the Gridiron dinner, Mitchell picked up Rogers at his hotel and drove to Bolling Field. Mitchell orchestrated the event, for a crowd of newspaper reporters and photographers were already on the runway as Rogers climbed aboard Mitchell's plane. When they landed after a brief aerial tour of the city, Rogers was thrilled. "Here I was a thousand feet up in the air when you can't even get me to ride a tall horse."[60]

Mitchell told Rogers after they landed that he had made his last flight as a brigadier general, for at midnight he would be demoted to colonel and exiled to a post in Texas. The two men had a long serious talk about aviation and its future. Mitchell urged Rogers to take a stronger stance in promoting

Rogers, after a flight with Billy Mitchell

aviation and support his crusade for a separate air force. Rogers admired Mitchell, and their meeting was the beginning of a friendship that ended only with Rogers's death.

After his flight with Mitchell, Rogers campaigned even more enthusiastically for military aviation. He attacked the army and navy for bickering over who was in charge of military aviation, suggesting that taking away their airplanes would make them "howl like a pet coon."[61] Many of his remarks were more serious: "Why a battleship will be as obsolete in the next war as a sword was in the last one, because in the next war there ain't nobody going to shoot nothing at you. They are just going to drop it on you. So everybody better start flying or digging in."[62]

One of his columns, titled "Big Flying at Clover Field," was so critical of military aviation that a congressman read the article into the *Congressional*

Record.[63] Rogers took a swipe at Coolidge's refusal to fund military aviation, saying that the president, "on account of his economy plan has suggested that they fly as high as they can on what little gas they have, and then coast down. In that way they get twice the amount of distance." But overall Rogers was grim, concluding the state of military aviation was "so sad it wasn't even funny."[64]

Soon after their flight, Rogers condemned the army for demoting Mitchell, writing that the aviator "never squealed and he never whined. He knows that some day America will have to have a tremendous Air Force, but he can't understand why we are not training it now. But it does seem a strange way to repay a man who has fought for us through a war, and who has fought harder for us in peace to be reprimanded for telling the truth."[65]

Despite being demoted and transferred to a remote post, Mitchell continued to anger his superiors by speaking out for a larger, separate air force. He criticized the military after the crash of the navy dirigible *Shenandoah* in September 1925. The huge airship flew into a severe thunderstorm over Noble County, Ohio, and broke into pieces, killing fourteen crew members. Mitchell accused senior army and navy officials of "treasonable" incompetence. To the brass he had gone too far, and President Coolidge personally ordered him court-martialed for insubordination.[66]

Mitchell's seven-week trial began on October 28, 1925, in the old Census Bureau offices a few blocks from the White House. During the proceedings, Rogers rode the train from Baltimore, where he was speaking on a lecture tour, to Washington to attend the court-martial.[67] Sitting with Mitchell's lawyers, Rogers watched as a witness delivered a scathing attack on Mitchell. He hurried over and put an arm around the aviator. "The people are with you Billy. Keep punching. You'll rope 'em yet." Mitchell was moved and said years later, "It was a moment of tenderness—the one moment of all that nightmare which I'll never forget."[68]

In a speech a week later, Rogers defended Mitchell and criticized the president:

> I see where they had [Mitchell] on trial today, If he had cruticised [*sic*] the
> Navy instead of the Army he would have come clear on the first ballott.
>
> If they convict him for talking too much . Let's try the Senate. . . .

. . . They say Mitchell was wrong about the Shendoah, they had an entire investigation to find out about the Shenandoah and dident find out what it was, but still they say Mitchell is wrong

Coolidge says [he] had nothing to do with the Mitchell investigation . . .

Say, the heads of any department in Washington cant change shirts till Cal gives em the high sign, He makes out their Menus.[69]

Rogers's criticism of the president must have struck a nerve. He wrote later that Coolidge "hasn't been paying much attention to me lately."[70]

To no one's surprise, the court found Mitchell guilty of insubordination and suspended him from active duty for five years without pay. After Mitchell resigned, he spent the next decade writing and preaching airpower.

So did Will Rogers. Over the next ten years he aggressively promoted aviation in countless newspaper articles and radio broadcasts. He was one of the first to propose that the federal government directly support civilian aviation. "Why not a subsidy to commercial aviation?" he wrote. "Congress is waiting two more wars to see if they are practical."[71] His remark that "the airplane program turned out more air than planes" helped lead to a Senate investigation.[72] During the 1920s and '30s he did more than any other private citizen who couldn't fly an airplane to change aviation's image from barnstorming daredevilry to a mode of mass transport that was safe and dependable. His love affair with flying and his enthusiastic support for aviation progress lasted until his death, which resulted, with tragic irony, from an aircraft crash.

WHILE WILL ROGERS was performing in the *Follies* during the summer of 1925, a twenty-four-year-old high school science teacher named John Scopes stood trial in the rural town of Dayton, Tennessee. Local officials accused Scopes of violating a state law forbidding the teaching of Charles Darwin's theory of evolution that argued "man has descended from a lower order of animals." Initiated by the American Civil Liberties Union as a First Amendment test case for freedom of speech and separation of church and state, the trial became one of the most publicized and hotly debated of the decade.[73]

The trial's notoriety was owing to its two renowned protagonists. Defending Scopes was Clarence Darrow, sixty-eight, the most famous criminal defense lawyer in the country and a popular and powerful public orator. Tall, big-boned, and slouching like a rumpled country lawyer, Darrow was an atheist who spent a lifetime deriding Christian beliefs. He helped over a hundred clients, including the infamous murderers Leopold and Loeb, escape the death penalty. He was among the first attorneys to use the insanity plea, prompting Rogers to criticize Darrow for always "trying to prove the defendant was sane enough to plead guilty, but too insane to hang."[74]

The prosecutor was William Jennings Bryan, sixty-five, the three-time Democratic candidate, staunch prohibitionist, and the country's leading and most vocal Christian fundamentalist. With his great bald head shining like a beacon and sweat pouring down his brow, Bryan vigorously defended the Tennessee law, arguing that "the people have the right and must have the right to regulate what is taught in their schools."[75]

The riveting trial lasted for two scorching weeks in July, beginning in a second-floor courtroom but later moving outside to a crude wooden platform to escape the heat. The trial degenerated into what *Time* magazine called a fantastic cross between a circus and a holy war.

The town leaders of Dayton invited Will Rogers to attend the trial, but he turned them down. Nevertheless, he devoted considerable attention to the event, as the entire episode angered him. To him, the trial not only politicized religion but made a spectacle of it. "After all," he said, "we are not so much concerned as to where we came from and where we are going."[76] He felt that both Bryan and Darrow were making fools of themselves, writing:

> If I was in either one of those men's places I wouldn't spend the best years of my Chautauqua life trying to prove or disprove my ancestry. With the condition of the Democratic Party is in at present, instead of trying to prove he didn't come from a monkey, Bryan had better be spending his time trying to prove he didn't descend from a Democrat.
>
> And as for Clarence Darrow, he just don't naturally believe in anything. If the sun is shining, Darrow will put you up an argument, assisted by expert testimony, to show you that it is raining and that you are cock-eyed and just can't see it. If, in your mind, a snake crawls, Darrow will introduce some snakeologist to show you that the snake is in reality skipping hither and thither like a gazelle, and that you don't know enough to see it. What Darrow should be doing and trying to disprove is that he didn't come from Chicago.[77]

Rogers was irritated with Bryan's rabid fundamentalism, writing in his weekly column:

> Tennessee claims they didn't descend from a monkey, but their actions in this . . . case prove otherwise.
>
> You can't stop a man thinking; neither do I think Bryan could start a serious man thinking.
>
> There is a terrible lot of us who don't think we come from a monkey, but if there are some people who think that they do, why, it's not our business to rob them of what little pleasure they may get out of imagining it. . . .
>
> Why don't Bryan and a lot of other people let the world alone? What has been the matter with it up to now?[78]

Rogers's criticisms revealed his strong views favoring freedom of religion. "The Lord put all these millions of people over the earth," he wrote. "They don't all agree on how they got here, and ninety per cent don't care. But he was pretty wise when he did see to it that they all do agree on one thing, (whether Christian, Heathen, or Mohammedan) and that is the better lives you live the better you will finish."[79]

On July 21, 1925, the court found John Scopes guilty and fined him $100, but a Tennessee appeals court later cleared him on a technicality.

Five days after the close of the trial, William Jennings Bryan, exhausted from his ordeal in Dayton, died. Rogers had kind words about a man whom he had criticized often but respected deeply. Shortly after Bryan was buried in Arlington National Cemetery, Rogers wrote:

> I am going to miss him. I guess I have told a thousand so called Jokes about him, some in favor, and most of them against him. Most of them I have repeated to his face. I feel and I hope he knew personally I always admired him.
>
> So here's good luck to you WJ. YOU WERE A NOVELTY AMONG POLITICIANS. YOU WERE SINCERE, YOU MIGHT HAVE MISSED THE WHITE HOUSE, BUT YOU DIDN'T MISS THE HEARTS OF THE PLAIN PEOPLE.[80]

WILL ROGERS starred in Ziegfeld's *Follies* for the last time in 1925. He left reluctantly, for he thoroughly enjoyed performing nightly in New York City where he had many close friends. He loved to stand before the footlights, rope his favorite celebrities in the audience, and drag them onto the New Amsterdam stage. That summer he introduced Thomas Edison to the audience, which stood and cheered the seventy-eight-year-old inventor. Tom Mix, then an international film star of silent Westerns, also showed up to see his old friend perform. Rogers reminisced from the stage about their days touring with Wild West shows twenty years before. "We didn't get much money, in fact our salary was supposed to be $20 a week," he remarked. "That was one time we were not overpaid actors, because we didn't even get the twenty."[81] Nevertheless, it was time for Rogers to move on. By the midtwenties, the *Follies* were fading, while he was a rising star, having outgrown the slapstick routines and scantily clad chorines of the Ziegfeld show.

Glad to be on the road again, Rogers left New York after the *Follies* closed in the fall and began an eleven-week lecture tour across the country. He loved it, writing from Vermont that "there is nothing thickens one like travel."[82] His New York agent booked him to do sixty lectures for $1,000 each. The tour was grueling, with a two-hour monologue at each stop, sometimes twice, his only rest often a couple of hours of sleep on the late-night train. Betty, who enjoyed the road as much as Will, accompanied him on part of the tour.

Rogers began the tour on October 1, 1925, with a lecture from the pulpit of the Park Church in Elmira, New York. Carrying only a small Gladstone bag "that packed itself" in one hand and his portable typewriter in the other, he crisscrossed the country lecturing social groups, business organizations, women's clubs, and almost every Elks Club and American Legion post he passed.[83] Stepping onto empty stages dressed in his modest double-breasted blue suit, he appeared in theaters, school auditoriums, concert halls, courthouses, and churches, while giving impromptu talks to crowds who gathered around him in train stations and greasy-spoon diners. If a community had a "railroad and a hall," he promised, "we'll be there sooner or later."[84] He made one-night stands in Cleveland, St. Louis, Pittsburgh, Detroit, Indianapolis, Minneapolis, Milwaukee, Chicago, and other midwestern cities and towns. In Des Moines he arrived during a vicious snowstorm. While appearing in Tulsa he visited with his Oklahoma relatives, then swung south to perform in Nashville, Memphis, and Montgomery, where he attended a Negro football game. In New Orleans he dined at Antoines, and in Houston he played in a local polo match. He swung back north, hitting Sioux City, Duluth, Buffalo, Rochester, and then east to Washington DC, where on November 28 he stopped by the White House to visit President Coolidge. He made a huge loop down through Richmond and Atlanta, then out to South Bend and Cincinnati, and back to Washington DC for the Billy Mitchell court-martial.

Whenever Rogers arrived at a new city or town, he buttonholed anyone he found to get the latest political scuttlebutt, then tailored his talk to the townfolk. He liked to get gossip on the town mayor so he could poke fun at him and other local politicians. "I talked with every Editor in each town, all the writers on the papers, Hotel Managers, Ranchmen, Farmers, Politicians, Head Waiters, Barbers, Newsboys, Bootblacks. Everybody I met I would try to get their angle."[85] When he stopped in Birmingham in November, he took shots at the city commission and its board of revenue and criticized a recent election rumored to be corrupt. He rebuked the Alabamans for spending $25 million for roads, then spending another $75 million "to make them meet."[86]

On the road Rogers spoke about politics and everything else, from football to rumrunners, from motion pictures to the comics, to the latest gossip about "Peaches," a fifteen-year-old New York schoolgirl who married a fifty-one-year-old real estate millionaire. He talked about the Florida land boom, where some of his rich Jewish friends were busy buying and selling lots. "When will the boom end?" he asked the audience. "Well, you'll know when it is over. Some morning when you wake up and find that all the land has been purchased by Gentiles. Then you'll know the boom has ended."[87]

He defended Billy Mitchell and ridiculed Billy Sunday. He pounced on his perennially favorite target, Congress, where he suggested that "every time they make a joke, it's a law. . . . And everytime they make a law it's a joke."[88] Funny one moment, he quickly turned dead serious. He attacked the Ku Klux Klan, warning that the organization was "coming into New York and kinder got it in for the Jewish People, Now they are wrong[.] I am against that."[89]

Traveling back and forth across the country filling theaters and lecture halls with overflow crowds, Rogers strengthened his connection with the American people. His popularity spread across the country like a prairie wildfire.

Despite his hectic schedule giving lectures every night, Rogers still ground out his weekly column, pecking away with two fingers on his Corona. When finished, he raced to the town's train station and gave the article to the local telegraph operator to meet his deadline. Besides containing humor and a heavy dose of politics, Rogers's column provided readers with a running travelogue of his whistle-stop tour, with complaints about the weather in one region, the food in another, and most of all descriptions of how wonderful the people were across the country.

When he wasn't lecturing or writing articles, he visited veterans hospitals, attended fairs and rodeos, accepted the keys to dozens of cities by the same mayors he joked about, and performed benefits for needy causes. "I make it a rule to play every Sunday night for charity," he told a reporter while rushing for a train.[90]

On December 14, Rogers ended the 1925 tour after eleven weeks on the road and seventy appearances. He pocketed at least $75,000, a huge amount for the time. His last performance was at Symphony Hall in Boston. Everywhere he performed he received flattering reviews, but in Boston he didn't please everyone.[91] Henry Taylor Parker, the music critic of the *Boston Transcript*, commented that Rogers's "diction was poor" and his "selections were extremely bad." The thin-skinned Rogers devoted an entire column to ridicule the music critic, even attacking his masculinity. "Now can you imagine yourself raising your son up to be a 'Male' Musical Critic?" he wrote. "If one of my boys ever starts shedding off to be a Male Musical Critic the rope that I have played with for life will be put to some practical use." Rogers also chafed after Parker accused him of being a small-town performer:

> In short, Parker, when you looked me over you were "slumming." . . . But you unconsciously paid me a Bear of a compliment when you said, "Will is a small town actor."
>
> You bet your life I am small town. I am smaller than that, I am NO town at all, and listen, that is what I am going to stay is Small Town.[92]

BY THE END OF 1925 Will Rogers had written his column for three years. Every week he appeared in several hundred newspapers across the country. Millions of Americans arose in the morning to read what he had to say. He was immensely admired. In Washington DC, he stood in the gallery of the

House of Representatives and received a standing ovation from the congress-men. According to a *New York Times* reporter standing nearby, Rogers was surprised by the honor and "turned a fiery red and bowed."[93]

Why was Rogers, a poorly educated part-Cherokee, soaring in popularity? There were other humorists and there were other political columnists, but only Rogers combined the two crafts so effectively. No other writer was more skillful at coating a sound idea with a little humor. He wrote in a very per-sonal and casual style as if he were talking face-to-face with his reader. He wasted few words. "Examine any statement that [Rogers] has ever made," the novelist Ben Dixon MacNeill observed, "and there is a nugget of pure sense in it. It was his gift that he could refine it into sixteen words when any-body else would write a book about it."[94]

Rogers's bad grammar, homespun vernacular, and poor spelling allowed him to communicate more effectively with the average American, whose education level averaged about the same as his own ten years of formal schooling. He was successful because he brought balance and reason during the Roaring Twenties, an age of extremes and excesses. It was Rogers, more than any single elected official, who represented the people.

More importantly, Rogers earned the trust of his readers. He was not always accurate or roaringly funny, but he was consistently honest and sin-cere. The high esteem he possessed enabled him, as a private citizen elected to no public office, to gain power and influence that, in many ways, remains unparalleled in American history. Few men have been so universally listened to and believed as was Rogers during the 1920s and 1930s.

Rogers provided evenhandedness during a period when many newspapers were decidedly biased. Cities often had several rival morning dailies, each aligned with a different political camp and supporting its own faction. Using both humor and nonpartisanship, Rogers stuck to the issues, and his column was a welcome relief from the political divisiveness of the day.

In both his writings and lectures Rogers explored complex, controversial political issues. He frequently made backhanded swipes at the self-centered Babbittry and commercialism of the 1920s, attacking the younger Gatsbys for their hedonistic lifestyles and excesses of booze, sex, and instant gratification. Rogers, however, was not one of the many bitter critics of the era who, like Sinclair Lewis in *Main Street*, scorned traditional American culture and hometown values. Nor was Rogers one of those iconoclasts who, whether from the far left or far right, wanted to dismantle democracy and build anew American government and society.

Rogers claimed often that all he knew was what he read in the papers, but he was much better read than he admitted. As early as 1908 he revealed an interest in deeper subjects when he mailed Betty Blake two novels he had read.[95] One was *A Little Brother of the Rich*, by the socialist writer Joseph Medill Patterson. The muckraking novel criticizes the inhumanity of modern industrialism and capitalism and deplores poverty and the evils of the idle rich. In a pessimistic view of the industrial world, Patterson describes how "grimy gnomes toiled in the dark underground to bring fuel to the light; . . . children of five years spun clothing for the race."[96] The novel ends by depicting capitalistic life as a "horrible lie, a poisonous blunder, a soul destroyer."[97]

The other book was Robert Herrick's *Together*, another muckraker and a best seller of 1908. *Together* deals with determinism and free will, corrupt professionals and businessmen, and the ways in which individual liberty clashes with materialism and power. Herrick indicts the capitalism of his day, labeling it "the most material age and the most material men and the least lovely civilization on God's earth."[98] He had little faith in government and business to cure society's ills and was suspicious of political doctrines and utopian legislation. "The effort by organization to right the human fabric, seemed futile, for the most part," the novelist wrote. "If man were right with himself, square with his own soul, each one of the millions, there would be no wrongs to right by machinery, by laws, by discussion, by agitation, by theories or beliefs."[99]

The social and political issues explored by both novels imply that Rogers had a keen interest in the complex social issues of his day. He took the two books seriously enough to send them to the woman he soon would marry. In his later writings and lectures, Rogers supported many of the social causes that Patterson and Herrick crusaded for. Together, Patterson and Herrick called for sweeping economic reform that would narrow the huge gap between the haves and the have-nots. Rogers would echo that call, albeit less radically. While he was in favor of many progressive reforms and embraced change as inevitable, he never turned against his own rock-solid, middle-of-the-road, small-town principles, remaining steadfastly loyal to his country, its people, and American democracy.

By the mid-1920s Rogers held a growing and well-deserved reputation as a wise, down-to-earth commentator of the political scene, a reputation that guaranteed him an influential role in the shaping of public opinion and national policy. Although he was still regarded primarily as a humorist, the American public nevertheless began to take his writings and speeches seriously. He alluded to his new, more influential role, remarking later, "Everything is changing. . . . People are taking their comedians seriously and the politicians as a joke, when it used to be visa versa."[100] An editorial in *The Nation* concluded: "His droll comments on men and events have become so popular that he finds himself—probably to his surprise—a national figure. It is just as well for Mr. Rogers that his caustic observations are wrapped in humor. If they were delivered without the funny tags, his audience would set the dogs on him."[101]

At this stage of his writing career Rogers was most biting when he wrote about politics but still most touching when he wrote about people whom he loved and admired. In November 1926 when three of his old friends died within a week of each other, he set his humor aside to bid farewell to them. One was Harry Houdini, whom Rogers called "the greatest showman of our time by far." Houdini headed the billing when Rogers first appeared on the Keith's Theater stage twenty-one years before, and the two remained friends. Charles Russell, the great artist of the West, was another good friend who passed away. "To have known Charley and just sit down and listen to him was the greatest remembrance of anyone's life who had had that pleasure," he wrote. "The best way to judge just how good a man is, is to find out how he stands around his home and among his kind of people. Well, he was the Cowpunchers' Painter. They swore by Russell." The third Rogers friend who died was Annie Oakley, "not only the greatest rifle shot for a woman that ever lived, but I doubt if her character could be matched outside of some Saint. . . . She was a marvelous woman, kindest hearted, most thoughtful, a wonderful Christian woman." Rogers concluded that Houdini, Russell, and Oakley "all lived so that their personal lives as well as their Professional ones will remain an everlasting credit to their various professions. So it's what you are and not what you are in that makes you."[102]

AS HE WROTE and lectured more and more, Will Rogers's comments about social and economic problems became more concrete, controversial, and often

Rogers with artist Charles Russell

contrary to the policies of the White House. He was particularly critical of the government's refusal to provide relief to the American farmer, who suffered dire economic conditions. He criticized President Coolidge for twice vetoing the McNary-Haugen bills that would have protected domestic farm prices. He also fought the high protective tariff enacted by Republicans, as he knew the tariff hurt farmers and damaged international trade. In March 1923, he opposed legislation granting federal loans to farmers, for he believed more credit drove destitute farmers deeper into debt:

Now this Farm Loan bill is going to be one of the best things to bankrupt the Farmers I know of, outside of running a Thrashing Machine. That used to be the surest indication of becoming poverty stricken.

Well, as I say, that, and borrowing money on what's called "easy terms" is a one-way ticket to the Poor House. Show me ten men that mortgage this land to get money and I will have to get a search warrant to find one that gets the land back again.[103]

In late 1923 Rogers again disagreed with "Kareful Kal" when he wrote a powerful piece urging Congress to give a bonus payment to World War I veterans and fund it with a tax on tax-exempt securities. A few congressmen favored the idea, quoted Rogers on the floor of the House, and read his column into the *Congressional Record.*[104]

Rogers's humor remained robust as ever, but between the lines there was a jagged edge to his message. In November 1924, for example, he linked his serious proposal for a national sales tax with his humorous dislike for golf:

Why don't they use a sales tax? That is the only fair and just tax. Have no tax on necessary foods, and moderate priced necessary clothes, but put a tax on every other thing you buy or use. Then the rich fellow who buys more and uses more certainly has no way of getting out of paying his share. Collect it at the source.

Put big taxes on everything of a luxury nature.

Golf and polo, hang it on them with plenty tax. If a man really feels like he wants to swing something Sunday morning, give him an axe and head him towards a woodpile. Let his wife give him a broom and see how many strokes he can go round the room in.[105]

In April 1925, Rogers fought a proposal to forgive France's war debt. The United States loaned more than $10 billion to several foreign nations during World War I, but the repayment of these loans was exceedingly difficult. Many of the indebted nations were overwhelmed with reconstruction costs, economic instability, and scarcity of surplus finances. France believed the loans were America's equivalent to the blood and money that France expended to win the war.[106] Rogers met with President Coolidge and Speaker of the House Nick Longworth in the White House to discuss the French debt issue. When Coolidge later took a hard line on the repayment, Rogers supported him:

There has been a terrible pack of Americans over in Europe the past few weeks telling them that we don't want or need the money they owe us, not to take us too seriously and that we are only kidding. Now I am sorry to hear this . . . but the boys are wrong.

. . . but we WANT THAT DOUGH. Don't let anybody kid you about that. And Calvin wants it too.[107]

Rogers's comments on the foreign debt alienated him from those congressmen and financiers who wanted to ease the reparation-debt problem. They proposed that the U.S. Treasury lend money to Germany, who would pay reparations to France, who in turn would make debt payments back to the United States. Rogers thought the plan was ludicrous, but it was backed by Treasury Secretary Mellon and other powerful policy makers, eventually starting American foreign lending on a massive scale.[108]

Rogers's increasingly hard-nosed opinions attracted so much attention that, by March 1925, five of his weekly columns had been read into the *Congressional Record*. When he mentioned that it might be a good idea to let Congress know how the country felt about certain legislation, thousands of letters flooded Capitol Hill.[109]

Rogers took his role seriously, sometimes so seriously that he lost both his temper and humor. In March 1925 he couldn't control his anger after a congressman criticized him on the floor of the House for several controversial articles. The articles faulted Congress for refusing the veterans bonus, ignoring aviation and building battleships, and allowing an overall lack of military preparedness. Rogers tartly responded to the congressman:

So, when a gentleman quoted me on the floor the other day, another member took exception and said he objected to the remarks of a Professional Joke Maker going into the Congressional Record.

Now you can beat that for jealousy among people in the same line? Calling me a Professional Joke Maker! He is right about everything but the Professional. They are the Professional Joke Makers. Read some of the Bills that they have passed. . . . Besides, my jokes don't do anybody any harm. You don't have to pay any attention to them. But every one of the Jokes those Birds make is a LAW and hurts somebody (generally everybody).

"Joke Maker!" He couldn't have coined a better coin for Congress if he

Rogers and
Nicholas
Longworth

had been inspired. But I object to being called a Professional. I am an Amateur beside them. If I had that Guy's unconscious humor, Ziegfeld couldn't afford to pay me I would be so funny.

Of course I can understand what he was objecting to was any common sense creeping into the Record. It was such Novelty, I guess it did sound funny.

And by the way, I have engaged counsel and if they ever put any more of my material in that "Record of Inefficiency," I will start suit for defamation of Character. I don't want my stuff buried away where Nobody ever reads it.[110]

It seemed easier and easier to get Rogers riled up over politics and politicians. He particularly lost his temper whenever the United States fouled up its foreign relations and treated other nations poorly.

————

FIVE

Nobody Knows Anything about Russia

F OR THE LOVE of Mike," Will Rogers griped to his readers.
"Why don't we let Mexico alone and let them run their country
the way they want to!"[1] American foreign policy was always a sore
spot for Rogers—he lost his temper every time the United States
intervened in another country's affairs. "Our gunboats are all in the Chinese
war, our marines have all landed in Nicaragua, Kellogg is sending daily ulti-
matums to Mexico, and Coolidge is dedicating memorials to eternal peace."[2]
He got especially irate whenever the United States imposed its will upon
weaker nations that posed no military threat but were of economic impor-
tance to American business. "Take the sugar out of Cuba," he wrote, "and we
would no more be interested in their troubles than we would a revolution
among the Zulus."[3]

An outspoken isolationist, Rogers argued strongly the United States
should avoid foreign entanglements. As a part-Cherokee who never forgave
the dishonest and inhumane treatment of his ancestors by the U.S. government, he was sympathetic to less advantaged peoples of the world, appreciat-
ing their simpler lifestyles. He chafed whenever Americans stereotyped others as "uncivilized." In one article he facetiously described the Mexican
people as "so primitive they have never tasted wood alcohol or know the joys

of buying on credit. They are evidently just a lot of heathens that are happy."[4]

In 1926, relations with Mexico deteriorated after the State Department sent a series of diplomatic notes protesting Mexican treatment of Americans. Rogers spent an entire column, titled "Meddling in Mexico, A Summer Sport," criticizing Secretary of State Frank B. Kellogg and the State Department:

America has a great habit of always talking about protecting American interests in some foreign Country. PROTECT 'EM HERE AT HOME! There is more American Interests right here than anywhere. If an American goes to Mexico and his Horse dies, we send them a Note wanting American interests preserved and the horse paid for.

We don't guarantee investments here at home. Why should we make Mexico guarantee them? . . . Why don't you let every Nation do and act as they please? What business is it of ours how Mexico acts or lives? Every village and community in Mexico has a church (and they go to it, too) where up here if we have a filling station we think we are up to date. . . .

The difference in our exchange of people with Mexico is, they send workmen here to work, while we send Americans there to *work* Mexico.[5]

In dozens of newspaper articles Rogers urged that the people of the Third World be left alone to determine their own fate. He insisted the U.S. grant independence to the Philippine and Hawaiian Islands, lambasted the British for their empire, and attacked the Japanese for terrorizing the Far East and taking "another hunk out of China."[6] In 1928, he pointed to Mexico as an example of U.S. discrimination:

See where they got a bill in Congress to make a road from Brownsville, Texas, up along the Rio Grande to El Paso, then on out to San Diego along the Mexican boundary.

It's a good idea and should be built, but it's called in the bill a military highway. Now, if we was building a road along the Canadian border we wouldn't insult our neighbors by calling it a military road. Can't you get Government aid without calling it military?

This case is like calling a hospital "the home for incurables." There is a tactful title for you.[7]

Rogers often poked fun at Mexicans with his comic exaggerations, sometimes condescendingly so, but he was one of few in the mainstream press who
understood and sympathized with that country's frustration in dealing with
the U.S. government. "Will somebody please write and tell me and then I will
shut up, why are we always picking on Mexico?"[8]

WHEN TWO ARIZONA delegates nominated Will Rogers for president at
the Democratic National Convention in 1924, most people refused to take
them seriously, including Rogers. He never could imagine holding public
office but liked to joke about the prospect: "I was born on election day, but
never was able to get elected to anything. I am going to jump out some day
and be indefinate enough about everything that they will call me a politician,
then run on a platform of question marks, and be elected unanimously, then
reach in the treasury and bring back my district a new bridge, or tunnell, or
dam, and I will be a statesman."[9]

Rogers may have dismissed notions about running for public office, but
others were serious when they suggested he enter politics. His popularity
increased to the point that some regarded him as an electable and potent
political force. In March 1925 Hollywood columnist Louella Parsons wrote to
Rogers, telling him, "if you were to run for president at any particular
moment every newspaper woman would go out and take the soap box for
you."[10] A few months later the Kiwanis Club of Rogers, Arkansas, invited him
to run for governor of that state. He sent back a curt reply, thanking the
Arkansans for the compliment, but refusing to run, and adding that Arkansas
was "one state I could not govern. I got the best part of Arkansas [his wife
Betty] here now, but I have never been able to govern her."[11] During the same
month the *New York Times* reported that prominent politicians in Oklahoma
tried to entice him to run as the Democratic candidate for governor. Rogers
quickly sent a letter to former Oklahoma congressman James Davenport to
stop any movement to put him on the ballot:

My dear Jim:

*Why did you want to slander me? I was going along in my own way
and not bothering anybody when you and some accomplices headed a
black cat across my trail.*

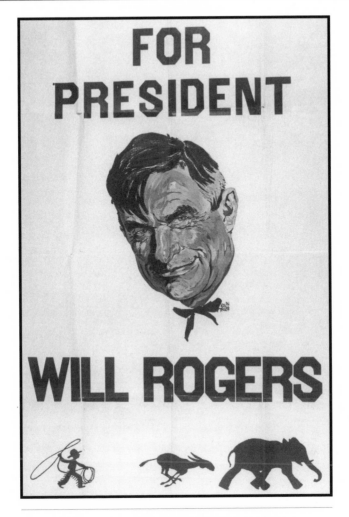

A mock political poster

Now, you might have meant well by knowing I couldn't be elected, but if you thought that I could then it was malicious. . . .

Jim, I couldn't be a Politician in a million years. I like to go my own way, and I don't believe I could take dictation. It sure would be an honor, and worth all the monetary sacrifice, but I am going through life making up my own mind, even if it is foolish enough to be considered worth paying for.[12]

IN JANUARY 1926, after vacationing for two weeks at the King Cole Hotel in Miami, relaxing on the beach and playing polo at the Nautilus polo fields, Will Rogers embarked on another grueling cross-country lecture tour. For thirteen weeks he performed one-night stands, stopping in towns across the southern tier of the country, heading west to San Diego, up through the heartland, and finally back to the east coast. On the way he was the dinner guest of the governors of North Carolina, Arkansas, and Texas and a host of mayors and other dignitaries.[13]

Rogers climaxed the lecture tour on April 11, 1926, when he appeared at Carnegie Hall. It was a rarity for a comedian to perform alone in the country's grandest venue, but he was a big hit. According to the *New York Times*, "It was a Rogers house . . . and roared uproariously at his every sally."[14] He talked about everything, from Prohibition to the Ku Klux Klan to Charles Darwin. "But as for this evolution stuff," he remarked, "it's not where we come from but where we're going that counts."[15] Noting that many women in the audience wore scanty flapper dresses, he said he "approved of a speaking acquaintance between the bottom of their skirts and the tops of their stockings."[16] He took a jab at his friend H. L. Mencken, remarking that the columnist "was coming tonight but he had to sell a book in Lansing, Michigan."[17] Turning to politics, Rogers told the New Yorkers that "Al [Smith] has the best chance of any Democrat. . . . Some have suggested that he would be elected if he changed his religion and turned Protestant. I think it would do more good if he would keep his religion but turn Repiblican [*sic*]."[18]

After his performance at Carnegie Hall, one critic explained why Rogers was so successful on stage: "Will Rogers always talks to us privately and confidentially. Even before he opens his mouth to speak, the barrier of the footlights is down and we are in the same room with him. If he didn't have supreme command of this informal mood, some of the things he says, the cracks he gets off at big people, all the way up to the President, would sound fresh and in poor taste. But his drawling tact always saves them from that."[19]

A week later he was in Philadelphia, where he watched the "Fillies" beat the Boston Braves, 8–4, and closed the tour that night with his last lecture.[20] He immediately began planning a trip to Europe. When Florenz Ziegfeld learned of the trip, he telegraphed Rogers and pleaded he postpone leaving, adding that conditions were "Rotten over there now anyway."[21] Ziegfeld hoped he would rejoin the *Follies* for the coming year, but Rogers had made up his mind. In planning the trip, he called upon his influential friends to arrange meetings with European leaders. While in Philadelphia, he lunched with George Lorimer, editor of the *Saturday Evening Post*, or as he called the magazine, "America's greatest nickelodeon." The two men were close and trusted each other. During the elections of 1928 Lorimer asked Rogers for his opinion of the political mood across the country. "It's Hoover," Will replied briskly. This time Lorimer commissioned him to write a series of articles on the European scene.[22] After the trip, Rogers would repackage the *Post* articles into *Letters of a Self-Made Diplomat to His President*, a book that sold well at two dollars a copy. Lorimer was fascinated with Benito Mussolini and proposed Rogers spend time in Italy and interview the fascist dictator. In a telegram to Lorimer, Rogers asked the publisher to "dig me up everything you have in the way of a credential even down to your marriage certificate."[23]

Rogers also met with *New York Times* publisher Adolph Ochs, who wrote a glowing letter of introduction:

> There is no one in this country who has so large an audience as Mr. Rogers. He has the happy faculty of presenting complex public questions in such a way as to bring them within the comprehension and understanding of the general public, whose confidence and respect he enjoys to a marked degree.
>
> Those who may have an opportunity of meeting Mr. Rogers will find pleasure and profit in his acquaintance.[24]

The *Times* had stopped publishing Rogers's weekly column in 1924 when the *New York World* picked him up, but Ochs told him he would publish any news items telegraphed from Europe. "If you run across anything worthwhile, cable it to us," Ochs said. "We'll pay the tolls."[25] Rogers then went to Washington DC to "try to get something from Calvin and Congressman Upshaw." While there he solicited letters of introductions from Vice President Charles Dawes, Secretary of State Frank Kellogg, and Speaker Nicholas Longworth. Senator William Borah wrote to "introduce Will Rogers, poet, philosopher, and America's greatest living humorist."[26] With the backing of high government officials, the excursion was gaining a more diplomatic purpose, albeit informal, in which Rogers began assuming the role of an unofficial ambassador of goodwill.

Overall, he accumulated about thirty letters of introduction, including two from Father Francis Duffy that recommended an audience with the pope and one from Charles Dana Gibson, editor of *Life* magazine, to his sister-in-law, Lady Nancy Astor. "This is our friend Will Rogers," Gibson wrote. "He has heard of you."[27]

AT MIDNIGHT ON MAY 1, 1926, Will Rogers and his fourteen-year-old son Will, Jr., sailed from New York on the *Leviathan*, the largest passenger ship of its day. Despite the ship's size, Rogers was seasick for most of voyage and arrived weary in Southampton six days later. In London they stayed at the Savoy Hotel, one of the city's most elegant and fashionable hotels, on the north bank of the Thames. The five-month trip to nine countries of Europe would be much different from Rogers's previous trips, as he now was an international celebrity possessing both the fame and fortune to travel in grand style. No longer just a vaudevillian, he performed only a few weeks on the London stage. He spent much of his time traveling about the continent meeting people and reporting on the international scene. His stay in England was frenzied and filled with formal dinners, afternoon teas, tours of the city's attractions, and nightly attendance at London plays, including the popular two-act comedy *No, No, Nanette* and the Gershwin musical *Lady, Be Good*, starring Fred and Adele Astaire.

While in London Rogers rekindled his friendship with the Prince of Wales. Arriving at St. James Palace, Rogers greeted the prince with, "Hello, old timer! How are you falling these days?"

"All over the place," the prince replied. "I got my shoulder broke since I saw you last." The two men spent several hours discussing horses, polo, travel, Prohibition, Mussolini, and the general labor strike then crippling England.[28] Rogers told the prince he thought the British newspapers overemphasized the strike by calling it a revolution. "Had it happened in America everybody would have thought they were having a retake of the later war," Rogers said.[29]

Rogers attended a stag dinner in the Savoy's Pinafore Room, where he met George Bernard Shaw, *Peter Pan* author Sir James Barrie, Lord Dewar of

Will and Will, Jr., on the Leviathan *headed for Europe*

Scotch whisky fame, tea magnate Sir Thomas Lipton, and British writer G. K. Chesterton. He visited the "great dignified comedy," the House of Lords, where he witnessed a bitter debate over the general strike between former prime minister David Lloyd George and Chancellor of the Exchequer Winston Churchill. From the gallery he watched members argue the merits of free trade versus a protective tariff.[30]

In the House of Commons he was the guest of Lady Astor, the beautiful and witty Virginia-born wife of Viscount Waldorf Astor and the first female member of Parliament.[31] The luminary of London's drawing room crowd, Lady Astor invited Rogers to stay at her grand London house at No. 4 St. James Square. She gave him a lavish dinner where she introduced him to some of the country's leading social, political, and literary figures. Rogers was fascinated by the sharp-tongued and independent Lady Astor, who, like Alice Roosevelt Longworth, had an unusual and deep understanding of politics and world affairs. Lady Astor and Rogers took an instant liking to each other and spent their time swapping political gossip from both sides of the Atlantic. Despite his opposition to women in politics, he defended her on several occasions. "She is the brightest Political mind I ever run into," he wrote.[32] After visiting one of the veterans hospitals she sponsored, Rogers was adamant: "If I ever hear social or political foes say aught against her. . . . I just rake up the vision of that woman walking among her boys with tears in her eyes, yet telling jokes of each one. So let no woman, mother of a son, ever say evil against her."[33]

Lady Astor sailed for the United States on the *Aquitania* in July. From the liner she wrote Rogers a letter that revealed the seriousness of their conversations:

> *Dear Boarder . . .*
>
> *I am positive that unless America helps in some way (not financially) we Shall have another war—You & I won't fight but our sons may—My heart aches for England. We[']re alone on that Continent & make no mistake about it. . . . I do hope that you will go slow about Europe. I feel exactly like you do—but . . . I hear that the cotton outlook is bad in the South also wheat—I wish you would pull the Republicans leg, not [the] League about the World Court! I don't believe they see Ireland to Come in. Tho' Mr. Kellogg vows he's all for it. . . . Nick L. [Longworth] will never be President. Smiths got a better chance![34]*

On the same day Rogers sent a short cable to the *New York Times* about Lady Astor's upcoming visit to New York:

> *Nancy Astor, which is the nom de plume of Lady Astor, is arriving on your side about now. She is the best friend America has here. Please ask*

*my friend, [Mayor] Jimmy Walker, to have New York take good care
of her. She is the only one over here that don't throw rocks at American
tourists. Yours respectfully,*

Will Rogers.[35]

The *Times* editor thought the telegram important enough to place it on the
top of the first page of the second section. The short missive became the first
of Rogers's daily telegrams and marked his return to the *Times* after an
absence of two years. The *Times* ran the daily telegrams exclusively until
October, when another ninety-two papers picked them up. Over the next few
years, over six hundred papers subscribed. Until his death, Rogers wrote 2,817
of the short newspaper articles, many beginning with "Will Rogers Says."

Rogers's daily telegram was a new and powerful vehicle for his humorous
commentary. Usually only a few sentences long, the telegrams broadened his
readership by millions and enlarged his influence on the American political
psyche. Unlike his weekly columns, which discussed topics in depth, the
shorter squibs reported on news as it broke. In an era before television prime-
time news, the public depended on journalists like Rogers to interpret events
shortly after they happened. Using his comic devices and down-home philosophy, he helped explain the mysteries of foreign affairs, disarmament conferences, government finance, and other issues baffling the public. Through
his daily telegrams he gave the American public, few of whom ever traveled
very far from home, an opportunity to live vicariously through his travels and
to accompany him, day by day, across the country and around the world. In an
important way, Rogers was shrinking the globe for his fellow Americans and
sharing with them a more personal view that made "this world of ours look
like the size of a watermelon."[36]

Besides writing his new daily telegrams, weekly columns, and *Saturday
Evening Post* feature articles, Rogers gave several performances while in
England. On May 12, 1926, he spoke at the American Club where he told his
audience, "England has the greatest statesmen and the poorest coffee of any
nation in the world. I just hate to see morning come because I know I will
have to drink some of that coffee."[37] Soon after he arrived in England, British
National Pictures contracted him to appear in a film entitled *Tip Toes*. He
also performed at the Pavilion Theater in Piccadilly Circus in the Charles
Cochran *Revue*, a British imitation of the *Ziegfeld Follies*.[38]

As before, Rogers was well received by the British, despite their different taste in comedy. Their quaint sense of humor reminded him of the old remark about telling the Englishman a joke one year and going back and hear him laugh the next.[39] Britain, however, was in a nationalistic mood and more sensitive to criticism, especially from an American. Rogers's comments about making the European nations pay their war debts were not popular in England. While most reviews praised him, London's *Everybody's Weekly* criticized him soundly, telling him simply to "go home" and describing him as an "irresponsible street-corner tub-thumper" who compelled his audience to listen to a "diatribe which mainly consisted of gratuitous insults aimed at Great Britain, France, and Belgium . . . insulting, insolent, presumptuous and in the worst of bad taste."[40]

Rogers left England early in the tour and visited Geneva to attend the League of Nations Disarmament Commission. The session turned out to be a failure, as both France and Italy refused to attend. Rogers was not surprised, as he had little faith in diplomatic negotiations. Time and again he argued the United States remain militarily strong and that "less diplomats is what you want, not less arms."[41] He added later that "Congress ought to pass a law to prohibit us conferring with anybody on anything, till we learn how."[42] He had little faith in attempts to disarm nations, writing in June 1927: "For two weeks last summer I sat at Geneva and listened to one argument on disarmament, and if I could reproduce it on the stage I would have a better show than Ziegfeld ever had. Of all the fool things that we go into (and we don't miss any) why, these disarmament conferences will go down as the prize. No nation can tell another nation how little it shall protect itself."[43]

Rogers then headed to Italy, stopping first in Milan and then moving on to Rome, a city he discovered to have "no more culture than Minneapolis or Long Beach, California." He wrote that when he found out ancient Rome had senators he realized "why it declined."[44] On May 26, 1926, he visited the Vatican, where Pope Pius XI received him.[45] His audience with the pope, like his own religious beliefs, was a private matter and he never wrote about being received or his opinion of Pius XI.

Two days later he had a private session with Benito Mussolini, who by then had turned Italy into his own dictatorship. The country became a Fascist police state in 1924 when Mussolini and his Blackshirts won corrupt national elections and silenced the opposition. Despite the oppression and injustices inflicted upon the Italian people, Rogers approved of Mussolini's efforts to bring order and efficiency to the country. "I have never yet seen a thing that he has done that wasn't based on common sense," Rogers wrote. "He has done more constructive things for his country since the war than any hundred men in any other country. . . . He is one wise wop."[46]

During the interview Rogers told Mussolini he had just left the disarmament conference at Geneva. Il Duce laughed and replied, "No Disarmament; we disarm when England dissarm at sea; when France in Air and land. So you see we never have to dissarm."[47] Rogers agreed with the dictator's stance on military preparedness, writing later that Mussolini

> knows the Nations that are great are the ones that have something in the way of side arms. He knows that without an Army and Navy they will never be able to find room for his growing population.
>
> That fellow has kept Italy on the up-grade for all these years. . . . He has done more for his Country than any man ever did for one in a like time.[48]

Rogers, who always feared chaos and breakdown in society, admired Mussolini for taking control of Italy. "Say, Mussolini could run this country with his eyes shut. In fact, that's the way our Congress has been running it."[49] Rogers seemed unconcerned that the Fascists crushed democratic government. "No sir Mussolini is a knockout. If we had him here he would do away with elections, even more useless than parades. He's some guinea, that kid."[50]

It is not surprising that the Italian dictator made a favorable impression upon Rogers. As he did with the Teapot Dome conspirators and later with professional baseball players who confessed to fixing ball games, Rogers quickly forgave people he met personally. He warmed up to them and became surprisingly loyal. "When you meet people," he wrote soon after the European trip, "no matter what opinion you may have formed about them beforehand, why, after you meet them and see their angle and their personality, why, you can see a lot of good in all of them."[51] He looked for the best in his fellow man, not the worst, claiming he never met a man he didn't like, even if he was a dictator.

Although Rogers continued to admire Mussolini for several years, his defense of the controversial dictator brought criticism. Rogers wrote in 1933 that "Mussolini, with no money, no natural resources, no nothing, has kept his country going; while us with a surplus of everything under the sun, are mangy with Representatives and liberty. But we can't digest either of 'em."[52] Soon after, an editorial in the *San Diego Union* censured Rogers for praising the dictator, reminding him that Italy had no elections, no independent newspapers, no political opposition, and a policy of repression and terror. As usual, he didn't take the criticism well and sent a reply to the *Union* that was impulsive and belligerent. "Mussolini is an amateur compared to [Franklin] Roosevelt's power and the whole country is tickled to death," he wrote. "Dictatorship is the best government in the world provided you have the right dictator."[53] James Thurber, who scorned Rogers's lowbrow witticisms, never forgave him for praising Mussolini. In a *New York Times* article twenty-three years after Rogers's death, Thurber remained upset over his "irresponsible observations" about the Italian dictator, warning that Rogers-style "political satire can be as dangerous as an unguided missile when it is unsound."[54]

Rogers did not change his mind about Mussolini until Italy threatened to invade Ethiopia and their troops clashed in December 1934. Only when hostilities broke out did Rogers realize that Mussolini went too far and, like Hitler, posed an international threat.

———

AS WILL ROGERS continued his whirlwind tour of Europe through the summer and fall of 1926, he discovered the joy of flying about the continent. Air transportation there was much more commonplace and reliable than in the States. On one junket he took off from London in the morning, flew over Holland and stopped in Amsterdam, and then went on to Berlin where he arrived before supper.[55] On another side trip he flew from London to Paris in a large new French airliner. The flight was a rough one for the seasick-prone Rogers, but nevertheless he was impressed with the advanced state of European air transportation. After observing the speed and convenience of commercial aviation there, he redoubled his effort to promote aviation progress back home.[56]

When he flew to Paris he stayed there only a couple of days, seeing the sights and visiting the House of Deputies, "a Satire on our Congress . . . the best thing I ever saw in Europe in the way of entertainment."[57] Throughout his career he never warmed up to the French and never performed in their country, realizing his humor did not translate well and would not appeal to the stiffer French taste. He also never accepted their snobbery. "A bunch of American tourists were hissed and stoned yesterday in France," he wrote that August, "but not until they had finished buying."[58] While Rogers criticized the French, he also had little patience for unruly American tourists. "They generally make more noise and have more to say than anybody, and generally create a worse impression than if they had stayed at home," he wrote. "There should be a law prohibiting over three Americans going anywhere abroad together."[59]

In Madrid, the Duke of Alba took Rogers to watch a polo game where King Alfonso XIII of Spain was playing, and Rogers talked with the king before and after the match. While in Madrid, he met with Spanish dictator Miguel Primo de Rivera. Over a glass of sherry they discussed the Geneva disarmament conference. Like Mussolini, the Spanish dictator stated, "When everybody else disarms, I will disarm." Rogers found Primo de Rivera to be "a very capable man—perhaps the best that Spain has produced in a long time."[60]

In July, Rogers visited Warsaw and met with Marshal Józef Piłsudski, who only two months before had led a coup d'état to become de facto dictator. Rogers found the country to be on a war footing. "Poland is rarin' to fight somebody so bad that they just get up and punch themselves in the jaw," he wrote. "They can't make up their minds whether to jump on Russia, Germany, or go up and annex Lithuania."[61]

In September, a month after Betty and the other two children arrived in Europe to join him, Rogers traveled to Ireland to meet with that country's president, W. T. Cosgrave. Rogers delighted in the Irish landscape, the friendly people there, and their efforts to free themselves from British control. "England is debating about giving Ireland home rule," he had once written. "Somebody should tip England off to give Ireland home rule, but reserve the moving picture rights! There's one thing about an Irish Parliament. There's never going to be a dull moment there!"[62] Rogers also found time for charity. After he learned that a tragic fire in a Dromcolliher theater had killed scores of citizens, he immediately volunteered to do a benefit in Dublin. He donated the two thousand dollars of proceeds, plus five hundred of his own money, to the sufferers.

———

"IF I WANTED to start an insane asylum that would be 100 per cent cuckoo," Will Rogers wrote, "I would just admit applicants that thought they knew something about Russia."[63] Rogers was fascinated with the Soviet Union and the communist experiment, having read Karl Marx and Russian history before the trip. He was determined to visit Russia during the European tour and see firsthand what living conditions were like there. He was a little skeptical about his ability to report on Russia but believed he was just as qualified as anyone, arguing he was "the only person that ever wrote on Russia that admits he don't know a thing about it. And on the other hand, I know just as much about Russia as anybody that ever wrote about it. Nobody knows anything about Russia."[64]

What Rogers saw and reported was a Russia at a moment in history never to be recaptured. When he visited that summer, Russia was caught in a peculiar and chaotic period between the severe repression of the czarist government and the even more restrictive government under Stalin. At the time the Communists allowed some forms of competition in business and gave the Russian people more freedom than they would in 1930. Nevertheless, times were hard during the early 1920s, for the revolution dislocated thousands and obstructed the production of food and industrial materials. The Communists tried new economic plans only to have them fail within a short time. After Lenin died in 1924, a period began of bloody power struggles within the Communist Party. Several party leaders plotted to take control, and, by the summer of 1926, Stalin emerged as the dominant power. The following year Leon Trotsky, one of the Bolshevik founders of the revolution, was exiled to Siberia.

Rogers's journey to Russia was his most ambitious venture during the 1926 trip. When he prepared to go to the communist state, he left behind anything that could be interpreted wrongly by the Soviets: books, newspapers, notes he made for articles, and reduced the amount of clothing he carried to two pairs of socks, an extra set of underwear, and one suit, for fear that he be accused of flaunting capitalism. He explained his nervousness: "I had seen pictures of long trains wending their way across the Trans Siberian Railway hauling heavy loads of human freight, when nobody had a return ticket but

THERE'S
NOT A
BATHING
SUIT IN
RUSSIA

▽

WILL
ROGERS

*The cover of Rogers's
1927 book, which reported
on his trip to the Soviet
Union*

the Conductor. . . . So if I thought of an alleged Wise Crack, it was immediately stifled before reaching even the thorax."[65]

Because Rogers was determined to see more of the daily life of the people than when visiting other countries, he scheduled his own air transportation. He departed Berlin at two in the morning aboard a Junkers trimotor, stopped in Königsberg at daybreak for breakfast, then boarded a single-engine Fokker as the sole passenger. After a stop in Smolensk, he arrived in Moscow late that afternoon.[66] In the Soviet capital, he toured the Kremlin and explored the city alone on foot. He also made an overnight trip to St. Petersburg.

To Rogers's disappointment, the Communists did not allow him to meet with Trotsky, then losing the power struggle with the Stalinists. "Trotsky is not in so good with the present government. It may seem rather funny to some to hear he is too conservative for them."[67] Rogers concluded, "If I had met him and had a chat with him, I would have found him a very interesting and human fellow, for I have never yet met a man that I dident like."[68] Rogers serialized his trip in three issues of the *Saturday Evening Post*, and the articles eventually turned into his book *There's Not a Bathing Suit in Russia & Other Bare Facts*.

Rogers showed some sympathy for the Bolshevik revolt that overthrew the aristocratic exploiters who ruled ruthlessly under the czar. But he also observed many of the same injustices that existed before the revolution. "Siberia is still working. It's just as cold on you to be sent there under the Soviets as it was under the Czar," he wrote.[69] "I wanted to tell them that what they needed in their Government was more of a sense of humor and less of a sense of revenge."[70]

Most of Rogers's observations of Russia were critical. He discovered the Soviet Union to be no workers' paradise and found the classless society not to exist: "It seems the whole idea of Communism, or whatever they want to call it, is based on propaganda and blood. . . . There is as much class distinction in Russia today, as there is in Charleston, South Carolina."[71]

Rogers was angered at the Soviets' attempt to exterminate all religion, writing that "there never was a nation founded and maintained without some kind of belief in something." The Communist government, he remarked, chose to repress the one thing that was "absolutely necessary to run a Country on, and that is Religion. Never mind what kind; but it's got be something or you will fail at the finish."[72]

Rogers derided the Soviet economy, saying that "there's no income tax in Russia, but there's no income."[73] After watching the Russians trying to cope, he realized that the Communist system simply was not working. "The Russians figured out everything in their Communistic system, except how to get enough to eat." He noted that state efforts to create new collective farms destroyed private property, sapped individual initiative, and created a new top-down tyranny. As he saw it, the state in the Soviet Union "owns everything . . . a little like the bankers here."[74] He concluded that "Communism is like Prohibition, it's a good idea but it won't work."[75]

WILL ROGERS and his family boarded the *Leviathan* in Southampton on September 22, 1926, and headed home. Former secretary of state Charles Evans Hughes was aboard, and the two men spent several hours discussing foreign policy. Rogers was angry about events in Nicaragua where four months before U.S. Marines had landed to thwart a leftist revolution and protect U.S. interests.[76] He later got even angrier when the United States pressured the Nicaraguan congress to elect Adolfo Díaz as president: "We say that Díaz is the properly elected president of Nicaragua, but Brazil, Argentina, Peru, Chile, Mexico, Ecuador, Costa Rica, Cuba, Guatemala, Colombia, Uruguay, Paraguay—all those say that the other fellow is the properly elected president. It's funny how we are the only ones that get everything right. I'd rather be right than Republican."[77] Rogers criticized the U.S. intervention so soundly that Congressman Edgar Howard arose on the floor of the House and stated Rogers was the only man with the "stomachical courage" to ask the great question, "Why are we in Nicaragua and what in the hell are we doing there."[78]

Soon after the *Leviathan* departed Europe, news reached the liner that a savage hurricane had hit south Florida, devastating Miami and killing over three hundred residents. Rogers quickly organized a three-night benefit to raise donations for the hurricane victims. Assisted by Hughes, he raised over $40,000 from passengers, including $1,000 from his own pocket.[79] After one of the benefit performances, a modest, retiring man approached Rogers and handed him a check:

> I looked at it, on some little bank out in Pennsylvania, then I looked at the amount, and I thought he had written the numbers wrong. It was for $8,000 which brought our fund to $42,000 and was from Mr. [Milton] Hershey of Hershey's chocolates, a man that I suppose had done more for other people than any man in America. He has an Orphan's home of over 200, and has built a model town just for his people. Nobody even knew he was on the boat.[80]

Rogers arrived in New York on September 27, 1926, after having been gone for five months. Two days later he received a telegram from President

Headed home from Europe with Jock,
a Sealyham dog given by Lord Thomas Dewar

Coolidge's secretary stating that "the President hopes you will stay at the White House during your visit wire arrival and car will meet you."[81] Coolidge customarily invited U.S. ambassadors to visit him in the White House upon their return home and gave Rogers the same privilege. Rogers immediately accepted by telegram. "Just think the only non officer [*sic*] seeker that ever slept in the White House," he wrote. "I have an awful lot to report."[82]

In Washington, the president's secretary met Rogers at the train and took him to the White House in a limousine. After a simple fish dinner, Rogers and Coolidge retired to a small upstairs sitting room where they stayed up late discussing European affairs and world leaders. Rogers knew it was a rare opportunity for a private citizen to spend time alone with the president. "When I have the good fortune to be able to talk to some big man, I don't spend the whole time by spouting off a mess of my jokes," he wrote afterward. "I am there to learn something from him. It's his ideas I want to get, not to try out any of my own on him."[83]

While Coolidge leaned back in his chair, put his feet on his desk, and puffed on a cigar, the two men thrashed out all sorts of topics, such as recent disarmament conferences, U.S. participation in the World Court, and the efficiency of air travel in Europe. Rogers told Coolidge the United States should "do more to foster commercial aviation, give the companies a government subsidy so they can exist." Rogers described his intense conversations with Lady Astor, adding that British people resented having to pay off their debts to the United States. "England's got a right to holler," the president replied. "They are paying!" When they discussed Philippine independence, a hot topic at the time, Rogers made it clear he wanted "to get out of everywhere but America." He also objected to American gunboats stationed in China and told the president "it was pretty tough on a country when they couldn't have their own civil wars without us and England butting in."[84]

After his visit with the president, Rogers wrote a long article in the *Saturday Evening Post*, giving many Americans their first glimpse of life in the White House. He revealed few details of his private conversation with Coolidge. "What I found out for him in Europe, and what I am to find out in America for him is none of your business," he told his readers. "But what I found out about the President is some of your business."[85] In the article, Rogers could have been describing any middle-class American family, making the charming, well-educated Grace Coolidge and her rather dour husband, whom she called "Papa," appear human and familiar, telling how they fed their collie dogs table scraps during dinner and served leftover fish the next day for lunch. In a larger and more important sense, Rogers reassured the American people that, in their democracy, the president was one of them, a simple New Englander with simple tastes, and not some European sovereign living in opulence and splendor.[86]

Although Rogers liked Calvin Coolidge, he never warmed up to him and considered him hard to read. "Coolidge is the only one nobody ever knew when he was acting and when he wasn't," Rogers wrote. "He was like a ukulele. You can't tell when somebody is playing one, or just monkeying with it."[87] He concluded that "Coolidge is the shrewdest politician that ever drew Government salary."[88] His opinion of the president, however, declined after Coolidge left office and the Great Depression descended upon his successor, Herbert Hoover. Rogers, who felt Hoover received too much blame for the stock market crash, laid some of the fault on Coolidge's laissez faire policy during the Roaring Twenties. "Coolidge went in and just turned his head," Rogers wrote. "And say, brother, if you didn't get yours then you was just dumb."[89]

Rogers summed up his feelings about the president when he later said he would "kinda enjoy seeing Calvin about half soused!"[90]

FOR WILL ROGERS, his 1926 tour of Europe provided a huge boost in his steady rise to becoming America's most widely read and eminently trusted source of political commentary. For five busy months he scurried back and forth across the continent, filling his days with fact-finding rambles and diving headlong into foreign cultures. Few men could ever soak up so much in so little time as Rogers, for beneath his cracker-barrel naïveté lurked a shrewd mind and a calculating eye that missed little. He developed a serious respect for post–World War I problems plaguing all European countries. He became more concerned with U.S. foreign policy in Europe and the lack of American preparedness in case of future war. "When you look up and see a cloud during the next war to end wars," he wrote, "don't you be starting to admire its silvery lining till you find out how many Junkers and Fokkers are hiding behind it."[91]

Rogers saw firsthand how other forms of government worked and compared them with the American system. He never was sure that republican democracy was the best form of government, if such a thing truly existed, but he continued to defend democracy religiously. Yet he possessed an open and critical mind and was fascinated about how other governments ran under parliamentarian, fascist, and Bolshevist regimes.

Rogers probed the motives of the intellectual and political leaders on the continent and formed well-founded opinions of their strengths and weaknesses. He not only met with heads of state, royalty, and the silk stocking set, he also talked with "regular birds" like cab drivers, waiters, and haberdashers. He heard and digested their concerns about the debts of war, the need to disarm, the urge to build navies, the justification for reparations, the rise of communism, the hypocrisy of Prohibition, the emergence of nationalism, the lowering of tariffs, and the crassness of American tourists. He realized that another world war was likely, predicting that "as soon as Germany gets strong enough so she thinks she can lick both of them [England and France] there will be another War."[92] He visited Russia during political upheaval, saw England suddenly immersed in a general strike, and spent enchanted evenings with the likes of Sir James Barrie and Lady Astor.

By the time he returned to America, Rogers was much more worldly and cosmopolitan, probably more so than he wanted people to believe. His horizons had widened, his insights had deepened, and his observations had become increasingly authoritative. After Rogers published several of his European articles in his book *Letters of a Self-Made Diplomat to His President* in October 1926, a *New York Times* reviewer commented: "there has rarely been an American humorist whose words produced less empty laughter and more sober thought. . . . Perhaps Will Rogers has done more to educate the American public in world affairs than all the professors who have been elucidating continental chaos since the Treaty of Versailles."[93]

On July 19, 1926, as Rogers hurried back and forth across Europe, *Time* magazine featured his photograph on its cover.[94] The cover of *Time* was not the only honor he received that year; when Rogers returned to California that winter, his friends from Beverly Hills had a surprise for him.

SIX

———

The Mayor of Beverly Hills

WHEN WILL ROGERS STOPPED in Grand Rapids, Michigan, to give a lecture just before Christmas in 1926, he received a telegram from Douglas Fairbanks, the famed actor and a good friend, telling him that a group of prominent Californians had elected Rogers as the first mayor of Beverly Hills.[1] In reality the mayor's position was honorary and unofficial, as the president of the city's board of trustees really ran the town government. But Governor Al Smith, New York City mayor Jimmy Walker, and even President Calvin Coolidge joined the charade, each sending Rogers a telegram congratulating him on his mayorship.[2]

In Los Angeles a week later, a large crowd met Rogers and his family at the train station and escorted them in a parade of forty Rolls-Royce limousines out Wilshire Boulevard. They stopped near the Beverly Hills Hotel, where, on a makeshift stage in front of several hundred local friends and fans, Fairbanks greeted them as master of ceremonies. After the Los Angeles Fire Department band serenaded the crowd with "The Old Gray Mare," Rogers gave his inaugural speech in the midst of a driving downpour. "I am by no means the first Comedian Mayor," he shouted through the raindrops. "That seems to be the one requirement of Mayor, I have never seen a Mayor that wasent funny." He promised better government, but not necessarily honesty:

Too many Mayors have been elected on honesty, That dont get you anywhere, John w davis ran on that last time for the Democrats, and Coolidge
dident suggest it at all and Davis lost by 70 mil. Now I don't say I will give
the old Burg a honest adminsitarti but I will at least split 50 50 with you.

I am bringing over a few of the syst[e]ms of Mussolini. There is the wis-
est cracking Wop in the world, every time he issues a statement it is a ifty
[nifty?].5

Rogers delighted in his first election to political office, albeit in jest, and
for a while signed his daily telegrams "His Honor the Mayor of Beverly Hills,
California," "the Meandering Mayor," "the Seated Mayor," "the Neutral
Mayor," and so on. His appointment did raise some eyebrows in Beverly Hills,
prompting the town to create an official mayor the next year. He later
claimed that the movie people impeached him because "they found out I was
opposed to polygamy."4 To this day, the town lists Will Rogers as its first
mayor.

The Beverly Hills mayorship was not the only "office" he held. In August
1927 the National Press Club "elected" him congressman-at-large, charging
him with duties "to roam over the country, pry into the state of the Union,
check up on prohibition enforcement and report at regular intervals to the
National Press Club."5 These honorary positions and other nominations for
public office were, in a way, more than mere jokes and publicity stunts. There
was a touch of wishful thinking in them, for Rogers represented what people
really wanted out of their politicians—honesty, compassion, straight talk—
but were not getting. The notion of Will Rogers in politics was a breath of
fresh air in an atmosphere that, to many Americans, reeked with incompetence and corruption.

After his mock inauguration as mayor, Rogers spent a two-week Christmas holiday with his family at their ranch in the Santa Monica Canyon. On
Christmas Eve he helped the Salvation Army give a thousand Christmas bas-
kets to the poor people of Los Angeles. He found time to play polo at a club
near his home where, during the match, he was thrown from his mount, tumbled in an arc over his pony's head, and landed in a heap. Luckily he was
unhurt, and more important to the competitive Rogers, his team won.6

Soon after the New Year, Rogers returned to another busy lecture circuit,
or, as he termed it, "barking for his dinner."7 He planned to open in Detroit

Rogers accepting the "mayorship" of Beverly Hills

on January 6, 1927, but left early so he could stop in Chicago to meet with baseball commissioner Judge Kenesaw Mountain Landis. Landis was then investigating charges that players had fixed games between the Detroit Tigers and Chicago White Sox ten years earlier. Like Billy Mitchell before, Landis was well aware of Rogers's widespread popularity and his increasing power to sway public opinion. With baseball taking a beating in the press over the game-fixing scandals, Landis welcomed the humorist to Chicago in hopes of drumming up some favorable newspaper coverage. According to Rogers, the judge "seemed very anxious to know what I had heard of the feeling in regard to all the baseball talk had been."[8]

On January 5, 1927, Landis summoned nearly the entire roster of both the White Sox and Tigers, including Ty Cobb and Tris Speaker. Landis allowed Rogers, who was friends with many of the players, to sit in his crowded office and observe the hearing. "It wasent funny," Rogers wrote, "to see thirty-four men that I had known personally and that had given from 10 to 20 years of healthful amusement and recreation to millions, be on trial practically for their lives."[9] To his delight, Landis exonerated the players, whom Rogers defended staunchly: "Baseball fans know these men are not crooked. They give their money's worth too much every day to be doing something crooked. Baseball is the greatest game in the world, for the greatest number of people. And it's the least crooked sport ever invented. And I am going to go to it, and believe in it, and admire the type of men that play it, till I get so old that my whiskers will get caught in the turnstiles."[10]

Rogers, who looked upon the pastime as not only a sport but an integral part of American culture, continued to defend the game in the future. "Baseball is still and will always be our national game," he wrote. "It requires more brains, more practice and more real skill than all our others put together. It's the only game when you see it played you know whether the ones playing it are being paid or not."[11]

WHILE IN INDEPENDENCE, Kansas, on his lecture tour that fall, Will Rogers kicked off the first nationwide radio broadcast of the National Broadcasting Company.[12] From backstage at the theater where he was performing, station WDAF linked him with nineteen other stations across the country. During the four-and-a-half-hour variety show Rogers talked mostly about politics. The Depression had not yet occurred, but farmers suffered dire economic conditions and many had lost their farms. Some politicians called for farm relief, but while Rogers agreed the farmers needed government aid, he objected to outright welfare. In a later article he argued against relief programs that "just give people money that couldent work, and not make them do something for it."[13] He feared direct relief undermined self-reliance and created a class of permanently dependent Americans. "England . . . was a fine country with only one drawback, the dole," he told the radio audience. "If you don't work they pay you. I told them that wouldn't do. We've tried it with Congress and the Senate for years and it's a failure."[14] The NBC broadcast reached eight million listeners, his largest audience to date.

Governors and mayors across the country continued to honor Rogers during his lecture tours. Everywhere he visited, local politicians sought his opinion about the national and world scene. During the first two months of 1927 he addressed the state legislatures in California, Nevada, Indiana, West

Virginia, Alabama, and New Mexico.[15] "I advised them but I doubt if they take it," he wrote. "These Legislatures are about hopeless."[16] Just before he spoke in California he watched the legislature pass a bill regulating the ethical conduct of the state's eight thousand lawyers. "Personally I don't think you can make a lawyer honest by an act of the Legislature," he told them. "You've got to work on his conscience. And his lack of conscience is what makes him a lawyer."[17] In Nevada, he spoke to both houses of the legislature and then watched them kill a bill to legalize gambling in the state. Four years later, after Nevada became the first state to legalize gambling, he congratulated them for being "smart enough to pass a law and get some tax money out of it."[18]

When Rogers lectured in Florida in February, John D. Rockefeller attended one of the performances.[19] After the show the eighty-seven-year-old billionaire invited the humorist to come to his winter home at Ormond Beach the next morning. After breakfast Rogers strolled with Rockefeller as he played several holes of golf. Before the two men met, Rogers had criticized Rockefeller several times in his writings. In 1924, after Rockefeller said that, "Love is the greatest thing in the world," Rogers snapped back, "You take a few words of affection and try and trade them to him for a few gallons of oil, and you will discover just how great love is."[20] But Rogers changed his tune after spending time with Rockefeller at his home. "Well, we just talked about everything," he wrote. "He is the most pleasant soft-spoken old Gentleman you ever saw."[21]

The unlikely friendship grew. Each time Rogers performed near Rockefeller's Florida home, the billionaire attended the show, brought all of his family and servants with him, and invited him to his home for breakfast and golf. Rogers, in turn, heaped praise upon the old man. "John D. Rockefeller . . . set the rich a great example by giving away hundreds of millions. The others just as well have done it, they lost it anyhow."[22] In 1935 he called Rockefeller "one of the very few men that knew how to give money away so that every dollar does good. That's more than our government can do. It's more than anybody can do. . . . All over the world there is a Rockefeller doctor swatting at a mosquito or trapping a poisonous fly. . . . There is no end to that old gentleman's talents.[23]

Rogers's fame on the lecture circuit grew to where he turned down dozens of requests to speak. There just wasn't enough time to accept every invitation,

Rogers with John D. Rockefeller

including one from General Douglas MacArthur. The U.S. military was in sad shape during the 1920s, and Rogers was one of a few writers calling for the nation to rearm, modernize, and expand the armed services. MacArthur was impressed with Rogers's pro-military stance and invited him to speak at a banquet of high-ranking officers. In his letter, the general wrote: "In these days, there are many it would appear who are, seemingly, trying to make the country believe that anyone who ever wore a uniform should sit forever upon the stool of repentance. Naturally we get a bit downhearted at times because of this attitude on the part of those idealists—and need cheering up! No one can better do it than you."[24]

Besides governors, millionaires, and generals, Rogers found time during his busy lecture tour to meet with average Americans, millions of whom barely eked out a living. He was particularly touched when he traveled through the hardscrabble parts of the South. In Georgia he found the backwoods people staunchly favoring Prohibition on one hand but illegally manufacturing and drinking liquor on the other. Rogers explained that the behavior of the local people at first seemed hypocritical, but actually became quite logical after he talked to them and began to understand their dilemma:

> Prohibition is never an issue in the South, their habits and their votes have nothing in common. They feel they are the originators of the still, and any legislation to permit large breweries would be unfair competition and would perhaps destroy the entire revenue of hundreds of thousands of small still owners, who have no other visible means of support. Corn likker is their product and I can't blame them for voting to protect its life.
>
> You see, you must not condemn a people until you have been among them and can see and know their angle. I don't blame them for not wanting big corporation breweries to be allowed by law to try and change their tastes. We would be a fine liberty-loving country if we allowed a few Yankees to dictate to us what we could make and what we could drink.
>
> Prohibition isn't an issue down here; it's a privilege.[25]

While lecturing across the South, Rogers read in the papers that Alabama senator Tom Heflin filibustered the Senate with a blustery tirade against the Catholic Church. "Cotton Tom" Heflin was a notorious segregationist who bragged that while a member of the House of Representatives in 1908 he shot and wounded a black man who confronted him on a Washington streetcar. Rogers was scornful when he pounded out his daily column from a Montgomery hotel room:

> Senator Heflin of Alabama held up all Senate business yesterday for five hours. That's a record for narrow views. Tonight in his home capital I am pleading with Alabama to not exterminate all Catholics, Republicans, Jews, negroes, Jim Reed, Al Smith, Wadsworth, Mellon and Coolidge and the Pope.
>
> Of course my plea will do no good, for Tom knows the intelligence of his constituency better than we do.[26]

Rogers interrupted his lecture tour for a week later in 1927 and traveled to Washington DC to film a silent comedy, *A Texas Steer*. Half seriously, he wired Coolidge asking permission to use the White House grounds for the filming. To his surprise, the president granted his request.[27] In the film Rogers plays a corrupt congressman named Maverick Brander from Red Dog, Texas, a place "where men are men and the plumbing is improving." The congressman declares at one point that since so many women were serving in legislatures and state houses, "politics has become downright effeminate." Rogers wrote most of his dialogue for the film, which according to him was about "a man elected to Washington on bought votes. We are bringing it up to date by not changing it all. In the stage version he didn't know what to do when he got in Congress. That part is allowed to remain as it was. He used to play poker more than legislate. That's left in. There was a little drinking among the members at that time. For correct detail in our modern version that has been allowed to remain in.[28] In its review of *A Texas Steer*, the *New York Times* raved about "that versatile genius, Will Rogers, who pals with princes and Presidents and wings his way across continents."[29]

The 1927 lecture tour was another grind. By the time Rogers stopped to lecture in Portland, Maine, in May, he had visited all forty-eight states in less than six months.[30]

WILL ROGERS'S WEEKLY newspaper columns continued to be increasingly popular throughout the 1920s. By the end of 1928 he had also published another twenty-three feature articles in the *Saturday Evening Post*. As his following grew, so did his recognition as a straight-talking political commentator. According to an editor of the *Dearborn Independent*:

> Will Rogers is serious. Did you ever see him tackle a subject for comment that was not serious? And did you ever feel that he had failed to get at the very heart and nub of the matter and split it open with a laugh? The answer is twice in the negative. The fact is, Will Rogers is a philosopher; so much of a philosopher that he has left the mechanics of philosophy far behind and has graduated into a higher region of humor.... Will Rogers tackles life, because he can. Humor is the highest gift; it is without alloy; Rogers has it. The editorial last week, or whenever it was, in this paper, that suggested

making Will Rogers Secretary of State for Pan-American Affairs is no joke. We need a serious-minded man like him in public affairs.[31]

Rogers continued to take harder stands on controversial issues and, when necessary, to "throw a cat into the electric fan." Often he hurled the cat at Congress, whose inattention to the nation's ills angered him constantly. On one occasion he proposed that a fat congressman be sent to destitute farmers, "so they can eat him."[32] On another he tried to spur the legislature into action, writing: "Did you know that the only bill that has already passed the House and Senate and been signed by the President is the bill appropriating the salary of the members of this extra session? The farmers can grow whiskers, the orphans can grow up, the tariff can tear out the vitals of the consumers' purse, but the boys there want theirs in advance whether they deliver any relief to anybody else or not."[33]

As Rogers became more strident, he attracted criticism from several quarters. His political satire had more bite, and it upset many who disagreed with what he wrote. If people had looked upon him as a mere humorist, they would not have taken him seriously or become upset over what they read, but many did take him seriously and their criticism reveals that what he said struck a nerve. In November 1928, for example, New York high rollers, including Mayor Jimmy Walker, became angry after Rogers implied gamblers involved in the murder of racketeer Arnold Rothstein were not gamblers but prominent New York citizens.[34] He upset some of the old guard in Congress when he wrote a column in February 1927 strongly supporting a bill to eliminate the lame-duck session. Reacting to the criticism, Rogers wrote:

> but it's got too much merit to it to pass. You know we got a lot of men in there that were defeated away last November. It takes seven months to blast you out after you have been fired. There is a very good Bill in there now to make it possible that newly elected men go in on January the first, at the beginning of the new Congress. Watch and see if you ever even hear of it. But you put some kind of appropriation to it and you will see it pass right now.[35]

Rogers irritated President Coolidge and conservative Republicans during congressional debates over farm relief when he decried the desperate conditions forcing farmers to lose their crops, property, and pride. The twenties were lean years for farmers, whose net income dropped over 25 percent after World War I. Hard times and low prices drove farmers from their land in record numbers; the 1920 census revealed that for the first time in the nation's history a majority of Americans no longer lived on the farm but were town dwellers.[36] Rogers's call for government aid to farmers was clearly a case where he attempted to influence legislative action. It was neither his first nor last attempt to do so. He exerted his influence closer to home when he sent a letter to Oklahoma senator John Harreld in February 1926 to lobby for an Indian hospital to be built in Claremore:

DEAR SENATOR:

I certainly was glad to hear of the bill you introduced, and hope you will be able to put it through.

Now, I certainly want to do anything I can to help the old home town. How is it getting along? Who is against it that I might be able to write to and try to convince? Anything you would like to have me do, just let me know.[37]

The bill passed and the hospital opened in 1929.

Rogers's articles sparked criticism from readers across the country. Such disapproval is understandable, given the enormous size of his readership and the controversial stands he took. Between October 1926 and March 1927 the *New York Times* received at least thirteen letters objecting to Rogers's commentary; some complained about a specific column, while others lodged more general complaints. One reader, for example, labeled his columns as "vulgar," proposing that "[a] paper such as the New York Times should *suppress* rather than encourage familiarity of [Rogers]," and declared, "Could there be any thing more obnoxious!"[38] Another appears to have tired of Rogers gallivanting around with the rich and famous, writing: "I hope Will Rogers isn't losing his sympathy with us common people by mingling with senators and congressmen."[39]

Rogers continued to anger millions of "drys" across the country with his opposition to Prohibition. In December 1928 he lost his temper when he read that a judge in Michigan had convicted Etta Mae Miller of selling two pints of liquor and sentenced her to life imprisonment under the state habitual criminal law. Comic exaggeration did not hide Rogers's irritation when he wrote:

For her fourth offense selling liquor the great State of Michigan sends the mother of ten children to the penitentiary for life. I guess that will just about blot out the liquor business in the State. I suppose she was the last one selling. Any woman that tries to raise ten orphan children in that cold state not only ought to be allowed to sell booze, but the State should furnish it to her to sell, and guarantee that it was pure. That would make her the greatest life saver in Michigan.

It certainly ought to be a lesson to people with ten children to never move to Michigan.[40]

Rogers felt the wrath of far-left writers who were put off by his down-home values and his frequent criticism of communists and other radicals. One socialist newspaper writer complained: "Will Rogers likes to pose as 'home folks,' but the truth is he's a millionaire. He has never written a word in support of a worker on strike. He has never spoken a sentence that doubted the divine justice of the capitalism system. Many of his wisecracks reveal a hidden sympathy for the Fascist type of Demagogue."[41]

In January 1927 Rogers upset the editors of the *New York Times* when he criticized a favorite target, American diplomacy. While making a lecture stop in Lexington, Kentucky, he wrote a one-line *Daily Telegram*, stating he had "been reading up on the early lives of our prominent men of today and find that Secretary of State Kellogg was scared very badly when a mere baby by a big ruff Russian."[42] Rogers was referring to Kellogg's attempt to blame Moscow for the deteriorating American relations with Mexico, the secretary testifying before the Senate Foreign Affairs Committee that there was a "Bolshevist threat" in Mexico and warning that "the government of Mexico is now on trial before the world."[43] Rogers knew that faulting Russia for Mexican-American troubles was far-fetched. The *Times*, however, felt his criticism too hard hitting and refused to print the piece.

Soon after, Arthur Sulzberger, a vice president of the *Times*, wrote to his publisher, Adolph Ochs: "Don't you think Will Rogers is getting pretty bad— and if so that we have been paying him long enough to feel that we have wiped out any obligation that we may have incurred last summer? . . . My suggestion would be that we give him due notice of desiring to stop at the earliest possible time."[44] Ochs wrote back to Sulzberger later and supported Rogers, albeit unenthusiastically. "I think Rogers is making a mistake in writing too much," Ochs wrote, "but that's his business.[45] The *Times* continued to print his daily telegrams until his death in 1935.

Rogers's disagreements with the *Times*, and they were numerous, suggest a more fundamental rift between those who liked and those who disliked what he said and how he said it. His lowbrow humor appealed mostly to the middle- and lower-class readership of the country, most of whom possessed only basic reading skills. They also were the ones most comfortable with his homespun homilies, cracker-barrel witticisms, and frightful grammar. On the other hand, there were those, mostly the silk stocking and literary set, who were put off by his earthier style. James Thurber, for example, was a sharp critic. Another was Frank Kent, a noted *Baltimore Sun* political writer who wielded a savage pen and labeled Rogers a "mercenary clown." The two men met for the first time in 1928 at the Republican Convention in Kansas City. "Why you durned little shrimp," Rogers said to Kent in jest. "If I had known you was no bigger than that I would have called you out long ago."[46]

In October 1929, the stuffy *Vanity Fair* published an open letter to Rogers written by Corey Ford, a frequent contributor to the magazine. Known for his satire and parody, Ford was a humorist who frequently inserted put-downs of Rogers in his writings. In the open letter he mimicked Rogers's style, saying he "was maybe just a boor who got his laughs by being Rude. . . . Only I just wish you wouldent try to be funny in print. I wish for example you wouldent write a book like Ether and Me, although I got to admit the title of that book is a pretty good suggestion how to read it."[47]

Rogers lost his temper when he read Ford's article, immediately scratching out an angry reply:

> Now Mr Ford we will just take you apart and see what makesyou so envious.
>
> Why should I get on your nerves, I never saw you in my life. . . . There is a bunch of you fellows back there that have your little so called Literary Clique, among you who have killed off more desrving talent than Editors have.
>
> Every laugh you aor anyone of you have [e]ver gotten has been at someone else's expense, You sit in New York and write for some magazine or apper [paper] and you are the last word, Well listen Brother, you hoppe[d] on the wrong Guy, I will get your name in more papers than you ever though[t] existed,

What we did used to call the fellows that lived off women, That's what you are doing. . . .[48]

Whether it was intellectual conceit or downright jealousy, there were some, like Corey Ford, who simply could not stand Rogers. O. O. McIntyre, the popular columnist who also wrote for McNaught Syndicate, later tried to explain why some writers disliked his friend Rogers:[49] "Something about Will Rogers fearfully upsets pseudointellectuals. He gets in their long hair. Everything he does grows increasingly irritating. His gum chewing . . . his ridgehopper twang . . . his scrambling of the Queen's English. . . . Will Rogers irritates because he has confounded these hooting intellectuals time after time. He always lands on top."[50]

IN MAY 1927 the president of the National Security League, Robert Lee Bullard, wrote Will Rogers to tell him that his writings and talks had accomplished so much for a strong national defense that the directors of the league had appointed him as a fellow director. The league was a nationalistic, militaristic, and nonpartisan organization supporting a strong military, universal conscription, the naturalization and Americanization of immigrants, meritocracy, and government regulation of the economy to improve national preparedness. Theodore Roosevelt, Jr., and George Haven Putnam were officers, and the group's honorary officers included some of the era's most influential politicians, including Franklin D. Roosevelt, Theodore Roosevelt, Elihu Root, Henry L. Stimson, Robert Bacon, and Alton B. Parker.[51] Many programs advocated by the league eventually materialized, such as a single department of defense, an interstate highway system, universal conscription, and a unified national budget. Rogers supported the league and its hard-line stance. "Here is a letter from General Bullard saying that any donation to the National Security League is deductible off the income tax," he wrote in his weekly column. "That's good news to know that they are not going to charge us for the sake of giving to our own security."[52]

Rogers did not agree with some of the hard-line conservatives, however. After Chicago mayor "Big Bill" Thompson started a xenophobic society called "America First" that opposed any foreign influence in America's schools, Rogers, who never got along with the heavy-handed mayor, countered with his own comically absurd society:

Bill has the nucleus of a good idea, but, like any good idea, it's the improvements that make it.

So I hereby offer stock in a society called "America Only" at $20 a share. Why be only first? Let's be the whole thing. . . . If everybody in America will give me $20 I will be more than glad to show them where we are the "only nation in the world." Besides, this money will not all revert to me. A small percentage will be spent in exterminating all other nations.

Who'll be the first to display super-patriotism and join "America Only"?[53]

While the right-wing National Security League courted Rogers's favor, he also was approached from the far left. According to Richard Whitney, the head of the ultra-right American Defense Society, federal agents seized Communist files in the early 1920s that mentioned several Hollywood performers, including Charlie Chaplin, Norma Talmadge, and Will Rogers. In his book on the Red Scare, Whitney wrote that "some of [the Hollywood performers] are known to be in hearty sympathy with Communism and to be close friends of Communists, to whose cause they have contributed greatly." In May 1922, Robert Morss Lovett, president of the radical Federated Press League, wrote to a leading Communist money raiser urging him to solicit donations from fifteen members of the movie colony, including William de Mille, Eric Von Stroheim, Chaplin, and Rogers. "These men are with us," Lovett wrote. "They helped us before and will do it again. Present the situation strong and don't let them get off easy, for we need the money and need it badly."[54]

It is not surprising that Communist-front organizations approached Rogers for money, as he was well known as a philanthropist with deep pockets and a man who supported causes across the political spectrum. There is no record, however, that Rogers contributed to any Communist organization and, if he did, it is doubtful he knew where his contributions went or approved of their leftist activities. Rogers was like most Americans, who were then less concerned about "bomb-throwing, bewhiskered Bolsheviks" than about what station they could tune into on their Philco radio set. To him, Communists were "likeable cusses and smart" but little more than political nuisances.[55] "These Reds are on their backs snoring," he wrote, "and they ain't keeping anybody awake but each other."[56]

As WILL ROGERS crisscrossed the country giving lectures throughout the winter and spring of 1927, cold torrents of rain poured down upon the southern states, week after week. The downpours drenched the region and soon gorged the Mississippi River until it roared past cities and towns, its swirling brown cataract rising until it was higher than any old-timer remembered. Huge earthen levees and piles of sandbags no longer harnessed the rising water. By April the river had broken through the dikes in hundreds of places, flooding over sixteen million acres of fertile Mississippi River valley and rendering seven hundred thousand people homeless in seven states.[57]

Rogers was speaking in Richmond, Virginia, when he learned the flood had reached catastrophic proportions. Rearranging his schedule, he flew back to New York City on a plane flown by famed air-racing pilot Roscoe Turner. He persuaded Ziegfeld to provide his Broadway theater for free and, along with tenor John McCormack, staged a benefit for the flood victims that raised $18,000 for Red Cross relief. Soon he traveled to New Orleans and gave another benefit at the Saenger Theater, where top seats cost five hundred dollars, and raised $48,000, a record for the Red Cross.[58] As he traveled across the country calling for help for the flood sufferers, hundreds of thousands of Americans answered his appeal and donated their time and money.

When Rogers arrived in New Orleans he canceled a lucrative engagement in Birmingham so he could spend several days touring the flooded areas. He took an air tour of the "sugar bowl" in Louisiana and Mississippi to see the damage firsthand and meet with those directing the relief effort.[59] "[Herbert] Hoover has done a wonderful work down here," he wrote. "I am flying all over the new part where the water has broken through and is still rising. Just saw today the cut they made to save [New Orleans] and saw the refugees. If you could see this you would double your donations."[60]

While in New Orleans Rogers received a telegram from Senator Pat Harrison of Mississippi thanking him for his work during the flood. "The Missi[ssi]ppi Valley appreciates your great labors in its behalf," Harrison wrote. "You have done more than any one else in the UnitedStates except Hoover and those directing the work to bring to attention American people the need and distress occasioned by the flood."[61] Late in June and soon after

Rogers accepting key to New Orleans from Mayor Arthur O'Keefe

he returned to California, John Barton Payne, chairman of the American Red Cross, notified Rogers he had been elected a life member of the organization.[62]

That fall, Rogers blew up after a senator suggested that the Mississippi flood relief effort was getting too much attention. In his daily column, Rogers attacked:

> One of our Western Senators says: "The Mississippi flood people say theirs is a national problem. Well, so is the Boulder Dam, and I will fight any effort to set it aside in favor of the flood."
>
> Well, there is no difference in the two problems to a politician; but to a human being there is a difference. One is to do nothing but save lives and property, while the other is to develop a dam for cheap water and power, the same as dozens of other projects on other rivers are developed every day, without dragging in the Mississippi.
>
> If the Colorado ever overflowed you can it turn out across the land anywhere on its lower course, and there is enough sand to soak up the Atlantic Ocean. The dam should be built, but not as a club over the Mississippi sufferers.[63]

During his benefits Rogers was one of only a few who spoke up for the blacks who suffered so terribly in the flood. In the Jim Crow South, he well knew, blacks were the last to get assistance, if at all. Rogers was no crusader for Negro causes, but at the same time he was no bigot, sympathizing in times of crisis with any and all sufferers. In his column he wrote:

> when you talk about poor people that have been hit by this flood, look at the thousands and thousands of negroes that never did have much, but now it's washed away. You don't want to forget that water is just as high up on them as it is if they were white.
>
> The Lord so constituted everybody that no matter what color you are you require about the same amount of nourishment."[64]

Rogers continued to seek aid for flood victims long after the waters receded. He kept criticizing Congress for "jawboning" and delaying flood-control legislation that would prevent such a disaster from happening again. In a *Saturday Evening Post* article he wrote: "If every man of every Committee that has gone to that river to investigate had put in one hour's actual work raising the levee, why, it would have been so high now you couldent have got water out over the edge with a hydraulic pump. So the next Committee you send to that river, give 'em a spade instead of a report sheet."[65]

On January 12, 1928, Rogers testified before the House Committee on Flood Control, describing his firsthand knowledge of the terrible conditions and dramatizing the need for direct governmental assistance. He urged that the federal government take full responsibility for flood control and pay Mississippi Valley victims for their losses.[66]

As Congress continued to delay providing flood relief, Rogers lost his patience as he gave a lecture in Montclair, New Jersey:

> Can anybody in this house tell me one constructive bill our Senate has passed since last December[?] ... They haven't done a thing—flood relief, farm relief, tax reduction—not a thing has been done about anything you can mention. They are arguing and arguing, always debating and messing around. ...
>
> If you've got any friends in the Mississippi Valley I'd advise you to assist them to get a boat. I'd rather have one canoe in a flood than a Senate behind

me. There is going to be nothing—Congress is going to do nothing about the flood.[67]

A month after Rogers's tirade, Congress passed the Flood Control Act and appropriated $325 million for relief work over the next ten years.

SEVEN

The Nation's Number-One Air Passenger

A FTER WILL ROGERS stopped in Concord, New Hampshire, on May 20, 1927, to raise more donations for Mississippi River flood relief and work the lecture circuit, he sat in his hotel room that night listening to the radio and, along with millions of other Americans, waited anxiously for the latest news. He typed away at his column, but his mind was elsewhere: "No attempt at jokes today. A slim, tall, bashful, smiling American boy is somewhere out over the middle of the Atlantic Ocean, where no lone human being has ever ventured before. He is being prayed for to every kind of Supreme Being that has a following. If he is lost it will be the most universally regretted single loss we ever had. But that kid ain't going to fail."[1]

Rogers was right, for the kid didn't fail. Just after eight that morning and amid a dreary rain, twenty-five-year-old Charles Lindbergh took off from muddy Roosevelt Field, Long Island, in his small monoplane, the *Spirit of St. Louis.* Thirty-three hours later, Lindbergh arrived in Paris to become the first pilot to fly solo across the Atlantic Ocean. Overnight, the handsome youngster became the most idolized man of the era. Will Rogers was among the millions of enthralled Americans who took Lindbergh to their hearts as they had no other human being in living memory. "The ones of us here now will never live to see a thing that will give us a bigger kick than his flight did," Rogers wrote afterward.[2]

In September, Rogers spoke at a banquet honoring the young aviator at the Hotel Coronado in San Diego. His remarks favoring air power impressed Lindbergh. "Get the biggest air force in the world," Rogers said, "and just sit here and take care of your own business and we will never during our life-time [have] to use it."[3] He also complained about the lack of progress in American commercial aviation, which then lagged far behind European air travel. "Flew into Russia," he told the dinner guests. "Russia has lots of air-planes. Everybody has more planes than we have. We talk more progress than we do. We build three golf courses to every flying field."[4] After the banquet Lindbergh invited Will and Betty to fly back to Los Angeles with him in a Ford trimotor; Rogers shared the cockpit with the world's newest hero. "You have never seen him at his best till you sit out in the pilot's seat by his side," a thrilled Rogers wrote afterward. "When he has a plane in his hands there is no careworn or worried look. That's when he is in his glory."[5]

Lindbergh's daring flight across the Atlantic in 1927 launched a golden era of flight, a period when aviators around the world clamored to set new records for flying the fastest, farthest, and highest: Richard Byrd and Floyd Bennett flew over the North Pole, and, a year after Lindbergh, Amelia Earhart flew from Newfoundland to Wales to become the first woman to cross the Atlantic, while the German dirigible *Graf Zeppelin* crossed from the opposite direction. Amateur pilots strove for fame, as in April 1929 when a seventeen-year-old chorus girl, Elinor Smith, stayed aloft for over twenty-six hours to set the women's solo endurance record.[6] New aviation technology advanced at breakneck speed, from Wiley Post setting a high-altitude record in a pressurized suit to Jimmy Doolittle landing a plane only on instruments. Pan American Airways launched its first passenger flight from Key West to Havana in October 1927. A month later the U.S. Navy commissioned its first modern aircraft carrier, the USS *Saratoga*.

Lindbergh's remarkable transatlantic flight, one of the most amazing feats of the century, had a huge impact on Rogers, for it increased his com-mitment to aviation, confirmed his belief in its potential to change the world, spurred his wanderlust, and led to lasting friendships with Lindbergh and other famous pilots. Rogers had not only caught the aviation fever that swept

Rogers with Charles Lindbergh

across the country, he was stricken with it. Less than a month after Lindbergh's flight, he took off as a passenger on his own record-breaking cross-country flight. No transcontinental air service yet existed, but Rogers made the flight on regularly scheduled airmail routes, paying $814 first-class postage because his ticket was priced by the pound of mail. He completed the trip in three and a half days, wearing goggles and a leather flying suit and stuffed in open cockpits with bags of mail. The flight made Rogers the first civilian to fly coast to coast with the airmail service. During the trip he emerged unhurt when his pilot made a forced landing on a muddy farm in Beaver Falls, Pennsylvania.[7] After he returned to California from his hop, he took another risky flight: "yesterday on the battleship Pennsylvania I took my first catapult in a plane from a ship. From a standing start, on a runway only sixty feet long, you are doing sixty miles an hour at the end of it, shot by compressed air. Just watch your head and see that you don't leave it behind you."[8]

Rogers and Lindbergh in the cockpit

Rogers became the number-one air passenger of his day, eventually making at least twenty-five crossings of the continent by airplane and logging over a half-million air miles. He flew in almost anything that could leave the ground, including army bombers, one of the first Goodyear blimps, navy planes when they took off from and landed on carriers, and rickety old biplanes that should have been scrapped years before.

By reading Rogers's newspaper accounts, earthbound readers experienced the thrill of flying. "Just flew in home," he wrote after flying across California in July 1928. "If you want a pretty trip, fly over the Imperial Valley and the Salt Sea, then over the desert, mountains, fig orchards, then 10,000 acres of grapes in one orchard."[9] A month later he wrote after flying over Arizona: "If you never take but one airplane trip in your life, make it the one where you fly over the Grand Canyon."[10]

As he barnstormed the country, Rogers described some of his more

*Will kisses Betty
before departing on
another flight*

harrowing airborne adventures. "Just flew in here 300 miles from Elko, Nev., by airplane," he wrote after landing in Salt Lake City. "Got lost over the mountains in a snowstorm. Oh, boy, we got real aviators in this country, even if the Government don't think they are useful."[11] After a flight through a Nebraskan blizzard, he told his readers that he "left Chicago last night at 10 o'clock in a snowstorm and flew to Omaha. These mail babies go through.

They can get through weather that most people couldn't find their way from the house to the garage with a well-lighted course. Good planes and good pilots!"[12]

But even Rogers realized he sometimes took too much risk. On one occasion he finished lecturing in New York City and wanted to get home to his family in California. "It was a dark, rainy, cloudy day on the New York end of the air mail," he wrote afterward. "No planes through in two days. . . . I insisted on going. It wasn't bravery—it was dumb ignorance and an unlimited confidence in all air mail pilots."[13] Rogers approached the scheduled airmail pilot, "Wild Bill" Hopson, pleading with him to ignore the bad weather and make the flight.[14] A former New York City cab driver and one of the more colorful and experienced airmail pilots of the era, Hopson agreed to make the risky hop. "And we got through, clear to Cleveland," Rogers wrote. "I kinder feel like his skill saved my life."[15]

Rogers became friends with many of the great aviators of the time, including Hopson, Lindbergh, Roscoe Turner, Frank Hawks, Casey Jones, Jimmy Doolittle, and Wiley Post. In his writings he portrayed them as modern-day heroes, admiring their bravery and independence. They must have reminded him of the soft-spoken but hard-boned cowboys of his days on the range. In dozens of articles and lectures, he supported those pilots with proposals to make their jobs safer and more efficient. On one occasion, he asked towns to paint their names on rooftops to help pilots navigate across the country. On another he suggested that golf courses, to him a waste of good pasture land, be designed as emergency runways:

> The big problem of aviation is having emergency places to land. Now you insist on every golf course having one fairway long enough and level enough to land a plane on, all marked with crosses to show it. Every golf club should be patriotic and humane enough to do this.
>
> Think what it would mean to an aviator with a missing engine to know that every golf course was a life preserver. If they don't do this voluntarily the Government will make 'em do it some day.[16]

Rarely did a week pass without Rogers promoting aviation and campaigning for the latest navigation and airport facilities, safer planes, more training for aircrews, and direct government subsidies to spur commercial aviation. During the decade prior to his death in 1935, he probably did more than anyone else except Charles Lindbergh and Billy Mitchell to promote civilian aviation as a safe, reliable, and efficient mode of transportation, as well as to argue that a modern and large military air force would be essential in future wars.

Rogers fumed every time newspapers treated an air crash as if it were a major catastrophe, as in September 1927: "Every paper is raving about legislation to stop ocean flying because thirteen people have been lost, just a fair Sunday's average in auto deaths. From ten to fifteen is just about the number that are always in a bus when it meets a train at a grade crossing, yet you never see an editorial about relief from that. You may not die as spectacularly in a machine as you would if you dropped in the ocean, but you are just as dead.[17] Two months later he complained again about newspaper coverage: "Five people killed in a plane yesterday and it is headlined today in every paper. Saturday in Los Angeles at one grade crossing seven were killed and six wounded and the papers didn't even publish the names. It looks like the only way you can get any publicity on your death is to be killed in a plane."[18]

From Salina, Kansas, six months later, he railed about the coverage. "When will the newspapers commence giving aviation an even break? There were eight people killed all over America in planes Sunday and it's headlined in every newspaper today."[19] In October 1928 he lost his temper while lecturing in Connecticut: "Seven people were killed in the whole of America over the weekend in airplanes, and the way the newspapers headlined it you would have thought Nicaragua had invaded us. Yet in New York City alone, fifteen was killed and seventy wounded with bad liquor, to say nothing about Chicago, so it's safer to take a flight than a drink."[20]

Whenever people tried to tell Rogers not to risk his own life in the air, he recoiled angrily: "This thing of talking about 'somebody's life being too valuable to risk in an airplane' is not only the bunk, but it's an insult to the men we ask to do our flying. Where does anybody's life come in to be any more valuable than anybody else's? Ain't life just as precious to one as to another?"[21]

Despite Rogers's insistence that flying was as safe as driving, he knew from firsthand experience that air travel was dangerous, having survived a number of crack-ups himself. Several pilots whom he knew and had flown with perished during the 1920s. By 1924, six years after the Postal Air Service began, only ten of the original forty pilots were alive.[22] On October 18, 1928, his friend "Wild Bill" Hopson, the same airmail pilot who braved stormy weather to fly him to Cleveland, died when his plane crashed into the top of a hill near Polk, Pennsylvania, during a bad storm. Rogers wrote from his heart after the crash:

> Yesterday he didn't get through.
>
> . . . so, "Hoppie" old boy, here's hoping you are piloting the best cloud the Boss has got in His hangar up there, and you don't have to worry about low ceiling, engine missing, head winds, or even whether the old rip-cord will pull in case—[23]

IN SEPTEMBER 1927, President Calvin Coolidge appointed his Amherst classmate Dwight Morrow as U.S. ambassador to Mexico.[24] A wealthy Wall Street attorney with a record as a brilliant financier, Morrow would turn out to be a popular and effective ambassador, but when he arrived in Mexico City, diplomatic relations between the two countries were dreadful. The new ambassador, well aware of Will Rogers's international popularity, his ability to make friends anywhere, and his sympathy for Mexico, invited Rogers to make a goodwill visit, a visit that might help break the ice in the frigid relations between the countries.

During his three weeks as Morrow's guest, Rogers made a whirlwind tour of Mexico to meet its leaders and absorb its culture. He was the dinner guest of former Mexican president Álvaro Obregón, was feted by dignitaries and wealthy businessmen, and was welcomed at government agricultural schools and irrigation projects. Piling into a huge caravan of motor cars one evening, Rogers's Mexican hosts drove him to an old hacienda about a hundred miles from Mexico City for a wonderful fiesta in his honor and a sumptuous banquet, alfresco, with tables strung with wreaths of flowers, music from a Mexican orchestra, champagne, and a guest list that included all of the high-ranking Mexicans and the diplomatic corps. "The audience decided to forget the Alamo," Rogers recalled, "[and] decided Texas wasn't worth taking back anyhow."[25]

The highlight of Rogers's trip was a ten-day tour of Mexico with President Plutarco Calles on the presidential train. To Morrow's pleasure, Rogers's humor was a hit with the Mexicans, prompting one American diplomat to report that Rogers "was all over the place, making jokes, very impertinent, making fun of everybody and getting away with it. The Mexicans roared with laughter and there was much good feeling and excitement."[26]

Before long, Rogers and President Calles struck up a friendship. "If you want to know a man," the humorist said, "travel on some extended trip with him."[27] On December 12, Morrow gave Rogers a lavish dinner that Calles and all of the cabinet attended, the first time a president of Mexico ever was in the American embassy. "We had many a laugh," Rogers wrote. "These are real people down here if we only knew them."[28]

Through his *Saturday Evening Post* and daily newspaper articles, Rogers provided the American public a warmly amusing but perceptive view of the people, politics, and culture of post-revolutionary Mexico. He admired the gentle campesinos who lived there and the rustic beauty of their land. Overall he fell for "the land of Manyana,"[29] but he did not ignore the weaknesses he observed. He was appalled at the poverty, especially in the small villages. He criticized a "kind of a socialistic scheme" whereby the Mexican government took land from the big landowners and gave it to the peons, a scheme that did not include the wealthy friends of President Calles.[30] During one banquet, Rogers was remarkably candid with the Mexicans: "Now if I was looking for comedy in Government, I dident have to come here. I could have stayed at home. I come down here to laugh with you and not at you. I dident come here to tell you that we look on you as Brothers. That would be a lot of bunk. We look on you as a lot of Bandits and you look on us as one Big Bandit. So I think we fairly understand each other, without trying to express it."[31]

While Rogers was in Mexico, Morrow invited Charles Lindbergh to fly to the country in another move to improve diplomatic relations. Lindbergh accepted the invitation, wanting to make one last, long trip in the *Spirit of St. Louis* before donating the airplane to the Smithsonian. The nonstop flight from Washington DC to Mexico City was almost as arduous and dangerous as his transatlantic flight, taking over twenty-seven hours. On December 14, 1927, Rogers was one of 150,000 spectators who waited seven hours to greet Lindbergh when he landed in Mexico City. Later, Lindbergh took Rogers on a flight over the Mexican mountains, flying a borrowed a plane so old it "had bandages on it and it was wrapped up in barbed wire."[32]

Morrow's effort to bring Rogers and Lindbergh to Mexico proved a huge success, as the tension in diplomatic relations seemed to disappear, at least for the time being. "You people up there can't realize what this trip of [Lindbergh] means to the two countries," Rogers wrote from Mexico City.[33] The trip also had another consequence, as it led to Lindbergh's first meeting with Morrow's daughter Anne, a quiet, shy girl only a year out of Smith College and who, in May 1929, became his wife.

BY 1928, the same year that the popular comedy *Amos 'n' Andy* first aired on station WMAQ in Chicago, radio networks were broadcasting variety shows that rivaled the star-studded Ziegfeld Follies. On January 4, 1928, the Dodge Brothers sponsored the most ambitious broadcast to date, the *Dodge Victory Hour*, which aired to the biggest audience in history. Will Rogers served as master of ceremonies from his Beverly Hills home, vaudevillians Fred and Dorothy Stone joined in from Chicago, Al Jolson from the Roosevelt Hotel in New Orleans, and Paul Whiteman and his orchestra from New York. On the air, Rogers departed from his normal routine and began mimicking Calvin Coolidge in the president's New England twang: "I am proud to report that the country as a whole is prosperous. I don't mean by that that the whole country is prosperous, but, as a whole it is prosperous. That is, it is prosperous for a whole. A hole is not supposed to be prosperous, and we are certainly in a hole. There is not a whole lot of doubt about that. Everybody I come in contact with is doing well. They have to be doing well or they don't come in contact with me."[34]

Rogers's imitation of the president must have seemed genuine, as many listeners thought it was really Coolidge. Unfortunately, some critics felt the prank went beyond the bounds of good taste. The harshest was an editor at the *New York Times*, whose high-brow column intentionally belittled the more rustic Rogers. The editor began with a quote from Shakespeare suggesting, "A jest's prosperity lies not in the tongue of him who makes it but in the ears of those who hear."[35] The editorial ended with a not-so-veiled threat: "And when the jest has for its object the President, and the occasion is an advertising stunt, the error of bad taste becomes even more unforgivable. Mr. Rogers is a national favorite, and he has been granted the unofficial rights of court jester, but there are marked bounds to his privilege. If he oversteps the limit like this, he will find his jests fallen upon adversity and growing flat upon his tongue."[36]

Two days after the broadcast, the head of the McNaught newspaper syndicate telegraphed Rogers: "Mr Ochs of Times asks us to convey to you the following idea. [H]e says your imitation of Coolidge on radio was so good that millions of people think it was really Coolidge talking and he thinks you might want to explain in daily dispatch that it was not really Cal but you. [W]e just transmit the suggestion to you at the request of Mr Ochs."[37] Rogers declared in his daily column of January 13 that he meant no harm to the president, adding that he thought it ludicrous that "any one could imagine it was [President Coolidge] uttering the nonsense that I was uttering! It struck me that it would be an insult to any one's sense of humor to announce that it was not him."[38]

Rogers traveled to Washington DC a week after the Dodge broadcast to testify before the House Flood Committee and speak at the Democrats' annual Jackson Day Dinner. Rogers made some biting remarks about Andrew Jackson, Democrats, and patronage politics, blaming Jackson for creating the spoils system by thinking up the "idea to promise everybody that if they will vote for you, why, you will give them an office when you get in, and the more times they vote for you the bigger the office you will give them." To Rogers, that was the real beginning of the Democratic Party. "It was called Democratic because you was supposed to get something for your vote. Then the Republicans come along and improved on the Democrats and Jackson's idea by giving them money instead of promises of jobs."[39]

While in Washington, Rogers wrote a long letter of apology to President and Mrs. Coolidge for his on-air imitation of the president:

> *I find that due to my lack of good taste, or utter stupidity, that I have wounded the feelings of two people who I most admire, and should have been the last to embarr[a]ss, had I purposvely started out to annoy the entire World....*
>
> *[I]t does hurt me, to think that I have to resort to bad taste to make my living from men who have befriended me....*
>
> *I just missjudged the intelligence of the people listening....*
>
> *If there ever was a sad Comedian, I am one, and I do ask all the forgivness that its in your and Mrs Coolidges power to give....*[40]

Rogers received a note from Coolidge the next day dismissing his impersonation:

> *Your letter has just come to me. I hope it will cheer you up to know that*
> *I thought the matter of rather small consequence myself though the*
> *office was informed from several sources that I had been on the air. I*
> *wish to assure you that your note makes it all plain that you had no*
> *[bad] intention [, only] some harmless amusement.*
>
> *I hope you will not give the affair another troubled thought. I am*
> *well aware how nicely you have referred to me so many times.*
>
> > *Cordially Yours,*
> > *Calvin Coolidge.*[41]

Rogers realized that his outright mimicry of the president had slipped past relatively harmless comic exaggeration into satire, potentially a humorist's most hurtful technique, and he seldom used such direct and personal satirizations again. To many critics, his impersonation had seemed mean-spirited. After the exchange of letters the incident appeared to be over, but the president did not invite Rogers to the White House during his remaining year in office.

From Washington, Rogers and his wife traveled to Cuba to attend the Sixth Annual Pan American Conference, where he claimed to be an unofficial representative-at-large. While in Havana, Will and Betty gave a dinner for their friends Ambassador Dwight Morrow and former secretary of state Charles Evans Hughes.[42] Coolidge attended the conference and gave the opening address. "The President made a good speech," Rogers observed. "He didn't say that we would do anything for these countries, but, on the other hand, he didn't say that we would do anything against them."[43]

WILL ROGERS spent the first half of 1928 on another lecture tour, hitting sixty cities from New York to Florida. That summer he quit the tour to attend both national political conventions. He left California on June 6 en route to the Republican Convention in Kansas City, but the trip proved to be more hair-raising than the convention. On the first leg he hitched a ride in a new airmail monoplane, but as the pilot attempted to land at a small field in New Mexico to refuel, the right wheel broke and the plane flipped over, nose first, and onto its back. Rogers was shaken but unhurt. A few hours later, he survived another crash while taking off from a small country grass field in Cherokee, Wyoming. When his Boeing air transport gained speed, one of the wheels hit a gopher hole, cracked a strut, and the plane cartwheeled onto its back. Again, Roger emerged unhurt, and he downplayed both accidents.[44] He remained undeterred from flying, even after surviving yet another crash in 1929 when the pilot ran out of gas and landed in a vacant lot near Chicago. The plane tumbled over and Rogers suffered fractured ribs.[45] Afterward he declared he was "going to keep on flying until my beard caught in the propeller."[46]

The Republican National Convention that convened in Kansas City on June 10, 1928, was so quiet and dull that one newsman labeled it the "dreariest public occasion since the burial of William McKinley."[47] To no one's surprise, the Republicans nominated popular secretary of commerce Herbert Hoover for president on the first ballot and Charles Curtis of Kansas for vice president.

To liven up the conventions, Rogers humorously declared himself as a third-party candidate for the presidency. His platform for his new Anti-Bunk Party was simple: "WHATEVER THE OTHER FELLOW DONT DO, WE WILL."[48] His only campaign promise was that if elected, he would resign. He told his readers that what the country needed was "cleaner minds and dirtier finger nails."[49] After the humor magazine *Life* endorsed him and placed his photo on its cover, the farcical campaign gathered some serious momentum. Fifteen prominent citizens announced their support, including Henry Ford, Billy Mitchell, Babe Ruth, Ring Lardner, and Father Duffy. "Don't get the idea that this is all just a big joke," a *Life* columnist wrote.[50] As Rogers went along with the mock campaign, he admitted that he did not have much faith in the electorate. "Our whole appeal is to the broadminded element," he wrote, "and I doubt if I receive over a hundred votes."[51]

Columnist H. L. Mencken was also at the 1928 Republican convention. Known for his acid pen, Mencken was the number-one curmudgeon of his age and a good friend of Will's. He was serious when he described Rogers as "the most influential editorial writer in America." On one occasion Mencken stood in the press box among a crowd of writers, pointed to Rogers, and announced loudly: "Look at that man! He alters foreign policies. He makes and unmakes candidates. He destroys public figures. By deriding Congress and undermining its prestige, he has virtually reduced us to a monarchy. Millions of American free men read his words daily, and those who are unable to read listen to him over the radio. . . . I consider him the most dangerous writer alive today." Rogers overheard Mencken and said, "Come on now, Henry you know that nobody with any sense ever took any of my gags seriously." "Certainly not," Mencken shot back. "They are taken seriously by nobody except half-wits, in other words by approximately 85 per cent of the voting population."[52]

Mencken was not the only journalist to recognize the serious influence Rogers wielded. At the time, the *Decatur Review* called Rogers "a national institution . . . [who] poked fun at both the Republican and Democratic conventions, but no dispatches from the conventions have been read with more interest than those sent by Rogers. Few if any correspondents have cut as deeply into the real facts as has Rogers. . . . His jibes and jolts are taken as humor, but they have a way of staying with you."[53]

While in Kansas City Rogers gave a charity benefit for the Salvation Army's Children's Fund at the Shubert Theater. Soon after, a gunman killed a Kansas City policeman, Happy Smith, when he tried to stop a daylight robbery near the convention headquarters. Rogers gave an hour-and-a-half benefit for Smith's widow and five children at the Ivanhoe Auditorium before eighteen hundred people. The theater filled two hours before he stepped onto the stage, and extra police were called out to control the overflow.[54]

Braving an oppressively hot summer in the South two weeks later, Rogers traveled to Houston for the Democratic National Convention. Fellow columnist O. O. McIntyre was also there, sharing the steamy press box with Rogers and describing his good friend: "Will Rogers' seat is next to mine and if there ever was a fibberty gibbety guy he is it. His jaws snap 100 times a minute and when he is not wriggling his feet he is shifting from one hip to another or rolling a lead pencil between his palms. I wasn't there a half hour before he had worked me into a spell of the jerks. . . . 'If you can't sit still, go home,' I finally told him."[55]

Early in the convention someone suggested Rogers run for vice president. He played along, and as a part-Cherokee declared, "Vote for Rogers and scalp the Kaws." His friend Charles Curtis, the Republican nominee for vice president, was part Kaw, an Indian tribe of the Osage Nation.[56] There also was an undercurrent of support for an Al Smith/Will Rogers ticket. The Catholic bishop in St. Joseph, Missouri, suggested Rogers enter the race, writing that he "has more genuine patriotism in his little finger than 10,000 bigots who are attacking Governor Smith."[57] According to the popular columnist Heywood Broun, there was no jest in the suggestion to put him on the ticket with Smith, writing that Rogers "is no clown, and his witticisms have a foundation in shrewd common sense. He could unite the party and under his leadership there might be a new era of friendliness in political encounter. . . . No man is better equipped to fight the Klan with useful weapons. He knows those people from the ground up. I think he could kid the Klan out of existence."[58]

While Rogers ignored any hints of nomination and tried to interject some humor from the press box, the fight among the Democrats on the convention floor was serious and bitter. The convention was the first held by either party in the South since the Civil War, and Jim Crow racial segregation still ruled in Houston and a chicken-wire fence separated black and white delegates.[59] The two controversies that had divided the Democrats four years before—Prohibition and religion—still dominated the floor debate. But eventually the delegates cooperated. After a single ballot and only one fist fight, they nominated front-runner Al Smith, the first Roman Catholic to capture the nomination. Along with Smith, who was anti-Prohibition, the Democrats nominated for vice president the pro-Prohibition senator from Arkansas, Joe Robinson, the first southerner on a presidential ticket since the Civil War.

Even though Smith's nomination was fairly quick, he remained controversial and opponents within his party continued to attack him. One of them, Texas governor Dan Moody, rallied the southern bloc to fight for a dry platform and oppose Smith's anti-prohibition stance. Evangelist Billy Sunday labeled Smith's supporters "the damnable whiskey politicians, the bootleggers, crooks, pimps, and businessmen who deal with them."[60] Rogers watched with frustration as the convention ultimately avoided the Prohibition issue and pledged only "honest enforcement of the Constitution."

Rogers defended Smith staunchly. In one daily column early in the campaign, his use of comic exaggeration was most acute:

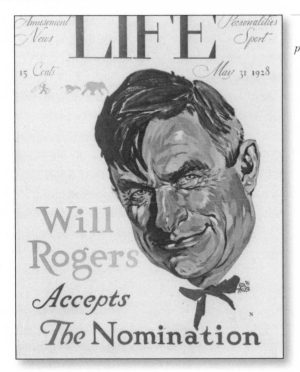

*The Anti-Bunk
presidential candidate*

If you want to read one of the only real straightforward statements ever issued by a politician, read Al Smith's, out today.

He explains that if elected president all Protestants would not be exterminated; that even a few of the present Senators would be retained, including Tom Heflin; that the Knights of Columbus would not replace the Boy Scouts and Kiwanis; that mass would not replace golf on Sunday morning; and that those that were fortunate enough to have meat could have it on Friday.

It's no compliment to a nation's intelligence when these things have to be explained.[61]

Rogers backed Smith so strongly that one observer remarked that he "sometimes somehow seemed to be running with Smith as his proxy."[62] Rogers also defended Smith for being a Catholic at a time when religion was enough to get a man licked, writing: "What do we care about a man's religion? We don't want to be saved spiritually, we want to be dragged out of the hole financially. He has been three times Governor of New York. The Jews elected him. Now if they can trust him to run the biggest state in the world where they own 90 percent of it and trust a Catholic over a Protestant why we shouldn't mind. . . . What do we care about a President's religion?"[63]

Rogers's support made little difference. As with the 1924 race, the disorganized Democrats made it easy for the Republicans to win the presidency in a landslide, Hoover amassing 444 electoral votes to Smith's 87. Rogers saw the defeat coming. Early in the convention he drew Smith aside and pleaded with him to withdraw from the race. "Wait four years," a Smith supporter remembered Rogers saying. "Nobody ever killed Santa Claus. Times are too good. You can't win in so prosperous year."[64]

———

WILL ROGERS stopped in Asheville, North Carolina, in March 1928 to spend a day visiting the brand-new Great Smoky Mountains National Park. "It's beautiful and can't help from being a big success as a public park for tourists. They got the stills in there already."[65] Later he spoke before three thousand Cherokees who continued to live nearby in the ancient territory of the tribe. It was a moving event for Rogers, as he was proud of the imprint that his Indian blood had on his upbringing. As he looked on the Cherokees standing stoically before him, he must have reflected upon his early years in Indian Territory.

The original home of the Cherokees was some forty thousand square miles covering parts of Georgia, North and South Carolina, and Tennessee. In 1838, after Congress passed the Indian Removal Act, a military force bodily removed fifteen thousand Cherokees to Indian Territory. During the trek, four thousand Indians perished in a tragedy later known as the Trail of Tears. Will Rogers's great-grandfather, Robert Rogers, saw what was coming, headed west voluntarily to settle in Arkansas, and later moved to the new Cherokee Nation in Indian Territory.

The years surrounding Rogers's childhood were turbulent times for the American West. When he was nine years old, Congress outlawed tribal government and abolished communal ownership of land among the Native Americans. Any hopes for an independent Indian state vanished. Two years later, the infamous Oklahoma land rush ended tribal rule when the government opened large tracts of the fertile territory to non-Indian homesteaders. The land rush was the tragic final chapter in the destruction of the Indians' traditional way of life. In 1893, the federal government paid $8.6 million to the Cherokee people for the lands seized. Of that settlement, the Rogers family received $365.70.[66]

Proud of his Cherokee blood, Will Rogers at times revealed a deep-seated anger about the inhumane treatment of the Indians. During one of his radio broadcasts, he was remarkably candid:

> Our record with the Indians is going to go down in history. It is going to make us mighty proud of it in the future when our children of ten more generations read of what we did to them. Every man in our history that killed the most Indians has got a statue built for him. The only difference between the Roman gladiators and the Pilgrims was that the Romans used a lion to cut down their native population, and the Pilgrims had a gun. The Romans didn't have no gun; they just had to use a lion.
>
> The Government, by statistics, shows they have got 456 treaties that they have broken with the Indians. That is why the Indians get a kick out of reading the Government's usual remark when some big affair comes up, "Our honor is at stake."
>
> Every time the Indians move the government will give them a treaty. They say, "You can have this ground as long as grass grows and water flows." On account of its being a grammatical error, the Government didn't have to live up to it. It didn't say "flown" or "flew" or something. Now they have moved the Indians and they settled the whole thing by putting them on land where the grass won't grow and the water don't flow, so now they have it all set.[67]

As Rogers spoke to the Cherokees that day in 1928 his memories of his own Indian heritage remained intense. The Cherokees who still lived in the Great Smokies of North Carolina were his distant relatives and "the ones that old Andrew Jackson wasn't able to run out of this country." He sympathized with his brethren. "They are pretty poor and their land is poor, and they don't get anything from the government, but they are not hollering for relief."[68]

As Rogers continued, the Cherokees showed no emotion, listening stoically and not cracking a smile at his jokes. After telling a few more humorous stories and giving his most energetic performance with the rope, he still got no response from the Indians. Rogers suddenly lost his temper and turned dead serious, tearing into Andrew Jackson, calling him a betrayer and attacking the former president for forcibly removing much of his ancestral tribe to the west during the 1830s. "I got no use for [Jackson] or any of his methods, for all he ever did was pounce on the Indians."[69] The novelist Ben Dixon MacNeill was in the crowd and watched as Rogers's face reddened with anger. "Then, suddenly, he became furious. His transformation was terrifying, and for three minutes his astonished audience was treated to a demonstration of what primitive, instinctive hatred could be," MacNeill wrote later. "Some long-forgotten, in-bred memory welled up in his heart." The Cherokees still listened silently and then, all of a sudden, the quiet was shattered by the screaming, blood-curdling war cry of the entire tribe, while Rogers stood "white, trembling, and actually aghast at himself."[70]

IN AUGUST 1928 Will Rogers's closest friend and Broadway star Fred Stone crashed his plane in a farmer's beet patch in Connecticut. Barely surviving, Stone broke his ankle, shin, thigh, and five ribs. Stone and his daughter Dorothy had planned to star in the play *Three Cheers,* scheduled to open at the Globe Theater in New York City in October. When Rogers heard of the crash, he canceled his lecture tour and sent word that he would take Stone's place so the show could go on. He arrived in Connecticut on September 11 to visit Stone in the hospital, then traveled on to New York to catch a Yankees game. On the next day he began rehearsal.[71]

Three Cheers got off to a flying start, as Charles Lindbergh was in the audience on opening night. The aviator called Rogers before the show and persuaded him not to introduce him. "Well I most generally introduce real celebrities and on an opening night it would be a great thing to point out the greatest one we have." But he yielded to Lindbergh's wish: "You talk about a struggle. There I stood with a pocket full of Gags that I had never used and I knew the audience would laugh at, especially with him there. But I stayed with it and dident say one word about him being there."[72]

Rogers enjoyed being back on Broadway amid the hustle and bustle of New York City. Betty stayed with him during *Three Cheers,* and the two kept

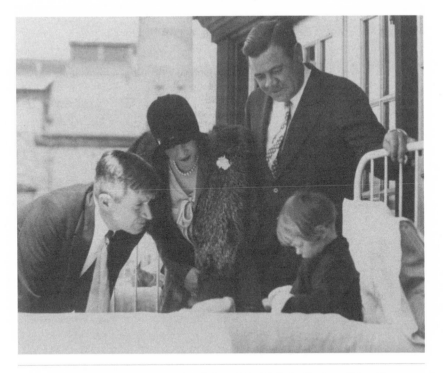

Rogers visits a Boston children's hospital with Babe Ruth and his wife

happily busy seeing old friends and meeting new ones. Lady Astor took in the show and afterward visited Rogers backstage. "Every time she comes to the show I try to get her to stand up and take a bow, but she won't," he wrote. "And over in the House of Commons they can't get her to sit down."[73] In September Betty and Will dined with Thomas Edison, Henry Ford, and Harvey Firestone at the Hotel Astor. Later they visited wealthy financier Bernard Baruch in his Manhattan mansion.[74] On March 4, 1929, they made a quick trip to Washington DC to attend the inauguration of Herbert Hoover, and two months later Rogers flew back to the nation's capital to dine with Speaker of the House Nicholas Longworth and to observe the Senate from a reserved seat in the gallery. As always, he found time for charity, such as a Madison Square Garden benefit for the Orphan Asylum and a visit to the Children's Hospital in Boston with Babe Ruth and his wife.[75]

After a successful 210-night run on Broadway, Rogers took *Three Cheers* on the road in April 1929. On the opening night in Boston, Will introduced Babe Ruth in the audience, as well as Secretary of the Navy Charles Francis Adams and a giant from the Ringling Brothers Circus.[76] The show closed in Pittsburgh on June 1. On the following day he flew to California to begin filming his first talking picture.

———

WILL ROGERS was disappointed but not surprised when Herbert Hoover won the presidency over Al Smith. But he was pleased with the outcome of the election for governor of New York, for Democrat Franklin Roosevelt bucked the Republican trend of wins across the country and edged Albert Ottinger by only twenty-five thousand votes to win the governorship. Roosevelt won by less than 1 percent of the four million ballots cast in one of the closest elections in the state's history.

Rogers and Roosevelt had met several times before and became fond of each other. Rogers admired the determination of the New York politician to defy his physical handicap and reenter politics, while Roosevelt, who saw Rogers perform on several occasions, enjoyed his quick wit and political humor. They spent time together during the 1924 and 1928 Democratic conventions, where both times Roosevelt nominated Al Smith for president.

As soon as he learned of Roosevelt's victory in New York, Rogers celebrated it in his daily column: "And this new Governor Roosevelt. Did you know what that guy has been doing for years at Warm Springs, Ga., for infantile paralysis victims? No, you didn't, for nothing has been said about it. Well, look it up. It's a real charity."[77] Roosevelt, stricken with the crippling effects of poliomyelitis since August 1921, had recently formed the Georgia Warm Springs Foundation, a nonprofit institution which operated a hydrotherapy center for the treatment of polio. Rogers had a soft spot for polio victims. "Any illness is terrible," he wrote later, "but there is something about this particular affliction that makes you just a little more sympathetic."[78]

Roosevelt responded to Rogers's column a few days later, writing:

Dear Wyll

That was a mighty nice paragraph of your[s] about Warm Springs. . . .

My spelling of your name is just to get square because when you were running your fine campaign for the Presidency you spelled my front name with a "y"!

Hope to see you in Albany on January first. It will do you good to come to one of those rare Dem. inaugurations.

> *Always sincerely,*
> *Franklin D Roosevelt.*[79]

A week later Roosevelt again wrote Rogers:

You are not only the most commonsensical person in the whole United States, but I think you have just about the biggest heart. . . .

I wish you were going to be Governor of New York instead of me. You thrive on work and I thought I was getting to the point where I had earned a holiday.[80]

Rogers already could see that Roosevelt was presidential timber, predicting the New Yorker would be the next Democratic candidate. A few months after taking office as governor, Roosevelt gave a Fourth of July speech before fifteen hundred cheering partisans at Tammany Hall. Roosevelt cautioned against the incestuous partnership between government and business. Rogers liked what Roosevelt was saying. "Now there is a fine man," he wrote soon after reading the speech. "You can start now trying to dig up something and in three years you won't have found anything wrong with Franklin D. Roosevelt outside of being a Democrat."[81]

As 1928 came to an end, Will Rogers and the rest of the country were in a carefree mood. The Roaring Twenties were still roaring, the economy was booming, and the nation charged happily ahead in a mindless euphoria. It seemed like the good times would last forever.

EIGHT

This Country Is Bigger Than Wall Street

THROUGHOUT the Roaring Twenties, Will Rogers filled his newspaper columns with mostly upbeat and harmless anecdotes, bringing chuckles to millions of Americans each day. In one such column he described his taste in the popular music of the day. "Now I personally have always considered the drummer the best part of a jazz band," he wrote. "I think if all the members of a jazz band play the drums it would make better music."[1] In another article he complained about shameless flappers flaunting their rising hemlines and strutting about with bobbed hair. "My wife can't appear in public with me," he griped. "She still has long hair."[2] He even took an absurdly lighthearted view of more serious conflicts in Europe: "The Balkan nations have gone into a huddle. It looks like Bulgaria's ball on Rumania's ten-yard line. Poland was penalized ten yards for being offside against Lithuania. Mussolini is the triplethreat man of the game. It will all wind up like the last one, just another incompleted war. They will have to bring it back and line up again."[3]

Rogers had reason to be carefree, for the Roaring Twenties was one of the most prosperous periods in history, a time when, according to F. Scott Fitzgerald, "America was going on the greatest, gaudiest spree in history."[4] Investors became overnight millionaires as stock prices soared, with General Motors stock rising from $9.62 a share in 1921 to $229 in 1928. RCA stock closed at $101 in 1927 and a year later peaked at $420.[5] The twenties "raced along under its own power, served by great filling stations full of money," Fitzgerald wrote. "Even when you were broke you didn't worry about money, because it was in such profusion around you."[6]

But the twenties also troubled Will Rogers. The rising stock market failed to disguise the economic inequities of the era. He was well aware that, while stocks still climbed at the end of the decade, nearly three-quarters of American families had an income below the $2,500 minimum for a decent standard of living.[7] He saw a society that blithely discarded the high-buttoned morals of the Victorian age and replaced them with a licentiousness he had never imagined. He watched as the divorce rate skyrocketed, increasing from one per eighteen in the 1880s to one in six in the 1920s. He half-joked about people flocking to Nevada, where at first a divorce could be obtained after living there six months, reduced to three months in 1927, and then to six weeks in 1931.[8] While he did not attend church, he watched church attendance drop off as more Americans bought automobiles and decided to take Sunday drives instead of attending services. He worried about American society, writing the following in the *Saturday Evening Post* in 1928:

Our children are delivered to schools in Automobiles. But whether that adds to their grades is doubtful. There hasent been a Thomas Jefferson produced in this country since we formed our first Trust. Rail splitting produced an immortal President in Abraham Lincoln, but Golf, with 20 thousand courses, hasent produced even a good A Number-1 Congressman. There hasent been a Patrick Henry showed up since business men quit eating lunch with their families, joined a club and have indigistion from amateur Oratory.[9]

The social turmoil of the twenties especially disturbed Rogers, a man with a fear of disorder and chaos. The front pages of the newspapers he read every morning were splattered with stories that scared him. He may have "never met a man he didn't like," but he feared that same man when he joined a mob. And there were plenty of mobs to fear during the twenties, a time of notorious crimes, race riots, labor strikes, Klan rallies, and lynchings. During World War I, the NAACP campaigned for a federal ban on lynchings.

A bill passed in the House in 1922 but failed in the Senate due to filibusters by Southerners who argued they were defending states' rights.[10] The Ku Klux Klan, with five million members in the 1920s, still possessed fearful power.[11] A series of race riots erupted across the country, beginning in Chicago in 1919. In May 1921, violence erupted in Tulsa, not far from Rogers's boyhood home, as gangs of whites and blacks clashed. Rioters burned over a thousand homes. Later, the Communist Party staged a demonstration for the unemployed in New York City's Union Square. The gathering turned into an angry, fighting mob scene, as thirty-five thousand demonstrators battled with police. Scores were injured.[12]

The usually cheerful humorist could not ignore the turmoil that seemed to rage across the country, writing at the time:

> Brothers, we are riding mighty, mighty high in this country. Our most annoying problem is, "Which car will I use today?" "Isn't that static frightful?"
>
> We are just sitting on top of the world. For every automobile we furnish an accident. For every radio sold we put on two murders. Three robberies to every bathtub installed. Building two golf courses to every church. Our bootleggers have manicures and our farmers have mortgages. Our courts are full, our jails are full, our politicians are full. If we can't house a prisoner, we burn him up.
>
> Truly Rome never saw such prosperity.[13]

Rogers watched as organized crime gained momentum in the 1920s, especially in urban areas where the underground sale of alcohol became a $60 million business. Overall, public disregard for the law was on the rise during the decade. Notorious criminals like John Dillinger, Bonnie and Clyde, and Baby Face Nelson became household names as they robbed and murdered across the country. "I just give up reading murders," Rogers wrote. "You no more than get a few details of one murder than the afternoon paper brings you news of another."[14]

Rogers was ever looking for solutions, writing half truthfully that, "we don't seem to be able to even check crime, so why not legalize it and put a heavy tax on it. Make the tax for robbery so high that a bandit couldn't afford to rob any one unless he knew they had a lot of dough. We have taxed other industries out of business; it might work here."[15]

More seriously, Rogers felt that one of the causes of increased crime was a criminal justice system that mollycoddled criminals. "Pardoning has been one industry that hasn't been hit by depression," he wrote.[16] "We don't give our criminals much punishment, but we sure give 'em plenty of publicity."[17] When the federal government put Al Capone on trial for tax evasion, Rogers had little faith in the system. "Now comes the out on bail, new trial, change of venue, habus corpus, stay of execution and twenty-one other things that the law has invented to hinder justice." After a jury sentenced the gangster to eleven years, Rogers felt the punishment too lenient. "See where they convicted Al Capone on five counts silk underwear."[18] He blamed the newspapers for making a folk hero out of Capone: "Everybody you talk to would rather hear about Capone than anybody you ever met. What's the matter with an age when our biggest gangster is our greatest national interest[?] Part is the government's fault for not convicting him on some real crime."[19]

Despite the popular image of the 1920s as a lawless era, bank robberies and other serious felonies were comparatively rare, but when they occurred the press sensationalized them to increase newspaper sales. According to Rogers, "the camera has made more criminals than bad environment."[20]

Rogers criticized the criminal justice system after famed attorney Clarence Darrow, who during his career helped over a hundred murderers escape the death penalty, was successful in having the lives of Nathan Leopold and Richard Loeb spared in one of the most sensational murder trials of the century. Rogers objected to the sentence, writing that a Chicago judge "let those two get away with life when they should have been given the extreme penalty."[21]

Rogers also believed there should be stricter control on guns:

You know what has been the cause of the big increase in murders? It's been the manufacture of the automatic pistol. It's all right to have it invented, but it should never have been allowed outside the Army. . . .

But I see where a lot of men are advocating letting everybody carry guns with the idea that they will be able to protect themselves. In other words, just make Civil War out of this Crime Wave.[22]

Unusual for a former cowboy, Rogers did not like guns, nor did he hunt or fish.[23] "I never killed anything in my life," he admitted.[24] When he was seventeen he mishandled a Winchester rifle and it accidentally discharged, the bullet passing through his hat and creasing his scalp. He feared firearms thereafter.[25]

Rogers was particularly moved by a notorious crime when he traveled to Massachusetts in 1921 and visited the governor of that state, Alvin Fuller.[26] Fuller was deliberating whether or not Nicola Sacco and Bartolomeo Vanzetti should be executed. A year before, they had been arrested for murdering two men during a payroll robbery of a shoe factory.[27] A jury convicted them in 1921, but, as appeals for a new trial followed, the case soon became a political crusade for those who believed the convictions stemmed more from the men's Italian birth, atheism, and radicalism than from any proven guilt. The appeals failed, and the fate of Sacco and Vanzetti rested with Fuller, who had to decide whether or not to set aside the death penalty.

When Rogers met Fuller, the governor was under intense pressure. As the two men talked in the governor's mansion, Fuller waded through testimony that was strewn about his office, including stacks of documents and even the guns used in the crime. The governor's dilemma moved Rogers, who wrote in his weekly column:

> Here he is day after day, night after night, studying over all the evidence, examining people and witnesses, trying from the bottom of his heart to get at the right solution of the case. . . . I don't know when I ever felt as sorry for a man, and I don't know when I have met a man that made a more favorable impression on me of his absolute fairness. . . . He made one remark that will always stand out in my memory, "I don't care whether they were Reds, Greens, Yellows, Pinks, or Pure Whites. WHAT I WANT TO KNOW, ARE THEY GUILTY?"[28]

After a special commission ruled the trial was conducted fairly, Fuller allowed Sacco and Vanzetti to be executed in the electric chair on August 23, 1927.[29]

WILL ROGERS distrusted the wealthy financiers of Wall Street, calling them "loan sharks and interest hounds" and questioning the ethics of the business practices they followed.[30] "You see there is a lot of things these old boys have done that are within the law," he wrote, "but it's so near the edge that you couldn't slip a safety razor blade between their acts and a prosecution."[31] On several occasions during the twenties, when few government regulations existed, Rogers warned about bogus holding companies selling worthless stock. "A holding company," he said, "is a thing where you hand an accomplice the goods while the policeman searches you."[32]

One of the few Wall Street financiers that Rogers did trust was Barnard Baruch, a multimillionaire investor and stock speculator. By the midtwenties, the two men of dramatically different backgrounds became close friends. Baruch was idealistic and independent, characteristics that Rogers admired, while Baruch described Rogers as a shrewd and original commentator who used humor to illuminate the serious.[33] "You have become . . . a Benjamin Franklin philosopher of our time," Baruch wrote in a letter to Rogers. "You have been taking the swelling out of a lot of heads, putting joy into lives, comfort into hearts and made many a man stand steadier upon his feet."[34]

Baruch was then one of the most influential men in America, and, over the years, he would be a close adviser to five presidents. He served brilliantly as chairman of the WWI War Industries Board, where he perfected modern economic warfare, establishing the first wartime priorities system for materials and labor, setting up production schedules, cutting down civilian industries, and putting the nation on an unprecedented war footing. A tall, handsome gentleman with snow-white hair and pince-nez glasses over his blue eyes, Baruch had a reputation for high personal integrity and a Lincolnian sense of humanity that was unique among wealthy Wall Street financiers.[35]

Baruch was a maverick among the Republican-dominated Wall Street barons. "I believe my people are pretty good people," he wrote, "and my people happen to be Democratic people."[36] Rogers and Baruch met often, including at Democratic conventions. In August 1925 Baruch invited Rogers to travel to Washington with him in his private railroad car when both headed to the Gridiron Club Dinner. A year later Rogers visited Baruch at the financier's castle in Scotland,[37] joking that Baruch went there to shoot grouse. "He names them after the Republicans and has never missed one."[38] Baruch frequented the *Follies* and visited with Rogers backstage after each show. In November 1928 after a *Three Cheers* performance, the financier took Rogers and General John Pershing to his lavish five-story brownstone on Fifth Avenue where they stayed late into the night discussing world affairs.[39]

In the spring of 1929, Baruch invited Will and Betty to his mansion for dinner, which was, as always, served precisely at 7:30. Afterward they relaxed over coffee in the large living room, sitting beneath a huge portrait of Woodrow Wilson that hung shrinelike over the mantle. Baruch idolized Wilson, referring to him as "the most Christlike man who ever lived."[40] While Rogers did not share Baruch's awe of the late president, the two men agreed on most political issues. Both were deeply disturbed by human suffering. They also feared the mob mentality. "Anyone taken as an individual is tolerably sensible and reasonable," Baruch wrote. "As a member of a crowd, he at once becomes a blockhead."

Baruch shared Rogers's concern that most Americans barely made a living. "You can talk about capitalism and communism and all that sort of thing," the financier wrote, "but the important thing is the struggle everybody is engaged in to get better living conditions, and they are not interested too much in government."[41] Rogers trusted Baruch absolutely and sought his wisdom often, soaking up the financier's vast knowledge of economics, public finance, international trade, and monetary policy. While Rogers had a large circle of prominent and brilliant friends, it was Baruch, perhaps more than any other, who had the greatest influence on the humorist's acute understanding of public policy.

During the conversation in the mansion, Rogers told Baruch he had just signed a contract with Fox films to make four films for $600,000.[42] When Rogers said he wanted to invest the money in the stock market, Baruch asked if he had any debts. Rogers said that a year before he had refinanced his California ranch and borrowed $440,000.[43] Baruch advised him to pay off the debt before he did anything else, but Rogers argued that a mortgage on property made it easier to sell. Besides, he admitted, rather than pay off his mortgage, he wanted to invest the cash in stocks. Baruch lost his patience, snapping back: "What you want to do is gamble. But I want to tell you that you're sitting on a volcano. That's all right for professional volcano sitters, like myself, but an amateur like you ought to take to the tall timber and get as far away as you can. There may come a time when the man that holds your mortgage will want his money and you may not have it, and your friends won't have it either."[44] Rogers slumped down in his chair, scratched his head, and chewed his gum as the financier lectured him. He followed Baruch's advice and within a year had reduced the outstanding mortgage on his property to $325,000. He also stayed out of the stock market.[45]

In 1927 Warner Brothers revolutionized the motion picture industry when it released the sound film *The Jazz Singer* starring Al Jolson. Using the new Vitaphone system, the film became an overnight sensation, drawing audiences as fast as movie theaters could be equipped to show it.[46] The popularity of talking pictures caused movie turnout to boom, from a weekly attendance of 50 million in 1922 to over 100 million eight years later. While the film industry prospered, many silent stars never adjusted to the new sound medium and disappeared, such as the great silent screen lover John Gilbert whose high-pitched voice doomed him and led to his suicide. Will Rogers, however, not only made the transition easily but saw his popularity soar on the sound screen.[47] According to one newspaper review, "Will Rogers is the man the talkies were invented for."[48]

During the summer of 1929 he filmed his first sound movie, *They Had to See Paris.* The film opened with great fanfare in Hollywood that September, with Jack Benny emceeing the ceremony. Rogers, who was in Wichita at the time, did not attend this or any other of his openings.[49] "They was opening my first talking picture tonight in Los Angeles," he wrote from Kansas, "and charging those poor people five dollars, and I just couldn't stand by and be a party to such brigandage."[50]

As other films followed, Rogers's fame on the screen rose quickly and further enhanced his influence upon the public psyche. According to the *Motion Picture Herald*, he was ninth on the list of top-ten stars in 1932, in 1933 he rose to second place behind Marie Dressler, and in 1934 topped the ratings. In 1935 he remained the top male actor, lagging behind only Shirley Temple.[51] But he never seemed to take his stardom too seriously. "Two things distinguished me in the movies," he told a lecture-tour audience. "The first was that I was the ugliest man out there, the second was that I came out with the same wife I went in with—my first one."[52]

Between 1929 and 1935 Rogers spent much of his time in Hollywood, where he starred in twenty-one films for Fox studios.[53] His name and profession were different in each of his films, but his personality never changed. He played a steamboat captain, a country doctor, a small-town banker, and an assortment of other humble but shrewd, archetypically American characters.

*Rogers with
Shirley Temple*

But his mannerisms, values, and general demeanor remained consistently Will Rogers.

Rogers's sound films, or "noisies" as he called them, often had political themes, and if they didn't, he ad-libbed political humor into the script. Films provided him another opportunity to address a range of current social issues, particularly the Depression and Prohibition. He frequently took shots at corrupt politicians, bumbling bureaucrats, and flaws in democracy. In several films he depicts men willing to fight against injustice while also discovering deeper truths about character, motivation, and ethics. In the comedy *Ambassador Bill* (1931), he plays an American ambassador who arrives in a small country that is plagued by political intrigue and civil unrest. He befriends the young prince who is to be the country's king and ensures that the young man is prepared to take on the crown. The film is an excellent use of the comically absurd comparison. Rogers teaches the young prince how to play baseball, a metaphor for American democracy. As royalty, the prince had never before experienced defeat, but on the baseball diamond, as Rogers instructs him, all players are democratically equal and apt to win or lose.

The County Chairman (1935) is a more serious film filled with political wisdom. Rogers plays the chairman of his political party in a Wyoming county who runs the political campaign of his idealistic young law partner. Although the candidate is honest, the party chairman is accustomed to dirty politics and uncovers some dirt on the corrupt opponent. If the slanderous information is made public, it would throw the election to the honest young attorney, but it would also hurt innocent people. Rogers, as the party chairman, must decide whether to tell the truth and let the chips fall where they may, or run a clean campaign and run the risk that his crooked opponent might win. The ethical dilemma he faces is as pertinent today as it was in 1935. Remarkable for the time, Rogers commented in the film about the Turkish slaughter of a half million Armenians in 1915. This was the twentieth century's first genocide, and an event the rest of the world tried to ignore.

Rogers best conveyed his view of American values and democracy in his classic film *Judge Priest* (1934). Like most of his movie parts, Rogers's judge provides a role model of the lovable but cantankerous individualist who uses humor to upset and reshape the ordinary workings of democracy. Set in a Kentucky town in the 1890s, the film conjures up a stream of small-town rituals—a taffy-pulling party, men gathered in the barbershop, a Veterans Day parade, a bucolic fishing hole, all linked by the proceedings of a one-room courthouse. As Judge Priest, Rogers defends democracy by using unorthodox methods to ensure that justice is served while also overcoming prejudice, hypocrisy, and pretentiousness. Directed by John Ford, Rogers's *Judge Priest* is both an affirmation and criticism of the fundamental structure of democracy.[54]

In 1934 Rogers starred in *David Harum*, playing a small-town banker and shrewd horse trader. The film is set in upstate New York during the panic of 1893, but its overriding theme of economic turmoil rang true to audiences mired in the Great Depression of the 1930s. Early in the film, one of the town elders admits that "these panics come in cycles every twenty-one years" and brings the movie close to the era of the audience. Traditionally a fiscal conservative, Rogers reveals through his portrayal of the optimistically laid-back horse trader David Harum that he had begun to accept the notion of deficit spending, an increased national debt, and Keynesian economics: "A panic is just like a war. You can talk your way in, but you've got to fight your way out. . . . The government has to spend some money. . . . I bet you this fellow [referring to Grover Cleveland in 1893 but more implicitly Franklin Roosevelt] will pull us through and we'll live to see the day when we'll have 100 million people in this country, and we'll have trouble remembering just when this panic was."[55]

David Harum was a box-office success, and audiences and most critics loved its Pollyannaish optimism. But it also came under criticism for treating dire economic conditions too lightly. In contrast to the cheerfulness of *David Harum* and other Rogers successes like *State Fair* (1933), the nation still struggled with the Great Depression, with millions standing in unemployment lines and farmers across the country facing economic ruin. One critic of Rogers's films, David Thomson, has written, perhaps too harshly, that "Rogers' philosophy was reactionary, dispiriting and provincial, despite every affectation of bonhomie and tolerance. It scorned ideas and people who held them, it relied on vague evolution rather than direct action, its fixed smile concealed rigidity of opinion that middle America need not be disturbed from its own prejudices and limitations."[56] Critics aside, Rogers's palliative films were immensely popular and gave the American theatergoers a much needed opportunity to smile, relax, and escape their troubles for a couple of hours.

Despite his busy film schedule, Rogers continued to write his daily wires and weekly columns. He carried his well-worn Corona with him so he could type out his page wherever he was, whether in a dressing room, in an airplane seat, or on a movie set. At Fox, actors and stagehands walking along the back lot were used to seeing Rogers sitting on the running board of his LaSalle roadster, hat pushed back on his head, reading glasses on the end of his nose, pecking away with two fingers. When he finished, he read the article over once, scribbled a couple of pencil changes, then grabbed a messenger boy and sent it off to Western Union. Everyone knew when he had finished because when they passed the roadster later, he was sitting in the front seat, his hat over his eyes, sound asleep for an afternoon nap.[57]

IN OCTOBER 1929, Henry Ford invited Will Rogers to attend a lavish dinner honoring Thomas Edison and celebrating the fiftieth anniversary of the

*Pounding out a
column while on
the movie set*

lighting of the first electric lamp. Held at Ford's Dearborn Village museum, the epic gala included over five hundred of the nation's notables: President Hoover, Charles Schwab, J. P. Morgan, Charles Dana Gibson, Jane Addams, Adolph Ochs, and Harvey Firestone were among the attendees.[58] While flying to Dearborn, Rogers's plane ran into thick fog and fought a headwind. The pilot headed back to Chicago but ran out of gas, crash-landing in a vacant lot and flipping the plane onto its back. Rogers fractured a rib. He never wrote about this latest crash, which was at least his third mishap.[59] Undeterred, he climbed aboard another plane and arrived at the celebration on time. Ironically, at dinner, he sat next to Orville Wright.[60] Rogers later admitted that being invited to Ford's dinner for Edison was "one of the crowning achievements of my little career."[61]

Three days later, on October 24, 1929, Rogers was in New York City on a day that is remembered simply as Black Thursday. With millions of other Americans, he watched in disbelief as the stock market collapsed, shattering the euphoria and financial gains of the Roaring Twenties and ushering in the deepest economic depression in history. Share prices on the New York Stock

Rogers with Henry and Edsel Ford

Exchange dropped sharply that day, with a record of 12.9 million shares traded, and continued to drop at an unprecedented rate for a full month. Losses during the first week exceeded $30 billion.[62] "You had to stand in line to get a window to jump out of," Rogers remarked with dark humor. "Speculators were selling space for bodies in the East River."[63] A week later he was in Oklahoma celebrating his fiftieth birthday but still keeping a close watch on the falling market. Like most Americans, he still did not realize the seriousness of the financial crisis, writing:

> What does it mean? Nothing. Why, if the cows of this country failed to come up and get milked one night it would be more of a panic than if Morgan and Lamont had never held a meeting. Why, an old sow and a litter of pigs make more people a living than all the steel and general motor stock combined. Why, the whole 120,000,000 of us are more dependent on the cackling of a hen than if the stock exchange was turned into a night club.
>
> And New Yorkers call them rubes.[64]

During the first months of the market collapse Rogers was among many who looked on the crash as a temporary event and expected the economy to improve. On February 18, 1930, six days after the *New York Times* proclaimed the country had "begun to recover," President Hoover announced that the unemployment rate was cut by almost one-half. With optimism growing, Hoover declared, "we have passed the worst and with continued effort we shall rapidly recover."[65] Rogers too remained somewhat upbeat, but advised his readers not to gamble in the market. "Take all your savings and buy some good stock, and hold it till it goes up, then sell it. If it don't go up, don't buy it."[66] He also tried to bolster confidence, writing that "the Country as a whole is 'Sound,' and that all those who's heads are solid are bound to get back into the market again. I tell 'em that this Country is bigger than Wall Street, and if they don't believe it, I show 'em a map."[67]

The catastrophic news from Wall Street did not surprise Rogers. For years he had worried about the false prosperity of the country and the possibility of a stock market crash. In 1924 he warned of the inflated stock market. "You mean to tell me that in a Country that was run really on the level, 200 of their National commodities could jump their value millions of dollars in two days?"[68] He worried about Americans being too far in debt, concluding that many lived beyond their means. "This would be a great world to dance in if we didn't have to pay the fiddler."[69] By 1927, consumer debt amounted to about $3 billion, with installment plans financing automobiles, refrigerators, radios, and other appliances.[70] He wrote in September 1928: "We don't have to worry about anything. No nation in the history of the world was ever sitting as pretty. If we want anything, all we have to do is go and buy it on credit. . . . So that leaves us without any economic problem whatever, except perhaps some day to have to pay for them. But we are certainly not thinking about that this early."[71]

Rogers was not alone in worrying about a stock market collapse. By 1928, his friend Bernard Baruch had liquidated his stock holdings and put his money into bonds, cash reserve, and gold. Baruch, who felt people should have taken warning from the collapse of the Florida land boom in 1926, blamed the stock market crash on the government, the banks, and the public.[72] He blamed the government for a long series of erroneous policies, including high tariffs, the ineffectiveness of the Federal Reserve Board, encouragement

*Rogers with James Farley, Bernard Baruch, Cornelius Vanderbilt; Edward J. Flynn
and Amon Carter standing in the back*

of public and private debt, and the failure to resolve the question of German reparations and foreign debt. He also believed that bankers and brokers were responsible for the collapse, as many of them ruthlessly abused the machinery of the stock exchange to take advantage of the speculative frenzy. And finally he blamed the public for its own undoing. "The stock market crash was a classic example of the madness of crowds," Baruch wrote later. "History records some of the most notorious of mass movements and the madness of the Twenties must certainly be added to the list."[73]

Long after the crash, Baruch ran into Rogers in a corridor of the Capitol. He stopped the humorist, backed him against a wall, and asked him if he had followed his advice and stayed out of the stock market. "Will, how did you come out of this?"

"I did what you told me," Rogers answered, "and you saved my life."[74]

"WATCH HIM, Herbert," Will Rogers warned President Hoover in a column in September 1929.[75] Britain's socialist prime minister, Ramsay MacDonald, was visiting the United States at the time and Rogers suspected the visit was more than just a goodwill gesture. "Englishmen are the only race of people that never travel for just fun." Rogers was right, as MacDonald and Hoover agreed to convene another naval disarmament conference in London in January 1930.[76] The purpose of the conference was to limit the naval capacity of Great Britain, the United States, Japan, France, and Italy. Rogers had attended earlier disarmament conferences in Washington in 1922 and in Geneva in 1926 and he wasn't going to miss this one. His skepticism continued: "Asking Europe to disarm is like asking a man in Chicago to give up his life insurance."[77]

Rogers rearranged his busy film schedule at Fox studios so he could take a month off to attend the London conference. He spent the Christmas holidays with his family on his California ranch. After watching Southern California defeat Pittsburgh 47–14 in the Rose Bowl on New Year's Day, he headed east. Shortly before midnight on January 10, 1930, he departed New York City on the SS *Bremen,* a turbine-drive flagship that had set a transatlantic speed record on its maiden voyage the year before. During this six-day winter crossing of the Atlantic, the liner encountered some of the worst sailing conditions its captain had ever experienced. Rogers spent the voyage seasick, but he did find the strength to cable the American ambassador at the disarmament conference. "Don't sink anything until you see them sink first."[78] Even while under the weather, Rogers worried that U.S. diplomats once again would come out the losers in the international arena.

Rogers arrived in London in time to attend the speech by King George to open the conference. While he praised the king for pleading to reduce navies and pursue peace, he had little faith in the conference. "I have always claimed that any International Conference does more harm than good," he wrote at the time, "for they engender more hate than good will."[79] He watched as the delegates made little progress. "Well the conference met today and appointed a commission to meet tomorrow and appoint a delegation who will eventually appoint a subcommittee to draw up ways and means of finding out what to start with first."[80] Rogers questioned the real motives of the attendees, doubting if anyone was really trying to reduce military power:

> Nations starting for the big London disarmament conference to disarm themselves of the things they figure won't be used in the next war, which will leave them more money to develop the things they will use. It's an economic, more than a humanitarian affair. It's like holding a traffic conference and just discussing the limiting of horses and buggies.
>
> I wonder if we ever will get so civilized that one will be held to limit submarines, airplanes and chemicals. You can't say civilization don't advance, however, for in every war they kill you in a new way.[81]

When France and Italy were not given parity by the other nations, both withdrew from formal discussions.

Rogers gave the American public a refreshing explanation of the rather dry and technical negotiations taking place in London. He also gave them a view that was contrary to the official U.S. negotiating position. The average American at first may have believed disarmament to be a logical step in reducing the likelihood of war, but Rogers argued otherwise. In language easily understood by the average citizen, he explained why nations would never agree on disarming themselves:

> Every editorial you pick up is discontented with the way the disarmament conference is going and they think that Europe is very warlike and that they ought to go on and disarm and agree to everything that we want them to. Now let's just kind a look it over and put ourselves in their position and see what we would do under similar circumstances to them. Suppose you took Germany, for instance, and you trade places with Mexico and you let Germany be living where Mexico is, and then you took France up with our good friends on the North, your Canadians—why you put France up there and they are living there with all the big army and everything, and they live up there and England, we move them into about where Cuba is now, you know.

Then Japan comes into Honolulu, around, around the Hawaiian Islands there you know. Now just surround us with those four gorillas and see how much disarmament we start hollering about, see if we want any disarmament.[82]

The editors of the *New York Times* believed Rogers's relentless criticism of U.S. foreign policy and the conference went too far. *Times* publisher Adolph Ochs cabled him in Geneva. "Am sure you share our hope for success of disarmament conference," Ochs wrote. "In that belief suggest you do not unwittingly embarrass this country's noble purpose in endeavoring to produce good lasting results. Lets try to be helpful."[83] Rogers did not reply.

As with disarmament conferences before, Rogers was disgusted that the United States agreed to physically destroy warships while other nations simply refrained from building new ones. To him, the real victor of the conference was Japan. "I met Admiral Takarabe, one of their principal delegates, out at Ambassador Dawes's last night, and on leaving I shook hands with him very warmly and said: 'Admiral, I am going right home to America and I want to say that I have shook hands with the winner.'"[84]

Rogers believed that only when leaders understood the true human cost could wars be avoided. In his weekly column he wrote:

I believe that a child could prevent all wars. Let a Congress, or a Reichstag, or a Parliament, or a House of Deputies be on the verge of breaking off diplomatic relations with some other country, and you let a child enter that Chamber and say: "What about me? What is to become of us? We have no say. Are not you men smart enough and generous enough to settle this without war? It won't hurt you. We are the sufferers; it will leave us fatherless; and after we grow up we will have the debt to pay, so please think twice before breaking off relations, are you sure that it can't be prevented."[85]

While in London Rogers kept busy. He visited the House of Commons several times to listen to its members, including a stirring speech by David Lloyd George favoring free trade that, according to Rogers, brought "laughs, logic, and slow death for the opposition."[86] He lunched with Dwight and Elizabeth Morrow, with Henry and Mabel Stimson, shared tea with Lady Astor and Lloyd George, and dined at the residence of Ambassador Charles

Dawes.[87] H. L. Mencken was also in London, and he and Rogers planned to spend a day together at Hyde Park listening to the soap box oratory at Speakers' Corner, but a heavy winter rain kept them indoors.

Rogers spent a delightful evening with famed playwright George Bernard Shaw[88] at his Whitehall Court residence. Rogers had met Shaw briefly on his visit to London in 1926, but this time the two men spent an evening alone, sharing their ironic wits and forging a friendship. As Rogers entered Shaw's flat, the dramatist bounded into the room, shook hands, pushed Will onto a sofa, seated himself on a backless stool, and crossed his long legs before him. Shaw talked so fast for an hour that Rogers continually held up his hand for permission to speak.[89] While their backgrounds could not have been more different, they both adopted the same approach to humor. "My way of joking is to tell the truth," Shaw said. "It's the funniest joke in the world."[90] Rogers admired Shaw immensely and was awed by his great intellect, writing, "He never says what you are looking for him to [say], but he always says what you are glad he did say."[91] Rogers listened intently to the famed writer, known for his wide-ranging Shavian criticisms of education, religion, class inequities, and the exploitation of the working man. Shaw's biting observations were complex and sometimes contradictory. "He is one crossword puzzle that has never been worked," Rogers wrote.[92]

While Rogers did not agree with Shaw's passion for socialism, the two men shared many philosophical beliefs. Both men mistrusted overzealous patriotism that too often led nations to war. "You'll never have a quieter world until you knock the patriotism out of the human race," Shaw wrote.[93] They shared a keen interest in Russia. "Shaw told me that the United States and Russia are the most unique countries in the world today," Rogers wrote. "Russia was trying a great experiment, too—was trying everything that come along—and that we were both in the experimental stage."[94]

They also shared a deep mistrust of politicians. Shaw's description of a politician could have been penned by Rogers. "[A politician] knows nothing; and he thinks he knows everything," Shaw wrote. "That points clearly to a political career."[95] Rogers struck a similar note, albeit less grammatically correct. "That's like a dumb guy with an argument," he wrote. "He don't think there can be any other side, only his. That's what you call politicians."[96]

ROGERS LEFT Europe on January 30, 1930, on the *Ile de France*. The ship left a day late, as a seamen's strike in Le Havre hampered the departure, and then the liner ran into a fierce Atlantic storm that further delayed them. The trip was another wretched one for the queasy Rogers, and his arrival in New York was just as miserable, as the temperature in the city dipped into the teens. Rogers took the train to Washington DC, where he met with top government officials, including Vice President Charles Curtis and Senator William Borah. He lunched in the Senate dining room with Senators James Watson, Pat Harrison, and James Couzens, wondering afterward "if they realize the harm they do."[97] Then he visited with Alice Longworth, "where you get the smartest and most authentic political dope in Washington."[98]

Back in New York City, Rogers attended the opening of the musical *Ripples,* starring his friend Fred Stone, since recovered from his injuries in an airplane crash. O. O. McIntyre was also at the play. "I sat with Will Rogers through one act at the opening of his friend Fred Stone's play," the columnist wrote, "and turned suddenly to find the big stiff crying like a baby."[99]

Rogers then headed west. On his flight from St. Louis to Oklahoma the aircraft ran into a snowstorm and made an emergency landing. He continued his journey by train, stopping in Claremore, Oklahoma, to visit relatives and dine in the brand-new sixty-two-room Will Rogers Hotel. He arrived home in California in time to attend a dinner with former president Coolidge and his wife at the home of *Los Angeles Times* publisher Harry Chandler. Rogers immediately went to work filming *So This Is London* at the Fox studios, followed by *Lightnin'* on location in Lake Tahoe.

The first months of 1930 were hectic. Besides filming and writing his columns, Rogers traveled to Globe, Arizona, where he spoke at the dedication of the Coolidge Dam. Coolidge attended the ceremony, where he "did a mighty fine job of dam dedicating here this afternoon."[100] In April the army held maneuvers on the West Coast and flew in 150 planes for the exercise. Assistant Secretary of War Trubee Davison invited Rogers to observe the maneuvers and fly over Los Angeles in an Air Corps bomber. "Friday night we went over the city with some bombers," he wrote, "and where I stood in there was the place for 4,000 pounds of high explosives. Millions of lights

*Rogers broadcasts
during his first Squibb
radio show*

under you and hundred of thousands of defenseless people."[101] Rogers took
another military flight that winter after he hosted Assistant Secretary of the
Navy David Ingalls at his ranch. Ingalls flew his Navy Helldiver out to sea,
where he landed on the aircraft carrier USS *Langley* steaming off the coast of
San Diego. Sitting in the rear gunner's seat of the plane and happy as a
schoolkid playing hooky was Will Rogers.[102]

On Sunday evening, April 6, 1930, Rogers sat before a microphone in the studio of station KHJ in Hollywood. A month before he had signed a contract
with E. R. Squibb & Son, one of the country's largest pharmaceutical companies, to broadcast twelve radio talks across the nation. Each broadcast was fifteen minutes long and aired on the fledgling Columbia Broadcasting System.
The studio was filled that night, as Rogers had insisted he broadcast in front
of a live audience. He felt more comfortable in a packed radio studio so he
could see how the audience responded. His topic was foreign affairs. He

An ad for Rogers's radio show

rebuked the U.S. government for interfering in the affairs of lesser nations like China, Nicaragua, and Haiti. He complained that the Naval Disarmament Conference recently concluded in London weakened the United States. "America has a unique record," he told his audience. "We never lost a war and never won a conference in our lives. . . . We can lick any nation in the world single-handed, I think, and yet we can't confer with Costa Rica and come home with our shirts on."[103] Radio became yet another mass medium that Rogers successfully conquered. His broadcasts, like his newspaper columns, soon were enormously popular and influential.

Rogers donated his $70,000 salary from CBS to the Red Cross and the Salvation Army. He contributed to many other charities and kept busy with philanthropic activities, spending most Sundays doing charity work such as visiting a military veterans home in Sawtelle, California. In April he received a warm letter from Helen Keller,[104] to him "the world's most remarkable woman," asking him to support a fund-raiser for the American Foundation for the Blind.[105] A year before Keller had sent Rogers a copy of her book *Midstream*, which she inscribed, "To our Will Rogers by thanking him for the good many laughs he has given me and the golden grains of wisdom the laughs scatter, not always on barren soil."[106] This time she complimented him for his "cleverness in finding ideas for those who haven't any. You have made suggestions for the farmer, the Democratic Party and the Naval Limitation Conference. You have supplied the U.S. Senate with a fair substitute for brains and found sticking-plaster for the unseemly breach between President Hoover and the Republican Party."[107]

Along with his donation, Rogers wrote back to Keller a month later supporting her fund-raising. "If you can be fortunate enough to keep Mr. Hoover from appointing a Committee to help you raise that fund I believe you will make it."[108]

For the rest of his life Rogers devoted ever more of his time and money to help people in need. As the nation entered the 1930s, the needs of those people were overwhelming.

NINE

The Dark Humor of Depression

S OON AFTER the beginning of 1930, a year when "optimism was overrated and pessimism was underrated," Will Rogers realized the stock market collapse was no longer a joking matter and much more serious and prolonged than just a temporary Wall Street setback.[1] As the future looked bleaker and bleaker, the country turned gloomy, pessimistic, even cynical. The expectation of difficult times ahead not only caused stock prices to fall but led potential buyers of products to defer purchases. When demand waned, manufacturers cut back and laid off workers, who in turn could not pay their bills, much less purchase new goods, leading to more cutbacks, more layoffs, and more unsold goods. As the downward spiral continued, the country plunged into the Great Depression, a decade-long national tragedy that destroyed the lives, livelihoods, and dreams of millions of Americans. As he watched the economy worsen, Rogers's newspaper columns and radio talks took on a more sober tone, and his humor, while still present, was darker, more critical, and often bitterly sarcastic. He was also somewhat fatalistic when explaining the market collapse, as when he wrote: "The Lord was wise to the World and he just wanted to show 'em that, after all, he was running things, in spite of the New York Stock Exchange. Well, that was a terrible blow to finance to learn that the Lord not only closed the Market on Sundays, but practically closed it on week days."[2]

As the Depression deepened, Rogers provided his audiences with a running account of bank failures, joblessness, ineffective monetary policies, trade imbalances, depressed stocks, and scores of other sad results of the Depression. He watched forlornly as paper profits vanished and businesses tottered or went bankrupt: eight hundred banks closed their doors in 1930 and twenty-three hundred the following year. Unemployment skyrocketed, from one and a half million in 1929, to four and a half million in 1930, to eight million in 1931, to twelve million in 1932—or roughly 30 percent of the American workforce. Industrial production plummeted, putting 45 percent of all factory workers in the breadlines. By 1933, over 40 percent of the nation's home mortgages had defaulted, while thirteen hundred local governments went bankrupt, as well as the states of Arkansas, Louisiana, and South Carolina.[3]

Americans also felt the Depression in their stomachs. While bumper wheat crops broke records, the surplus of grain depressed prices below the farmers' margin of profit. Banks foreclosed on farm mortgages across the country. Millions went hungry for lack of bread. An angry Rogers told his radio listeners: "So here we are in a country with more wheat and more corn and more money in the bank, more cotton, more everything in the world— there's not a product you can name that we haven't got more of than any other country ever had on the face of the earth—and yet we've got people starving. We'll hold the distinction of being the only nation in the history of the world that ever went to the poor house in an automobile."[4]

In the small village of England, Arkansas, five hundred farmers and their wives who were denied credit stormed into town demanding food, which the merchants supplied. Rogers sympathized with the farmers, writing: "We got a powerful government, brainy men, great organizations, many commissions, but it took a little band of five hundred simple country people (who had no idea they were doing anything historical) to come to a country town store and demand food for their wives and children, they hit the hearts of the American people, more than all your Senatorial pleas, and government investigations."[5]

In Oklahoma City, several hundred hungry rioters raided a grocery store and were dispersed by police using tear gas.[6] The city of Detroit, deciding it could no longer justify operating its zoo, slaughtered the animals to feed hungry people.[7] Rogers was appalled at the government's inability to reduce the public suffering, writing in his weekly column: "If you live under a Government and it don't provide some means of you getting work when you really want it and will do it, why then there is something wrong. You can't just let the people starve, so if you don't give 'em work, and you don't give 'em food, or money to buy it, why what are they to do? What is the matter with our Country anyhow?"[8]

Rogers criticized many of the half-baked attempts to solve the country's woes. When Chicago's powerful mayor, "Big Bill" Thompson, proposed a lottery to raise $1,000,000 and stem the Depression in his city, Rogers slammed the idea in his column. "Mayor Thompson of Chicago has got the most original idea to help the unemployed. He wants to sell 'em four million lottery tickets at twenty-five cents apiece, and the one that draws the lucky number gets to eat."[9] Thompson, whose heavy-handed and corrupt politics were often the target of Rogers's criticisms, struck back:

> All I have to say is that if Will Rogers had made so much money that his head is so swelled that he thinks it is funny to crack jokes about people who are starving, I hope to God he goes broke and gets hungry himself and he won't crack any more jokes about those who have to accept charity.
>
> He has pulled some pretty brutal and unfair stuff about me in years gone by, which means nothing to me, because I consider the source from which it comes. When this nation is suffering and people are hungry, a wisecracker that belittles the condition and efforts of anyone to correct it is to me the cheapest skate on earth.[10]

Rogers did not respond to Thompson's tirade. The lottery was a failure, and within a year the flamboyant mayor was out of office.

Rogers attacked the Federal Farm Board for another far-fetched attempt to ease the country's economic despair. At the time there was a surplus of cotton and the price per bale was so low that farmers went bankrupt. The Farm Board proposed that farmers plow under every third row of cotton so a reduced harvest would raise prices. Rogers thought the idea absurd, writing with comic exaggeration:

> Destroying every third row of cotton is the nub of a great idea. What would give more relief than extinguishing every third Senator, every third

congressman, every third committee, every third stock broker, every third law. Make a third of the vice presidents of concerns go back to work. Turn the cows back into every third golf course. Convict every third gangster arrested. One-third of all millionaires that issue optimistic reports from aboard yachts. Too many banks, bump off a third. Stop up every third oil well and every third political speaker.

Destroy one-half the newspaper columnists, and last, but the main thing, the matter with the whole world is there is too many people. Shoot every third one. This whole plan is inexpensive and a sure-fire scheme back to prosperity.[11]

Rogers searched for more realistic answers. In January 1931 he proposed the federal government create large-scale public works projects to provide employment, with a higher surtax on large incomes to fund the projects. While he urged that the government feed the hungry, he still opposed direct monetary relief:

We shouldent be giving people money, and them not do anything for it. . . .

So every City or every State should give work of some kind, at a livable wage so that no one would be in actual want. . . .

How can you equalize it [distribution of money]? By putting a higher surtax on large incomes, and that money goes to provide some public work. . . .

Now that we got that settled all we have to do is get by Congress and see if the Republicans will vote a higher Income tax on the rich babies. It might not be a great plan, but it will DAM sure beat the one we got now.[12]

Two months later, he proposed that the government help taxpayers by withholding federal income taxes from payrolls, writing:

This is income tax day and I am in no shape to be funny.

Why don't they do it all like they do the gasoline tax? You pay it when you buy it and you are through with it. Or, make the man that pays it to us take it out, or something.

The way it is they let us handle it one year, then two and a half months after it's all made and spent then they ask you to pay it.[13]

When his friend Bernard Baruch made several proposals to speed recovery, Rogers echoed the financier, calling for an increase in the income tax for higher brackets, a sales tax on all but necessities, and no debt cancellations.[14] Rogers was more controversial, however, when he called for an end to property taxes: "You can't legitimately kick on income tax, for it's on what you have made. You have already made it. But, look at land, farms, homes, stores, vacant lots. You pay year after year on them whether you make it or not. . . . Every land or property owner in America would be tickled to death to pay 45 percent of his profits, if he didn't have to pay anything if he didn't make it."[15]

Rogers also proposed a simple solution linking the nation's financial crisis with the repeal of Prohibition: "What would be the matter with using every cent [from a tax on legalized liquor] just for charity and unemployed relief? And make the tax very high, even as high as 50 per cent. If it was a 50 per cent tax and it went to charity, you couldn't drink alone. Some poor family would be drinking with you."[16]

WILL ROGERS, essentially a Jeffersonian who mistrusted big government, blamed the dire economy on a bloated federal bureaucracy, an impotent Congress, greedy industrialists and bankers, and Wall Street financiers who "over-merged and over-capitalized and over-everything else."[17] While Rogers faulted the federal government for a large part of the Depression, he believed that Herbert Hoover received far too much blame. In a radio broadcast, he said Hoover "just happened to be the man that was left watching the dam when the dam busted and we expected [him] to put the water back."[18] It seemed to Rogers that everyone blamed all of the troubles on the president. "If the weather is wrong, we blame it on Hoover."[19] While visiting his family in Oklahoma, Rogers listened as one of his relatives criticized the president. "I like him and I always will," Will countered testily, ending the conversation.[20]

In April 1930 Rogers devoted an entire radio broadcast to praising Hoover, a man he described as a "wonderful character" who practically won World War I with his food programs.[21] Hoover had shown he was a man of deep humanitarian concern and generosity by heading the Belgian food relief during the war and coordinating the Mississippi River flood relief in 1927, when he and Rogers first met.

Rogers sympathized with the president but criticized him for being too slow in responding to the market crash. A shy man, Hoover was unwilling to reveal his emotions, unable to stir an audience, and came across to the public as cold and uncaring.[22] When unemployment rose during the end of 1929, the president sought to avoid panic by urging some reform in the banking system, calling for increased spending for public works and ordering belt tightening at the federal level. These efforts failed to boost either the economy or public confidence.

In June 1930 Rogers took the train from New York City to Washington, where he "had a nice chat" with Hoover in the White House. They discussed a variety of items, including a new protectionist tariff being debated in Congress. The Smoot-Hawley tariff bill, which the president supported, would raise U.S. tariffs on twenty thousand imported goods to record levels. But, in the opinion of many opponents, it would prolong and deepen the Depression.[23] Rogers opposed tariffs and believed they hurt the small American farmer and protected big business. He told a lecture audience that "Argentine exports meat, wheat, and gigolos, and the United States puts a tariff on the wrong two."[24] Despite advice from over one thousand economists to the contrary, Hoover signed the new tariff into law a week later, leading to an increase in rates on imported raw materials by as much as 100 percent and causing a huge decrease in exports and imports.[25]

As the Depression continued to worsen, the Hoover administration shouldered the blame. In the congressional elections of November 1930, the Republicans lost eight seats in the Senate and their majority in the House.[26] For the first time since 1918 the Democrats controlled the House, where Rogers's good friend, Texan John Nance Garner, soon became Speaker.

Despite the political backlash and his own misgivings, Rogers still defended the president, never attacking him personally. "Now, let's don't lay all of our troubles on Mr. Hoover and the Republican administration," he wrote. "There are so many things that happened to us in the last year that I wouldn't want it to happen to them purposely. I hate to down a fellow when he is down."[27]

Hoover recognized Rogers was a powerful voice who could sway public opinion. He valued the unique role that Rogers played, later saying that the humorist's political commentary provided a safety valve for public anger and fear and that he had "a great understanding of the background of public events."[28] According to the *American Magazine,* "If the President of the United States says a thing is so, the Democrats may doubt him. But if Will

Rogers backs him up, even the Democrats believe. In Washington they say that the Senate fears Will Rogers more than all the editors in America."[29] Gaining Rogers's support became more crucial for passing controversial legislation. In July 1931, for example, Congressman John Tilson, then Republican House majority leader and a close Hoover adviser, visited Rogers in Beverly Hills to discuss the president's proposed debt plan.[30]

Hoover issued a national plea for Americans to stop hoarding, claiming that for every dollar stashed away, ten dollars of credit was lost. He turned to Rogers for help, asking him to think up a joke that would stop the public from hoarding.[31] Rogers quickly responded with a humorous piece about events back in Oklahoma:

> Out on the Rogers ranch at Oologah, where I spent yesterday, Herb McSpadden, my nephew, had to take a milk stool and whack an old cow over the rear end. She was hoarding her milk.
>
> A Jewish farmer at Claremore named Morris Haas hid $500 in bills in a barrel of bran and a cow ate it up. He has just been able to get $18 of it back, up to now.
>
> This hoarding don't pay.[32]

In August 1931 Hoover created the ironically named President's Organization on Unemployment Relief (POUR) to generate private funds for unemployment relief and community chests. To kick off the relief effort and to restore public confidence, the president scheduled a nationwide radio broadcast. He asked Rogers to join him during the broadcast. It was an unprecedented request for an American president to ask a private individual who held no official office to join him in enlisting the public's support to alleviate the national crisis. By having only the humorist with him, Hoover also acknowledged that Will Rogers was probably the most influential and trusted man in the country.

On October 18, 1931, Hoover and Rogers broadcast their joint radio appeal across the country. Linked to 150 stations, the president aired from the White House and Rogers from California.[33] Hoover tried to be upbeat, telling his audience that the worst of the Depression had passed. He stressed that federal monies not be appropriated for direct relief and that care for the unemployed resided with state and local governments. When Rogers spoke after the president, he discarded his humor. His speech was blunt, critical, and void of optimism. Its title, "Bacon, Beans, and Limousines," implied that millions were worried about their next meal, while the wealthy few were doing quite well. As Rogers talked, he was respectful of Hoover, "a very human man,"[34] but went on to describe the bitter irony of hungry people in a land of plenty:

> There's not really but one problem before the whole country at this time. It's not the balancing of Mr. Mellon's budget. That's his worry. That ain't ours. And it's not the League of Nations that we read so much about. It's not the silver question. The only problem that confronts this country today is at least 7,000,000 people are out of work. That's our only problem. There is no other one before us at all. It's to see that every man that wants to is able to work, is allowed to find a place to go to work, and also to arrange some way of getting more equal distribution of the wealth in the country.[35]

Rogers must have aggravated the staunchly conservative president when he proposed a more equal distribution of wealth. He went on to rebuke the administration for failing to provide relief funds for the unemployed. A week after his radio talk, he donated $5,000 to the Los Angeles Community Chest.

Rogers's remarks during the broadcast with Hoover were often and widely quoted. An RCA vice president sent Rogers a telegram saying broadcasters received hundreds of requests for copies of his speech. His sober expressions touched on the core concerns of millions of Americans.[36] The mood of the country, and Rogers himself, had darkened since Black Thursday.

It would have been easy for Rogers to attack Hoover and Republican policy makers personally and hold their policies up to public ridicule. But Rogers knew he would not have been acting in the best interests of the country. He knew his duty was to lift public morale, to try to explain to a confused people exactly what was happening to their country.[37] Years before, Rogers had promised he would "just watch the Government and report the facts."[38] His statements reflected accurately the situation as it was, offering no silver lining because he knew there was none to be found.[39]

Rogers did not have many answers, but he suggested reforms in ways that did not increase the disillusionment the public had developed in their elected government and in the democratic process. He had too much respect for the presidency to malign Hoover directly. He understood the difficulties, but he hoped the president would do something positive to alleviate them, recognizing it was the policies, not the man, that caused the trouble. Rogers therefore directed his criticisms at the bankers, economists, and conservative politicians who since the Harding years had run the government. In doing this he tried to take some of the blame off of Hoover's shoulders and lessen public animosity.[40] He reported what he saw, as depressing as it might be, but also in a way that brought a much-needed smile to the faces of his readers.

IN JUNE 1930, Will Rogers again lost his temper over Prohibition. This time he was incensed over a government report that refused to recommend any changes to a ban on liquor that, to Will, was causing more problems than it was solving. A year before President Hoover had appointed former attorney general George Wickersham to determine whether or not the enforcement of Prohibition was successful, to identify criminal activity, and to make recommendations for appropriate public policy. For over a year the commission documented the widespread evasion of the ban on alcohol and the numerous counterproductive effects it had on American society.

After the commission issued a report filled with contradictions and inconsistencies, widespread rebuke followed. While the report provided overwhelming evidence of the unenforceability of Prohibition, its eleven members, all moderate on the issue, could not agree on either retention or repeal of the Eighteenth Amendment. Rather than recommending repeal, as many expected, the report concluded that more aggressive law enforcement be continued.

As expected, Rogers criticized the report's feeble findings and the commission's inability to take a hard stand. "I was down in west Texas last week and they are feeding goats the Wickersham report," he wrote.[41] He also claimed to be confused: "I have been out studying the Wickersham report. There is only six men in the world that understand Einstein. They say Einstein issued a statement that only six men can understand. I'll tell the world that there ain't anybody that can understand Wickersham. He improved on Einstein."[42]

Rogers was especially angry that the administration and Congress still debated Prohibition, and he fumed that the federal government spent huge sums of money and energy on enforcement while millions of Americans were unemployed and the country sank deeper into depression. "It's food, it ain't drink that we are worried about today," he told a radio audience.[43] Frustrated, Rogers saw the Wickersham report as the final straw:

> I try to write my little jokes without getting riled up over anything, but tonight I am on the warpath.
>
> For the first time in our lifetime our country is in need. . . . Seven million people's minds are on their next cup of coffee.
>
> And what happens? The prohibition report is turned in! . . .
>
> Prohibition! Our grandchildren will be arguing over that, and here we are taking it serious at a time like this.
>
> If we could butter that report and put it between two loaves of bread, it would be welcome now.[44]

Rogers continued to be exasperated over Prohibition. A year after the Wickersham report, Congress scuttled a bill to legalize beer, prompting Rogers to write:

> Prohibition originally started out with us as a moral issue. It was either good or bad for you to drink. Then it drifted to economics: Did people save more when not drinking? Then into racketeering. But now it's drifted into the worst angle of any, that is politics. . . .
>
> The vote in the Senate the other day shows that morals, economy, less taxes, nothing entered their minds; only "how can my party get part of the beer and all the credit?" Beer has lined up with the post offices as political loot.[45]

IN THE FALL OF 1930, Will Rogers warned Americans about the danger of Adolf Hitler, a man who "has Germany like Capone has Chicago."[46] Rogers followed events in Europe closely and knew the nations there would always quarrel. He believed another war was inevitable, predicting as early as 1925 that as soon as Germany rearmed there would be another war. But as an isolationist, he was not as concerned with conflicts in Europe as he was with keeping the United States out of them. "Boys, it's your cats that's fighting," he wrote as tensions rose, "you pull 'em apart."[47]

Rogers had watched Germany with interest, at least since 1923 when Hitler staged his Beer Hall Putsch in Munich and seized the city government. After the Depression hit Germany in 1930, Hitler's Nazis suddenly rose from obscurity to win 107 Reichstag seats. Two years later the Nazis won 230 seats and became the largest party in the government. Thousands of Germans later cheered as Adolf Hitler was sworn in as chancellor.

At first Rogers saw Hitler as yet another in a long line of European saber rattlers and expressed little concern over the dictator's rise to power and the threat he posed to peace and stability. He revealed more unease with Hitler's racial bigotry, especially his anti-Semitism, than with his war mongering. "Papers all state Hitler is trying to copy Mussolini," he wrote in March 1933. "Looks to me like it's the Ku Klux that he is copying. He don't want to be Emperor, he wants to be Kleagle."[48]

OVER FOUR MILLION Americans were unemployed in 1930 and thousands more were laid off every day. To worsen the nation's misery, a severe shortage of rainfall that year began to affect parts of the eastern and central United States, followed by a far more widespread and severe drought stretching into early 1931. The drought left much of the Great Plains with scorched earth, evaporated ponds, and barren farms. Particularly hard hit were the southern plains, where the agricultural economy already was crippled by years of collapsed commodity prices, increased operating costs, and mounting debt. Farmers who owned their land defaulted on their mortgages, while tenants who rented their land, unable to feed their families, just walked away.

Will Rogers watched in frustration as the government took no action to help those in need. On January 12, 1931, he flew by airmail plane from Los Angeles to Fort Worth where he met with local volunteers who organized a drought relief crusade for Arkansas, Texas, and Oklahoma.[49] Three days later he was in the nation's capital where he met with House Speaker Nicholas Longworth, Minority Leader John Nance Garner, and other congressmen. On the next day he went to the White House to discuss the drought with President Hoover. Rogers proposed the federal government give money directly to the Red Cross to help alleviate the Depression in general and the suffering of the drought victims in particular.[50] He failed to get Hoover's support, and wrote afterward: "Had a long talk with the President this morning. He sincerely feels (with almost emotion) that it would set a bad precedent for the government to appropriate money for the Red Cross. He feels once the government relieves the people, they will always expect it, and you have broken down the real spirit of American generosity and spoiled all that our great American Red Cross has worked years to achieve."[51] Roger was not only upset over the president's hard stand on Red Cross relief but was irked by the legislature's reluctance to pass a food aid bill. "They seem to think that's a bad precedent to appropriate money for food—it's too much like the 'dole.' They think it would encourage hunger."[52]

On January 20 Rogers took his plea for drought relief to New York City, where he lunched with Al Smith at the Democratic Club. Smith was occupied with the construction of the Empire State Building and was a front-runner, along with Franklin Roosevelt, for the upcoming Democratic presidential nomination.

Getting no results from the federal government, Rogers launched his own relief effort. He quickly made plans for a private tour of the drought area to publicize the farmers' plight and drum up donations for the Red Cross. On January 21, after the Red Cross approved his plan, Rogers left Washington in the official plane of Secretary of the Navy Charles Francis Adams, III. Frank Hawks, a veteran pilot of the Army Air Service who had set hundreds of flight speed records, agreed to fly him on the tour.[53]

Rogers made more than fifty stops in his eighteen-day circuit through Texas, Oklahoma, and Arkansas. "Starving ain't so bad," he told the crowds. "It's getting used to it that is rough. The first three years of a Republican Administration is the hardest. By the end of that time you are used to living on predictions."[54] So frenetic was the trip that his troupe did three shows simultaneously in Little Rock, with Rogers and members of his cast being shuttled by car between a downtown theater, a white high school, and a black high school. Hawks, who died in an air crash in 1938 when his plane hit telephone wires, often appeared on stage during the performances and spoke of his flying exploits.

While in Little Rock, Rogers joined a national radio broadcast on NBC launching the Red Cross campaign. President Hoover, former president Coolidge, and John Barton Payne shared the microphone. A few days later Rogers broadcast his plea for more contributions on CBS, speaking during the intermission of a stage appearance in Waco, Texas.

Rogers with pilot Frank Hawks

On February 2, Rogers lunched with Oklahoma governor William "Alfalfa Bill" Murray, a family friend who had served with Clem Rogers as a delegate to the Oklahoma constitutional convention in 1906.[55] A populist who claimed to champion the little man, the colorful and controversial Murray was best known for his excessive use of gubernatorial powers, calling out the National Guard and declaring martial law over thirty times. Rogers liked the rambunctious governor. "They will never impeach this baby, he's too slick for 'em. He's got lots of common sense, and if the people want a good government he will give it to 'em. Sometimes I doubt if they do."[56]

Rogers with Red Cross officials and children in drought-stricken Arkansas

After lunch with Murray, Rogers spoke to a joint session of the Oklahoma state legislature, lending his support to the governor's emergency relief measures then being debated. Through money collected from state employees, businessmen, and even his own salary, Murray financed programs to feed Oklahoma's poor. With no federal relief existing at the time, Murray soon became a national spokesman for the victims of the Depression, calling for a national council for relief that was held the following June in Memphis.

That night, speaking to a packed audience at Oklahoma City's elegant India Temple Shrine, Rogers gave one of his more emotional performances. He pleaded with his fellow Oklahomans to help those in need, lamenting the dire straits of the sharecropper, the one-mule farmer who "raises nothing but children and dogs all the time. Those two crops never fail and they both eat." At the end of his performance Rogers picked out wealthy people in the audience that he knew and challenged them to donate. "Oh my Lord, there never was a time in the history of my country when the need was so great."[57]

Rogers ended the tour on February 12 with five appearances that day in Arkansas. Among the stops was a visit to England, Arkansas, the site of the earlier food riot by desperate farmers. Three days later Hawks flew Rogers home to California, landing on a field near his ranch.[58] By the end of the tour, he had traveled fifteen thousand miles and raised $225,000 for the Red Cross.[59]

Getting back to California did not lessen Rogers's frustration. Near the end of February he still was angered at the federal government's refusal to help people in need:

> The stock market is picking up, so that makes the rich boys feel a little better. Lots of appropriations bills for government expenditures have been passed. Business in general in the last four or five weeks looks better. But, all that has nothing to do with the folks that the Red Cross has to feed.
>
> United States Steel can go to a thousand and one, Auburns to a million, but that don't bring one biscuit to a poor old Negro family of fifteen in Arkansas, who haven't got a chance to get a single penny in money till their little few bales of cotton are sold away next fall.[60]

SOON AFTER returning to California, Will Rogers was back in the movie studio, finishing *A Connecticut Yankee* early in the year and beginning *Young as You Feel*. On March 31, 1931, near the end of production, he learned that a devastating earthquake had hit Managua, Nicaragua, killing some two thousand people and leaving the city in ruins. Wrapping up his movie, he departed Los Angeles on a two-week airplane trip to Central and South America.

Rogers spent three days touring Managua and other parts of earthquake-ravaged Nicaragua, sleeping in a tent as aftershocks still shook the city and fires burned uncontrolled, with rebel skirmishes on the outskirts adding to the crisis.[61] "They tell you pictures don't lie," he wrote from the rubble, "but the ones you saw of this earthquake did, for they didn't tell that eight days after it happened there is from one to three hundred bodies still under those ruins."[62] Before departing, he donated $5,000 to a Red Cross disaster fund.

MARTINIQUE
ANTIGUA
GRENADA
TRINIDAD
COLOMBIA
COSTA RICA
NICARAGUA
BRIT. HONDURAS

DOMINICAN REPUBLIC
VIRGIN ISLANDS
St. LUCIA PORTO RICO
DOMINICA
VENEZUELA
PANAMA
CANAL ZONE   CUBA
HONDURAS   HAITI
MEXICO

*Rogers touring
Nicaragua after
earthquake*

On April 11 Rogers arrived in Panama for a five-day visit, where he gave several benefits for the Nicaragua earthquake victims.[63] He flew to Maracaibo, Venezuela, then to Guatemala, El Salvador, Nicaragua, Costa Rica, Trinidad, Puerto Rico, and the Virgin Islands. The trip covered eight thousand miles.[64]

After Rogers completed his goodwill mission to South America, as well as his grueling drought relief tour, the *New York Times* temporarily abandoned its animosity toward him and commended him for his charity efforts. In an editorial the paper praised him, in almost saintlike terms, "for flying over great stretches of God's earth to make it as much of heaven as possible while still a very human mortal." Rogers's missions, according to the *Times*, suggested "a kind of angelic service, though the angel be of a very masculine type and very different from the conventional one."[65]

As soon as he arrived back in the United States from South America, Rogers headed to Washington DC to brief government officials on what he had observed, especially his experiences in Nicaragua. While Rogers was there, Secretary of State Henry Stimson called him into conference.[66] Stimson wrote to Rogers afterward, saying he "was very glad to learn that such a staunch American as you, who had just been to Nicaragua and had seen the

Rogers entertains U.S.
sailors in Panama

conditions there at first hand, believed that what I am trying to do is the right thing and was kind enough to come and tell me so."[67] Rogers came away from the meeting satisfied, writing that Stimson "knows things about Nicaragua that none of these critics of his do."[68] For a change, Rogers was pleased with U.S. diplomatic policy, as both Hoover and Stimson opposed intervention in Central America and the Caribbean. The administration implemented a good neighbor policy that led to the eventual removal of marines from Nicaragua and Haiti. In the spring of 1931 American business interests in Nicaragua sought further protection for American citizens there, but Stimson and Hoover refused.[69]

After his trip to Washington, which also included a speech to the Daughters of the American Revolution, another Gridiron Dinner performance, and visits with Nicholas and Alice Longworth and other Washington insiders, Rogers returned to California. Soon he was back on the movie set to finish his third picture of the year, *Ambassador Bill*. When he completed the film that fall, he kept busy, including a visit to William Randolph Hearst's ranch in Chihuahua state, Mexico. Rogers hosted Secretary of War Pat Hurley at his Santa Monica home and appeared on another national radio broadcast on unemployment with President Hoover, Calvin Coolidge, Al Smith, Mary Pickford, Amos and Andy, and others.[70] Later he participated in an NBC broadcast paying tribute to Knute Rockne, who had died in a plane crash in March. Rogers helped raise funds for a new field house on the Notre Dame campus in honor of the legendary coach.[71]

Meanwhile, rumors of Rogers running for office continued to pop up. A Kentucky newspaper reported, "it is beginning to look as if the possibility exists of Rogers being taken seriously as a possible [presidential] candidate."[72] In June 1931 an editor of the *Columbus Dispatch* asked, "Why not name Will Rogers president of the U.S. by acclamation? His so-called 'applesauce' seems to be just what the world needs right now."[73] Six months later an article in the *New York Times* recommended him as governor of California. "I'd rather be a poor actor than a poor governor," Rogers responded.[74]

Over the years Rogers rejected separate movements to run for governor of Oklahoma, Arkansas, and California. Democrats urged him to run for senator from California and, in May 1933, the *Los Angeles Times* suggested he run for mayor of Los Angeles. A splinter party later announced he was their presidential candidate.

Most of the offers for Rogers to enter politics were mere jokes, much like his mayorship of Beverly Hills, his appointment as congressman-at-large, and his campaign for the presidency in 1928 as the Anti-Bunk Party candidate. But some of his supporters continued to see him as a potent political force. After the *Home Friend* magazine proposed that "Will Rogers [is] the man we need in the White House," the magazine received a flood of letters, surprising the editors that their suggestion "would arouse so much favorable comment, and strike such a sympathetic chord in the hearts of our readers."[75]

While most people, including Rogers himself, did not take his candidacy for public office seriously, Henry Ford thought otherwise. The millionaire once snapped at the press, "the joke of Will Rogers's candidacy for President is that it is *no* joke."[76]

AT THE END OF October Rogers flew back to Mexico City where he called on U.S. Ambassador Reuben Clark, afterward visited with his friend, former president Plutarco Calles who then was minister of war, and dined with foreign correspondents at the plush Hotel Regis. On the trip with Rogers were director Hal Roach and polo star Eric Pedley. The three spent much of their time on the polo field of the Reforma Club.[77] While all of the players wore spiffy polo uniforms, the humorist galloped recklessly up and down the field garbed in overalls and a cowboy shirt.[78] Rogers, who never could stand to see an animal suffer, declined an invitation to a bullfight in the Mexican capital.

From Mexico City Rogers flew to San Antonio, Texas, then drove across eighty miles of mesquite brush to Uvalde, Texas, to spend his fifty-second birthday with his friend John Nance Garner at the congressman's ranch. Rogers loved talking politics with the grizzle-faced Garner, who was known for inviting fellow congressmen to his office for drinks and poker. Known as Cactus Jack, Garner was one of the most powerful men in Washington, having been first elected in 1902 as a Democrat to the House of Representatives from a congressional district that covered tens of thousands of square miles of rural Texas. Since then he had won reelection fourteen times. Garner's hard work and integrity made him one of the most respected leaders in the House, the Democrats choosing him as minority floor leader in 1929 and, when his party took control in 1931, selecting him as Speaker. Whenever Rogers was in Washington he used Cactus Jack's office as his own.

From Garner's ranch Rogers flew to Kingsville, Texas, where he spent the night at the legendary King Ranch, one of the largest spreads in the world at over a million acres. The ranch was noted for its huge herds of prime-rate cattle, especially its own crossbred Santa Gertrudis line. That year the ranch shipped twenty-five thousand of them to market.[79] After his visit, one of the family owners of the ranch sent Will a purebred Brahma calf named Sarah. The Rogers family treated her as a pet, with Sarah soon becoming a prized possession that "followed the children around like a big dog."[80]

Rogers with John Nance Garner

As fall turned to winter in 1931, Rogers looked forward to spending the Christmas holidays with his family at his California ranch. It was not to be, as world events thousands of miles away upset his plans for a quiet vacation. He soon found himself on the high seas, headed to one of the most remote and dangerous spots in the world, and smack in the middle of a war.

TEN

———•◦•———

Journey to the Brink of War

P
ICKING UP the newspaper one morning in September 1931, Will
Rogers read that a Japanese army of twenty thousand troops had
invaded China and quickly captured a seven-hundred-mile
stretch of Manchuria. Knowing the Far East was filled with quarreling nations, each trying to dominate the region, Rogers feared that the latest incident could touch off a major war. "Japan has been trying to match a
war with China for years," he wrote at the time. "Looks like they finally
made it. Russia is rehearsing to get in. This Manchuria must be a pretty valuable country."[1]

American officials viewed the invasion with alarm, as they feared the
Japanese planned other conquests in the region, particularly an invasion of
the U.S.-held Philippines. When the Manchurian attack occurred, Secretary
of War Pat Hurley was in the Philippines making an inspection of the
islands. He too worried about Japanese intentions in the Far East.[2] On his way
back to Washington he stopped in California to visit with Rogers at his Santa
Monica ranch.

Rogers and Hurley, who also was born in Indian Territory, were close
friends from the old days. The two men had first met in 1898 when working
as cowhands on a ranch in Texas.[3] Since then Hurley had had an impressive

career as a colonel in World War I, a successful attorney practicing in Oklahoma, and a powerful Republican politician. After the war he became wealthy through oil exploration and real estate investments. President Hoover appointed him assistant secretary of war in 1929 and promoted him to secretary eight months later after the death of James William Good.

Hurley had traveled to the Philippines to determine if the United States should grant the islands independence, concluding afterward that the islands were neither ready for self-government nor able to defend themselves. Rogers disagreed with his friend, arguing that the Philippines deserved independence. "Let people do their own way and have their own form of Government," he wrote in 1924. "We haven't got any business in the Philippines. We are not such a howling success running our own Government."[4] Two years later Rogers had not changed his mind. "We are in wrong with them now. Why we don't give 'em to them, and come on home and get our little Army together, and pass a law to never let them leave the country again."[5] One of the nation's most outspoken isolationists, Rogers believed the United States should avoid any conflict between China and Japan, writing that "America could hunt all over the world and not find a better fight to keep out of."[6]

At the ranch meeting on October 21, Hurley told Rogers the Philippines were vulnerable to an attack by Japan. Since the end of the Russo-Japanese War of 1904, Japanese economic, political, and military interests in the Far East had grown more threatening to the United States. The invasion of Manchuria only heightened Hurley's worries. "Wouldent Japan pounce on [the Philippines] and take 'em over the very day we got out?" Rogers asked. "No!" Hurley replied. "Not till maby the following morning."[7] Even though Rogers favored Philippine independence, he conceded that the islands were incapable of defending themselves. If Japan invaded the Philippines, he wrote, they would "have a Crop planted before we could get a Feet [sic] across that Ocean."[8]

During their meeting at the ranch, the two men agreed that Rogers would make a last-minute trip to the Far East, stopping in Japan and then traveling on to Manchuria to observe the hostilities. Hurley complained he was not getting a complete picture of the Manchurian situation from the State Department, confiding to Rogers that he was "not permitted to correspond with State Department officials outside of the territorial limits of the United

*Rogers with
Secretary of War
Pat Hurley*

States."[9] He needed someone he could trust to enter the war zone, get a better understanding of Japanese intentions in the Far East, and determine the strength of Chinese resolve to defend their territory. Hurley also was concerned about how nearby Russia would react to the Japanese invasion. Like Japan, Russia coveted resource-rich Manchuria and already had significant economic interests in the area, including ownership of the southern branch of the Trans-Siberian Railway.[10] Hurley feared Manchuria could be the spark to ignite another major war. He was right. The Japanese invasion touched off a Sino-Japanese war that lasted for the next fourteen years until the end of World War II.

The plan was for Rogers to visit the Far East, then continue on across Asia into the Mediterranean and Europe, and finally return home, having completed another trip around the world. The trip would be a hectic end to an already busy 1931 when he starred in three motion pictures, barnstormed the South to raise donations for drought victims, visited nine countries in Central and South America, including earthquake-devastated Nicaragua, made two more trips to Mexico, traveled several times to Washington to root out the latest political gossip, and made a number of national radio broadcasts, including three with President Hoover. Instead of spending a quiet Christmas holiday with his family, he left them on his California ranch and headed off alone to explore one of the more remote and dangerous parts of the world.

Hurley knew that his friend Rogers was ideal for observing what was happening in Manchuria. Since the early 1920s, Rogers had watched the tense situation in the Far East with interest. Besides, his status as an international celebrity made it difficult for any country to deny him entry, his celebrity often opening doors to top foreign leaders that even U.S. ambassadors found difficult to access. Unlike his many international travels in the past, the trip was not going to be a carefree excursion, as he was headed into a dangerous war zone and to a region where, even in the best of circumstances, transportation was scarce and unreliable. He would be traveling in the dead of winter in Manchuria, which had one of the harshest climates in the world. He told his readers the trip was to be "long, and it's hazardous, and it's inconvenient, but you want the facts, and that's what I'm going after for you."[11]

In November, as soon as he decided to make the trip, Rogers telegraphed Adolph Ochs requesting the *New York Times* provide him with correspondent credentials. Before the 1926 European trip Ochs wrote Rogers a glowing letter of introduction, but this time he refused. The publisher turned down the request after the managing editor, Frederick Birchall, argued strongly against Rogers making the trip:

It should be remembered that neither the Japanese nor the Chinese know Mr. Rogers, nor will they be able to understand his keen wit. These two are perhaps the most sensitive nations on earth. They have no sense of humor, and if he is going to be humorous, he will be misinterpreted and misunderstood. . . .

Whether the situation be drawn out or short lived, Mr. Rogers will be better able to comment from Beverly Hills, basing his material on what he reads in The Times.[12]

Rogers's relationship with the *Times* editorial staff was always strained, the paper having treated him condescendingly for years. They never regarded him as a bona fide correspondent despite the fact that he had traveled to most parts of the world and met many of the great leaders. Rogers had better results from George Lorimer, the editor of the *Saturday Evening Post*, who commissioned him to write five feature articles on the Far East trip.

More importantly, Rogers had the official backing of the U.S. government. Pat Hurley had Secretary of State Henry Stimson provide a letter to American diplomats in the Far East advising them to grant Rogers "such courtesies and assistance as you may be able to render." Hurley gave him a list of contacts, ministers and military officers at U.S. embassies who could assist him with visas, arrange audiences with foreign dignitaries, and could "kill the fatted calf" for him. In his letter to Rogers, Hurley added the handwritten comment that, "If you can go to the Philippines cable me and I'll fix you up. That's in my jurisdiction." Hurley also worried about his friend's safety. "If you do get to where it's happening," he wrote, "I hope you will wear the tin hat."[13]

WEARING HIS blue serge suit and carrying only a portable typewriter and an "old soft, flat red grip that packed itself," Will Rogers left California on November 21, 1931, and headed north to Vancouver.[14] There he boarded the SS *Empress of Russia*, sailing west across the Pacific en route to Yokohama, Japan. Built in 1912, the *Empress of Russia* was neither the most modern nor the fastest liner, but she was one of the favored ships plying the Pacific, offering some of the most comfortable, tastefully furnished first-class accommodations afloat: a dining saloon, library, card room, smoking room, veranda cafe, and lounge with a fireplace. As soon as he boarded, Rogers explored the ship, even venturing deep into the engine room to watch in fascination as a

Empress of Russia.
Courtesy Canadian Pacific Archives

giant Russian shouted orders at sweating, shirtless Chinese coolies shoveling coal into the hot furnaces.

Rogers did not like ocean voyages owing to chronic seasickness, but this time he looked forward to the trip. The nine days at sea offered a time to relax, to cast aside his celebrity status, to collect his thoughts and take stock of the last two years of economic turmoil. He told another passenger that the voyage was the first time in years he felt free from care; he "wanted to get away from things, wanted to be alone on his own."[15] While Rogers was not a heavy reader, he took along a stack of books he wanted to wade through, including Sandburg's *Abraham Lincoln,* Harold Lamb's *Genghis Khan,* and Fred Pasley's *Al Capone.* He later admitted that he had read more on the voyage than at any other time in his life.

As soon as the *Empress of Russia* departed Vancouver, Rogers discovered his fellow first-class passengers were a fascinating bunch who made the voyage one of the most entertaining trips he ever took. The group included international war correspondent Floyd Gibbons, professional golfer Nathan Cornfoot, Japanese physicist Dr. Toshio Takamine, George Walden, who managed Standard Oil operations in Indonesia, two German businessmen traveling to Japan, a colorless little salesman from a paper factory, and a beekeeper from Canada named George Riedel.[16]

Twice each day, the group met in the ship's lounge for cocktails, each sharing their vast experiences and knowledge. They amused themselves with humorous stories and the latest jokes and held spirited conversations that ranged from the world political situation to their favorite writers and poets. After they got to know and trust each other, they held loud, heated arguments over the causes of the Depression, the existence of God, the emergence of communism, and any other controversial subject they happened upon. Rogers seemed to relish the meetings on the *Empress* more than anyone. It was a time when, according to one passenger, "no one cared whether the time stopped, went on and on, or round and round."[17]

Rogers, of course, captivated the group with stories that "set everyone alive as if they had been hit by an electric current."[18] Rogers entertained them with gossip about the movies and the stars he worked with. "Chaplin is the only real genius the movies have produced," he said, "the only one who will live."[19] He talked about the politicians he knew and had befriended over the years such as John Nance Garner, Pat Hurley, Joe Robinson, and especially Bill Borah, his friend and the leading isolationist in the Senate and "the only man in public life in his time with independent thought, when everybody else's ideas are as standardized as Ford parts."[20]

Floyd Gibbons also entertained them with his stories. He was the only passenger that Rogers had known earlier, the two having met in Warsaw in the summer of 1926 when they "were covering Piłsudski's revolution."[21] By this time Gibbons was one of the world's premier news correspondents, who, according to Rogers, "covered an awful lot of wars, and a lot of awful wars too."[22] Starting with the *Chicago Tribune* in 1907, Gibbons became well known for covering the Pancho Villa Expedition in 1916. As a World War I correspondent at the Battle of Belleau Wood, he lost an eye from German gunfire while attempting to rescue an American marine.

Since the war, Gibbons had become a radio commentator and narrator of newsreels. He was loud and dominating, always spiffily dressed, and wore an eye patch that made him look like he had just left the set of a Douglas Fairbanks swashbuckler. He told interesting yarns about everything from riding Mongolian ponies to dodging around in New York City taxicabs with heavyweight champ Gene Tunney.[23] Gibbons had the group speechless one evening when he described when a German submarine torpedoed and sank a ship he was on. Like Rogers, Gibbons was interested in the tensions building in the Far East, and was heading to Manchuria equipped with a short-wave radio to report live from the war zone.

Rogers enjoyed sitting in a corner listening to his fellow passengers tell their tales. Dr. Takamine, a professor of physics at the Imperial University at Tokyo, was returning from a world tour during which he consulted with the leading physicists of Europe and America. "He was might pleasant," Rogers wrote, "but he wouldent tell us exactly what we asked him. He was smart though. He had been down to Pasadena, and studying with Prof. [Robert] Millikan [of Cal Tech] and all those fellows that Einstein was with."[24] Nathan Cornfoot was another passenger that Rogers enjoyed listening to. The personable golfer had learned to play at St. Andrews in Scotland, but during the war his left arm was riddled with shrapnel. In spite of his injuries he could still hold his own. He designed the golf course at Heliopolis outside of Cairo and was on his way to Tokyo where a new golf club had hired him to teach Japanese noblemen how to play the game.

Rogers found none of the passengers more intriguing than George Riedel, the beekeeper from Alberta, Canada. Riedel was a successful entrepreneur and a salesman who could sell anything. He claimed to have brought the first banana trees to California and had business ventures in real estate, avocados, mahogany, and gold mining on the West Coast. The owner of several apiaries in Canada, he planned to be the first large-scale beekeeper to supply the Chinese market. That summer in Alberta he prepared a big shipment of twelve hundred swarms headed by new queens and delivered them in a special container to Vancouver, where he loaded them on the *Empress of Russia*. Rogers was fascinated with the cargo of bees, often relaxing on the ship's stern at sunset while Riedel checked how the swarms were surviving the voyage. On one occasion the beekeeper turned to Rogers and told him that "a bee was more interesting than a person, and he looked me right in the face when he said it."[25]

Drinking a fifth of whisky a day and smoking a box of cigars a week, Riedel was one of the most brilliant and eccentric men Rogers ever met. The beekeeper spoke five languages fluently and seemed to have read every book written, easily quoting from the classics and poetry from memory. To Rogers, "He was what you call a kind of a well read Nut."[26] Riedel gave him a copy of Pearl Buck's *The Good Earth* and insisted he read it. Rogers stayed up late and finished the book in one reading, captivated by Buck's tale of the peasant Wang Lung and village life in rural China. He wrote afterward that the Pulitzer-winning classic was "the greatest thing I had ever read."[27]

Riedel was so liberal he bordered on anarchy, and such a die-hard iconoclast it seemed every time he talked with Rogers the two ended up in a hot argument. Rogers loved it, describing Riedel as a "Komical Cuss and got everybody on the Boat sore, because in every argument he knew more about everything than anyone else; and what made us all sorer still, he did know it."[28] During one discussion Rogers said he liked mimicking Calvin Coolidge, claiming he could imitate the former president better than Grace Coolidge herself, putting the group in stitches when he described staying at the White House where in the evening Cal pulled out his watch and said, "Well, its nine o'clock, folks. Time to go to bed. Good night everybody." Rogers then pretended to be Coolidge giving a keynote speech:

> Fellow citizens: Tonight I'm going to speak to you about the most important problem confronting the Nation. . . . Do you know what it is? I will tell you. It's Thursday. Now let me tell you something about Thursday which in the hurry and bustle of everyday life you may not have learned. Thursday is a very great day, in fact one of the greatest we have. Don't forget that Thursday comes just before Friday; and further more—and I want to impress this on your minds—it also comes right after Wednesday, which is another important day. And now, fellow citizens, since we all know about this matter, I feel sure you will back up the administration on this important legislation.[29]

When Rogers finished, Riedel abruptly told him that he thought Coolidge was a dunce. "No, Bees, you're wrong there," Rogers snapped back, adding that Coolidge "was a whole lot smarter than a lot of people give him credit for. He wasn't dumb at all. He knew politics, and he knew politicians, and he didn't let any of them put anything over on him. He was hep to 'em all the time. He knew the depression was coming."[30]

Rogers then asked Riedel what he thought of Wilson. "He was a good schoolteacher," the beekeeper said, "and wrote an exhaustive book about Constitutional history." Riedel didn't consider any president since Lincoln a great man—they were all politicians first and great men second. He told Rogers: "I almost feel ashamed to know that I am a member of a Nation that was governed as it was during the Harding administration and of the chicanery that made his election possible." Riedel urged Rogers to read the muckraking novel *The Plum Tree* by David Graham Phillips, "if you want to learn why so many second class men become Presidents."[31]

Riedel surprised Rogers when he described two of America's best-known journalists, Arthur Brisbane and H. L. Mencken, as shallow and out-of-date thinkers. "Well, I'll be damned," Rogers grunted. "Why Brisbane knows more in his little finger than all the rest of us columnists put together, and here you lay him on the shelf." He also defended Mencken, the tart columnist of the *Baltimore Sun.* "What? Mencken old fashioned? Why, he's supposed to be the last word in new ideas." When Riedel argued that Thoreau, Emerson, and Whitman were greater men than, say, Edison or Ford because they gave values that will endure, Rogers just shook his head in dismay.[32]

During one of their meetings, Rogers talked about the flight he had made with Frank Hawks across the South raising money for destitute farmers during the drought. Riedel stunned Rogers by saying that the trip was "monstrous and stupid." The beekeeper argued that there was no excuse for poverty, that it was downright criminal for the nation to allow people to go hungry:

> Think of you and Hawks trying to entertain those poor farmers and make them happy when they saw their children without clothes and food: and to think that all those things were right there bulging out of stores and ware houses, and you and Hawks making a few collections to give them only the dregs of charity when they had already produced it all themselves. There was cotton in the warehouses and idle factories ready to make it into cloth. There were beans and corn and meat in the warehouses, and on the other hand a lot of empty stomachs and you can't get the two together except by charity. Why, it makes my blood boil when a representative of the Community Chest comes around and tries to high pressure me into giving charity for the poor. Charity! When it ought to be the poor laborers themselves giving charity to us idlers who get a good living by kidding them along and making them forget their misery.[33]

Rogers was dumbfounded that anyone regarded his relief efforts as monstrous and stupid. He argued with Riedel for another twenty minutes before finally giving up.

When Riedel and Cornfoot shared their love for poetry, Rogers sat quietly in a corner and listened, half dozing away. He also enjoyed listening to Riedel and Takamine hold long talks comparing occidental and oriental literature, history, and culture. Rogers wrote that Riedel "had also read a lot of Chinese stuff. He and the Japanese would argue over that. I tell you this old Bee man was a freak."[34] Riedel and Takamine also talked for hours about scientific topics, covering the spectrum of physics, chemistry, and biology and their relationship to mysticism and religion. At one point, the Japanese physicist spoke at length about the connection between hydrogen and uranium and nuclear physics.

During a violent storm off the Aleutians, Riedel, Takamine, and Rogers stayed in the lounge in front of the fire. Most of the passengers were under the weather and "even the bees were seasick." Rogers, however, felt fine and never had even the slightest attack. He could not understand why he was not sick himself. One reason may have been that he was drinking on this voyage. He told Riedel that at home he never drank, "except a little 'dago red' occasionally with friends in the evening," but during this voyage he was drinking sometimes as many as five or six cocktails a day. He joked that the only reason he drank cocktails was to eat the cherry at the bottom.[35]

Later in the voyage Rogers spoke about his experience at the London Disarmament Conference, sparking a long debate about the possibility of war. The group argued over the weakness of the League of Nations and the possibility of the United States getting into the Far East conflict. The ship was receiving messages every day about the Manchurian crisis. Since Gibbons and Rogers were going there, everyone was intensely interested. "Gibbons sure seems to want to get where the cannon balls are," Riedel observed, and "to delight the world with the carnage that was about to break out there." The beekeeper considered Gibbons "a light-weight and fairly ignorant." Rogers asked Dr. Takamine, a very polished gentleman, if Japan was going to stay in Manchuria and if there was going to be a war or not. The physicist answered cautiously, saying that he thought the Japanese were not willing to "lose their sphere of influence" in Manchuria.[36]

Rogers talked about things going on in Washington that only he knew about, but, according to Riedel, he was almost as cagey and cautious as Dr. Takamine had been. Riedel later wrote: "as everyone knows, in his later years

[Rogers] was very close to things going on in Washington and they did not hesitate to use him whenever they could. As a matter of fact some of us thought—and I believe the Japanese government did too—that he was on his way over there as a good-Will ambassador and general sounder-out of the situation."[37]

Despite their constant squabbles, Rogers and Riedel took a liking to each other by the time the ship reached Japan. While he disagreed with much of what Riedel said, Rogers had great respect for his intellect. "Old Bees was pretty tough to down in all argument," he wrote afterward, "and you would about have to buy him a drink to beat him."[38] When the trip was over, Rogers gave Riedel his copy of Sandburg's *Lincoln*. Riedel also saw a deeper Rogers, a man who was much more complex than merely a jokester. The beekeeper wrote later: "One rarely noticed his other side, except when he was in repose as I saw him that stormy day when Dr. Takamine and I were settling all the problems of infinity, and Will was alone with his thoughts;—and this sad wistful quality was very apparent."[39] After they parted on the dock in Yokohama, Rogers and Riedel never saw each other again.

WHEN THE SS *Empress of Russia* docked in Yokohama just after dark on December 5, 1931, Will Rogers took the train to Tokyo where he was welcomed as a celebrity and lodged at the Imperial Hotel, the recently completed masterpiece designed by Frank Lloyd Wright. "Talk about a 'rube' in town," he wrote. "I got off the boat last night standing rubbering at everything with my mouth open and got run over by a ricksha. That's a taxicab propelled by a man."[40]

In the Japanese capital Rogers met with Minister of War Jirō Minami. A Japanese general who became governor-general of Japanese-occupied Korea, Minami was a dominant figure in the Japanese cabinet. When the Japanese army invaded Manchuria, it ignored the orders of the civilian leaders who had prohibited any invasion. It was unclear to outsiders whether or not Minami had given his approval for the army to cross the border and invade Chinese territory. When Rogers met with the war minister, the two men sat cross-legged on the floor eating "a real Japanese feed" with chopsticks.[41] With them were several high-ranking Japanese intelligence officers who told Rogers about the war in Manchuria, "of course from their angle."[42] For a cou-

*Always on
the go*

ple of hours they grilled him as to why he was visiting the war zone. "Well, they couldent figure me out at all. I dident tell them what I had in mind to do over in Manchuria, for I had nothing in mind."[43] Rogers never disclosed the exact conversation with Minister Minami, although he did obtain permission to enter the Japanese-occupied area of China. When reporters asked Rogers why he was in Tokyo and meeting with Minami, he cast aside the question, responding only that he was checking out the geishas and "over here 'scouting for Ziegfeld's Follies.'"[44]

While in Tokyo, Rogers met with the Soviet ambassador to Japan, Alexander Troyanovsky.[45] Rogers was not sure whether he would travel through the Soviet Union on the trip but needed the ambassador's permission if he decided to do so. He also wanted to learn what the Soviet Union's intentions were in Manchuria, as Soviet troops were massing on the other side of the Chinese border. A war between the Soviet Union and Japan would be far more serious than the current hostilities between Japan and China.

On the morning of December 7, Rogers left Tokyo in a Fokker triplane, arriving in Osaka late in the afternoon in time to tour the ancient city's theater district. He left the next morning and flew across the Sea of Japan to Seoul, Korea, where he spent the night. On December 9, Rogers landed in Dairen, Manchuria, then took the train to Mukden, the Manchurian capital.

Mukden, a good-sized city of four hundred thousand, was the scene of a train explosion that had ignited the Japanese invasion. The Japanese blamed Chinese Nationalists for dynamiting a section of railway track and used the explosion as the reason to march into Manchuria. The Chinese claimed that the Japanese committed the act as a ruse to invade.

When Rogers stepped off the train, he noticed dozens of heavily armed Japanese soldiers dressed in khaki uniforms and red-banded hats standing guard around the station. The Chinese army had fled the city, but some fighting still broke out. The Japanese military declared martial law throughout the city, commandeered government offices, railways, telegraphs, banks, and major Chinese industries, and plundered the homes of wealthy Chinese. The Japanese army soon impressed Rogers. "Don't you let anyone tell you these little Japanese are not Soldiers," he wrote. "They fight, and will be hard to lick."[46]

Trudging about the snow-covered ancient city, Rogers visited the walled fortress and the palace once used by the Qing Dynasty in the 1600s. He explored narrow alleys filled with curio shops, fur stores, and open-air food stalls serving things he never imagined could be eaten. He stayed at Mukden's Yamato Hotel along with a large group of journalists, diplomats, Japanese military officers, and others wanting to catch the first glimpse of war. According to one war correspondent, the Yamato was "one of the greatest rumor factories in the world."[47] Journalists raced around the city trying to outdo each other and scoop the next story. William Randolph Hearst cabled his correspondent in Mukden a promise of $1,000 for the first story of shots between Japanese and Russian troops.[48]

Of all of the correspondents there, Rogers puzzled the Japanese intelligence officers the most. Like their fellow officers in Tokyo, they were not sure why he was in Manchuria and probably suspected he was there for a more serious reason than writing his columns. Japanese military officers tightly censored the newsmen in Mukden, including China experts Edgar Snow,

John Powell, Hallett Abend, and Frederick Kuh, but they were most befuddled by Rogers.[49] The censors "were cranky as goats" and did not understand his humor or his rustic writing style.[50] The Japanese delayed for several hours one column after Rogers wrote: "League of Nations is sending here a commission to look over the ground. That's like a sheriff examining the stall after the horse has disappeared."[51] They took his article to various American correspondents trying to get an explanation, one of them saying afterward that "it required considerable diagramming before the Japanese military censors and staff officers could understand that!"[52]

Nevertheless, Rogers ignored the censors and described the Japanese disparagingly. From Mukden he wrote: "These Japanese! Now, here is something I better tell you right off the reel: Don't ever call a Japanese a 'Jap.' Now, I dident know that till I got over here; I just thought it was like Englishmen calling us "Yanks"; . . . But this Jap business is a serious matter with them. . . . Then, too, the word 'Jap' is short, and they are very sensitive about their size anyhow, and 'Jap' makes 'em sound shorter still."[53]

Rogers then traveled farther north, crossing the front lines to the Chinese-held city of Harbin, Manchuria, near the Siberian border. When he arrived the temperature was 32 degrees below zero, so cold that "Vodka is not a beverage, but a necessity."[54] In Harbin, Rogers met with General Ma Zhanshan, the commander of the Chinese forces making the last stand against the Japanese. Rogers was impressed with the general's determination. Ma had a hardened army of tough-looking Manchurians, each dressed in uniforms padded so thick they could hardly move, but they proved incapable of stopping the invasion.[55] The Chinese army still controlled Harbin when Rogers arrived, but the city fell to the Japanese a month after he departed. General Ma then retreated into Russia.

Harbin had the feel of old Russia, with onion-domed churches and black-bearded Cossacks driving droshkies along wide, cobbled streets. Besides the Chinese, the city was the home of many White Russians who had escaped the Bolsheviks during the revolution. The city was a melting pot of oriental and occidental cultures, with almost every nationality in the world seeming to have settled there. The American consul, George Hanson, gave Rogers an insider's view of the fascinating city, wearing him out with an all-night tour of Harbin's dingy bars, coffee houses, and sadly exotic cabarets.

Despite Hanson's attempt to show the humorist a good time, Rogers found Harbin to be a cheerless city riddled with vice. "It's not lively, it's not amusing, it's just depressing," he wrote. He was most appalled when he learned that thousands of young, beautiful Russian girls were exploited as prostitutes. In a *Saturday Evening Post* article, Rogers departed from his customary humor to bluntly deplore the harlotry in Harbin. He also revealed a rather strong racial prejudice when he described the white Russian girls plying their trade:

> These Girls, simply to eat have had to live under the most degrading circumstances—at the mercy of the lowest class of every race of people under the sun.
>
> There is nothing happened during our generation that has done more to lower the standing of the White Race than what has taken place right here in this Town and all Manchuria and China. Years ago, the White Man had a standing, especially Social, that put him apart. But since these thousands of white Women have been, for the sake of their very existence, thrown at the feet of people who, before this time, couldent have even spoken to them. . . .
> "Why it is that you don't do more to protect your White Women?"[56]

Rogers returned to Mukden, where he planned to take the train to Peking. When he learned that the train was the frequent target of bandits who robbed and kidnapped wealthy passengers, he decided to go to the port of Dairen on the Yellow Sea where he took a boat to Tientsin. He regretted the decision, as the boat was "just six inches longer than a Ford" and barely weathered a vicious storm.[57] From Tientsin he traveled to Peking by train, as a heavy snowstorm grounded all planes.

In Peking, Rogers met for several hours with Marshal Zhang Xueliang, the warlord of Manchuria who retreated when the Japanese invaded his territory. Xueliang had controlled the region since 1928, when the Japanese assassinated the former warlord, his father Zhang Zuolin. Rogers found the marshal to speak good English and "a very pleasant young fellow. . . . One thing you got to say about these Chinese. They are good losers. There is no yapping or excuses. . . . He thinks that China will eventually absorb the Japanese the same as they absorbed the Mongolians who captured China so much they got tired."[58]

According to one journalist, Xueliang was a "broken down skeleton of a man, addicted to enormous quantities of opium."[59] Nevertheless Rogers seemed impressed with the young warlord, writing that he "has put more progressive things into Manchuria than all the others proceeding him put together, or anywhere else in China."[60]

———

WILL ROGERS arrived in Shanghai on Christmas day, "the first one I had ever spent away from my Family since committing the Overt Act."[61] He spent the next five days lonely, cold, and homesick. "I didn't know that Christmas did mean so much till you have to spend one away off like this from home."[62]

China was in turmoil when Rogers arrived in Shanghai that winter of 1931. Over the past six years disorder throughout the country had escalated into a long civil war between Nationalists and Communists. The recent invasion of Manchuria by the Japanese only served to increase the bitter internal conflicts. Outsiders were no longer welcome, as popular resentment against foreigners led to several violent, deadly demonstrations; antiforeign attacks continued to occur against missionaries, Christian churches, and schools, and rioters looted both the U.S. and British consulates. The raging civil war led to more foreign military intervention, including a thousand U.S. Marines who landed to protect American property and American and British gunboats stationed near the Chinese capital of Nanking.

In Shanghai, Rogers found time to gather his thoughts about China, a country he found fascinating, confusing, and sadly beautiful. Holed up alone in the Cathay Hotel, he pored through issues of the *Far Eastern Review* and *China Digest*, scribbling notes in the margins about Chinese history, culture, and philosophy.[63] While there he wrote several feature articles for the *Saturday Evening Post* that were in many ways the best and most penetrating he ever produced. He described a Chinese culture that was not just one nationality but a widely diverse mix of races that spoke dozens of languages and dialects. He tried to put himself in Chinese shoes, to understand why there was such a strong antiforeigner undercurrent in Chinese society. He expressed high regard for the Chinese people and their veneration for family life in a society where generation after generation lived under the same roof, but was appalled at the widespread, wretched poverty of the peasantry, many of whom lived in trembling straw lean-tos that were scarcely larger than dog kennels. He concluded that "the last man that knew the Chinese was Confucius, and he died feeling that he was becoming a little confused about 'em."[64]

Rogers always disapproved of the way the world, including the United States, treated China. "Why, they forgot more about living than we will ever know."[65] He strongly opposed any foreign intervention, writing: "Every nation in the World has always felt privileged to dictate some particular policy to China. . . . They all grabbed off territory in China for what they termed as a Coaling Station, or Eastern Naval Base, always claiming it was necessary for their protection. They gobbled up Hong Kong entirely. A Chinaman himself can't get into Hong Kong without a passport."[66]

Rogers also disagreed with sending missionaries to tell other countries what to believe: "What we ought to do is import some Chinese missionaries from over there to come and show us, not how to be saved but how to raise something every year on our land. We just got the missionary business turned around. We are the ones that need converting more than they do."[67]

Rogers wanted to visit Pearl Buck while in China, but bad weather kept him from flying to her home in Nanking. Six months later he spent several hours with the novelist, whose *The Good Earth* he admired greatly, when they both passed through New York City. Buck agreed with him on missionaries in China. "She claims they send the wrong ones, the one who couldent make a living here," he wrote. "She claims a dumb missionary hasent any more business in China than he has [in America], in fact not as much."[68]

Rogers criticized a Chinese government that was riddled with graft, corruption, and nepotism. But he also saw an energetic China whose economy was fundamentally capitalist and based on free trade. "All this open-door stuff is a lot of hooey. Any door is only open to those that have the best product at the cheapest money."[69] He described the Chinese as the best merchants in the world for centuries, who would continue to be so in the distant future: "And don't waste too much pity on Poor Old China; she will be here when some strange Race of people will be excavating some of our Skyscrapers and wondering what Tombs they were. There is none of us that don't feel that China will be here five thousand years from now, and none of us are sure that other Nations will be here through the life of two more flivvers."[70]

Years before it occurred, Rogers predicted that China, despite then being militarily weak, would become one of the most powerful countries in the world. "Nobody is going to take China. . . . You could move the whole of Japan's seventy millions into the very heart of China, and in seventy years there wouldn't be seventy Japanese left."[71]

ON DECEMBER 30, 1931, Will Rogers boarded the SS *President Taft* in Shanghai, spending New Year's Eve at sea heading for Hong Kong. He arrived there late and missed his connection to Manila, disappointed that he was not able to "go by and set the Philippines free."[72] Quickly changing his plans, he sailed to Singapore, then to Bangkok, and on to Penang, Malaysia. There he boarded a KLM Fokker on January 10 to begin a nine-day odyssey on "the longest airplane route in the world from Java to Amsterdam Ten thousand miles with the same pilot, same crew, same plane all the way."[73] He stopped in Karachi, Pakistan, followed by an unscheduled stop in Allahabad, India, when the plane broke a piston. He crossed Persia in the morning, with the pilot flying low across the fertile valley between the Tigris and Euphrates rivers. In Cairo he visited Jerusalem, the Dead Sea, and Bethlehem. He spent the night in Athens where he met with Greek premier Eleutherios Venizelos. After a stop in Rome he arrived in Paris on January 19, 1932. A week later he was in Southampton where he met Betty, who had arrived from America aboard the *Bremen*.

Will and Betty flew to Geneva on February 1, where he attended the latest disarmament conference. Before he departed he wired from Paris for the State Department to not "send delegates with hardened arteries, as usual, but get some with hardened hearts."[74] Rogers saw little hope in the conference, saying that "there is nothing to prevent their succeeding now but human nature."[75] Will and Betty then boarded the SS *Europa* in Cherbourg and headed for New York. Having been gone for twenty weeks, he was eager to get home. "If this boat don't hurry up and get in, I will be too late to vote for Al [Smith]."[76]

As soon as he arrived in New York City, Rogers flew immediately to Washington DC, where he appropriated the huge office of his friend and new Speaker of the House, Jack Garner. There he received scores of congressmen and briefed the leadership, including Senator Bill Borah, on what he had observed during his round-the-world junket. He headed to the White House early the next day, where he spent several hours with President Hoover and

Secretary of War Hurley, discussing "serious matters" that included his Far East observations. Afterward they talked about the nation's economy.[77] "We fixed up all the affairs of the world," Rogers told reporters when he left the White House. "I think we got the situation in China in pretty good shape now if Secretary Stimson don't start it again."

During his White House visit Rogers also discussed with the president a variety of domestic issues, including the widespread unemployment plaguing the country and what to do about it. "The only thing we didn't take up was Al Smith and Huey Long," Rogers said. "We agreed to take them up later."[78] At the time the Senate was debating the Costigan–La Follette bill, a $500 million federal relief program for direct aid to the unemployed. Rogers favored the bill, Hoover opposed it, and a week later the Senate killed the measure. After a trip to New York City where he met with Al Smith, Rogers returned to the nation's capital for meetings at the War and State departments, including a private session with Secretary of State Stimson. That night he took a break with Betty, the two of them enjoying Ziegfeld's musical revue *Hot-Cha*, with its lavish sets and leggy showgirls.

BY THE TIME he returned from his latest round-the-world expedition, Will Rogers was a recognized authority on foreign affairs. *Life* magazine noted Rogers's far-reaching expertise: "Will Rogers has seen something of the world. He knows more about our foreign relations than do all the eighteen august members of the Senatorial Foreign Relations Committee. He was famous as an Ambassador of Good Will when Lindbergh was still toting mail between St. Louis and Chicago."[79]

While most Americans were not aware of Rogers's new role and still regarded him as a witty political commentator, there were powerful government officials who knew that when he spoke about world events, they should listen. These included the men who made U.S. foreign policy, such as Hoover, Stimson, Hurley, Borah, and Garner. Policy makers now listened to Rogers not only because he brought them keen observations of other countries but because he was well qualified to judge the intentions of foreign governments and their leaders. Unlike most so-called political experts and academics, Rogers had actually *been* to the countries he spoke or wrote about, and had met their top leaders as well as their common folk. He knew people and was

*Rogers reads a
studio gag of his
fame*

an excellent judge of character, as when he met with various Japanese officials to gauge their aggressive intentions in the Far East, or in 1926 when he concluded that the Prince of Wales did not really want to be king, ten years before the prince actually abdicated.

Well aware of Rogers's reputation, embassy officials around the world bent over backward to provide him access to people and places otherwise denied to diplomats and journalists. Rogers had little difficulty obtaining an audience with a Japanese minister of war, a Manchurian warlord, or an Italian dictator. An intense observer of human nature and society, Rogers had a deep understanding of the cultures of the foreign countries he visited. Few had a better understanding of the Chinese conundrum and the complexity of the Far East. He was not a military expert, but he knew the difference between crack Japanese troops and ragtag Chinese conscripts. While not a pilot himself, he was an authority on civil and military aviation and could recognize how well trained were foreign aviators and how technologically advanced were their aircraft.

This was neither the first time nor the last that government officials used

Rogers as a surrogate. Presidents Wilson, Harding, Coolidge, and Hoover all recognized his ability to sway public opinion, and each of them, in their own way, turned to him to help their cause. Increasingly Rogers was recognized as someone who could serve a very useful public purpose while still appearing to be a harmless, humorous entertainer. Rogers's fellow passenger on the *Empress of Russia*, the insightful beekeeper George Riedel, saw through Rogers's comedic façade, believing he was traveling around the world with a much more serious and quasi-official purpose than just gathering funny anecdotes.

Secretary of War Patrick Hurley, also aware of the humorist's value, undoubtedly insisted that Rogers travel to the Far East to gather information about a conflict that not only puzzled most Americans but baffled policy makers and intelligence experts as well. Rogers provided another set of sharp eyes and keen ears for the U.S. government. He may not have traveled in an official capacity, but his observations were of no less value to American leaders. A year after Rogers returned from the Far East, a new president would, more so than any in the past, recognize the powerful influence that he exerted. Franklin Roosevelt would not only turn to him to sway public opinion but encourage him to take on more ambitious ventures to observe the international situation and to report back to the White House.

Back in the United States, Rogers shifted his attention from a foreign war zone to a pitched battle on the domestic political scene. By the summer of 1932, with the campaign for the presidency heating up, Rogers again found himself in the political fray, not just as a humorous commentator but, increasingly, as a partisan participant.

ELEVEN

No Longer an Impartial Observer

A S THE SUMMER OF 1932 approached, Will Rogers looked forward to the upcoming party conventions and the presidential election the following fall. He may have joked that "our national politival [*sic*] conventions are glorified Mickey Mouse affairs," but he also realized they were serious affairs that determined the country's political future.[1] The Republican Convention threatened to be another anticlimax, as everyone expected Herbert Hoover to be nominated to run again. Rogers arrived in Chicago on June 12, 1932, where three days later delegates overwhelmingly nominated Hoover. The only controversy was whether or not to renominate Vice President Charles Curtis, considered by some Republicans to be too old, dry, and dull to run again. In hopes of strengthening the Hoover ticket, party leaders pushed other candidates forward and advised Curtis not to seek reelection and instead to consider running for the Senate. A one-eighth Kaw Indian, Curtis was a good friend of Rogers. "I am strong for Charley," Rogers wrote, "because he's an Injun and he is close enough to Oklahoma to understand the farmers' problem."[2]

Soon after learning of the movement to dump Curtis, Rogers jumped to his friend's defense, calling him in his Capitol office to offer support, working behind the scenes to gather votes, and launching sharp attacks on those who tried to oust him. When Curtis won renomination after a heated fight, Rogers took some credit for his success. "And say, I saved my 'Injun' Charley Curtis for vice presidency. The rascals was just ready to stab him when we caught 'em."[3] A week after the convention Curtis wrote Rogers, thanking him for "sounding the alarm in your article. It was of great assistance as it brought a number of wires to me and caused quite a number to be sent to delegates at the convention."[4]

While the Republican Convention offered little excitement with Hoover's renomination, the race for the Democratic nomination was a different story. Also held in Chicago, the 1932 convention loomed as another of the party's legendary donnybrooks.

Three strong candidates were running—John Nance Garner, Al Smith, and Franklin Roosevelt. Rogers was torn between them, as each was a good friend. They roughly represented three competing factions of the Democratic Party. Of them, the darkest horse was Garner, the Speaker of the House from Texas who had the support of William Randolph Hearst and Senator William McAdoo. Garner never bothered to campaign and his chance at winning the nomination was slim, but the faction supporting him controlled enough delegates to break a deadlock between Smith and Roosevelt. Writing in May, Rogers knew the Democratic nomination remained undecided: "Al Smith's big spurt in the East has shown that Governor Roosevelt can't possibly go to the convention with enough to nominate. Give Garner California and Texas and he will be sitting prettier than any of the three, for there is one thing about a Smith delegate, he is sure loyal to Smith, and won't go for anyone else at the finish only who Smith tells 'em to."[5]

Rogers adored Al Smith, the loser in the 1928 presidential race. Of the three candidates, Smith most closely shared Rogers's political philosophy. While the two came from very different backgrounds, they had similar personalities and loved people, humor, and politics. Smith was supported by the Tammany Hall machine in New York City and important members of the Democratic National Committee. The third candidate, Franklin Roosevelt, was steadily building the support of a solid majority of delegates. He had the backing of Senators Burton Wheeler, Cordell Hull, Alben Barkley, and Huey Long, who held the Deep South. This new Democratic coalition would unite at the convention, allowing Roosevelt to bring into the Democratic fold west-

*Rogers arriving at the
1932 Democratic
Convention*

ern progressives, ethnic minorities, rural farmers, and intellectuals. While
Rogers was not as close to Roosevelt as he was to Garner and Smith, the two
had met, corresponded several times, and had already built a strong admiration for each other.

Franklin Roosevelt, probably better than the other candidates, recognized
the value of gaining Rogers's support and courted him aggressively. The correspondence between Rogers and Roosevelt prior to the convention reveals
not only a growing friendship but Roosevelt's desire to have the influential
columnist in his corner. At times Roosevelt bordered on obsequiousness as he

sought Rogers's favor. In April 1931, for example, Roosevelt wrote Rogers after seeing one of his films:

> *By the grace of the movie people we had a special showing of the "Connecticut Yankee" at the Mansion the other night and I want to send you this line to tell you how much I liked it and especially the part you take in it. . . .*
>
> *Some of these days when you are proceeding to or from New York on a plebeian train do please stop off in Albany and come and talk to me of cabbages and Kings! I want to see you, Oh, most excellent of philosophers!*
>
>

Very sincerely yours,
Franklin D Roosevelt.[6]

Roosevelt must have chuckled when, in the film, King Arthur asks Rogers if he is a magician. "I'm just a Democrat," the humorist replies. "But maybe I could do a few little tricks. Where I come from nowadays you pretty near got to be a magician to make a living."[7]

Rogers also confided in the New York governor, writing him two months later to offer his thoughts about the next presidential election:

> *If people in 32 are still as hungry as they are now, and from the looks of things they will be "Hungrier," why the Democrats have got a fine chance, They only vote for our Gang when they are starved out, we fatten 'em up then they turn Republicans again, If I get east anyways soon, I am coming up to see you, from what I hear, you seem to be keeping impeachment from the door, thats harder to stave off than the wolf nowadays with most Governors. Well good luck to you, and Mrs Roosevelt, and your troop.*
>
> *Meet you at the convention anyhow, Looks like Reno will get the next one. . . .*[8]

In May 1932 Roosevelt invited Rogers to visit him at his retreat in Warm Springs, Georgia, but Rogers was on the Fox set working on the film *Down to Earth* and could not go. He telegraphed Roosevelt from Beverly Hills, saying, "under Hoover you cant leave home for fear they will foreclose on it but I am hoping to see you at the Democratic jubilee." Rogers's remark came as foreclosures threatened the homes of millions of Americans because of the failed economy and the collapse of the banking system. By 1933 the rate of foreclosures reached one thousand a day, and more than two-fifths of all residential loans defaulted.[9]

A month later and only four weeks before the convention, a concerned Roosevelt wrote Rogers to keep him out of the race. While Rogers never took rumors of his running for office seriously, the shrewd Roosevelt was not one to take any chances. He could not allow a dark horse like Rogers to enter the political arena and siphon off even a few delegates. "Don't forget you are a Democrat by birth, training and tough experience," Roosevelt wrote, "and I know you won't get mixed in any fool movement to make the good old Donkey chase his own tail and give the Elephant a chance to win the race."[10]

Rogers flew to Chicago on Monday, June 27, 1932, in time to observe the opening ceremony, the last he was to attend. His wealthy Texas friend Amon Carter,[11] seeking support for John Nance Garner, tried to persuade him to make the trip on a special train for Garner, writing, "your presence on this train will be tremendous value to our cause."[12] Having to stay in California filming, Rogers took a plane at the last minute. Nevertheless, he stood behind "Cactus Jack" during the early balloting. When Senator Tom Connally nominated Garner for president, more than a thousand marchers paraded through the aisles. Leaping down the steps from the press box, Rogers joined them, yelling Indian war whoops and waving the Oklahoma flag as he marched around the convention floor.[13]

On the third day of the convention, Rogers took the rostrum and spoke for twenty minutes to the twenty thousand delegates. The mood was gloomy, for the day before the Dow Jones Industrial Average fell to 41 points, its lowest during the Depression. Sensing this was no time for jokes, Rogers gave the conventioneers some serious advice, calling for party unity and a solid platform. "I'm going to stand here and act a fool until the Democratic party agrees on prohibition," he said. "I'll be here from now on. As soon as they can get enough of the platform committee sober enough they will turn in a platform." As he continued, Rogers abandoned his prepared remarks and persistently lectured the delegates:

> Now, you rascals, I want you to promise me one thing. . . . No matter who is
> nominated, . . . don't go home and act like Democrats. Go home and act like

Rogers with Eleanor Roosevelt and Amon Carter

he was the man you came to see nominated. Don't say he is the weakest man you could have nominated; don't say he can't win. You don't know what he can do, or how weak he is until next November. I don't see how he could ever be weak enough not to win. If he lives until November he's in.[14]

The crowd went wild when Rogers finished, giving him such a raucous standing ovation that several of Roosevelt's backers became uneasy. "They fear it will wind up with Will being nominated for President," Damon Runyon wrote, "but they may calm their fears. Will wouldn't accept. He makes more money at his own racket." Heywood Broun was also struck by Rogers's speech, writing, "It seems a little ironical that the same Convention which thinks Will Rogers is a clown accepts Huey Long as a statesman."[15] That night, Carl Sandburg invited Rogers to his room, where, along with Groucho Marx, they all spent the wee hours of the night playing guitars and singing ridiculous songs.[16]

When the balloting began on July 1, delegates nominated their favorite sons as the front-runners jockeyed for votes. On the second ballot Oklahoma cast all twenty-two votes for Rogers.[17] "I was sitting there in the press stand asleep and wasn't bothering a soul when they woke me up and said Oklahoma had started me on the way to the White House."[18]

Roosevelt remained the front-runner, but he still needed to overcome serious opposition. Chicago mayor Anton Cermak packed the hall with Smith supporters, but Rogers knew that Smith was losing headway. Several popular columnists, including Rogers, Walter Lippmann, H. L. Mencken, and Heywood Broun, all favored Smith and helped slow Roosevelt's momentum.[19] Political maneuvering became intense as Roosevelt supporters tried to break the deadlock. Clare Boothe Luce, the politically active writer, worked behind the scenes for Roosevelt trying to gain the support of several important Democrats, including Rogers, Josephus Daniels, New York mayor Jimmy Walker, and James Forrestal.[20]

The stalemate lingered for several days until Joseph Kennedy, then a leading Democrat and Roosevelt supporter, made a late-night call to Hearst saying that if the convention continued in the same way, Al Smith or progressive Newton Baker would be nominated, two people that the conservative Hearst detested. After Kennedy's call, Hearst convinced Garner to bow out of the race and support Roosevelt. When McAdoo learned of this, he threw California's delegates to Roosevelt. The other states fell in line, and, on the fourth ballot, Roosevelt swept past Smith, 945 to 190, to capture the nomination. As Roosevelt's running mate the delegates chose John Nance Garner, who supposedly said that the vice presidency was not worth a bucket of warm spit.

On Valentine's Day, 1932, Will and Betty Rogers drove into the rural Sourland Mountains of New Jersey to spend the day with Charles and Anne Lindbergh. As soon as they arrived they fell for the Lindbergh's twenty-month-old son, Charles, Jr. Totally smitten, Rogers noted the baby had "his father's blonde curly hair. . . . It's almost golden and all in little curls. His face is more of his mother's. He has her eyes exactly."[21] For an hour that afternoon, Will, Betty, Charles, and Anne sprawled on the floor of the sun parlor playing blocks with the toddler.

Four days later, Rogers headed west to California. On his way he stopped in Detroit to visit with Henry Ford,[22] who "drove me around in everything he had."[23] The millionaire automaker was one of the first of many public figures Rogers ridiculed on the stage. Ford was very touchy when criticized by the press but surprisingly took no offense at Rogers's cracks and accepted his comments because they were not only couched in humor but based on fact. Ford never interpreted Rogers's remarks to be a personal attack, and the two men became close friends. Describing Ford as another Brigham Young who "originated of mass production,"[24] Rogers greatly admired the industrialist for proving he could "pay the highest wages, gives everybody a square deal and still wind up being the richest man in the world."[25] In June 1930 he devoted an entire radio broadcast praising Ford:

> I like him because he sees more music in an old-time fiddler than he does in a long-haired one with a foreign name. He has caused more dirty dishes to be left in the sink after supper than all the leading men on the screen put together. He has broken more wrists than all the osteopaths combined. He has caused more profanity than a Senate investigation. He has given more value for the least money. . . .
>
> He is a great old fellow and he is very, very human. I always liked Mr. Ford. I think he is a great man, and I wish we had a lot more like him.[26]

Though Rogers admired Ford, he didn't hesitate to criticize the automaker's outspoken bigotry and anti-Semitism, concluding that Ford's hatred of Jews and Catholics was morally wrong and writing, "Uncle Henry may not be packing a full head of facts on past historical events."[27] When Ford apologized for anti-Semitic remarks he made in the *Dearborn Independent,* Rogers remarked half seriously that Ford "used to have it in for the Jewish people until he saw them in Chevrolets, and then he said, 'Boys, I am all wrong.'"[28] Rogers summed up his mixed feelings for Ford later when he said, "It will take us a hundred years to tell whether he helped us or hurt us, but he certainly didn't leave us where he found us."[29]

From Detroit, Rogers traveled to Chicago, which he reveals "is located just north of the United States. I am well acquainted with the American consul there."[30] While there he interviewed Al Capone, spending two hours with the jailed gangster who was serving an eleven-year prison sentence for tax evasion. Rogers, however, did not mention the interview in his next columns, not wanting to make Capone any more of a celebrity than he already was. Rogers had finally met a man he *didn't* like.

On March 1, two weeks after the Capone interview and not long after Rogers's visit with the Lindbergh family in New Jersey, an intruder entered the aviator's second-floor nursery and kidnapped the Lindbergh baby from his crib. Along with the rest of the country, Rogers was devastated. "What a shock to everybody," he wrote. "I wish we had taken him home with us and kept him."[31] The Lindbergh kidnapping was the crime of the century, pitching the nation into a media frenzy as police searched for the baby. "Did you ever see such a day?" Rogers wrote. "Nobody don't feel like doing anything, taking any interest in anything. The attention of the world is on a little curly haired baby. Till he is found we can't get back to normal."[32]

Soon after, newspapers nationwide carried a sensational, headline-screaming interview with Al Capone by Arthur Brisbane, one of the nation's leading newspaper columnists and a good friend of Rogers. Capone told Brisbane he would offer a reward for information leading to the recovery of the Lindbergh baby and would use his underworld connections to locate the child. He offered to post bond and conduct the hunt accompanied by a federal agent. Coming within days of the kidnapping, the interview upset Rogers. In his next column he sharply criticized Brisbane for demonstrating the difference between "a good reporter and a punk one." Rogers seldom showed so much anger in his writings, rarely criticizing another journalist personally, but this time he did not hold back:

> Two weeks ago I had two hours with Al Capone. (That raises Arthur one hour.) He told me all that I read today that he told Mr. Brisbane and more. But there was absolutely no way I could write it and not make a hero out of him, and even as superb a writer as Mr. Brisbane couldn't either. Everybody you talk to would rather hear about Capone than anybody you ever met. What's the matter with an age when our biggest gangster is our greatest national interest? Part is the government's fault for not convicting him on some real crime. Now will somebody please suggest what to do with the story I got bottled up with me and be fair to everybody.[33]

Eleven days after the baby was kidnapped, police found the child's murdered body five miles from the Lindbergh home.

Charles and Anne Lindbergh later sought refuge from the relentlessly hounding press, flying to California where they secluded themselves at the Rogers ranch in Santa Monica. Afterward Anne wrote Betty to thank her, saying, "Perhaps Charles and I appreciated the place especially because it was so quiet and far away and protected," and adding that she and her husband had felt completely private and free.[34] The Lindberghs left California by plane when New Jersey state police informed them they had arrested the alleged kidnaper, Bruno Hauptmann. Hauptmann was convicted and executed in 1936.

Rogers worried the murder would affect his friend Charles Lindbergh, wondering whether the aviator continued to take pride in America. "Will it make him still proud that he did it for them?" Rogers asked his readers. "Or in his loneliness will it allow a thought to creep into his mind that it might have been different if he had flown the ocean under somebody's colors with a real obligation to law and order?"[35]

BY THE SPRING OF 1932, twelve million American workers were jobless, including a thirty-four-year-old cannery worker from Portland, Oregon, named Walter Waters. An aggressive ex-sergeant who had served overseas in the 146th Field Artillery, Waters was fed up with being in the bread line and decided to do something about it. He hatched a plan to lead three hundred World War I veterans from the Pacific Northwest to the nation's capital where they were determined to collect a bonus for their service in the war. Waters believed his "bonus march" might spur the passage of a bill being debated in Congress calling for the immediate payment of a World War I veterans' bonus. The original bill, passed in 1924, called for the money to be paid in 1945, with each veteran receiving $1.25 for every day overseas. The veterans felt the advance payment of a few hundred dollars would be more useful to them alive in 1932 than dead in 1945.[36]

As Waters and his ragtag bonus marchers made their eighteen-day trek toward Washington, other jobless veterans started drifting into the capital. Within a few weeks their ranks swelled to twenty thousand marchers. By the middle of that summer and while the Republican and Democratic conventions were held in Chicago and the Olympics were about to begin in Los Angeles, a huge shack city had sprung up on the mud flats along the Anacostia River within sight of the Capitol.

The bonus marchers had little support in Washington. President Hoover, who claimed to be "so tired that every bone in my body aches," was overwhelmed with the deepening Depression and a hostile Congress. He refused to meet with any of the marchers, as did most legislators and War Department officials. Rogers's friend and fellow columnist H. L. Mencken opposed the veterans, describing their fight for a bonus as a "bold and shameless effort to loot the public treasury for the benefit of professional heroes of the war, three-fourths of whom never heard a shot fired in anger."[37] Will Rogers, however, sympathized with them and believed they deserved the bonus. "I think the best insurance in the world against another war is to take care of the boys who fought in the last one," he wrote. "YOU MAY WANT TO USE THEM AGAIN."[38] In December 1923, when Congress debated the first bonus bill, Rogers had proposed a bonus financed by taxing tax-exempt securities. He visited Harding in the White House to discuss his plan, but the president took no action and vetoed the first bonus bill, as did Coolidge afterward.

As Rogers continued to plead for a veterans' bonus, some Republican congressmen and other critics complained that his writings and speeches interfered with legislative affairs. Newspapers across the country also attacked him, a *New York Times* editor writing, "when Will Rogers suggests a plan for the payment of the soldiers bonus by taking it out of the profits made by people during the last war, he is simply stimulating the ill feelings always being fostered by some of the politicians."[39]

Ignoring the critics, Rogers did not let up, attacking both Congress and the White House for breaking its promise to the veterans: "We promised them EVERYTHING and all they got was $1.25 a day and some knitted sweaters and sox. And after examining them, they wore the sox for sweaters and the sweaters for sox."[40] Again he suggested the way to pay for the bonus was to levy a tax on tax-exempt bonds, prompting sympathetic congressmen to enter his columns supporting the bonus into the *Congressional Record.*[41]

Rogers favored the bonus for the veterans, but he was less supportive of their march on Washington. Again, he feared any sort of disorder or chaos, and a demonstration by twenty thousand unemployed men made him nervous. Nevertheless, he defended their right to come to Washington, writing, "They have the same right there as any other 'lobbyist.' They at least were not paid."[42] He also felt sorry for the bonus army; watching the bedraggled veterans trudge through Washington may have reminded him of the Trail of

Tears when his ancestor Cherokees were forcibly uprooted to the West. Over time, the marchers earned Rogers's respect: "They hold the record for being the best behaved of any fifteen thousand hungry men ever assembled anywhere in the world. They were hungry, and they were seeing our government wasting thousands and millions before their eyes, and yet they remained fair and sensible."[43]

On June 17, 1932, the House of Representatives passed the bonus bill, but the Senate killed it, 62–18. The marchers refused to return home. Eleven days later, after President Hoover ordered the army to remove the veterans from their tent camps, General Douglas MacArthur led fifteen hundred infantry troops carrying rifles with fixed bayonets plus the Third Cavalry Regiment under Major George Patton onto the Anacostia flats. As MacArthur's troops burned the camps and clashed with the marchers, hundreds of veterans were injured and several killed.

Pictures of the bloodshed were blazoned across the front pages of the nation's papers. The American people were disgusted by the sight of U.S. armed soldiers confronting poor unemployed veterans of the recent Great War. Rogers too was appalled: "Wouldent Mr. Hoover had come out here and opened those [Olympic] games like he should have done he would have not been in Washington during that mess they had, in fact they wouldn't have had it. What made it look so bad was the army going in with tanks and full war equipment."[44]

Both the press and the public rebuked Hoover for the severity of his actions. By the time the last bonus marcher had returned home, the image of a heartless president and an unsympathetic Republican government was set firmly in place.

"OUR WORLD OF 'make believe' is sad," Will Rogers wrote in July 1932. "Scores of comedians are not funny, hundreds of 'America's most beautiful girls' are not gay." Rogers, along with the rest of the entertainment industry, was stricken over the loss of Florenz Ziegfeld, who passed away at the age of sixty-five after a long illness with pleurisy.[45]

Rogers revered Ziegfeld, the man who more than anyone else was responsible for his early and meteoric success as an entertainer. The two men remained close friends, even after the *Follies* folded and after Ziegfeld lost

Florenz Ziegfeld

everything in the stock market. Despite failing health and mounting debts, Ziegfeld, who Rogers said "brought beauty into the entertainment world," continued to visit Will years later, always showing up at the ranch dressed immaculately in riding habit.[46]

Rogers personally planned and paid for the funeral arrangements. When he delivered the eulogy, written on the back of a blank telegram, he brought the huge crowd in the Hollywood cemetery to tears:[47]

> this is the first time that i have ever appeared as a witness before the court
>> of the lord. i have no credentials, i am not an [accredited] witness, i am
>> just [an] ex hired hand that wants to speak a few words for our "boss" . . .
> our [profession] of acting must be honorable and it must be necessary for it
>> exists in [e]very language and every race. its as old as life itself,
> amusement must be necessary, for its given to babes and [children] to
>> laugh and to play.

in our life the curtain plays a great part,

the curtain either rises or falls, the curtain has fallen for our boss,

  our master.

we stand before our lord to give back all that is mortal of our friend. . . .

among us gathered here, our religious beliefs are many, but one belief is

  universal with all. and that is there is some divine higher than earthly,

  we can speak to him in many devious ways, in many languages, but he

  sees us all in the same light, and judges us according to our actions, as we

  judge the actions of our children different [because] we know they are

  each different.

among all our earthly accomplishments, the greatest is to beautify, for

  beauty speaks no language, beauty appeals to every eye thats put into the

  human head, well certainly our divine being above welcomes back into

  his fold a man who has been on earth and given to it beauty. . . .[48]

Ziegfeld's funeral was an emotional event that brought Rogers's beliefs into the public eye. As Rogers seldom attended church services and kept his religious feelings to himself, his tribute to Ziegfeld was a rare episode when he revealed his deep, inner faith.

"So, goodbye, Flo," he wrote afterward, "save a spot for me, for you will put on a show up there some day that will knock their eyes out."[49]

DURING THE SUMMER OF 1932, the city of Los Angeles hosted the tenth Olympiad. Rogers attended the opening ceremonies and returned several times to enjoy a variety of sporting events. He was impressed with the huge delegation of Japanese athletes who swept the swimming events. "If any country wants to pounce on Japan, now is the time, for every able-bodied Japanese man, woman and child is here to compete in the Olympics."[50]

Fearing that the Depression would damage attendance, Olympic organizers enlisted Hollywood stars, including Will Rogers, to promote the games in a worldwide radio broadcast. Airing from California, Rogers tried to be upbeat, but the sad state of the world economy put an edge on his comments: "Whats the use kidding ourselvs. we are broke, you are broke, the whole world is broke, we are not nearly as 'cocky' in America as we used to be, we are a humble people now, come and see us before we start getting rich again. Never was the world more on an equal. Never was the world as friendly, poverty has made us human, and poverty has made us all kin."[51]

In the fall of 1932, after the Olympics ended and as the presidential election campaign was heating up, Rogers was hit with another attack of his
chronic wanderlust. "I think it's a good time to go," he wrote, and headed to
South America, where "revolutions are thicker down there than Roosevelt
Republicans."[52]

Rogers left California on October 5, arriving in Mexico City two days later.
He spent a night in San Salvador, then went to Honduras and on to Panama.
"Rain? Brother, you never saw rain."[53] Next he flew to Managua, Nicaragua,
where a year before he had visited earthquake victims. He then began a
string of Pan American flights across the equator and down the west coast of
South America, visiting Ecuador, Peru, and then Chile for a stopover in the
remote Tacna-Arica region under dispute by Peru and Chile. Soaking up the
breathtaking panoramas, he flew to Argentina and on to Brazil. "Say, had a
great trip over those Andes Mountains. Our highest altitude was 21,500 feet.
They have oxygen tubes at each seat, but I guess I am so windy anyhow that
I didn't use any."[54]

Arriving in Buenos Aires in time to enjoy a polo match, Rogers then char-
tered an aircraft to take him to the Gran Chaco region, the scene of fighting
between Paraguayan and Bolivian troops, then struggling to capture territory
thought to be rich in oil. The bloody Chaco War would last for the next three
years. In Argentina, Rogers visited the pampas and watched the gauchos, a
reminder of the time he spent there thirty years before. He arrived in Rio de
Janeiro on October 23, a day late after his aircraft had to skirt violent thun-
derstorms. He then headed back to the United States, stopping in Trinidad
and San Juan, where he made a theater appearance for the benefit of sufferers of a hurricane that had devastated the island a month before. After stopping in Miami, he flew to New York where Betty met him. During his first
night there, President Hoover was in the city giving a campaign speech, but
the couple skipped it and went to see the play *Dinner at Eight*.[55]

FRANKLIN ROOSEVELT launched his West Coast campaign for the presidency on Saturday night, September 24, 1932, before sixty thousand cheering
supporters in the Los Angeles Memorial Coliseum.[56] As master of ceremonies, Will Rogers introduced his friend: "I have known you before you was
governor, or even secretary of state, I knew you when you first started in on
your career of nominating Al Smith to office, as a young man you used to

come to the Follies, and I would call on you from the stage to say a few words in appreciation of our show, and you would get up and nominate Al Smith for something."[57]

Rogers's introduction of Roosevelt, along with his twenty-minute speech at the Democratic Convention that summer, marked yet another turning point in his career, for it was a time when he took a clearly partisan role in a political campaign. While he never outwardly opposed Herbert Hoover, he staunchly supported Franklin Roosevelt and, in all of his writings and talks during the 1932 campaign, never wavered in his strong devotion to the New York governor. But it was not just his admiration for Roosevelt that caused Rogers to take a much more active role. Always immersed in politics, he finally succumbed to the excitement of it all, much like the anti-intellectual critic who derides intellectuals for so long that eventually he becomes one himself. While Rogers condemned politicians, he was deeply fascinated by the political process, studying it so closely for years that by 1932 he was swept up and, in more ways than not, became somewhat of a politician himself and definitely part of the process. He could no longer remain an impartial observer.

As Rogers became more partisan, he attracted criticism. In 1932 he was the highest-paid male film star in the world as well as one of America's most successful columnists and radio personalities. But his celebrity, combined with his Democratic political leanings, opened him up to attacks from many pro-Hoover readers. *Los Angeles Times* publisher Harry Chandler jumped to Rogers's defense. Chandler, himself a powerful Republican and Hoover supporter, wrote Rogers to spur him on and tell him to ignore the "weak sisters," those editors who were timid in the face of criticism.[58] Never relenting, Rogers resumed his attack not only on Hoover but Roosevelt as well. On November 1, as the waning campaign became tiresome and bitter, he wrote a column calling for both candidates to go fishing until after the election:

> There should be a moratorium called on candidates' speeches. They have both called each other everything in the world they can think of. From now on they are just talking themselves out of votes.
>
> The high office of the President of the United States has degenerated into two, ordinarily fine men being goaded on by their political leeches into

Rogers introducing Franklin Roosevelt during the 1932 campaign

saying things that if they were in their right minds they wouldn't think of saying. . . .

So you two boys just get the weight of the world off your shoulders and go fishing.[59]

His proposal that the Hoover and Roosevelt stop campaigning caused another spate of criticism, but he remained cynical about the election. "I honestly believe there is people so excited over this election that they think the President has something to do with running this country."[60]

Rogers continued to attract criticism when again he insisted the United States collect the war debts owed by foreign nations. A one-year moratorium was about to expire, and soon after five countries, including France, would default. The Democratic platform of 1932 opposed cancellation of the debt and Roosevelt demanded full payment. So did Rogers, who always opposed the "cancellationists," as he called them. After some senators suggested disarmament be a prerequisite for extending the moratorium on European war debts, Rogers responded tartly.

If I had suggested such a "nut" thing I doubt if even my own papers would have run it, but somebody in official life done it on the level—suggested that England pay us her debts in battleships, that they had more than we have.

Now, can you see England bringing over a couple of big dreadnoughts to us and turning the sailors loose on the "dole?"

Why not Italy pay in Spaghetti and France in perfume and berets?[61]

Rogers's comic exaggeration struck a chord with his friend Senator William Borah, another staunch opponent of debt cancellation. Writing Rogers a few days later, Borah congratulated him on his hard line. "Your communication of October 13, appearing in the *New York Times*, among other papers, is a gem. You state in three paragraphs that which it will take volumes of diplomatic correspondence to conceal."[62]

After Rogers called for repayment, his friend and fellow columnist Walter Lippmann attacked him, claiming he was using incorrect facts. Meanwhile, the *New York Times* received a number of critical letters. "It might improve conditions a bit if Will Rogers took a much-needed long rest," one reader wrote. "By all means bottle up Will Rogers," another wrote. "He is not even funny. Once upon a time when he was a comedian, his comments were witty observations of timely subjects, but since he has begun to take himself seriously, he is a most undesirable columnist." A third reader wrote that if Rogers "will keep away from politics, the international debt question and other matters about which he knows so very little, limiting himself to write about cows and similar subjects, I think it will be a great improvement."[63] A couple of days later the *Times* published Rogers's short, simple response on the debt controversy: "I would suggest they pay, that might silence me." The paper also ran seven more critical and five complimentary letters, with one fan writing, "More power to Will Rogers. He is a rare bird. An unhyphenated American." The *Times* headed them with an editorial that opened sarcastically with, "Anyhow, Will Rogers is read. . . . Let the raw, untutored voices be heard."[64]

The *Times* would not let the issue die. On December 7 it ran an editorial stating Rogers's opinions were his alone and not the editorial views of the paper. Up until then Rogers had held his temper, but the latest slur from the *Times* set him off. He fired off a tongue-in-cheek reply from Beverly Hills for the next day's edition:

*I would like to state to the readers of THE NEW YORK TIMES that
I am in no way responsible for the editorial or political policy of this
paper.*

*I allow them free reign as to their opinion, so long as it is within the
bounds of good subscription gathering.*

*But I want it distinctly understood that their policy may be in direct
contrast to mine.*

Their editorials may be put in purely for humor, or just to fill space.

*Every paper must have its various entertaining features, and their
editorials are not always to be taken seriously, and never to be con-
strued as my policy.*

Yours,
Will Rogers.[65]

Soon after the *Times* rebuttal, Secretary of War of Pat Hurley wrote his
friend Rogers and tried to convince him to stop losing his temper whenever
he was criticized by the press:

*Don't get in any more rows with our friends the pen-pushers. The great
majority of them are clean, conscientious, bright fellows, always anxious to be right. On the other hand, some few of them do not think they
are writing anything unless by doing so they are unjustly injuring
someone. You would get no place in an argument with the latter kind.
You have never in your life intentionally hurt anyone. Your generosity
and kindliness have done as much toward building your splendid reputation as has your wit and humor.*[66]

Rogers ignored Hurley's advice and continued to fire off bitter responses
when criticized. The ruckus over the debt cancellation only served to increase
Rogers's notoriety.

Just after the New Year, Rogers angered the *Times* editors when he criticized the lame-duck Hoover administration for advocating a plan to help the
needy by "percolation," a plan now known as "trickle-down theory." The
theory assumed that by having the government help banks, large industries,
and railroads, eventually prosperity would emerge for small businesses and
individual workers. Rogers argued otherwise:

The Reconstruction Finance Corporation is made up of fine men, honest, and mean well and if it was water they were distributing it would help the people the plan was meant to help. For water goes down hill and moistens everything on its way, but gold or money goes uphill. The Reconstruction loaned the railroads money, medium and small banks money, and all they did with it was pay off what they owed to New York banks. So the money went uphill instead of down. You can drop a bag of gold in Death Valley, which is below sea level, and before Saturday it will be home to papa J. P. [Morgan].[67]

When Rogers sent the column to the *Times*, he received a terse telegram from the paper. "We did not use your piece tonight. We do not carry attackes on character or credit."[68] While the New York paper did not publish the piece, the *Los Angeles Times* and others did.

Rogers was most touchy when people criticized his opinions on foreign affairs. One such incident occurred after the Manchurian crisis when he wrote in his daily column:

After drinking at least two barrels of tea and wanting to be fair, here is about how Manchuria looks to me:

China owns the lot. Japan owns the house that's on it. Now who should have the policemen? China is trying to save its country, Japan is trying to save its investments, and the League of Nations is trying to save its face.

Now somebody has got to lose.[69]

Rogers's comments criticizing the League of Nations and questioning who was going to police the Far East brought immediate criticism from the press, the Hoover administration, and the public. A political science professor at a small college in Washington State told a group of parents and students that Rogers lacked knowledge about foreign affairs, adding that anyone who adopted his thinking risked similar inaccuracy. After the *Pullman Herald* published the professor's remarks, Rogers struck back with a telegram challenging the professor to a debate. "I want to tangle with a guy like that," he wrote. "Why don't these professors lay off me I dont bother them In fact I dont read them why do they read me?"[70]

After one *New York Times* reader asked, "Why does Will Rogers butt into these international problems he knows nothing about?" Rogers shot off a long column defending himself and his ability to discuss foreign affairs:

> Well I have been in almost every country in the last few years. I have talked with prominent men of those countrys, our Ambassadors, or Ministers, and I would have to be pretty dumb to not soak up some information. . . .
>
> If I write about Mexico, I have been down there half a dozen times. Nicaraugua, I been there twice and found out things that I couldent ever have by reading about it. Crossed India at the heighth of their troubles, been in Europe and talked debts till I had everybody's angle over there. There is not a state in this country that I am not in ever once in a while. Talk to everyone, get the ranchers' and farmers' angle.
>
> Those New York writers should be compelled to get out once in their lifetime and get the "folks" angle.[71]

Rogers had no patience for writers and critics who had not traveled extensively, never visited the hot spots of the world, but claimed to be experts in foreign relations. "Where do these other fellows get all of their vast stores of knowledge?" he asked. "I never heard of 'em going any place."[72]

WILL ROGERS was not surprised when his friend Franklin Roosevelt won the presidency in a landslide on November 8, 1932. Roosevelt captured forty-two states and amassed 472 electoral votes to Herbert Hoover's 59. Overnight, Rogers's writings became more upbeat, for he was optimistic the new president would make the much-needed changes to halt the Depression and return the country to prosperity. Increasingly, Rogers would help Roosevelt restore public confidence, not only becoming an unofficial spokesman for the new president, but at times shaping public opinion, influencing legislation, suggesting recommendations for economic recovery, and, on occasion, criticizing Roosevelt if he thought he was going too far or in the wrong direction. Will Rogers's influence upon the American political scene would never be greater.

TWELVE

—————

The Opening Act for Franklin Roosevelt

WILL ROGERS waited a few days after Franklin Roosevelt's election and then sat down and wrote a long, heartfelt telegram to the president-elect. Rogers gave him lots of advice:

I didnt wire you on your election for I knew you was too excited to read but now that all the folks that want something are about through congratulating you I thought maby a wire just wishing that you can do something for the country and not just wishing you could do something for me would be a novelty and not unwelcome Your health is the main thing Dont worry too much. . . .

He counseled Roosevelt, then resting in Warm Springs, Georgia, on his leadership style and warned him to not try to do everything himself: "pick you out some good men and make em responsible. . . . If Europe don't pay up fire your secretary of the treasury and get one that will make em pay If people are starving and our farmers granaries are full of wheat that's your secretary of agricultures business to feed em."

Turning to foreign affairs, Rogers suggested, "If Nicaragua is holding an election, send em your best wishes but dont send the Marines Dont worry your life away over Europe disarming they are not worrying about it." In dealing with congressmen and senators, he suggested, "dont scold em. They are just children thats never grown up." He warned the president-elect that the higher educated are the ones who will give him trouble: "The illiterate ones will all work You will have no trouble with them but its the smart ones that will drive you nutty for they have been taught in school that they are to live off the others In fact this last paragraph is about all that is the matter with the country now If you don't like these rules I can send you some more, but the next bunch will be collect Yours with all good wishes Will Rogers."[1]

On March 4, 1933, as a cold rain fell and sleet hung on the trees in Washington DC, Franklin Roosevelt took the oath as president. Rogers was invited to the inauguration but could not attend as he was on the West Coast filming *Dr. Bull.*

Soon after the inauguration, an upbeat Rogers wrote in his daily column:

America hasn't been as happy in three years as they are today.

No money, no banks, no work, no nothing, but they know they got a man in there who is wise to Congress, wise to our bankers and wise to our so called big men.

The whole country is with him. Even if what he does is wrong they are with him. Just so he does something. If he burned down the Capitol we would cheer and say, "Well, we at least got a fire started anyhow." We have had years of "Don't rock the boat," go on and sink it if you want to, we just as well be swimming as like we are.[2]

One day after he was sworn in, Roosevelt called Congress into special session to deal with the Depression and to announce a nationwide bank holiday. Four days later the House and Senate passed his Emergency Banking Act, and the bill was sitting on the president's desk for signature by dinnertime. Within two weeks 90 percent of the banks had reopened, with popular confidence in them greater than at any time since the crash.[3]

Rogers was as effusive as ever after Roosevelt closed the banks, writing: "Say this Roosevelt is a fast worker. Even on Sunday when all a President is supposed to do is put on a silk hat and have his picture taken coming out of church, why this President closed all the banks and called Congress in extra session, and that's not all he is going to call them either if they don't get something done."[4]

IN APRIL 1933 the Gulf Oil company hired Will Rogers to make seven nationwide radio broadcasts, paying him $50,000 for the series. As with his Squibb broadcasts in 1930, he donated his entire salary to charity. He gave half to the Salvation Army, which promised him "that if ever you want for a bed or a meal you will find it in the Salvation Army."[5] He donated the remainder to the Red Cross, which created a Will Rogers Fund that supported public health nursing services in fifty-three rural communities across the country.[6]

Broadcasting live was hardly new to Rogers, and the twelve earlier radio shows he had made for Squibb had been a huge success. So too were the new broadcasts, with Gulf Oil renewing his contract each time it expired. Rogers eventually made fifty-three Gulf shows up until his death. During the lean Depression years, listening to the radio was the only diversion for many Americans. At nine every Sunday evening some thirty million of them made a ritual of tuning in to hear Rogers, so many in fact that ministers across the country complained of a 50 percent decline at Sunday evening services.

Rogers broadcast the first Gulf show from the NBC studio in New York City on April 30. After a medley by Al Goodman's Orchestra and a song from the Revelers, the quartet that accompanied him on the benefit tours, Rogers began his monologue.[7] A *New York Times* reporter wrote: "It was plainly evident that the 'Sage of Beverly Hills' was a frightened man when he stepped up to the microphone. Immediately prior, he sat with his head in his hands nervously glancing now and then at a watch. He strode to the microphone at 9:00 PM, grimaced at it, then at the crowd and the show was on."[8]

Rogers spoke mostly about Roosevelt, who was sweeping the country "like a new toothpaste."[9] For the first time in years Rogers sounded downright optimistic. "That bird has done more for us in seven weeks than we've done for ourselves in seven years," he began. "We elected him because he was a Democrat, and now we honor him because he is a magician. He's the Houdini of Hyde Park."[10] Rogers ended by talking directly to the president, who "somebody told me was listenin' in." He expressed a deep trust in Roosevelt: "We've given you more power than we ever give any man—any man was ever given in the history of the world. . . . So you take it and run it if you want to, you know, and deflate, or inflate, or complicate, or, you know, insulate. Do anything, just so you get us a dollar or two every now and again."[11]

In one of his daily columns, Rogers was more graphic. "I don't know what additional authority Roosevelt may ask, but give it to him, even if it's to drown all the boy babies, for the way the grown up ones have acted, he will be perfectly justified in drowning any new ones."[12]

Rogers shuttled between Washington and New York City that week. In the nation's capital he gave a speech for Roosevelt at the Gridiron Club, getting the president to laugh loudly as he tossed gags around a room brimming with the famous, including Irving Cobb, Fred Stone, O. O. McIntyre, socialist Norman Thomas, and Walter Winchell. While Rogers did not criticize the president, he took a swing at New York senator Robert Wagner, a powerful member of Roosevelt's "Brain Trust." According to Rogers, Wagner "from the start has fought for relief for the unemployed. When he started fighting for them there was only a million. Now there is ten million. So it shows what a senator fighting will do."[13]

While Rogers was in Washington, the new vice president, John Nance Garner, turned over his office to Will, who spent much of his time meeting with top government officials then trying to repair the economy. "Had a long chat with Speaker Rainey," he wrote. "Saw Congress pass the inflation bill, the biggest bill ever to pass any Legislature in the history of the world." After lunch with Senators Joe Robinson of Arkansas and Tom Connally of Texas, he visited Secretary of the Treasury William Woodin, who took him to a meeting of the Federal Reserve Board. Later, he met with Lewis Douglas, the director of the federal budget. "Not a one of all these men knew what inflation was," he joked afterward.[14] On the following evening, Jesse Jones, the head of the Reconstruction Finance Corporation, took him to the U.S. Chamber of Commerce to hear a speech by Roosevelt.

Back in New York he was happy to see the stock market rising. On Sunday, May 7, he gave his second Gulf radio broadcast. On that night he immediately preceded the president, who was broadcasting one of his fireside chats live from the White House. The timing of the two shows was just right, for it enabled Rogers to set the stage for the president, to be the opening act for Roosevelt's main event. In his comments, Rogers pleaded with his audience to support the president as he made major changes to a devastated economy:

Now tonight, I am on here with President Roosevelt. He is on here. We are both on here. I am selling Gulf Oil, and he is selling the United States, and both of them are good propositions, and don't sell either one of them short. . . .

We have only two big problems in this country: one is to balance the budget, and one is to keep my old friend Huey Long still.[15]

As soon as Rogers finished his broadcast, the White House called NBC to request a transcript. The speech was read over long-distance telephone and taken down by shorthand by a White House secretary, as Roosevelt demanded to see the transcript before he went on the air.[16] After Rogers finished, the president gave one of his most important talks. His first fireside chat had been eight weeks before, when he announced the closing of the banks, but this talk was more significant for he explained his New Deal program for economic recovery, combating inflation, and fostering international cooperation. Roosevelt described new legislation for massive public works to get men back working, creation of the Civilian Conservation Corps, completion of the Tennessee Valley Authority, mortgage relief for farmers and homeowners, and a half-billion-dollar relief fund for state and local governments. Rogers praised the speech, writing afterward:

Mr. Roosevelt made us a mighty fine speech over the radio Sunday night.

He spoke our language, not "ballyhoo the nation to prosperity," "nation in a tailspin," "can't make a hit every time we come to bat."

And in addition to all this he has the best radio voice in America. . . .

You know, I don't believe there is a thing this man Roosevelt couldn't put over if he was a mind to.

He is so strong with the people, and so convincing over the radio that if he ever got in a fight with Congress, all he would have to do is take it to the people, via the air, and he would lick any of 'em.[17]

As Rogers and Roosevelt teamed up again several times on Sunday nights, the similarities between their remarks became strikingly obvious. In a later Good Gulf show broadcast from Texas, Rogers interviewed "Hired Hand" Huff, a *Fort Worth Star-Telegram* reporter. During the show, Huff asked Rogers why his remarks and the president's were so akin, pressing Rogers that "some people are wondering if the President is writing your speeches or you're writing the President's speeches." Rogers quickly denied any collaboration with the president. He explained simply that he and Roosevelt had a similar grasp of political matters because they both had traveled much and understood power. Rogers ended his conversation by telling Huff he was proud that he and Roosevelt were of like minds.[18]

Rogers broadcast his third Gulf program from Hollywood on May 14, 1933. "I haven't got my partner on the radio with me tonight," he began, referring to the fact that Roosevelt would not be following him. Rogers reinforced the president's call for farm relief. "He gave the farmers a little bad deal last week. He is not going to let the banks or loan companies foreclose on them. So, I guess the farmer is going to have to keep his farm now." The number of foreclosures peaked that year when two hundred thousand farms were lost. The new legislation provided some mortgage relief but did not stem the tide of foreclosures. Rogers finished by ridiculing a proposal to change the name of Hoover Dam. Secretary of the Interior Harold Ickes, attempting to vilify the former president, ordered that Hoover Dam be renamed Boulder Dam. "That is the silliest thing I ever heard of in politics," Rogers said. "They are going to take the name of Hoover away from that dam. Lord, if they feel that way about it, I don't see why they don't just transfer the two names."[19]

—•••—

WILL ROGERS spent only a week in California before he hopped aboard an airplane and headed back to Washington, sometimes described as "Roosevelt, DC," or even worse, "cuckooland." Arriving on May 19, 1933, he rushed to Griffith Stadium to watch the Senators lose to the White Sox, 10–1, then to the Capitol to meet for several hours with Democratic senator Carter Glass.[20] They discussed a controversial new banking bill creating the Federal Deposit Insurance Corporation, guaranteeing deposits from bank foreclosures and prohibiting commercial banks from using their own assets to invest in stocks and bonds. After Glass convinced him the bill was critical, Rogers dashed off a column for the next morning's newspapers: "Carter Glass, who knows more about money than any man in America, talked in the Senate today on his new bank bill. It protects deposits and makes bankers responsible to each other. In other words he wants to set a banker to watch a banker, instead of leaving it to the depositor to try. He also stops banks from racketeering in trusts and holding companies. It really sounds too good to pass."[21] Despite strong opposition from the banking community, the bill passed.

On Sunday, May 21, Rogers delivered his Gulf broadcast from Washington's Mayflower Hotel. He pretended he was addressing the Senate; in fact, several senators were in the audience:

> Order! I want order here in the House. Huey Long. Quit prowling around there. Sit down somewhere. Sit down. Come on. Huey, find your place to rest. If you can't find your place to rest, I am sure there is people in your home state of Louisiana that will be glad to dig you a place to rest. . . .
>
> Borah, I told you eight times that I am not going to recognize Russia. . . . Why should Roosevelt and me recognize Russia? It took them five years to work a plan that it has taken Mr. Roosevelt to work the same plan in eight weeks. Sit down there.[22]

While he joked about Russia, Rogers knew the relationship with the Soviet government was a serious matter. He agreed with Senator Borah that recognition of the Soviet government would win the friendship of a nation that might restrain the ambitions of Japan and Germany, as well as boost Russian economic development. During a later Gulf program, Rogers said the United States was arrogant for not recognizing Russia and predicted the president would soon establish diplomatic relations. "We'd recognize the devil with a false face on if he'd contract for some pitch forks."[23] Soon after, the president recognized Russia, but only after appeasing Catholics with a promise from the Soviets to extend religious freedom to Americans in the Soviet Union.

Rogers traveled to New York City for two days and then returned to the capital. When he arrived he received a telegram from the president inviting him and Betty to spend the night at the White House. In his next radio broadcast Rogers gave his listeners an inside view of life in the executive mansion. He said the president, despite his enormous responsibilities, was in high spirits. "He has a grin on his face . . . he has got some kind of divine feeling. He knows that things is going to be all right." Rogers said that when he got up in the morning he asked Eleanor Roosevelt where the president was. She answered simply, "Wherever you hear the laugh." Rogers ended his broadcast by advising his listeners to follow the president's example and adopt his zest for life.[24]

THE ELECTION OF Franklin Roosevelt in 1932 was not only a repudiation of Herbert Hoover's inept attempts to stave off the Depression, it also served as a national referendum against Prohibition. Roosevelt campaigned on a wet platform, personally agreeing with Will Rogers and millions of other Americans that the ban on alcohol was a huge mistake. The American people were tired of the crime and corruption attributed to Prohibition and, more simply, they wanted a legal drink. But most of all, they were tired of being told what they could *not* do. "I have always claimed America didn't want a drink as bad as they wanted the right to take a drink if they did happen to want one," Rogers wrote.[25] As Prohibition became increasingly unpopular, especially in the big cities, repeal was eagerly anticipated.

Rogers, too, looked forward to repeal, but in May 1932 he wrote a column that probably hurt his cause more than it helped:

> See a lot of pictures of Mrs. Vincent Astor and society women of New York taking up nickels on the street to aid the anti-prohibition campaign.
>
> Such antics as that are sure to win the small town and the farm women over. Yes sir, right over to the other side!
>
> I'll bet there is more fool things done for publicity's sake that defeat their own purpose than ever aided it.
>
> There is but one reason that prohibition won't be repealed, and it's not numbers either. It's because the wrong people want it repealed.[26]

Many readers wrongly interpreted Rogers's column as opposing the repeal of Prohibition, which was certainly not his intention. He favored repeal but felt it would fail if it did not get the support of the rural voters. His column implied that the efforts of the urban elite such as Mrs. Astor were not effective in swinging the country vote. Nevertheless, he received dozens of protest letters from wets across the country accusing him of abandoning their cause. One protester reprimanded Rogers for succumbing "to the bootlegger's dollar," another called him a hypocrite, and another labeled his column as "most ill advised, in poor taste, and utterly devoid of your usual keen sense of humor."[27]

As the critical letters poured in, Rogers, who was never very good at apology, tried to explain himself to the protesters:

The other day I wrote a little "gag" about the main thing that handicapped repeal of Prohibition was the wrong people are for it. I still claim it's true.

Prohibition is not a party issue. You will find it is country against city. Your city's wet and the country is against it, more because it's the city dictating to them what to do.

And if you don't think it's that way, you wait till you count the votes. Country folks know the whole thing won't work, but they are not going to let "town folks" tell 'em so.

That's why I say the wrong people are for it to get through. Yours, Will Rogers.[28]

By the time Rogers wrote the protesters, the repeal movement had reached full speed. Near the end of the Hoover administration Congress had voted to allow repeal to begin, but a new constitutional amendment would take many months to get the required three-fourths of the states to ratify it. Roosevelt did not wait. Only a month after his inauguration, he had the new Democratic Congress revise the Volstead Act to remove the ban on drinks containing no more than 3.2 percent alcohol. After almost fourteen years of Prohibition, Americans could drink beer legally. When he signed the amendment to the Volstead Act, Roosevelt remarked jovially, "I think this would be a good time for a beer."[29]

Rogers was glad that the repeal of Prohibition was under way, but he worried that Roosevelt's quick action to legalize beer might weaken the repeal effort still being debated the states. Rogers did not want to see the Prohibition amendment lose momentum and fail. In his daily column he wrote:

Beer is supposed to be coming. From what I can read from all the States, nobody knows who is going to sell it, where you are supposed to get it, what it will cost, or what it will taste like.

The whole thing came up so quick that the boys can't hardly arrange how the graft will be distributed, all but New York. Tammany Hall, of course, got the privilege there.

I tell you what I will lay a little bet on. I bet they mess this thing up so that it will do away with the passing of the real prohibition amendment.

The whole country is buying a blind horse. Suppose this stuff don't taste like we think it will.[30]

Rogers need not have worried. On December 5, 1933, Utah ratified the Twenty-first Amendment, becoming the thirty-sixth and last state necessary for the end of Prohibition.

————

DURING THE early months of the New Deal, Franklin Roosevelt needed all of the favorable press coverage he could get. At the time, four out of five newspapers were editorially hostile to him and his policies.[31] Loud and irritating critics soon emerged to challenge the president's efforts to cope with the Depression. Huey Long, who had presidential aspirations of his own, originally supported Roosevelt but turned against him. Long created his Share Our Wealth scheme that would redistribute capital and make "every man a king." Philosophically, Rogers agreed with the Kingfish that wealth needed to be redistributed, but he also criticized Long's plan for being too utopian.

> There ain't nothing wrong with the plan, only this one little defect: Nobody ain't going to share it with you, that's all.
>
> I know a lot of tremendously rich people that should share their wealth with me, but they just don't see it that way.[32]

Father Charles Coughlin, who had earlier supported Roosevelt, also turned against the New Deal. In 1934 the priest used his popular "Shrine of the Little Flower" radio program to organize the National Union for Social Justice, claiming nine million members. Coughlin accused Roosevelt of leaning toward socialism and creating "radical inflation." Other schemes to end the Depression and help the needy abounded, including the proposal by socialist writer Upton Sinclair to "End Poverty in California" and Dr. Francis Townsend's plan to grant old-age pensions to all retired persons over sixty.[33] Rogers favored old-age pensions and supported Townsend in his columns. "There is nothing more terrifying than that thought of facing the future with nothing to carry on with," he wrote on his fifty-fifth birthday. "I don't know where they will get the money. . . . Take it out of increased income tax."[34] The popularity of Townsend's plan helped force Roosevelt to push through the Social Security Act of 1935, which Rogers endorsed.[35]

To help counter his opposition and sell the controversial New Deal, Roosevelt turned to Rogers and the few other journalists whom he could trust. In dozens of newspaper columns, radio broadcasts, and lectures, Rogers shored up public support for the president's monetary policies, relief programs, regulation of big business, increased taxes, and large-scale spending. When Roosevelt created the Federal Housing Administration to stimulate home construction, Rogers wrote a hearty endorsement:

> They are finally starting something that should have been started a year ago, and that's this house building and repairing.
>
> The local bank, or local organization loans the money, up to $2,000. The government don't spend anything. It only guarantees 20 per cent of it in case of loss. And these loans are made almost entirely on a man's name alone.
>
> Well, just the idea of a man being trusted again is going to make the whole thing 100 per cent honest. It's the best of all the plans. . . .[36]

Rogers openly supported the Civilian Conservation Corps, National Industrial Recovery Act, Agricultural Adjustment Act, Public Works Administration, and the Good Neighbor Policy in Latin America. In the summer of 1934, when critics claimed the New Deal was not working, Rogers wrote a quick rebuttal from Maine:

> Vacationers and everything have improved 30 per cent over last year. Roads have been fixed up with Federal money. Newspaper advertising has increased over 50 per cent. All these things have been done, yet the editorials say that the New Deal is a failure.
>
> It's a funny world. You feed a dog and he bites you.[37]

With the exception of only Franklin Roosevelt, Will Rogers probably did more than any other American to convince the public to accept the New Deal.

THE MOST CONTROVERSIAL New Deal program was the National Recovery Administration. The NRA allowed industries to reduce "destructive competition" by letting them collectively set minimum prices. Critics charged that the NRA encouraged monopoly, collusion, and legalized corruption. In August 1933 the president invited Will Rogers to Washington to meet with him and General Hugh Johnson, head of the NRA. "You better not monkey with him," Rogers wrote of Johnson. "He is hard-boiled and is liable to make you do what you are supposed to do."[38] During the meeting Roosevelt and Johnson persuaded Rogers to actively support the NRA in his nationwide broadcasts and newspaper columns.

On a Sunday night two weeks later, Rogers made his "Blue Eagle Drive" speech on a joint NBC and CBS broadcast. Bing Crosby, Eddie Cantor, and popular torch singer Ruth Etting joined Rogers in a show designed "to help pep things up for the National Recovery Administration."[39] In his talk Rogers appealed to the American public to give the NRA a fair test as well as pled with industries to hire more people. He liked the proposal to ensure fair competition on an industry-wide basis and to prohibit child labor. But he did not disguise the reservations he had about the NRA. He suggested it was "kinder nutty" for the government to tell a businessman to limit the hours of his workers so he can hire "somebody you don't need."[40] Deep down Rogers had doubts about the legality of the NRA. He was right, as the Supreme Court declared the NRA unconstitutional in 1935. According to the court, the NRA violated the constitutional separation of powers by delegating legislative authority to the executive branch and granting powers that exceeded congressional mandates under the Commerce Clause.

Rogers came to Roosevelt's defense when the president proposed restricting holding companies and halting their monopolistic control over gas and electric utilities. The Public Utility Holding Company Act outlawed such practices and allowed federal commissions to regulate the rates and financial practices of utility companies. In his daily column, Rogers wrote:

> Say did you read about what Mr. Roosevelt said about those "holding companies"? I wouldn't want my worst enemy to call me names like that.
>
> Now Huey Long and Father Coughlin and General Hugh Johnson can call each other names, but theirs is all in good clean fun. They don't really mean it, any of 'em. But Mr. Roosevelt ain't kidding.
>
> And what makes it worse is that it's true.[41]

Rogers received so many complaints about his crack about holding companies that he penned a canned letter that more or less dodged an apology:

> Roosevelt is the fellow you ought to take it up with, I cant do you any damage, anyhow I hope I havent. . . .
>
> This is no time to do injury to business. We all got our rackets, and I doubt if any of us would stand too close inquiry.[42]

As the complaints kept pouring in, Rogers drafted a second backhanded response:

The other day I went "Popping off" about holding companies. Now as a matter of fact I don't know a thing about a "Holding Company." . . . Then when I read Mr. Roosevelt's tirade against them, I said to myself, well here is a man who must know what he is talking about. . . . Well I dident figure that my little half witted remark would upset the whole holding company business. But I forgot that a remark hurts in proportion to its truth. If it's as untrue as to be ridiculous why nobody pays any attention to it.[43]

Rogers supported Roosevelt's efforts to clean up government. During the summer of 1933 the president placed all postmasters under the civil service system, thus removing thousands of government positions from patronage politics and angering many Democratic ward heelers. With comic exaggeration, Rogers "attacked" the president in his daily column:

This fellow Roosevelt can close the banks, he can tell industry how much to pay and how many hours to work, he can hold back the sun, he can evaporate the water, but when he demands that a postmaster has to be able to read, that's carrying dictatorship too far.

When he takes the postmasters out of politics he is monkeying with the very fundamentals of American political parties. How is the army going to fight if they don't get any of the loot?

I tell you this suggestion of his is bordering on treason. The idea of a postmaster being able to read. It looks like an undemocratic move to favor the college man. I tell you he will ruin the Democratic party. We mustn't let him get away with it.[44]

While Rogers overall supported Roosevelt's policies, he did not hesitate to criticize the president when he felt the administration was headed in the wrong direction. He opposed several specific New Deal programs that tended toward a welfare state, questioning relief programs that enabled people to receive "more for not working than . . . working, and more for not raising a hog than raising it." Rogers blamed Roosevelt for the collapse of the NRA, the president's inability to make his gold policy "quite clear" in radio broadcasts, and the government's cancellation of commercial airmail contracts.

Sometimes he refrained from criticizing the president directly, instead making nastier attacks on the "brain trusters" and cabinet secretaries charged with carrying out Roosevelt's policies. He attacked the unrealistic theories of the college professors in the president's inner circle, particularly

Raymond Moley, writing: "Theories are great, they sound great, but the minute you are asked to prove one in actual life, why the thing blows up. So professors back to the classroom, idealists back to the drawing room."[45] He criticized Secretary of Agriculture Henry Wallace for futile attempts to restrict farm production and failing "to teach the farmer corn acre control and the hog birth control."[46]

Rogers was nervous about the inflationary measures then being put in place. In May 1933 he wrote that "the phenomenal popularity of the Roosevelt administration now meets its severest test. They are starting to decide where all this money they have been appropriating will come from."[47] In another column he butchered Shakespeare's *Hamlet* as he discussed the inflation problem:

> To inflate or not inflate, that is the Democratic question. Whether it's nobler in the minds to suffer the slings and arrows of southern politicians or to take up inflation against a sea of economists, and by opposing, end them.
>
> To expand, to inflate, to inflate perchance to dream. Aye there's the rub.
>
> For in that sleep of inflation, what dreams may come, puzzle the will and make us doubtful whether to bear those ills we have or fly to others we know not of.[48]

While Rogers supported most of Roosevelt's social programs, he doggedly argued that the budget should be balanced. More than once he suggested a national sales tax to create the funds needed for the New Deal and lessen the huge debt being incurred. He also opposed Secretary of the Treasury Henry Morgenthau's proposal to increase inheritance taxes, believing that if a businessman earned his money by working hard and honestly, his heirs should be entitled to his earnings.[49] Rogers distrusted costly federal projects that did little for unemployment, and blamed some of the joblessness on technological innovations that took away jobs.

Roosevelt angered Rogers when the president vetoed a bill that would have provided a cash bonus payment to veterans, claiming the payout would spur inflation. While Rogers also was concerned about inflation, he felt the World War I veterans deserved a bonus. The House overrode Roosevelt's veto, but the Senate sustained it a day later. Afterward, Rogers complained to his radio audience:

Well, the bonus had been the big thing the past week. They'd just as well
pay it. . . .

Mr. Roosevelt made a mighty good speech. It was a Hoover speech but
delivered with the Roosevelt personality. Shows you that Mr. Roosevelt can
put over pretty near any material, no matter how poor it—no, but it
was. . . .[50]

The comically critical nature of remarks like these made them acceptable
to people who normally rejected opinions on controversial subjects or who
were offended by remarks directly criticizing the president. Rogers's wit
remained positive rather than pessimistic and lacked the hatred and malice
that would have repelled many. Besides disarming his audience with humor,
he added validity to his remarks with his open-mindedness and general nonpartisanship.[51] His criticisms of the more radical aspects of the New Deal
were important for they bolstered his independence and credibility. By voic-
ing his objections, he could not be accused of being a propagandist for the
White House.

When Roosevelt's more radical New Deal policies began alarming the
more conservative policy makers in Washington, a few of them, notably Vice
President Garner, Senator Carter Glass, and Bernard Baruch, leaned on
Rogers to spread the word that the president was going too far. Garner was so
concerned that at one point he wrote Rogers, "Your friends over here in the
East need you ever so often to put the fear of God in their hearts, and this will
be a good time to do it."[52] No doubt the "friends over here in the East" that
Garner referred to were Roosevelt and his more liberal "brain trust."

Meanwhile, Glass and Baruch urged Rogers to question the Roosevelt
administration's decision to abandon the gold standard as the foundation of
the nation's monetary system, an action that ended Americans' right to sur-
render paper dollars for gold and even to own gold bullion. Baruch, recognizing Rogers's ability to sway public opinion, wrote his friend a long, detailed
letter not only justifying his criticism of Roosevelt's monetary policy, but
demonstrating his high regard for Rogers's ability to comprehend a complicated financial issue and translate it into words more acceptable to mainstream America. Baruch wrote:

*My dear Will: . . . You are familiar with the announcement the Presi-
dent made about the R.F.C. buying gold with its debentures. That of*

course is one form of inflation. If it continues much further, it will result in a loss of confidence in Government credit. This is already indicated by the small decline in Government bonds but of course this can be overcome if the fears of inflation now in the minds of the people are removed. If confidence in Government securities continues to lessen, the Government may find itself in the position where it cannot sell its securities except at very high rates of interest and then it will be forced to do either one of two things—either to retrace its step by making a permanent value of the gold dollar or go ahead issuing greenbacks. The President now has the right to issue $3,300,000,000 without further Congressional action. If they start on that road, we are headed for still greater trouble. The real destructive inflation will not come until people lose entire confidence in our money.[53]

Soon after, Baruch was on the West Coast staying with Rogers at the Santa Monica ranch. That week Rogers mentioned the visit in his daily column:

Yesterday I ran onto a fellow who had hitch-hiked his way out here from New York. Rather dignified looking old bird but kinder down at the heels. He gave me about the most information I have had.

He hopes they won't inflate. In fact he hopes they announce they will soon go back on gold, then everybody will know what their money is worth. Had optimistic hopes of our future. Thought too many people, both large and small, looked too much to the government to fix their trouble, and do nothing themselves. He wasn't sore at the world, and had a good word for everybody.

As I let him out of my car to catch a ride with some one else, I asked his name. Said his name was Baruch, Bernard Baruch.

So pick up all old men you meet, some of 'em are mightly smart.[54]

As a huge public outcry arose over abandoning gold, Rogers tried to calm things with a little down-home common sense. He agreed with Baruch that the decision to abandon the gold standard was potentially a bad one and could lead to runaway inflation, but he also pointed out that no one used gold anymore in daily transactions and that most nations, including England, did business with money not backed by gold. In late 1933 he wrote a daily column that was less a rebuke of Roosevelt than a tribute to the late William Jennings Bryan, who years before had called for abandoning the gold standard:

There is really not much new under the sun. Thirty-seven years ago a long-haired young man came riding a day coach out of the West and said something about, "You can't crucify us on a cross of gold. We want the wreath on our brow to be studded with about sixteen silver ducats to one gold dubloon." In the meantime silver was used as the sole medium of exchange by over three-quarters of the earth's population. With us it was a money, but never official, it just had a slot machine value. So lying under Arlington's hallowed soil tonight must be a satisfied smile. For it's something to be thirty-seven years ahead of your government.[55]

Rogers was back in Washington after the New Year. Sitting in the Senate gallery with Alice Longworth on January 27, 1934, he watched as senators defeated a bill to provide for the virtual free and unlimited coinage of silver by two votes. The proposal arose as an amendment to Roosevelt's gold bill, which gave greater government control over credit and currency and a limit on the devaluation of the dollar.[56]

Two days later Rogers was the guest speaker at a dinner given by Vice President Garner and his wife for President Roosevelt's birthday. Among the thirty-five guests, Rogers was the only man not in full dress, his old blue serge suit rather hideous among a room full of tuxedos. Roosevelt made him stand up, turn around, and display his shiny seat. When he rose to give his speech, Rogers bowed to Gene Buck, the Broadway impresario who had given him his first break on Broadway years before. After two nights in New York City, Will, Betty, and their daughter Mary returned to the capital to attend a reception at the White House. The reception, the only one held during 1934, was given in honor of officials of the Treasury, Post Office, Interior, Agriculture, Commerce, and Labor departments. As he entered the White House, Rogers got a round of applause from the bureaucrats as he bent to kiss the hand of Alice Longworth, also a guest but one of Roosevelt's most vocal opponents.

IN 1934, Walt Disney filmed the animated movie *Snow White*, the popular and timeless film featuring the charming little seven dwarfs, one of which was a shy and sentimental character with big ears and a winning smile named "Bashful." Disney, a close friend who often played polo on Will Rogers's ranch, had patterned Bashful after the real-life Rogers, for the cartoonist knew that deep down Rogers was not the gregarious, ever-smiling

Rogers with Walt Disney

celebrity as seen in the newsreels, but an introvert, a shy and retiring man subject to mood swings.[57] Rogers's agent Charles L. Wagner reached the same conclusion, admitting his client was "temperamental and hard to work with and he's not all sunshine and jolliness."[58] Biographer Herbert Croly said that the private Rogers was "vastly reserved; there was a wall that no one went beyond; and there were dark chambers and hidden recesses that he opened to no one."[59]

Spencer Tracy, another close friend and polo teammate, later told a writer that Rogers was the only man whom he confided in. Tracy once described Rogers as "a strange paradox . . . he is at the same time one of the best known and one of the least known men in the world, by inclination a great mixer, by instinct a hermit; when he talks about someone else he's brilliant, but about himself he's shy, ill-at-ease, embarrassed."[60] Ben Dixon MacNeill, the North Carolina journalist, also saw a deeper, more complex Rogers: "People think of

*Rogers with Spencer Tracy
at the racetrack*

Rogers as a humorist, a comedian, a clown. Maybe he was all of these things. He was, to me, just, and tremendously sane. He laughed because, at least when, people laughed. I think he was more comfortable with people who didn't laugh at every sentence he uttered. At best he was serious, tremendously practical, keen in observation and comprehension. . . . I doubt if anybody ever plumbed his mind."[61]

Surprisingly ambitious, Rogers was driven by an inner need to succeed, as reflected in his early years when he strove hard to please his father. He was very sensitive about his lack of education, so much so that he refused the many offers of universities to confer honorary degrees. "I got too much respect for people who work and earn em, to see em handed around to every notori[o]us character. I will let Oolagah kindergarden give me one DA— (Doctor of Applesauce)."[62]

Fiercely independent, Rogers had a strong streak of libertarianism and became testy any time someone tried to tell him what to do or say. As such, he never took criticism well. He was very adaptable, but only within his own rules. If pushed he could be quite stubborn. His writings could be fearless when he felt strongly about an issue.

To those who knew Rogers well like Croly and Tracy, the public impression he created as an outgoing entertainer was only a façade. While one biographer wrote that Rogers "was essentially what he seemed—a country boy who had come to the big city," he was a much more complex person.[63] There was, for example, an intellectual side to Rogers. After moving to California, Will and Betty developed warm relationships with an array of fascinating figures, including intellectuals like Charles Fletcher Lummis, John Burroughs, Carl Sandburg, and Will Durant. Their ranch became a favorite stop-off for an eclectic group of writers, actors, cabinet officers, and itinerant ranch hands.[64]

The Rogers family enjoyed the casual social life in southern California. Rogers was a kid at heart; Betty realized she had four children, not three, "and that Will was the greatest child of all."[65] On the ranch he wore blue jeans, boots, cowboy shirt, sometimes a handkerchief around his neck, and a small, light-colored Stetson. In later years he needed reading glasses, which perched on the end of his nose, and when he was talking to someone, he took them off and twirled them around. A perfectionist, he personally decided on all the details around his ranch house in California, seeing to the placement of every rosebush and bougainvillea.[66] He stayed in good, loose-jointed physical condition and was always in motion, both physically and mentally, ever needing to be outdoors. He seldom entered a restaurant without a rolled-up newspaper in his hand, and hardly sat through an entire meal.[67] He had simple tastes in food, especially beans, "kinder soupy navy beans cooked with plenty of real fat meat." Dessert? "Had any more room, would eat some more beans."[68]

Rogers was extremely inquisitive, always wanting to know what made things work and why people acted the way they did. Although he belonged to no church and rarely attended services, he was a deeply religious man on his own terms. He regularly donated to a small community church in Beverly Hills.[69]

If Rogers had a major fault, it was that he could be a naïve judge of character who often overlooked major flaws in people once he met them. His overriding desire to please everyone and anyone made him less critical than he should have been of the likes of men such as a Mussolini, a Manchurian war-lord, a crooked Senator Albert Fall, or a thickheaded Warren Harding, all of whom he should have judged more severely. Nevertheless, his view of mankind was acute and penetrating. Despite his tendency to see only the good in people, he was a serious student of human nature who had the gift of making people laugh at themselves because he was endlessly laughing at himself.

IN LATE 1933 the Roosevelt administration faced its first major scandal when evidence surfaced that the Post Office Department had conspired with the major airlines to award lucrative airmail contracts. When the Senate learned of the "air mail fiasco," Senator Hugo Black chaired a full-scale, well-publicized probe that revealed an unhealthy collusion between the government and United Airlines, TWA, and American Airlines. The investigation disclosed that the previous postmaster general had signed noncompetitive and extremely profitable contracts at the expense of smaller airlines.

In October, as the airmail controversy continued to build, Will Rogers flew to Uvalde, Texas, where he spent a couple of days on Vice President Garner's ranch. Postmaster General James Farley and Federal Director of Aviation Eugene Vidal were also there. A couple of days after Rogers returned to California, Secretary of the Navy Claude Swanson met with him at the MGM studio in Hollywood. All of these discussions undoubtedly concerned the building airmail scandal. Rogers likely was included so he could sway public opinion in favor of any actions taken by the Roosevelt administration.[70]

Soon after Black opened public hearings in January 1934, Farley canceled all civilian airmail contracts and shifted service to the Army Air Corps. Rogers disagreed strongly with Farley's decision, writing that he saw no reason to remove airmail from the airlines just because of some corruption in the top ranks:

> What's all of the hundreds of airplane pilots and the thousands of people who make an honest living in the airplane business going to do? It's like finding a crooked railroad president, then stopping all the trains.
>
> You are going to lose some fine boys in these army flyers who are marvelously trained in their line but not in night cross-country flying, in rain and snow.

I trust an air line, for I know that the pilot has flown that course hundreds of times. He knows it in the dark. Neither could the mail pilots do the army flyer's stunts and his close-formation flying.[71]

Rogers knew the civilian airline industry had modern aircraft, the latest navigation instruments, and trained pilots, while the Army Air Corps used obsolete aircraft flown by poorly trained pilots. "They're just kids," he told his radio audience.[72] Rogers's worry, unfortunately, was well founded, as ten army pilots died in crashes in the first two months of operation. A public outcry arose, with World War I ace Eddie Rickenbacker describing army airmail operations as "legalized murder." Charles Lindbergh, a founder of TWA, sent a 275-word telegram to the president saying that using the Air Corps to carry mail was "unwarranted and contrary to American principles." Lindbergh also released the telegram to the press, infuriating Roosevelt. The White House accused him of being a publicity hound.[73]

In February, Rogers flew from California to New York, landing in a blinding snowstorm so heavy that "the plane stuck in the snow after it landed."[74] He was in Washington the next day in time to attend the Senate airmail investigation. While defending the airlines, he admitted that "there was crookedness and the guilty must suffer."[75] On the following day he met with the president and one of his advisers, Nicholas Butler, at the White House. Eleanor Roosevelt poured the tea. "The cup really should be fortified with some kind of liquid with a short wave frequency," he later remarked to his radio audience.[76] Rogers and the president sat on the couch together deep in conversation about the airmail controversy. After questioning Rogers about his experiences flying in Europe on different commercial lines, Roosevelt explained why he had decided to cancel the civilian contracts and order the Air Corps to take over the mail.

The next day Rogers flew to New York City where he met with Charles Lindbergh at the Waldorf-Astoria. During their two-hour conversation, a still-angry Lindbergh told Rogers he felt TWA had been mistreated and that he had personally written every word of the telegram to the president. Rogers tried to get Lindbergh and Roosevelt to meet, but they refused. Each man never forgave the other for their role in the controversy.[77] "One is a hard headed Dutchman and the other is a hard headed Swede," Rogers told his radio audience. "These men could learn quite a bit from each other."[78]

While in New York City on Sunday, February 25, Rogers delivered perhaps his most emotional broadcast. Earlier that day he learned that a United Airlines passenger plane vanished near Salt Lake City. Just before he went on the air he received a five-word dispatch saying the plane was sighted, but no other information. Instead of performing in front of a live audience, a tearful and worried Rogers broadcast from an empty studio. "I just sneaked off in this room to myself," he told his listeners. "I just wanted to talk to you folks alone. I don't want a whole mob around hearin' this."[79] A week before, right after his previous Sunday broadcast, Rogers had left California on a flight from Salt Lake City to Cheyenne, Wyoming. As the plane climbed through dangerous mountain passes east of Salt Lake City and weathered blizzard conditions, Rogers leaned through the cabin door, watching the pilots and talking with them. "Well, that's the ship that's lost now," Rogers told his audience. The same pilots and stewardess he befriended were missing.[80] After the broadcast, he learned that the aircraft had crashed into a mountain twelve miles from Salt Lake City, killing all eight aboard.

Under intense public pressure, Roosevelt ordered on March 7, 1934, that the flying of airmail be returned to private companies in an open and competitive bidding system and flown by civilian pilots.[81] After the army suspended airmail service, TWA and United Airlines carried the first airmail under the new contracts.

The airmail fiasco did not lessen Rogers's love of flying and his commitment to commercial aviation. "All I know is, I'm going to keep on buying tickets and keep on flying."[82] Rogers also did not lessen his desire to travel, and soon he embarked on yet another of his round-the-world adventures.

THIRTEEN

Circling the Globe Again—and Again

I N J U L Y 1934 Will Rogers, never able to sit still for very long, decided to take another trip around the world. He traveled to Washington early that month to discuss his itinerary with Secretary of State Cordell Hull, who soon afterward wrote his ambassadors in Moscow and Istanbul to arrange for Rogers to meet with Joseph Stalin and Kemal Pasha. While in Washington, Rogers met with the Soviet ambassador, Alexander Troyanovsky, and discussed his plans to take a long train journey on the Trans-Siberian Railway across the heart of Russia. Troyanovsky, whom he first met in Tokyo in 1931, gave him permission to send his daily dispatches from Russia without censorship.

On July 22, 1934, Will, Betty, and their two boys sailed west from San Francisco on the SS *Malolo*. Their daughter Mary, an aspiring actress, did not make the trip, as she was in Maine playing in summer stock. While steaming to Hawaii, Rogers learned that FBI agents had ambushed and killed the legendary bank robber John Dillinger outside a Chicago movie house. He wondered what picture got Dillinger. "Hope it was mine," he wrote. It wasn't.[1]

Arriving in Hawaii five days later, Rogers spent his first evening dining with Franklin Roosevelt in the Royal Hawaiian Hotel's presidential suite. The president was taking a four-week vacation to escape the stifling

Washington summer, a major renovation of the White House, and to make the first presidential visit to Hawaii. Sailing on the cruiser USS *Houston*, Roosevelt had stopped in the Virgin Islands, Haiti, Colombia, and Panama; he later sailed from Hawaii to Portland, Oregon, to begin a cross-country train tour on his way back to Washington.

That night in Honolulu, Roosevelt and Rogers stayed up late discussing world affairs, particularly the latest events in Russia and their opinions of revolutionary Maxim Litvinov, Stalin's minister of foreign affairs and a key player in convincing Roosevelt to recognize the Soviet Union the year before. They also discussed the Far East where the Japanese invasion of Manchuria had Roosevelt on edge. "Will, don't jump on Japan," the president told Rogers. "Just keep them from jumping on *us*."[2]

While in Hawaii, or what he described as "some Japanese islands in the middle of the Pacific," Rogers found time to play polo and tour Oahu, including getting caught speeding by a local policeman.[3] He took a seaplane to Waimea to tour the half-million-acre Parker Ranch with its herd of thirty thousand purebred steers. He also visited the army fortifications at Schofield Barracks and the huge naval base at Pearl Harbor. At the time, and seven years before the Japanese attack, he observed firsthand the vulnerability of American forces. "If war was declared with some Pacific nation we would lose the Philippines before lunch, but if we lost [Pearl Harbor] it would be our own fault."[4]

On August 3, Rogers and his family left Hawaii and sailed for Yokohama on the *Empress of Canada*. He spent six days in Tokyo, where he "saw a lot of golf courses being put in. That's the beginning of a nation's commercial decline."[5] In Tokyo he met with Baron Takeichi Nishi, a charismatic Japanese army officer whom he had watched win an equestrian gold medal at the 1932 Olympics. "He was just about the most popular little rascal that was here," Rogers wrote.[6] Nishi would die in 1945 leading a tank regiment while defending the island of Iwo Jima.

From Japan the Rogerses traveled to Korea, then to Manchuria, renamed Manchukuo although the United States and other nations did not recognize Japan's annexation. They stopped in Mukden and Harbin, the region where fighting broke out when the Japanese invaded three years before. The two cities were quiet during Rogers's latest visit, but he sensed increasing tension

*Happiest when
traveling*

when he visited Hsinking, the railhead of the Japanese-owned South Manchurian Railway and the Russian-owned Chinese Eastern Railway. "This country [Japanese Manchukuo] is so mad at Russia that they've broken off diplomatic relations that never existed," Rogers wrote. "Looks like we're going to have peace over here all week long."[7] Throughout Manchuria he saw detachments of the Japanese army on a warlike footing, while just across the border in Siberia he observed an equally large Russian army massed for combat. "Tell you sometime about all the military preparations on both sides," he wrote from Siberia. "I said sometime I would tell you."[8]

After the Rogers family left Manchuria and crossed into Russia, they boarded the Trans-Siberian Railway to begin an eight-day, 5,800-mile train ride across the heart of the Soviet Union. The journey provided them a fascinating panorama of the Siberian taiga, with its endless evergreen forests, low mountains, and beautiful valleys. After skirting the shores of Lake Baikal, the train steamed through hundreds of miles of endless prairie where they saw "not a tree, not a fence, just grass up to your stirrups."[9] On the Russian plains Rogers watched the harvesting of wheat, with "women doing the harvesting and the men are at the depot. You know these folks got some good ideas at that."[10]

Arriving in Moscow on August 27, 1934, Rogers spent a week in the Soviet capital, including meetings with the American ambassador, William Bullitt. He took Betty to the opening of the Russian opera and made a side trip to Leningrad where she enjoyed the ballet. On September 2 he flew to the Black Sea port of Odessa in the Ukraine. The flights across the country allowed him to observe Russian aviation progress, leading him to conclude that the Soviets took aviation seriously:

> Say, these old Russians can really fly.
>
> We had about a 65 to 70 foot ceiling today and they stuck right under it.
>
> That's what the Japanese are more afraid of than any other thing, is that these guys will out fly 'em.
>
> Commercial aviation is not so hot but military is, and it looks like they got 'em by the thousands.[11]

From Russia Will and Betty took a quick tour through Scandinavia, making overnight stops in Helsinki, Stockholm, Oslo, and Copenhagen. They then flew to London but spent only one night there before heading back to central Europe. In Vienna they attended the opera, where they ran into their good friend Arkansas senator Joe Robinson. Rogers found the Austrian capital intriguing. "This is Vienna. Europe's hot box. If a war starts, this is supposed to be the place it starts. It's a beautiful city."[12]

Will and Betty then traveled to Bucharest and on to Budapest. After bouncing around Europe and observing increased friction between nations, Rogers concluded a future war was likely. "There is twenty countries over here in a bunch all thinking of some trick to pull on the others," he wrote, adding facetiously, "they do love each other."[13] He found Europe to be deceptively quiet. "Don't hear much war talk so I guess that means one will break out. That's when they have 'em when there ain't any reason."[14] European leaders were edgy over Adolf Hitler's increasing belligerence. After Hindenberg's death a month before, Hitler assumed both the German chancellorship and presidency, thus combining the highest offices of state, military, and party, and within six months repudiated the Treaty of Versailles, announced formation of the German air force, and restored full conscription. Rogers too looked ominously upon the Nazi dictator's action. "Hitler broke out on me," he told his radio audience. "I thought I had him covered. Hitler broke out on me and tore up the Versailles Treaty. It wasn't a good treaty, but it was the only one they had."[15]

Will and Betty Rogers returned to London where extremists from both the left and right demonstrated loudly. "These Englishmen are about the smartest white folks there is," he wrote. "It's one place where fascism, communism, Hitlerism or nudism will never get anywhere."[16] While in London Rogers broadcast his first overseas radio show back to the states, going on the air early Monday morning so the show could be heard at its usual time on Sunday night on the East Coast. He titled his program the "Bad Will Tour," pretending he was a traveler making a telephone call back home to his friends. "Is this America[?] It don't sound like your voice, It sounds sad." He faked a talk with a rich man in California who was upset because the stock market had gone to hell. "H. as in Huey, E as in the third letter of Huey, and L as in Long. And another L as in Long."

After making observations about the hardships of being a communist in Russia, Rogers cautioned Americans to be content with their less-than-perfect government: "We don't know what form of government it is. But whatever it is, its ours. And you can bet your life we wont change it. And as bad as we are off we are better than anybody else I have seen. If, your country looks bad to you go see some other, it will make you feel good."[17]

A week after the broadcast Will and Betty headed home on the *Ile de France*, arriving in New York City on September 25, 1934. Rogers then flew to Washington DC to meet with leading congressmen and cabinet officers.

—•◆•—

IN AUGUST 1933, Will Rogers again lost his temper after learning the United States was meddling in the internal affairs of another country. This time he was angered over Franklin Roosevelt ordering three American warships into Cuban waters after a bloody revolution erupted in the island nation. Soon a squadron of thirty ships surrounded Cuba, supposedly to protect American citizens living there. The revolution raged for eight months, ending with the ouster of President Gerardo Machado. Although Cuba had been an independent republic since 1902, the United States continued to dominate that country's internal politics and international relations. The Platt Amendment of 1901 allowed the United States to intervene in Cuban affairs whenever it deemed necessary, prohibited Cuba from negotiating treaties with any country other than the United States, and stipulated that Cuba could create no foreign debt without guaranteeing the interest be served from ordinary revenues.

Rogers thought the Platt Amendment was an insult to the Cuban people. "The trouble is we never did set Cuba plum free," he wrote. "We kept a clause in the contract where we were to remain the guardian. Take the sugar out of Cuba . . . and our altruistic feelings would kinder cool off."[18] Rogers called for Roosevelt to "take that godfather clause out of our Cuban treaty, and first thing you know we would be called 'brother' and not 'big brother.'"[19] In May 1934 the Roosevelt administration, to Rogers's relief, negotiated a new treaty with Cuba that abrogated the Platt Amendment and finally gave complete sovereignty to the island. Three months later Rogers learned that the last group of U.S. Marines stationed in Latin America had left Haiti, marking the end of nineteen years of American military presence in the Caribbean nation.

There were other international events that bothered Rogers. During one of his Gulf broadcasts he predicted the London Disarmament Conference scheduled for the end of 1935 would fail, adding that the United States was unwise to strip its navy and army during an era of disarmament conferences. Instead, America should begin preparations for the next war. Rogers blamed the current nationalist conflicts in Europe on the animosities caused by the Versailles treaty and Woodrow Wilson's naïve idealism.[20]

Closer to home, he supported a proposal by Republican Senator George Norris calling for an end to the Electoral College and electing the president by direct popular vote.[21] Rogers earlier proposed the president serve only one six-year term in office and receive a life salary when he retired.[22]

Rogers became upset during the summer of 1934 when a series of labor strikes broke out across the country. The strikes occurred at a time when Roosevelt was trying to get people back to work, prompting Rogers to write:

> It must be terribly discouraging to Mr. Roosevelt after eight months of hard work to try to get people a job to have them strike the minute they get it.
>
> It looks like if all these dissatisfied groups instead of striking would keep on working and lay their complaints before the government with the proviso that if it's settled in their favor they get the extra back pay.
>
> Labor has seen enough of Roosevelt to know he is in sympathy with them, and that in government arbitration they will get a square deal.
>
> Help your company to start making some money, and when they do Roosevelt will see that you get a fair part of it. If American labor would work while their case is being arbitrated, instead of striking, they would have the gratitude of our President and the sympathy of everybody.[23]

When a general strike erupted in San Francisco that put seventy-five thousand workers on the picket line, cost businesses millions in lost revenues, and sparked considerable violence and radical activity, Rogers "grabbed the quickest plane and up I went."[24] Arriving at the same time as General Hugh Johnson, Roosevelt's head of the NRA, he found the city to be quiet with National Guardsmen patrolling the streets. The strikers returned to work after three days of unrest.

Rogers sent mixed messages about strikes. He supported unions and eulogized Samuel Gompers when the legendary labor leader died in 1924, writing that Gompers had "done more for the working man than any man living."[25] Rogers was less supportive of strikes, however, writing simply in 1933 that, "I can think of nothing more unpopular than a strike, a strike of anything."[26] While he was not opposed to small strikes, he feared the chaos and unrest caused by larger, general strikes, especially when "the reds were running the thing." In a column in 1934 he was somewhat sympathetic: "Lots of times individual strikes when they are just, and conducted along fair lines have won their case, and they should, for manufacturers have associations for their mutual betterment, bankers have associations to see how they can help each other out, and there is nothing fairer than workmen having unions for their mutual benefit."[27]

When he wasn't writing and broadcasting, Rogers was jumping back and forth from the movie studio to speaking engagements to raising funds for many charities and, on New Year's Day, making his annual pilgrimage to the Rose Bowl game in the Los Angeles Coliseum. In Sacramento, he was a member of the state welcoming committee for the National Governors' Conference, speaking at the conference opening, attending many of the official functions, and hosting the governors at his Santa Monica ranch. In March 1934 he emceed the Oscars at the Ambassador Hotel in Los Angeles and entertained columnist Walter Lippmann back at the ranch.[28] In April he starred in Eugene O'Neill's three-act stage play *Ah, Wilderness!* The show played to rave reviews for three weeks in San Francisco and another six weeks in Los Angeles.[29]

ALWAYS FEARFUL of any sort of breakdown of society, Will Rogers took a hard line whenever he talked about crime. He favored strict enforcement of the law and long sentences for those convicted of breaking it. But he may have gone a little too far in the fall of October 1934 when he wrote a humorless daily column criticizing the prison parole system:

> There must not be such a thing in this country as what you would call an "amateur crook." Every person that is caught in some terrible crime you find where he has been "paroled, pardoned, and pampered" by every jail or insane asylum in the country. Some of these criminals' records and the places they have been freed from, it sounds like the tour of a "one-night stand theatrical troupe."
>
> It must be awfully monotonous belonging to one of those State pardon boards. There is days and days when they just have to sit around waiting for new criminals to be caught so they can pardon 'em.[30]

A week later Rogers received a terse letter from the California Board of Prisons accusing him of being misinformed about parole procedures and unduly criticizing the penal system. The letter ended with an invitation to visit San Quentin for a briefing. For a change, Rogers realized he had been too critical. In pencil, he wrote at the bottom of the Prison Board letter for his secretary to "tell this old Boy if I ever get a chance I will take him up and that I will lay off the Prison Board."[31]

Rogers's quarrel with the prison board produced only a minor embarrassment for the humorist, but one of his radio broadcasts humiliated him terribly. During his Sunday evening radio broadcast from Hollywood in January 1934, he used the word "nigger" four times in a description of Negro spirituals.[32] Overnight, NBC received a deluge of protests by telephone and telegraph from outraged listeners across the country. One upset viewer, Charles D. Washington of New York City, wrote:

> *I was surprised and disappointed tonight when you said* nigger *spirituals. I could not believe it at first and asked my wife to turn the radio on louder. . . . Candidly and frankly I donot believe you would intentionally and maliciously insult a group of people because of the color of the skin.*
>
> *But permit me to remind you Mr. Rogers that you are a public character, and a very popular one, and must be very careful for you are an emissary of either good will or bad will.*[33]

Rogers was deeply hurt by the criticism. In a long telegram to a prominent black civic leader soon afterward, he attempted to pour out his regret.

> *If the colored race has a more sympathetic friend than I have always been, I dont know who it is. . . . I reverted to the word that I had used since childhood down home, with never a thought of disrespect. . . . I think you folks are wrong in jumping too hastily onto someone or anyone who might use the word with no more thought of belittlement than I did, there is millions in the South use that word, and if the race has more real friends than it has among millions of people down there I don't know where it is, I am offering no excuse for using it myself, I was wrong.*[34]

Rogers returned to the Negro issue in his radio broadcast the following week, still trying to apologize and claiming to be a friend of African Americans, but not noticing that he still used a disparaging term. "I wasn't only raised among darkies down in Indian Territory, but I was raised *by* them. And Lord, I was five years old out on the ranch before I ever knew there was a white child." On March 4, Rogers again apologized "for using some word that was objectionable to some of them," and assured his audience that he meant no offense.[35]

Quite touchy about racial incidents, Rogers's record was mixed. He often described African Americans in less than flattering terms and situations. "They [Republicans] are a good deal like the Negro down home where I was raised," he wrote in one column. "They are better when they are broke. You keep a Republican broke and out of office and pretty near anybody can get along with them."[36] In other columns he referred to "the entire bent haired population of Birmingham"[37] and called Negroes "big burr head," "big jigg," and "coon."[38]

Probably most telling about Rogers's view of race relations is not so much what he said, but what he did *not* say. He never spoke out against lynchings. He never took a stand when Congress debated bans on lynchings and when presidential candidates debated them at national political conventions. He never mentioned the notorious case in March 1931 when nine black youths were sentenced to death for rape in Scottsboro, Alabama. Over the course of the next two decades, the crime produced an endless series of notorious trials, convictions, reversals, and retrials and divided America. Rogers also never mentioned the race riots that broke out in Harlem in March 1935 that reflected the deep resentment felt by black New Yorkers during the Depression.

In Rogers's defense, his language and condescension were the products of a time filled with prejudice, mistrust, and hatred. He did, however, take pride in his general acceptance of all races, as reflected by his charity work for African Americans during the Great Flood of 1927, as well as his visits to black colleges like Tuskegee Institute when other white dignitaries and entertainers shunned them. In June 1929 Rogers defended President Hoover's wife for inviting the wife of Oscar De Priest, the black congressman from Illinois, to a White House tea. When southern legislators offered resolutions condemning the incident, Rogers jumped to Mrs. Hoover's defense. "Who I entertain is my business. Who Mrs. Hoover entertains is her business."[39] He also attacked Jack Dempsey for refusing to fight an African American. "As far as fighting a colored man for the championship," he wrote. "What difference does it make who is heavy weight champion?"[40]

WILL ROGERS caught election fever again in 1934. While it was not a presidential election year, the hotly contested congressional elections served as a referendum to accept or repudiate Roosevelt's New Deal. Conservatives and many middle-class people who did not suffer terribly from the Depression saw the New Deal as radical, but the majority of ordinary Americans supported Roosevelt's agenda. In the November election, voters overwhelmingly backed the president and his allies in Congress. The Democrats took nine seats from the Republicans in the Senate and another nine in the House; the Republicans were reduced below one-fourth of the lower chamber for the first time since the creation of the party.

Although Rogers hated to see some of his Republican friends ousted from office, overall he was pleased with the wins by the Democrats, as his political comments and behavior were decidedly partisan. In July, shortly before Rogers's round-the-world trip, Louis Howe, Roosevelt's political adviser, asked him to record a speech supporting the reelection campaign of Maine Democratic governor Louis Brann. Roosevelt saw the election as another important test of public support for the New Deal.[41] Brann won reelection and the Democrats captured one of Maine's traditionally Republican Senate seats.

The most interesting political race of 1934 occurred in Rogers's home state of California, where the socialist writer Upton Sinclair[42] won the Democratic nomination for governor. "My Lord. Maine's gone Democratic and California's gone nuts," Rogers told his radio audience.[43] Running on a campaign known as EPIC (End Poverty in California), Sinclair galvanized the support of the more liberal arm of the Democratic Party. Alarmed that Sinclair's nomination was an attempted left-wing takeover of their state, California conservatives used massive political propaganda to portray him as an ardent communist. The California race of 1934 was the first race to use modern campaign techniques like motion pictures and saturated radio ads.

At first Rogers was sympathetic to the muckraking socialist and his platform to end poverty. He wrote that Sinclair "should not only be governor of one state, but president of all of 'em."[44] Later, after party liberals tried to pressure Rogers and other Hollywood celebrities to endorse the candidate, he had second thoughts. During an October 1934 radio broadcast Rogers said, "I ain't made up my mind yet [on this guy]. . . . Sinclair says he never did ruin the country, but he might."[45] In the hotly fought election, the Republican Frank Merriam won with 1.1 million votes, Sinclair getting 900,000. According to some newspapers, an endorsement by Rogers could have changed the results.

IN OCTOBER 1934, while Upton Sinclair was running for governor of California, Franklin Roosevelt wrote to his friend Will Rogers. The president had just seen his latest movie in the White House. "We saw 'Judge Priest' last night," Roosevelt wrote:

> It is a thoroughly good job and the Civil War pictures are very true to life as I remember the battles of that period! . . .
>
> I suppose the next thing you will be doing is making application for an appointment on the Federal Bench. I might take you up on that![46]

Roosevelt was half serious about appointing Rogers to the bench, for he worried about the Supreme Court. On the same day as the president wrote the letter, the nation's highest court opened its new term. The Court granted review of two lower-court decisions affecting New Deal laws—the Gold Reserve Act and the National Industrial Recovery Act (NIRA). Although Roosevelt had been successful in the majority of New Deal cases in the lower courts, he now faced his first constitutional tests before the highest tribunal.

Roosevelt's fears were well founded, as the Supreme Court on January 7, 1935, voted eight to one to declare a section of the NIRA unconstitutional. The decision was the New Deal's first judicial defeat, ruling unconstitutional a provision that gave the president authority to control interstate shipments of oil. The action appeared to doom other major pieces of New Deal legislation. On the same day, the Court began to hear arguments on the Gold Clause cases that concerned the power of the president to regulate currency.[47] Rogers, who doubted the judgment of abandoning the gold standard, hoped that the Court's decision would clear up a great deal of confusion and controversy over monetary policy. "Whatever the decision is," he wrote, "it will break these Democrats from sucking eggs without first finding out the condition of the egg."[48] The Court later voted five to four in favor of the Gold Clause cases. The decision affirmed federal control over the monetary system, but the close vote again boded ill for other New Deal cases.[49]

In June the Supreme Court declared the National Recovery Administration to be unconstitutional, ruling the NRA illegally regulated commerce that was not interstate in character. During his Gulf radio broadcast, Rogers jumped to the president's defense and attacked the "nine old men in black kimonos." He questioned the usefulness of a Court that prevented a nation from flexibly coping with its challenges. He told his audience that he feared for a country whose institutions were not keeping pace with the times.[50]

Rogers's attack on the Court brought immediate criticism. An angry listener wrote to the *New York Times:* "I protest against the campaign Will Rogers seems to be carrying on in your paper to undermine and belittle the American judiciary. Mr. Rogers whether intentionally or from ignorance is aiding the forces which are trying to overturn our form of government and destroy our liberties."[51] Rogers did not respond.

Rogers criticized the Supreme Court often, concluding early on that the judiciary held excessive power over the other branches of government and accusing the Court of frequently making decisions not in the best interest of the American people. "Did you know the U.S. is the only country in the world where the court is higher than the legislative branch of government," he complained in one speech. In another, he railed against the Court for opposing child labor legislation: "Take child labor. For sixty years there had been an outcry against child labor. It battled hot through the Senate for ten years. In 1916 a bill was passed 52 to 12 in the Senate and 337 to 46 in the House, but the nine old gentlemen in the kimonos said no. Endorsed by the people and President Wilson, in 1919 they passed another one. But to this day they have never got one by those old boys."[52]

Rogers also lost his temper over the Court's resistance to minimum wage legislation. After Harding appointed two conservative justices, the Court struck down legislation passed during the Wilson administration guaranteeing a fair minimum wage. "By one stroke, these five men whose average age was 67 had done away with the votes of millions and millions, the judgment of dozens of state supreme court justices."[53]

In criticizing the Supreme Court, Rogers again linked his comedy with the dominant principles of democracy. He put the Court itself on trial and allowed his readers to consider the constitutional implications. His satirizations of the Court were not attacks on democracy but rather on the ways in which democracy had been distorted by a powerful and superannuated small body of jurists.[54]

⁂

"WAS YOU EVER down in Long Valley?" Will Rogers asked his readers. "There is a wonderful, beautiful, poetical valley along the length of our great

Mississippi River. Cities, beautiful prosperous ones, hanging moss from century old trees. Charming and delightful people in this valley. It's not called Long Valley on any of your maps, its labelled Louisiana."⁵⁵ When Rogers landed at the airport in Baton Rouge, Louisiana, on January 28, 1935, National Guard troops still patrolled the runways while machine-gun nests lined the nearby roads. Only a week before a large angry mob protesting Senator Huey Long's iron-fisted reign over the state clashed at the airport with the guardsmen, who scattered the protesters with tear gas.

Rogers admired strength in political leaders, having written admiringly of dictators in Italy, Spain, and Poland, but a dictatorship at home in Louisiana was too much for him. He flew to Baton Rouge to get a firsthand view.

Huey Long scared the hell out of a lot of people, including Franklin Roosevelt and Will Rogers. From 1929 until his violent death in 1935, Long seized more control over an American state that any politician before or since. By the end of his reign, he dominated almost every aspect of government in Louisiana. He controlled the hiring of thousands of government workers, proposed a gag law that prohibited newspapers from criticizing him, deployed the state militia as his personal police force, packed the courts to ensure his increasing power went unchecked, ordered the state legislature to pass hundreds of bills that increased his power, destroyed his enemies, and stretched the very limits of constitutionalism. Since Long had taken power in the state in 1928, corruption and despotism were so rampant that Roosevelt at one point contemplated sending federal troops to reestablish republican government in Louisiana. With his radical proposals and rude demeanor, Long became Roosevelt's arch enemy and most vocal critic of the New Deal.⁵⁶ In 1935, Long announced he was running for president.

Tensions still ran high in Baton Rouge when Rogers arrived. On a personal level, he seemed to like Long, or at least was amused by the senator's colorful antics. When in Washington, Rogers often dropped by Long's Senate office, flirting with his secretaries and joking with the Kingfish, as Huey liked to be called. After Long finished one of his legendary filibusters, Rogers remarked: "Imagine just ninety-five Senators trying to out-talk Huey Long. That many can't get him warmed up, and Huey has got just enough of a sprinklin' of the truth of what has been going on in our high finance that Wall Street is just on the verge of calling him a 'menace.'"⁵⁷

Huey Long.
Courtesy State Library of
Louisiana

Fascinated by Long's demagoguery, Rogers made him a favorite target of his humor, often comparing the Kingfish to European dictators: "Mussolini has his Rome, Stalin his Moscow, but Huey has his Baton Rouge."[58] In February 1933, after the U.S. Senate investigated a notoriously corrupt election in the state, Rogers wrote: "From what we can gather from the evidence, the investigation is held to determine who is the biggest liar in Louisiana, and with the amount of competitors they are having a tough time finding out."[59]

Rogers never accepted Huey's heavy-handed methods but showed some sympathy with the Kingfish's plan to reduce the incomes of millionaires and dole out their wealth to the poor. Long proposed that Congress give a thirty-dollar pension for all needy persons over sixty, limit work hours to thirty a week, and give a free college education to deserving students. By 1935, he had organized his followers into the Share Our Wealth Society, with eight million members nationwide. Although economists discarded his notion to redistribute wealth as rash and impractical, a vast and growing number of poor Americans believed his plan was workable.

During his visit to Baton Rouge, Rogers met with O. K. Allen, Long's puppet governor, and tried to meet with some of Long's opponents. He had to go to the rescue of Mrs. J. S. Roussel, one of the leaders of the anti-Longs, when the Kingfish's goons prevented her from entering the Heidelberg Hotel. Rogers raced to the lobby and took her to his room for an hour conference.[60] "I visited [the Louisiana] Capitol today," he wrote. "They have buttons on the desks and they vote by electricity. It's a marvelous way to vote, but Huey runs the switchboard, so it don't matter much which button the boys press, all the answers come out yes. But they are great folks."[61]

ALTHOUGH WILL ROGERS sided with Franklin Roosevelt in the court battles over the New Deal, he opposed the president's effort to join the World Court. As an isolationist, Rogers saw U.S. membership in the court as an unnecessary entanglement in international disputes. He devoted several Gulf radio broadcasts to objections to World Court participation. "For if this thing was put up to the voters right now it—it not only wouldn't git to Europe, but it wouldn't git to the docks in Hoboken."[62]

In January 1935 he arrived in Washington just before the Senate was to vote on the court. "Well I get in here and what do you think I find this Senate arguing over?" he wrote. "The World Court! Now, I don't want to split the party, but the World Court is the deadest thing in this country outside of prohibition. It's all right to fix the world, but you better get your own smokehouse full of meat first."[63]

On the following day Roosevelt sent a brief, earnest request to the Senate asking it to consent to U.S. admission to the court. "The movement to make international justice practicable and serviceable is not subject to partisan considerations," the president wrote. "At this period in international relationships, when every act is of moment to the future of world peace, the U.S. has an opportunity to throw its weight into the scale of peace."[64]

Two days after Roosevelt sent his note to the Senate, the motion to join the World Court fell seven votes short of the required two-thirds. According to Secretary of State Cordell Hull, Rogers's resistance to membership "hurt painfully" and may have caused the U.S. Senate to defy the president.[65] Historians too have credited Rogers with stimulating last-minute opposition to membership in the court.[66]

As expected, Rogers was criticized for his hard stand against the World Court. One angry reader wrote: "Is Will Rogers a sort of unofficial assistant to Father Coughlin? He certainly did jump into the arena to help the Michigan Rasputin keep the U.S. from joining the World Court. . . . Many of his wisecracks reveal a hidden sympathy for the fascist type of demagogue . . . a bad writer, ham actor, cheap jokester, and shallow thinker. And, besides he can't spell."[67]

Rogers answered his critics on his Gulf radio program from Carnegie Hall. Early in the program Amelia Earhart visited with Rogers, talking about her flight to Hawaii. Rogers then praised the defeat of the World Court, shrugging off any complaints that his comments had any effect on Congress: "If anybody could accuse me of influencing anybody, it would have to be a half-witted Senator. . . . If I'd a known what they was going to do, I wouldn't have been blatherin' around last Sunday night."[68]

Despite Rogers's dismissal of his own influence, William Randolph Hearst, who also opposed the World Court, concluded that Rogers's opposition was significant, telegraphing him on the day of the Senate vote: "Hello Will Thank goodness there are some Americans left You said a few mouthfuls which helped immensely to bring about this blessed result Your radio speech was marvelous. . . . Congratulations on the World Court."[69]

As 1934 ended, Will Rogers was busy as ever. In October he joined Henry Ford in Detroit where they sat in front-row seats for the first two games of the World Series between the Tigers and the "Gas House Gang" of the St. Louis Cardinals. Swept up in the excitement of his favorite sport, Rogers went on to St. Louis to see the third game. He then made a quick trip to Oklahoma for an old-timers' reunion, broadcast his Sunday night show from Tulsa, and then hired a plane to take him back to Detroit to see the final games of the series. Rogers watched with glee as his Cardinals, led by Oklahoman brothers Dizzy and Paul Dean, came from behind to take the series. After the seventh game, he could not stop shaking Dizzy's hand. "We done it, didn't we boy?" Dean shouted to him.[70]

Rogers ended the year with a number of charity benefits, including a nationwide radio broadcast to benefit the Salvation Army Christmas Drive. Two weeks after the New Year he was in Washington, having made the hop from Pittsburgh in a commercial plane piloted by Helen Richey, the first woman licensed as an airmail pilot.[71] In the capital Will and Betty attended Vice President Garner's birthday party for the president at the Washington Hotel. On the next day he was in Philadelphia to speak before the Poor Richard Club and address a joint session of the Pennsylvania legislature.

Later, after a snowstorm grounded his plane, he took the train to Indianapolis to give a benefit for the James Whitcomb Riley Hospital for Children. While there he addressed the Indiana general assembly. On the following evening he was back in Washington to speak at the Alfalfa Club, with the president and most of the Senate in attendance.[72] Covering a range of domestic and international topics, his remarks were particularly biting. "We are always saving the Chinese," he said. "Why the Chinese had a religion and civilization when we was hanging by our tails and throwing cocanuts at each other." The debate over U.S. membership in the World Court was still hot, and Rogers did not hesitate in letting the president and senators know where he stood. According to Rogers, "the World Court has got just as much business in this session of our Congress as the Supreme Court would have in interferring with the laws of the principality of [Louisiana]."[73]

He was in New York City the next evening for a benefit for the Actors Fund, then headed west just in time to escape the heaviest snowfall since 1888, which paralyzed the East Coast and took two hundred lives. On his way he stopped in Austin to give a benefit for the Texas Society for Crippled Children.

During this period Rogers corresponded with Helen Keller, who asked him to do a benefit broadcast for the production of ten thousand talking books for the blind. The broadcast was on the same evening as Garner's birthday party for the president. Rogers spoke at the party for about fifteen minutes, did some rope tricks, and then left to appear at the benefit for the blind being broadcast on NBC. "Your broadcast has put me in the seventh heaven of happiness!" Keller wrote Rogers the next day.[74]

Rogers persuaded Roosevelt to help support Keller's talking-book project. "Dear Will," Roosevelt wrote afterward. "Anything that Helen Keller is for I am for—I say this because of the splendid work for humanity that she has done during these many years."[75] Keller later met with the president to get his help. In 1936 the government began manufacturing talking books as a work-relief program.[76]

<hr>

DURING THE SUMMER of 1935 Will Rogers decided to take another trip around the world. It would be his fourth. This trip was not to be a family vacation like the previous summer but would be a much more adventurous and dangerous circumnavigation in a plane flown by Wiley Post. A good friend of Rogers and a fellow Oklahoman, Post was one of the most famous fliers of his day. A short, stocky pilot who wore a white patch after losing his left eye in an oil rig mishap, Post set a world record in 1931 when he and his navigator circled the globe in eight days. In 1933 Post made the trip using one of the first autopilots, breaking his previous record and becoming the first pilot to circumnavigate the globe alone. In 1934 he set the high-altitude record, flying above forty thousand feet while wearing a pressurized suit.

Rogers completely trusted Post's flying ability and his toughness—he had the "endurance of a burro."[77] In early 1935 Post became interested in surveying a mail-and-passenger route from the West Coast of the United States to Alaska and across the Bering Strait to Russia. When Rogers found out about the trip, which the airlines were to fund, he told his friend that he wanted to go along. Together they sketched out a plan to fly to Siberia and then on to Moscow where Betty would meet Will.

In February 1935 Post purchased a Lockheed Orion, originally a six-passenger monoplane, and replaced the engine with a new, more powerful one that weighed 145 pounds more than the factory version. He exchanged the wing with the solid wing of a Lockheed Explorer that could accommodate pontoons so he could land on lakes in remote areas. He made other changes, including using larger fuel tanks that increased the overall weight. Post privately told mechanics, "that's the screwiest damn plane I ever flew."[78]

While Post prepared the plane on the West Coast, Rogers traveled to Washington DC to make his rounds meeting with the nation's leadership. On what would be his last visit to the Senate he visited Garner's office, watched proceedings in the gallery, and ate lunch in the Senate dining room with William Borah, Gerald Nye, Pat Harrison, Arthur Capper, and Henrik

Rogers and Post in Alaska

Shipstead. As they were eating, Huey Long barged in to dominate the conversation.[79]

On August 2, 1935, Post flew the airplane to a repair facility in Renton, Washington, where he exchanged the wheels for pontoons. Two days later Rogers took a late Sunday flight to San Francisco where he visited the Soviet consulate. The Russian ambassador, Alexander Troyanovsky, was in San Francisco at the time and granted Rogers and Post approval to fly across the Soviet Union. The two visas confirmed permission to fly over vast regions of secretive Russian territory to Moscow via Uellen, Nogaev, Jakutsk, Irkutsk, Novosibirsk, and Sverdlovsk.[80] The Soviets routinely denied clearance to famous aviators, but Rogers was too much of a celebrity to turn down. If Russia refused to grant him access, the ambassador knew the denial would be on the front page of the *New York Times* the next day.

Trying to keep the trip quiet, Rogers flew to Seattle on a commercial flight that listed him as a passenger named "Mr. Williams."[81] In Seattle he visited the Boeing plant and "saw the world's greatest bombing plane being finished."[82] There he joined Post, who had finished preparing their plane.

On August 7, Post and Rogers roared across Seattle bay in the bright red seaplane, lifted into the air, and headed north to Alaska. They arrived in Juneau later that day and a week later were in Fairbanks. Early on August 15, they took off from Fairbanks and headed northwest toward Barrow, the northernmost settlement on the continent. They flew across five hundred miles of some of the most breathtaking yet forbidding wilderness of mountains, snow, and ice. Rogers was excited. In one of his last articles, he wrote, "You know who I bet would like to be on this trip. Mr. Roosevelt."[83] As Post and Rogers headed to Barrow, the weather soured and thick clouds and fog made navigation impossible. Running low on fuel and unsure of where he was, Wiley circled the area looking for a break in the weather. Finally, a gap in the clouds opened up and he spotted a large lagoon on the Alaskan tundra. He lowered the nose of the plane and headed downward.

Postscript

Setting of the Midnight Sun

---·⦁·---

A SMALL BAND OF ESKIMOS had just finished a day of hunting seals and were skinning their kill on a beach alongside the Arctic Ocean. It was a summer evening in the northern Alaskan wilderness, and although the mist-shrouded sun dipped low near the western horizon, the natives knew it would never set, for this was the land of the midnight sun, a treeless desolate place over two hundred miles north of the Arctic Circle. As the Eskimos sat beside a lagoon they called Walakpa, the distant drone of an airplane approaching from the southeast interrupted the quiet twilight, growing louder as it broke through the low-hanging clouds and circled the lagoon. Minutes later, the plane lowered its nose, banked steeply down, and landed smoothly on the water. When the pilot saw the native hunters gathered on the water's edge, he taxied the seaplane toward them, cutting its engine and drifting into the shore.

Wiley Post and Will Rogers climbed out of the plane and stood on the large pontoons, beckoning the natives to come closer to talk. The leader of the Eskimos, Claire Okpeaha, spoke no English, but his wife had learned some words in a Presbyterian Sunday school. Struggling to understand, she learned the two fliers were lost while trying to fly to the village of Barrow, Alaska. Using hand signals and pidgin English, she pointed straight north and said Barrow was about twelve miles away. Post and Rogers climbed back into the plane, but before they did, Rogers smiled at them and asked what they were fishing for. Seals, the Eskimos answered.

Okpeaha and his wife watched as the shiny red plane taxied to the end of the lagoon, revved its huge engine, and roared across the water spewing a trail of spray. At the last moment, the plane struggled into the air and veered sharply to the right towards Barrow. When the plane was about a hundred feet above the water, its engine missed, coughed, and went silent. To the natives' horror, the aircraft dropped from the sky, its pilot struggling in vain to stay in the air, and smashed steeply into the lake, the violent impact flipping the crushed plane onto its back and tearing one wing from the fuselage, the metal ripping like a crack of thunder, followed by a sudden and horrifying stillness.

Terrified, Claire Okpeaha ran along the shore to get closer to the wrecked plane, yelling to the passengers but hearing nothing. After calling the other Eskimos to help, Okpeaha ran through miles of muddy Arctic tundra toward Barrow, finally reaching the only store in town to breathlessly tell a government weather agent, "bird men dead." While Okpeaha ran to Barrow, the other natives rowed their umiaks across the shallow lagoon to the plane, now a pile of half-submerged splintered wood and twisted metal surrounded by a sheen of aviation fuel. Struggling through the wreckage, the Eskimos could not remove Post's body, trapped in the cockpit, but they pulled the lifeless Rogers from the back of the plane.[1]

WILL ROGERS was fifty-five years old on August 15, 1935, the day he perished in the plane crash on Walakpa lagoon. His sudden death shocked the country, immediately becoming one of those clock-stopping tragedies people remembered for the rest of their lives; they would recall exactly where they were and what time it was when they heard the news that Rogers had died.

The nation grieved dreadfully. A week after Rogers's death, fifty-one thousand people waited five hours in the scorching sun to pass his bier in a Los Angeles cemetery.[2] It was believed to be the largest funeral since the death of Abraham Lincoln. The studios shut down that day, as hundreds of Rogers's Hollywood friends attended, including Louis B. Mayer, Mary Pickford, Eddie Cantor, Billie Burke, Amelia Earhart, Walt Disney, and Spencer Tracy.

Tragic news

In cities and towns across the country, motion picture theaters darkened their screens for two minutes at the hour Rogers's funeral began. In Washington, Vice President John Garner presided over the U.S. Senate at the time. The crusty old Texas politician seemed unable to comprehend his good friend's death, adjourned the session, and walked out of the chamber in silence.[3]

More than seven decades after his death, Will Rogers remains the most renowned entertainer of his era. From just before World War I, through the Jazz Age, the Great Depression, and up until his tragic death in 1935, his humor captivated the nation. During the last two years of his life he was the top male box office star at the movies, one of the most widely read newspaper columnists, and a popular radio personality with an audience of over sixty million.

Rogers had an amazing entertainment career, but he was much more than merely a talented humorist. He was the most incisive political commentator of his day, who, beneath his humor, provided his countrymen with an often impassioned account of current events and a critically honest appraisal of American politics and world affairs. Few men touched the American moral and political conscience more deeply than Rogers.

History has not taken Rogers seriously enough. His legacy as a humorist is so profound and entrenched that it overshadows the true contributions he made as one of the country's most influential public figures. Rogers's impact upon the political scene is somewhat difficult to grasp, only becoming clearer when the humorous one-liners are stripped away from his story, thus allowing a more sobering view of his influence to emerge. An examination of whom he met, where he traveled, and the subjects of his writings and speeches reveals a more complex picture, a picture displaying an impact on public policy that was quite significant, enduring, and effectual.

Why have historians and biographers discounted the more serious side of Will Rogers? One reason may be the refusal of academics to accept that a poorly educated humorist, whose grammar was a disaster, had something serious and sharp to say. Another reason may have been a deep-seeded racial bias against his Native American upbringing. History has done a disservice to Rogers by painting him in caricature as merely a cowboy comedian. Some truly exceptional men such as Will Durant, George Bernard Shaw, H. L. Mencken, Bernard Baruch, and Carl Sandburg saw through Rogers's home-spun façade and recognized his true brilliance, seeing him, despite his lack of schooling, as a savvy commentator, well read and widely traveled, and possessing keen knowledge of human nature not to be found in the most philosophical of books. They knew that behind his beguiling grin was a streak of genius.

How could a part-Cherokee with a tenth-grade education so greatly influence public policy? Rogers's influence on the nation's political conscience was unique for his time. The sheer magnitude of his audience was unprecedented, as no other person has so dominated the entire media spectrum of newspapers, radio, motion pictures, and lecture halls. Few men, especially one not holding public office, have made such an impact. Mark Twain, for example, captivated his readers with timeless literary talent and wit a generation before Rogers. But Twain did not delve as deeply into politics; nor did he alter the political landscape or have the modern media of radio and film to reach a wider audience. Walter Lippmann, Arthur Brisbane, and other intellectuals of Rogers's period had a great impact on public policy, but none of them resonated with the average American as did Rogers. H. L. Mencken, for example, was influential in politics and justly regarded as one of the country's greatest journalists and essayists, but the typical man on the street probably took Mencken less seriously than Rogers. The public enjoyed reading Mencken, as his bombastics and meticulous use of the English language were to some even more humorous than Rogers's. But Mencken was so iconoclastic that it was hard to take him seriously or trust what he really meant. Rogers, on the other hand, was eminently trusted, what he said mattered, and his humor made his criticisms easier to swallow. Mencken and the other well-known scribes of his era, after all, could not walk unannounced into the White House or the Senate cloak room.

Beginning in the mid-1920s, Rogers visited Washington frequently to attend congressional sessions, testify at hearings, meet with cabinet officers, attend official receptions, and speak at the exclusive Gridiron and Alfalfa clubs. Senators and congressmen recognized his influence and sought his support on pending legislation. "This country could never go to war unless Will Rogers was for it," one politician reported in 1930. "He'd destroy the plans of

A more serious side of Will Rogers

the jingoes in a week"[4] If he told the American people to write their con-gressman about certain legislation, thousands of letters flooded the Capitol.

Rogers spoke or wrote convincingly on almost any subject important to the American people, serving as their source of reason and their interpreter of difficult social and political issues. He deftly used poignant humor to pen-etrate controversial subjects that otherwise would have offended his audi-ences. By using comic exaggeration he was able to critically examine the democratic process in all of its complexity, admitting that democracy was not perfect but adding, "that as bad as we sometimes think our government is run, it's the best run one I ever saw."[5] Overall, he convinced America that performing political humor was not merely good entertainment but served an essential public service and, in the long run, actually strengthened democracy.[6]

Rogers gave the American people a refreshingly candid appraisal of cur-rent events and public policy. From him, millions formed their opinion of President Wilson's quest for a League of Nations, debated freedom of speech and religion during the Scopes Monkey Trial, questioned the success of several disarmament conferences, took pity upon the sufferers of the Great Flood of 1927, and tried to grasp the awful reality of a nation struggling with the Great Depression. Rogers was remarkably prescient. Years before the stock market crash of 1929, he concluded the American people were living beyond their means, warning of overspeculation and the eventual economic havoc it bred. Seven years before the Japanese attack that thrust America into World War II, he traveled to Hawaii where he warned of the vulnerability of American forces. He was among the first to recognize the rise of fascist and Nazi threats in Italy and Germany. An isolationist but not a pacifist, he demanded that the country rearm as tensions rose around the world.

While many historians have created a one-dimensional portrayal of Rogers as a harmless comedian, there remains abundant evidence of his political influence. He supported government subsidies to boost aviation, sympathized with the World War I veterans who marched on Washington demanding a bonus, condemned the Ku Klux Klan, and argued that the United States grant the Philippines independence. During the turbulent Depression years, he was a voice of political stability when radicals from both sides of the political spectrum vied for power. He distrusted political extremes, including the right-wing tirades of Father Charles Coughlin, the left-wing panaceas of Huey Long and Upton Sinclair, and the naïve idealism of Woodrow Wilson. Herbert Hoover recognized Rogers's valuable role, writing that his political humor provided a safety valve for public anger and fear and that he had "a great understanding of the background of public events."[7] Franklin Roosevelt also recognized Rogers's powerful influence, saying, "above all things, in a time grown too solemn and sober, he brought his countrymen back to a sense of proportion."[8]

Rogers's impact on public policy was usually subtle and couched in humor, but he frequently stepped into the political arena to make serious calls for change. He could be devastatingly direct when angered at policy failure. Although he seldom drank, he believed Prohibition was a disastrous mistake, his constant hammering at the Volstead Act playing no small part in convincing the American people to favor repeal in 1933. After helping to deliver aid to refugees during the Flood of 1927, he appeared before a congressional committee to lobby for more effective flood-control measures. He may have caused Upton Sinclair to lose a close election when he refused to endorse him for governor of California. He helped spur the Senate to deny U.S. membership in the World Court. When the federal government refused to aid victims of the drought of 1931, he single-handedly raised huge sums for the Red Cross. An expert on world aviation who flew often and crusaded for aviation progress, he was asked to appear before the Federal Aviation Commission. With the exceptions of Charles Lindbergh and Billy Mitchell, Rogers probably did more than any other American to promote civilian aviation as a safe and efficient mode of transportation and argue that a modern, large military air force would be vital in future wars.

Presidents Wilson, Coolidge, Hoover, and Franklin Roosevelt all recognized Rogers's ability to sway public opinion; each of them, in his own way, turned to him to help their cause. Rogers was certainly not a spy, and there are no mentions of him as a source of foreign intelligence, but as an ambassador without portfolio he provided another set of sharp eyes and keen ears for the U.S. government.[9] The Coolidge administration invited him to travel to Mexico to help mend diplomatic relations with that country. During Hoover's tenure he traveled to Nicaragua to help after an earthquake devastated that country. In 1931, at the urging of the War Department, he traveled to Manchuria to observe hostilities between Japan and China, and, as soon as he returned, reported his observations to the president and secretary of war. When Hoover made a nationwide radio broadcast calling for public support to combat the Depression, he asked only Will Rogers to join him on the radio.

During the early years of the New Deal, President Franklin Roosevelt turned to Rogers to sell his controversial programs to the American people. When Roosevelt began his Sunday evening fireside chats on nationwide radio, several of the broadcasts were immediately preceded by Rogers's live radio show. Rogers previewed what the president was going to say and urged the public to support him. In dozens of newspaper columns, radio broadcasts, and lectures, he shored up public support for the president's monetary policies, relief programs, social security program, regulation of big business, higher income taxes on the rich, and large-scale deficit spending to provide jobs through public works. With the exception of only Franklin Roosevelt, Rogers did more to convince the public to accept the overall New Deal program than any other American.

In 1935, as tensions continued to build in Europe and the Far East, Rogers embarked on yet another fact-finding trip around the world that ended with his tragic death. The fateful trip with Wiley Post would have been the fourth time he circled the globe, taking him across Russia and Europe as the storm clouds of World War II gathered. Franklin Roosevelt, unable to travel abroad because of his domestic responsibilities as well as his physical infirmities, would have welcomed the insights that his friend Will Rogers brought from overseas. Undoubtedly, the president would have chortled at his quips, but also would have listened with rapt attention to Rogers's observations of world affairs and appraisals of foreign leaders. Roosevelt never received that last report, and Rogers's sudden death grew ever more grievous during the challenging years ahead. When Rogers perished in the plane crash in the Alaska wilderness, the president and the American people lost more than a popular humorist and a good friend; they lost a voice of reason and balance and a most trusted source of their political and moral conscience.

ON AN AUGUST MORNING in 1935, a middle-aged man was walking down busy Market Street in San Francisco. Suddenly he was startled, as a roar of excited shouts from a dozen newsboys broke out from a nearby alley next to the *San Francisco Examiner* building. The herd of newsboys came on the run, lugging their bales of papers and yelling with all their might. Everyone on the street stopped to listen, finally catching their words.

"Will Rogers dead! All about Will Rogers and Wiley Post!"

"Unbelievable!" thought the man as he stopped to buy a paper and read the huge headline. "Impossible! Will Rogers dead? It couldn't be."

The man watched as the hustle and bustle on Market Street seemed to come to a halt, people on the sidewalks standing around, looking into each other's faces in stunned amazement. And strangers though they were, they started talking to one another about Rogers's death and the utter incredibility of such a tragedy. Only the night before, the papers had displayed pictures of Rogers and Post in Alaska, standing on their plane and waving at the camera.

The man walked on as a pall seemed to fall over downtown San Francisco. All that day, wherever he went, everyone talked in hushed, solemn tones about the sad and terrible news. When the man returned to his hotel room, alone, he was overcome with grief. "I never realized how much Will Rogers meant to me until then," George Riedel wrote afterward.[10] Riedel was the eccentric beekeeper who was Will's friendly antagonist on their 1931 voyage across the Pacific on the *Empress of Russia*. For two weeks Rogers and Riedel hotly debated almost every controversial subject, but by the end of the voyage they had gained a mutual respect and liking for each other. During the cruise, Riedel upset Rogers when he argued there were no great men in the world. Now, on this sad August day, Riedel sat down on his bed and put his head in his hands and wept for the loss of a man who was "the greatest and most lovable personality I ever met, or ever expect to meet."[11]

Sources and Acknowledgments

THE IDEA FOR THIS BOOK emerged slowly. While doing research covering the first thirty years of the twentieth century for my earlier books and articles, I often came across quotations from Will Rogers. Usually they were humorous one-liners, inserted by authors to liven up otherwise dry manuscripts. But over time I realized there was more to Rogers's comments, that beneath his humor was a more serious message, and that his involvement in politics may have been more than just making people laugh. Rogers always seemed to be closer to the center of political power than the average journalist. During one incident, for example, he was eating lunch in the Senate dining room with a group of powerful senators. Huey Long joined the group, but was reluctant to talk about inside politics while Rogers was present. Senator Tom Connally turned to Huey and told him to not hold back, that Rogers was one of *us*. This was only one anecdote, but, over time, the anecdotes became a pattern, and eventually developed into a hypothesis that Rogers was more than just a humorist and truly an influence on politics and policy during his time.

Will Rogers's life has been well documented. Oklahoma State University Press and the University of Oklahoma Press have compiled and published his newspaper articles, radio speeches, and papers into a priceless collection. Several biographies describe Rogers's life, most notably the fine work of Ben Yagoda. But none of the biographia of Rogers truly uncovers the serious and influential political role he played. This book intends to fill a serious gap in the story of Will Rogers.

Many individuals contributed to my efforts. First and foremost is Steve Gragert, director of the Will Rogers Museum in Claremore, Oklahoma. When first approached, Steve immediately recognized the need for a political biography of Rogers. His support has been enthusiastic and unwavering. He opened up the museum archives to my use, provided me with unpublished manuscripts, meticulously edited several drafts, and made my visits to Claremore both productive and enjoyable. Steve's dedication and professionalism are nonpareil. Will Rogers would be pleased that his legacy is in such good hands.

I received excellent support from the staff of the National Archives in College Park, Maryland, and, as always, from the LSU Libraries. In California, the curator of the Will Rogers State Historic Park, Rochelle Nicholas-Booth, opened the park's archives to my use. Randy Young, source extraordinaire of the Pacific Palisades Historical Society, was a fascinating host.

I must thank my agent, David Madden, who continues to guide me through the publishing world. Also, Jim Richardson and my other colleagues at LSU have provided the perfect scholarly environment that allows me to pursue my passion in political biography. John Mulvihill did a superb job in copyediting the manuscript and making overall improvements. My friend Wendy Myers read an early manuscript and made several helpful suggestions.

From our first meeting, Judith Keeling, editor in chief at Texas Tech University Press, eagerly recognized the need for a political biography of Will Rogers. Overcoming huge obstacles, she has made this book a reality, giving guidance and encouragement where needed and ensuring that the final manuscript was of the highest academic quality. An author could not ask for a better editor than Judith.

Finally, without the support of my wife, Cynthia, our children and grandchild, and our wonderful circle of close friends, this book would never have been.

Notes

Introduction

1. Mukden is modern-day Shenyang, China.
2. *TDW*, February 7, 1932; *WA* 1:117.
3. May, *The Big Tomorrow*, 11. In 1935, Rogers was second to Shirley Temple at the box office.
4. For compilations of articles, see: *Will Rogers' Weekly Articles*, 6 vols.; *Will Rogers' Daily Telegrams*, 4 vols.; *Radio Broadcasts of Will Rogers*, all published by Oklahoma State University Press; and the *Papers of Will Rogers*, 5 vols., published by University of Oklahoma Press.
5. *PWR* 4:77.
6. *TDW*, December 18, 1932; *WA* 5:214.
7. Jenkins, "Representative Clowns," 129.
8. Brown, *Imagemaker*, 18; from Hoover speech on NBC broadcast, November 19, 1935. Roosevelt radio broadcast made on November 4, 1938.
9. *Toledo Times*, January 21, 1923; *CA* 32.
10. An extensive search of War Department intelligence files in the National Archives revealed no mentions of Rogers as a documented source of intelligence.

Chapter One

1. Betty Rogers, *Will Rogers*, 13.
2. *PWR* 3:59; Betty Rogers, *Will Rogers*, 39.
3. Robinson, *American Original*, 18–19.
4. Betty Rogers, *Will Rogers*, 38.
5. Yagoda, *Will Rogers*, 3. According to Cherokee rolls, Will Rogers was 9/32 Cherokee.

6. Homer Croy, "Will Rogers: Methodist Philosopher."

7. Rollins, *Will Rogers*, 3; Brown, *Imagemaker*, 175.

8. Sterling and Sterling, *Rogers: A Photo-Biography*, 17.

9. "Kemper School Monthly Report, March 26, 1907, WRM.

10. Robinson, *American Original*, 34. The Spanish-American War lasted from April 24 through December 10, 1898.

11. *Vinita Leader*, February 27, 1902.

12. Chron 67.

13. WR letter to "Folks," May 3, 1902, WRM.

14. Robinson, *American Original*, 53; Rollins, *Will Rogers*, 161.

15. Keith, *Will Rogers*, 181; Yagoda, *Will Rogers*, 56–59.

16. Robinson, *American Original*, 56.

17. *OCT*, February 3, 1931.

18. Robinson, *American Original*, 61.

19. Robinson, *American Original*, 61–63.

20. Brown, *Imagemaker*, 84–85, 154; Yagoda, *Will Rogers*, 259–60; *Los Angeles Argonaut*, September 7, 1914.

21. O'Brien, *Will Rogers*, 268.

22. Florenz Ziegfeld, Jr. (1869–1932). Theatrical producer. Born Chicago. Known for spectacular *Ziegfeld Follies*, 1907–31. Highlighted composers such as Irving Berlin, George Gershwin, and Jerome Kern, and featured elaborate costumes and sets. Well-known performers included Fanny Brice, W. C. Fields, and Eddie Cantor. Produced other landmarks, including *Show Boat*. (*DAB*)

23. For descriptions of Henry Ford's peace mission, see Steven Watts, *The People's Tycoon: Henry Ford and the American Century;* Robert Lacey, *Ford: The Men and the Machine;* Douglas Brinkley, *Wheels for the World: Henry Ford, His Company, and a Century of Progress, 1903–2003.*

24. Day, *Will Rogers;* Rogers, *Will Rogers at the Ziegfeld Follies*, 9.

25. Yagoda, *Will Rogers*, 142.

26. Sterling and Sterling, *Rogers: A Photo-Biography*, 77.

27. *NYT*, August 24, 1915; Chron 131; Rogers, *Will Rogers at the Ziegfeld Follies*, 7.

28. Rogers, *Will Rogers at the Ziegfeld Follies*, 8.

29. Klapp, "The Clever Hero," 34.

30. William Jennings Bryan (1860–1925). Political leader. Born Salem, Illinois. Graduated Illinois College; practiced law. Elected to Congress 1890. Editor, *Omaha World Herald.* Democratic presidential candidate, 1896, 1900, 1908. Secretary of State, 1912. Resigned in protest against way Wilson dealt with sinking of *Lusitania.* Fully supported World War I. (*DAB*)

31. *WA* 1:112.

32. *NYH*, December 17, 1922, remarks at anti-Prohibition meeting in New York City.

33. *NYA*, Scrapbook 20, WRM; Yagoda, *Will Rogers*, 142.

34. *NYT*, February 17, 1924; *WA* 1:194.

35. *NYT*, February 17, 1924; *WA* 1:194.

36. Yagoda, *Will Rogers*, 144.

37. *NYT*, February 17, 1924; *WA* 1:194.

38. Ketchum, *Will Rogers*, 150–51.

39. *NYT*, February 17, 1924; *WA* 1:195.

40. *NYT*, May 31, 1916.

41. *NYT*, February 17, 1924; *WA* 1:192.

42. *ID* 93.

43. *NYT*, February 17, 1924; *WA* 1:192.

44. Keith, *Will Rogers*, 226.

45. Chron 139.

46. Robinson, *American Original*, 125

47. John O'Hara, "A Big Shot," *Collier's*, April 13, 1956; Yagoda, *Will Rogers*, 143.

48. Yagoda, *Will Rogers*, 39; Robinson, *American Original*, 42.

49. Betty Rogers, *Will Rogers*, 12–13; Rollins, *Will Rogers*, 161.

50. Robinson, *American Original*, 42.

51. Jim Hopkins, oral history, Tape T7-087-1, WRM.

52. Betty Rogers, *Will Rogers*, 97.

53. Betty Rogers, *Will Rogers*, 110–11.

54. Correspondence file, November 12, 1910, WRM.

55. Chron 235.

56. Rollins, *Will Rogers*, 163.

57. Unidentified London newspaper clipping, microfilm reel 1, Will Rogers State Historical Park.

58. Alice Roosevelt Longworth (1884–1980). Socialite. Oldest child of Theodore Roosevelt. Two days after her birth her mother and paternal grandmother died, as her father, then New York assemblyman, hovered over deathbeds. Dubbed "Princess Alice," attractive, outspoken, source of songs, poems, and even a color—Alice Blue. Married Nicholas Longworth, Ohio congressman, later House Speaker. Staunchly Republican, she worked behind scenes to kill Wilson's League of Nations. Opposed FDR and New Deal. (*DAB*)

59. Chron 132.

60. Betty Rogers, *Will Rogers*, 125.

61. *TDW*, July 19, 1931; *WA* 5:49.

62. Chron 50.

63. Betty Rogers, *Will Rogers*, 168.

64. *NYT*, November 3, 1935; Brown, *Imagemaker*, 15–16. Supposedly Roosevelt said this to Albert D. Lasker.

65. Roosevelt handwritten note, August 4, 1918, WRM.

66. Roosevelt handwritten note, "The Langdon" hotel stationery, WRM.

67. *TDW*, February 22, 1925; *WA* 1:369.

CHAPTER TWO

1. *NYT*, April 11, 1930; *DT* 2:155.

2. *RB* 165, June 2, 1935.

3. *NYT*, August 26, 1930; *DT* 2:205.

4. *TDW*, March 31, 1929; *WA* 4:7–8.

5. *TDW*, November 16, 1930; *WA* 4:205.

6. *TDW*, July 8, 1928; *WA* 3:179–80.

7. *NYT*, October 16, 1930; *DT* 2:225.

8. *NYT*, February 24, 1930; *DT* 2:138.

9. *NYT*, January 21, 1923.

10. Correspondence file, WRM; Ketchum, *Will Rogers*, 151.

11. Certificate dated December 24, 1918, WRM.

12. *NYT*, September 14, 1924.

13. *New York Telegraph*, May 16, 1917, Billy Rose Theater Collection, New York Public Library.

14. *HTBF* 4.

15. *TDW*, April 13, 1930; *WA* 4:134.

16. *Chicago Examiner*, March 3, 1918; *PWR* 4:121.

17. Unidentified clipping, April 16, 1918, WRM; *PWR* 4:123.

18. Letter to Maud Rogers Lane, ca. November 29, 1918, WRM; *PWR* 4:150.

19. *NYT*, February 11, 1923; *WA* 1:9.

20. Klapp, "The Clever Hero," 21–34.

21. *NYT*, February 17, 1924; *WA* 1:10; *ID* 167.

22. Chron 148.

23. *PWR* 4:77.

24. *NYT*, March 9, 1924; *WA* 1:204.

25. Unidentified clipping, WRM.

26. *PWR* 4:131.

27. Ketchum, *Will Rogers*, 165.

28. *TDW*, February 7, 1932; *WA* 5:115.

29. *WA* 5:187; *TDW*, September 25, 1932.

30. The true number in WWI was much greater; over 110,000 soldiers died.

31. *NYT*, November 20, 1918.

32. Behr, *Prohibition*, 29.

33. *PWR* 4:166; Behr, *Prohibition*, 80.

34. *BG*, January 17, 1919.

35. Yagoda, *Will Rogers*, 200.

36. *TDW*, January 22, 1928; *WA* 3:123.

37. Rogers, *Will Rogers at the Ziegfeld Follies*, 116.

38. *NYT*, August 28, 1928; *DT* 1:248.

39. Rogers, *Will Rogers at the Ziegfeld Follies*, 124.

40. Rogers, *Will Rogers at the Ziegfeld Follies*, 116.

41. On October 28, 1919, President Wilson vetoed the Volstead Act, officially known as the National Prohibition Act, on both constitutional and ethical grounds. Congress overrode the veto the same day.

42. *NYT*, February 4, 1923; *WA* 1:20.

43. Handwritten notes from lecture at Montclair, New Jersey, April 16, 1928, WRM; *PWR* 4:563.

44. *TDW*, April 18, 1926; *WA* 2:179.

45. *HTBF* 3.

46. Ketchum, *Will Rogers*, 139.

47. Unidentified clipping describing Houston, Texas, performance, Scrapbook A-3, WRM.

48. Combs and Nimmo, *The Comedy of Democracy*, 6.

49. Rogers film archives, WRM.

50. Unidentified newspaper clipping, ca. November 14, 1926, WRM.

51. Chron 270.

52. *NYT*, June 24, 1923; *WA* 1:84.

53. Handwritten speech notes, WRM.

54. *NYT*, March 2, 1924; *WA* 1:204.

55. Sterling and Sterling, *Rogers: A Photo-Biography*, 133.

56. *NYT*, March 4, 1923; *WA* 1:30.

57. Robinson, *American Original*, 144.

58. *NYT*, August 26, 1923; *WA* 1:112.

59. Ketchum, *Will Rogers*, 176–78.

60. Yagoda, *Will Rogers*, 194; Ketchum, *Will Rogers*, 176–78.

61. "Will Rogers Talks to the Bankers," May 31, 1923, Victor Records, 45374, WRM; *PWR* 4:306.

CHAPTER THREE

1. *PWR* 4:12.

2. *CA*, June 7, 1920.

3. *CA*, June 5, 1920.

4. Boies Penrose (1860–1921). Lawyer, political leader. Graduated Harvard University.

Practiced law in Philadelphia. Member, Pennsylvania state house of representatives, 1884–86; state senate, 1886–97. U.S. Senate, 1897–1921. (*DAB*)

5. *CA*, June 9, 1920.

6. *ID* 152.

7. *CA*, June 15, 1920.

8. *CA* 3; Rollins, *Will Rogers*, 165.

9. Russell, *The Shadow of Blooming Grove*.

10. Miller, *New World Coming*, 79.

11. Allen, *Only Yesterday*, 45.

12. Betty Rogers, *Will Rogers*, 147; *PWR* 4:13.

13. William Gibbs McAdoo (1863–1941). Lawyer, politician. Born Marietta, Georgia. Graduated University of Tennessee, practiced law in Chattanooga. Moved to New York City to sell investment securities. Worked for Wilson presidential campaign. Vice chairman Democratic National Committee. Secretary of treasury, 1913–18. Married Wilson's daughter Eleanor in 1914. Turned Federal Reserve System into operational central bank. Director general of railroads during World War I. Ran for Democratic nomination for president in 1920 and 1924. U.S. senator from California, 1933–38. (*DAB*)

14. *CA*, July 25, 1920.

15. *CA*, June 2, 1920.

16. *PWR* 4:85; unidentified newspaper article by Rogers, September 5, 1916, WRM.

17. *CA*, July 25, 1920.

18. *NYT*, June 10, 1923; *WA* 1:79.

19. Miller, *New World Coming*, 60. Quotation attributed to Frederick Lewis Allen.

20. Typewritten speech notes, WRM.

21. James Alexander Reed (1861–1944). American politician. Born Richland County, Ohio. Attended Coe College. Practiced law in Kansas City. City councilor. Prosecutor of Jackson County. Kansas City mayor, 1900–1904. Elected to U.S. Senate, 1910–29. Opponent of corruption and inefficiency. Unlike many Democrats, opposed League of Nations and Prohibition. Lost Democratic presidential nomination to Al Smith in 1928. (*DAB*)

22. *NYA*, November 3, 1921.

23. *TDW*, August 4, 1929; *WA* 4:49–50.

24. *NYA*, November 3, 1921; *PWR* 4:226.

25. *NYA*, November 3, 1921; *PWR* 4:226.

26. *LSMD* 108.

27. Typewritten speech notes, WRM.

28. Betty Rogers, *Will Rogers*, 190.

29. *NYA*, November 3, 1921; *PWR* 4:226.

30. *TDW*, January 25, 1925; *WA* 1:355.

31. *NYT*, May 4, 1924; *WA* 1:228.

32. Sterling and Sterling, *Rogers: Reflections*, 113.

33. *NYT*, January 7, 1923; *WA* 1:9.

34. Unidentified clipping dated February 11, 1922, Scrapbook 20, WRM; *PWR* 4:231–32.

35. *NYT*, November 11–27, December 7, 1924; *WA* 1:329–33.

36. *TDW*, February 1, 1925; *WA* 1:361.

37. *Congressional Record*, vol. 66, pt. 1, December 18, 1924, p. 796; *Washington Post*, December 7, 1924.

38. *TDW*, December 7, 1924; *WA* 1:332.

39. *TDW*, December 7, 1924; *WA* 1:329–33.

40. Ogden Livingston Mills (1884–1937). Lawyer, businessman, and politician. Born Newport, Rhode Island. Inherited in excess of $40 million from banking, railroad, and mining. Graduated Harvard Law School. New York Senate, 1914–17. Elected to Congress, 1921–27. Undersecretary of the treasury, 1927–32. Secretary of the treasury, 1932–33. (*DAB*)

41. *NYT*, October 27, 1922.

42. *NYT*, October 28, 1922.

43. *NYT*, January 14, 1923; *WA* 1:12.

44. *NYH*, December 18, 1922.

45. *NYT*, April 29, 1923; *WA* 1:59.

46. *NYT*, January 6, 1924; *WA* 1:177.

47. *NYT*, September 26, 1928; *DT* 1:258.

48. *CA* 90.

49. *NYT*, October 1, 1930; *DT* 2:218.

50. *NYT*, April 3, 1933; *DT* 4:12.

51. *NYT*, June 1, 1924; *WA* 1:241.

52. *TDW*, May 24, 1925; *WA* 1:32–34.

53. *WA* 2:xiii.

54. Original typed manuscript, WRM.

55. *NYT*, December 31, 1922; *WA* 1:6; *ID* 30.

56. *ID* 323.

57. *NYT*, June 8, 1924; *WA* 1:244–45.

58. Cassette #1975, WRM; recording made February 6, 1923; *PWR* 4:295.

59. *TDW*, November 9, 1924; *WA* 1:101.

60. *NYT*, June 10, 1923; *WA* 1:78.

61. *NYT*, May 13, 1923; *WA* 1:66.

62. *NYT*, May 13, 1923; *WA* 1:66.

63. *PWR* 4:226.

64. Will Hays (1879–1954). Attorney, Republican party official. Born Sullivan, Indiana. Chairman Republican National Committee, 1918–21. Postmaster general,

1921–22. First president of Motion Picture Producers and Distributors Association of America, 1922. Responsible for restrictive Hays Code in 1934. (*DAB*)

65. Hays, *The Memoirs of Will H. Hays*, 468.

66. *NYT*, June 10, 1923; *WA* 1:71.

67. *NYT*, June 29, 1929; *DT* 2:44.

68. Yagoda, *Will Rogers*, 188–89; Rogers, *Will Rogers at the Ziegfeld Follies*, xviii.

69. Yagoda, *Will Rogers*, 190.

70. Rogers, *Will Rogers at the Ziegfeld Follies*, 150.

71. *NYT*, May 5, 1923; *WA* 1:61–62.

72. *NYT*, June 24, 1923; *WA* 1:86.

73. *NYT*, August 19, 1923; *WA* 1:111.

74. *TDW*, April 12, 1925; *WA* 1:16.

75. Ketchum, *Will Rogers*, 183.

CHAPTER FOUR

1. *NYT*, April 6, 1924; *WA* 1:215.

2. Ervin, *Henry Ford vs. Truman H. Newberry;* WA 1:376.

3. *TDW*, October 12, 1924; *WA* 1:304.

4. *TDW*, March 29, 1925; *WA* 2:9.

5. *NYT*, March 2, 1924; *WA* 1:203.

6. John Calloway Walton (1881–1949). American politician. Born Indianapolis. Mayor Oklahoma City, 1919–23. Elected governor of Oklahoma in 1923, serving shortest term and first impeached. Outraged state legislature when he declared martial law as result of Tulsa race riots of 1921. During impeachment, state house filed twenty-two charges, eleven sustained. Convicted and removed from office, 1923.

7. *TDW*, December 13, 1925; *WA* 2:121.

8. See Bates, *The Origins of Teapot Dome: Progressives, Parties, and Petroleum, 1909–1921;* Diner, "Teapot Dome, 1924"; Noggle, *Teapot Dome: Oil and Politics in the 1920s;* Stratton, *Tempest over Teapot Dome.*

9. Miller, *New World Coming*, 107. Albert Fall (1861–1944). Lawyer, senator, cabinet officer. Born Frankfort, Kentucky. U.S. Army during Spanish-American War. Studied law, practiced in New Mexico. District judge, 1893. U.S. Senate, 1912. Secretary of the interior, 1921. (*DAB*)

10. Miller, *New World Coming*, 83.

11. Diner, "Teapot Dome, 1924"; *PWR* 4:151–52.

12. *TDW*, March 25, 1928; *WA* 3:147.

13. *NYT*, February 10, 1924; *WA* 1:190–91.

14. *NYT*, February 24, 1924; *WA* 1:181.

15. *ID* 126.

16. *NYT*, July 21, 1931; *DT* 3:55.

17. Stratton, *Tempest over Teapot Dome*, 312; *PWR* 4:153.

18. *TDW*, December 26, 1926; *WA* 1:286–87.

19. *NYT*, March 19, 1930; *DT* 2:147.

20. *TDW*, July 5, 1931; *WA* 5:45–46.

21. *TDW*, April 22, 1928; *WA* 3:154.

22. *NYT*, June 9, 1924; *CA* 33.

23. *NYT*, June 11, 1924; *CA* 36.

24. *NYT*, June 3, 1923; *WA* 1:76.

25. *NYT*, June 11, 1924; *CA* 37.

26. *NYT*, June 11, 1924; *CA* 37.

27. Slayton, *Empire Statesman*, June 28, 1928; Murray, *The 103rd Ballot*.

28. *NYT*, June 28, 1924; *CA* 59.

29. *DT* 1:228.

30. *NYT*, June 30, 1924; *CA* 65.

31. *NYT*, July 6, 1924; *WA* 1:257–60.

32. *NYT*, July 9, 1924; *CA* 84.

33. *NYT*, July 6, 1924; *CA* 45.

34. *Washington Post*, June 29, 1924.

35. Telegram on Western Union letterhead, WRM; *PWR* 4:345.

36. *WA* 4:233; Slayton, *Empire Statesman*, 31.

37. *TDW*, November 9, 1924; *WA* 1:318.

38. *NYT*, June 10, 1924; *CA* 87.

39. *New York Evening Telegram*, November 10, 1928.

40. Telegram from Rogers to Smith, July 10, 1924; *PWR* 4:348.

41. Telegram from Rogers to McAdoo, July 10, 1924, WRM; *PWR* 4:347.

42. *NYT*, July 1, 1924; *CA* 65.

43. Statement appears in typewritten notes at dinner for Jimmy Rolph, ca. October 1930, WRM. Rolph, a Republican, was running for governor of California.

44. *NYT*, April 8, 1923; *WA* 1:51–52.

45. *NYT*, April 29, 1923; *WA* 1:61.

46. *NYT*, September 30, 1923; *WA* 1:131.

47. Prince of Wales (1894–1972). Later Edward VIII, later Duke of Windsor. Served in World War I. King of England from death of father George V in January 1936 until abdication in December 1936. Forced constitutional crisis by proposing to American divorcée Wallis Simpson. Only monarch to voluntarily relinquish throne. During World War II, stationed with British Military Mission to France, but after accusations he was pro-Nazi was moved to Bahamas as governor. (*DAB*)

48. *NYT*, September 5, 1924.

49. *NYT*, September 19, 1924.
50. Sterling and Sterling, *Rogers: A Photo-Biography*, 128.
51. *NYT*, May 15, 1926; *PWR* 4:427n3.
52. *LSMD* 51.
53. Miller, *New World Coming*, 125.
54. *TDW*, May 3, 1925; *WA* 2:25.
55. *NYT*, April 24, 1925.
56. The Gridiron Club, founded in 1885, is the oldest and most prestigious journalistic organization in Washington DC. Sixty-five active members represent major newspapers, news services, and broadcast networks. Membership by invitation only.
57. *NYT*, September 21, 1924.
58. Betty Rogers, *Will Rogers*, 200; Ketchum, *Will Rogers*, 132; Brown, *Imagemaker*, 225.
59. *NYT*, November 18, 1923; *WA* 1:153.
60. *TDW*, May 10, 1925; *WA* 2:27–28.
61. Davis, *The Billy Mitchell Affair*, 209–10; *TDW*, October 4, 1925; *WA* 2:89.
62. *WA* 1:308; *TDW*, October 19, 1924.
63. *Congressional Record*, vol. 68, pt. 1, January 17, 1927, p. 1758, entered by Rep. Bingham, from *Washington Post* article, January 16, 1927; *WA* 2:293–96.
64. *TDW*, January 16, 1927; *WA* 2:294, 295.
65. *TDW*, May 10, 1925; *WA* 2:29.
66. Davis, *The Billy Mitchell Affair*, 209–10.
67. Davis, *The Billy Mitchell Affair*, 319.
68. *NYT*, December 12, 1925.
69. Typewritten notes for speech, December 17, 1925, WRM; *PWR* 4:403–4.
70. Unidentified clipping, Scrapbook 21, WRM.
71. *NYT*, April 15, 1927; *DT* 1:77.
72. Betty Rogers, *Will Rogers*, 200; Ketchum, *Will Rogers*, 132; Brown, *Imagemaker*, 225.
73. For a description of the Scopes trial, see Edward J. Larson, *Summer for the Gods: The Scopes Trial and America's Continuing Debate over Science and Religion*.
74. *TDW*, November 1, 1925; *WA* 2:103.
75. Larson, *Summer for the Gods*, 58.
76. *Elmira Advertiser*, October 2, 1925, Scrapbook 8, WRM; *PWR* 4:390.
77. *TDW*, July 26, 1925; *WA* 2:57–58.
78. *TDW*, July 19, 1925; *WA* 2:55–56.
79. *TDW*, July 19, 1925; *WA* 2:56.
80. *TDW*, August 9, 1925; *WA* 2:65–66.
81. *WA* 2:18–19; *TDW*, April 19, 1925.

82. *NYT*, May 8, 1927; *DT* 1:86.

83. Ketchum, *Will Rogers*, 345.

84. Betty Rogers, *Will Rogers*, 185.

85. *TDW*, December 13, 1925; *WA* 2:122; Betty Rogers, *Will Rogers*, 186.

86. *Birmingham Post*, November 4, 1925.

87. *Birmingham Post*, November 4, 1925.

88. *RB* 146.

89. Original typed manuscript, WRM; *PWR* 4:275.

90. *NYT*, April 13, 1926.

91. *PWR* 4:380; Sterling and Sterling, *Rogers: Reflections*, 25.

92. *TDW*, January 3, 1926; *WA* 2:132.

93. *NYT*, May 29, 1924.

94. MacNeill, "Reminiscences," 119.

95. Letter WR to BBR, October 19, 1908, WRM; *PWR* 3:66–67.

96. Patterson, *A Little Brother of the Rich*, 113.

97. Patterson, *A Little Brother of the Rich*, 360.

98. Herrick, *Together*, 517.

99. Herrick, *Together*, 528.

100. *NYT*, November 23, 1932; *DT* 3:241.

101. Betty Rogers, *Will Rogers*, 157.

102. *TDW*, November 21, 1926.

103. *NYT*, March 18, 1923; *WA* 1:40.

104. *Congressional Record*, vol. 65, pt. 1, January 7, 1924, p. 672.

105. *TDW*, November 2, 1924; *WA* 1:313.

106. *LSMD* 123.

107. *TDW*, May 31, 1925; *WA* 2:36–37.

108. McElvaine, *The Great Depression*, 34.

109. Sterling and Sterling, *Rogers: Reflections*, 4.

110. *TDW*, March 22, 1925; *WA* 2:8.

CHAPTER FIVE

1. *TDW*, March 14, 1926; *WA* 2:165.

2. *TNBSR* xv.

3. Ketchum, *Will Rogers*, 355.

4. *NYT*, October 2, 1931; *DT* 3:74.

5. *TDW*, June 28, 1925; *WA* 2:46–49.

6. *NYT*, April 28, 1927; *DT* 3:238.

7. *NYT*, January 4, 1928; *DT* 1:152.

8. *TDW*, December 5, 1926; *WA* 2:277.

9. *NYT*, March 12, 1933; *WA* 6:2.

10. Parsons letter dated March 20, 1925, WRM.

11. *NYT*, August 2, 1925.

12. Letter from Rogers, on Will Rogers letterhead, New Amsterdam Theater, NYC, WRM.

13. *PWR* 4:28.

14. *NYT*, May 12, 1926.

15. Unidentified clipping, Scrapbook 21, WRM.

16. *NYA*, April 12, 1926.

17. *New York Herald Tribune*, April 12, 1926.

18. Typewritten performance notes, WRM.

19. Betty Rogers, *Will Rogers*, 128.

20. *TDW*, April 25, 1926; *WA* 2:84.

21. *LSMD* xviii–xix.

22. Tebbel, *George Horace Lorimer*, 190.

23. Telegram from Rogers, on Western Union letterhead, WRM.

24. Letter on *New York Times* letterhead, April 28, 1926, WRM.

25. *DT* 1:xiii.

26. Letter from Borah, correspondence file, WRM.

27. Letters of introduction, WRM.

28. *NYT*, May 15, 1926; *PWR* 4:427.

29. Assorted newspaper clippings, Scrapbook 21, WRM.

30. *TDW*, August 8, 1926; *WA* 2:227.

31. Nancy Witcher Astor, Viscountess Astor (1879–1964). First female member of British Parliament. Born Danville, Virginia. Formerly Nancy Langhorne, sister-in-law of *Life* editor and illustrator Charles Dana Gibson. Wife of Waldorf Astor, 2nd Viscount Astor. Elected in November 1919 to Parliament, serving as Conservative, 1919–1945. Fierce debater, championed women's and children's rights, unreconstructed elitist. (*EWB*)

32. *Los Angeles Examiner*, July 28, 1929.

33. Langhorne, *Nancy Astor and Her Friends*, 70.

34. Letter from Astor, on *Aquitania* letterhead, WRM; *PWR* 4:437.

35. *NYT*, July 30, 1926; *DT* 1:1.

36. *NYT*, June 30, 1931; *DT* 1:47.

37. Typewritten speech notes, WRM.

38. *NYT*, July 7, 1926; *LSMD* xxi.

39. *LSMD* 117.

40. *Everybody's Weekly* clipping, Scrapbook 21, WRM; Betty Rogers, *Will Rogers*, 195–96.

41. *BG*, September 26, 1927.

42. *NYT*, February 2, 1927; *DT* 1:53.

43. *NYT*, June 15, 1927; *DT* 1:90.

44. *LSMD* 73, 75.

45. *NYT*, May 27, 1926.

46. *Kansas City Times*, July 28, 1929; *DT* 2:55–56; *NYT* replaced "wop" with "man."

47. *LSMD* 115.

48. *TDW*, June 8, 1930; *WA* 4:154–55.

49. *NYT*, February 11, 1933; *DT* 2:274.

50. *TDW*, November 20, 1927; *WA* 3:98.

51. *TNBSR* 52.

52. *NYT*, February 11, 1933; *DT* 3:248.

53. Ketchum, *Will Rogers*, 331; Robinson, *American Original*, 219.

54. Thurber, "State of the Nation's Humor," 26.

55. *TNBSR* 22.

56. *PWR* 4:447.

57. *TNBSR* 9.

58. *NYT*, August 3, 1926; *DT* 1:2.

59. *LSMD* 113.

60. *LSMD* 92–95.

61. *LSMD* 109.

62. Unidentified clipping, WRM; *PWR* 4:123–24.

63. *NYT*, September 15, 1930; *DT* 2:212.

64. *TNBSR* xvi, 6.

65. *TNBSR* 47.

66. *NYT*, July 15, 1926; *TNBSR* 25.

67. *TNBSR* 53.

68. *TNBSR* 52; Rollins, *Will Rogers*, 52. This may be the first public mention of Rogers's famous phrase.

69. *TNBSR* 82.

70. *TNBSR* 52.

71. *TNBSR* 73, 82.

72. *TNBSR* 88, 89; Ketchum, *Will Rogers*, 314.

73. *RB* 114, April 7, 1935.

74. *TNBSR* 52; May, *The Big Tomorrow*, 43–44.

75. *TDW*, November 6, 1927; *WA* 3:93.

76. Betty Rogers, *Will Rogers*, 204.

77. *NYT*, January 11, 1927; *DT* 1:41.

78. *Congressional Record*, vol. 69, pt. 1, January 1928, p. 1323.

79. *PWR* 2:30; Robinson, *American Original*, 178–79.

80. *TDW*, October 10, 1926; *WA* 2:251.
81. Telegram from White House, correspondence file, WRM.
82. Telegram from Rogers, correspondence file, WRM.
83. *SEP*, January 8, 1927.
84. *SEP*, January 8, 1927.
85. *SEP*, January 8, 1927.
86. *ML* 3–17.
87. *NYT*, August 18, 1928; *DT* 1:225.
88. *NYT*, August 4, 1927; *DT* 1:115.
89. Yagoda, *Will Rogers*, 286.
90. Unidentified clipping, Scrapbook 21, WRM.
91. *TNBSR* 79.
92. *TDW*, June 28, 1925; *WA* 2:49.
93. Ketchum, *Will Rogers*, 209.
94. *Time*, July 19, 1926.

CHAPTER SIX

1. Telegram from Douglas Fairbanks, December 3, 1926, on Western Union letterhead, WRM; *PWR* 4:33.
2. Telegram from Coolidge, December 18, 1926, on White House stationery, WRM; *PWR* 4:471.
3. Typewritten speech notes, WRM; *PWR* 4:471–72.
4. *St. Louis Post-Dispatch*, June 11, 1928.
5. *NYT*, August 28, 1927; *TDW*, September 11, 1927; *WA* 3:70–73.
6. *NYT*, December 28, 1926.
7. Collins, "Will Rogers."
8. *TDW*, January 23, 1927; *WA* 2:296.
9. *TDW*, January 23, 1927; *WA* 2:298.
10. *TDW*, January 23, 1927; *WA* 2:299.
11. *NYT*, October 15, 1929; *DT* 2:84.
12. *PWR* 4:32.
13. *TDW*, September 6, 1931; *WA* 5, 65.
14. *Kansas City Star*, November 15, 1926, Scrapbook 8, WRM; *PWR* 4:464–66.
15. *PWR* 4:35.
16. *TDW*, April 3, 1927; *WA* 3:13.
17. *NYT*, March 16, 1927; *DT* 1:67.
18. *NYT*, March 21, 1931; *DT* 3:6.
19. John D. Rockefeller (1839–1937). Industrialist, philanthropist. Born Richford, New York. Bookkeeper in Cleveland. Entered oil business, 1863. Organized Stan-

dard Oil Company, 1870. By 1872, purchased nearly all refining firms in Cleveland. Properties merged in 1882 into Standard Oil Trust. In 1896, gave up leadership of business and focused on philanthropy, establishing institutions highly influential in American science, medicine, and public health. (*DAB*)

20. *NYT*, January 27, 1924; *WA* 1:186.

21. *TDW*, February 20, 1927; *WA* 2:306–10.

22. *NYT*, July 8, 1933; *DT* 4:51.

23. *NYT*, July 9, 1935; *DT* 4:329.

24. Letter from MacArthur, correspondence file, WRM.

25. *NYT*, October 16, 1926; *DT* 1:16–17.

26. *NYT*, February 19, 1927; *DT* 1:58.

27. *NYA*, August 22, 1927.

28. *LAT*, September 1, 1927; *DT* 1:123.

29. *NYT*, January 2, 1928; *PWR* 4:39.

30. *NYT*, May 24, 1927; *DT* 1:91.

31. *Dearborn Independent* clipping, WRM.

32. *NYT*, June 8, 1929; *DT* 2:36.

33. *NYT*, May 25, 1929; *DT* 1:32.

34. *New York Telegram*, November 27, 1928.

35. *TDW*, February 27, 1927; *WA* 2:312.

36. Miller, *New World Coming*, 63.

37. *PWR* 4:405–6.

38. *PWR* 4:459–60.

39. *WP*, June 9, 1924.

40. *NYT*, December 13, 1928; *DT* 1:285.

41. Croy, *Our Will Rogers*, 279.

42. *BG*, January 17, 1927; *DT* 1:7. Neither the *NYT* nor *LAT* carried this article.

43. Yagoda, *Will Rogers*, 247.

44. *PWR* 4:481.

45. *PWR* 4:529.

46. *St. Louis Post-Dispatch*, June 11, 1928.

47. *PWR* 5:132.

48. Letter to Corey Ford et al., ca. October 1929, WRM; *PWR* 5:139–40. Unclear whether letter was mailed.

49. Oscar Odd McIntyre (1884–1938). Newspaper columnist. Born Plattsburg, Missouri. Began newspaper career on *Gallipolis Journal* (Ohio), 1902. Arrived in New York in 1912 as an editor at *Hampton's Magazine*. Syndicated with Scripps-Howard and McNaught. Column, "New York Day by Day," appeared in more than five hundred newspapers. Publicist for Florenz Ziegfeld and various entertainers. (*DAB*)

50. Milsten, *An Appreciation of Will Rogers,* 89.

51. *NYT,* May 12, 1927.

52. *TDW,* February 19, 1928; *WA* 3:134–35.

53. *NYT,* November 2, 1927; *DT* 1:145.

54. See Whitney, *Reds in America,* 50, 83, 150; Allen, *Only Yesterday,* 83. Rogers read *Only Yesterday,* but never publicly commented on his being mentioned in relation to communist activities. In August 1915, a splinter group broke off from the National Security League to form the American Defense Society, composed largely of Republicans unhappy with the NSL's support of Woodrow Wilson.

55. *NYT,* February 28, 1930; *DT* 2:140.

56. *TDW,* February 22, 1925; *WA* 1:369.

57. For descriptions of the Great Flood, see Frederick Simpich, "The Great Mississippi Flood of 1927," 243–89; and John M. Barry, *Rising Tide: The Great Mississippi Flood of 1927 and How It Changed America.*

58. Ketchum, *Will Rogers,* 222–23; Sterling and Sterling, *Rogers: Reflections,* 109; *PWR* 4:36–37, 498.

59. *PWR* 4:37.

60. *NYT,* June 2, 1927; *DT* 1:95.

61. Telegram from Harrison, WRM.

62. *NYT,* June 28, 1927.

63. *NYT,* September 28, 1927; *DT* 1:121.

64. *TDW,* May 8, 1927; *WA* 3:26.

65. *SEP,* June 2, 1928.

66. *NYT,* January 13, 1928.

67. Typewritten speech notes, WRM; *PWR* 4:540, 559.

CHAPTER SEVEN

1. *BG,* May 21, 1927; *DT* 1:90.

2. *TDW,* June 5, 1927; *WA* 3:35.

3. Typewritten speech notes, WRM; *PWR* 4:505.

4. Typewritten speech notes, WRM.

5. *NYT,* September 23, 1927; *DT* 1:130.

6. *NYT,* April 5, 1929; *DT* 1:20.

7. Rollins, *Will Rogers,* 128; Yagoda, *Will Rogers,* 246.

8. *NYT,* December 30, 1927; *DT* 1:164.

9. *NYT,* July 4, 1928; *DT* 1:230.

10. *NYT,* August 25, 1928; *DT* 1:248.

11. *NYT,* March 18, 1927; *DT* 1:68.

12. *NYT,* February 21, 1928; *DT* 1:182.

13. *NYT*, October 28, 1928; *DT* 1:266.

14. William "Wild Bill" Hopson (1887–1928). Born Hill City, Kansas. Began flying airmail in April 1920, logging over four thousand hours of flight time and covering 413,034 miles. Left the service when airmail was transferred to private companies. (National Postal Museum)

15. *NYT*, October 20, 1928; *DT* 1:266.

16. *NYT*, August 31, 1927; *DT* 1:123.

17. *NYT*, September 6, 1927; *DT* 1:125.

18. *NYT*, November 1, 1927; *DT* 1:144.

19. *NYT*, May 1, 1928; *DT* 1:207.

20. *NYT*, October 9, 1928; *DT* 1:262.

21. *NYT*, March 1, 1929; *DT* 1:313.

22. Miller, *New World Coming*, 318.

23. *NYT*, October 20, 1928; *DT* 1:266.

24. Dwight Whitney Morrow (1873–1931). Lawyer, banker, diplomat. Born Huntington, West Virginia. Graduated Amherst College, studied law Columbia University. Partnered at J. P. Morgan. WWI, directed National War Savings Committee. Aide to General Pershing. Headed Morrow Board recommending creation of Army Air Corps. Ambassador to Mexico, 1927–30. U.S. Senate, 1930–1931. (*DAB*)

25. Riedel, "Conversations," 37–38.

26. Yagoda, *Will Rogers*, 247.

27. Betty Rogers, *Will Rogers*, 215.

28. *NYT*, December 15, 1927; *DT* 1:158.

29. *ML* 68.

30. *SEP*, June 2, 1928; *ML* 69; Collins, "Will Rogers," 184.

31. *SEP*, June 9, 1928; *ML* 82.

32. *RB* 8, April 30, 1930.

33. *NYT*, December 15, 1927; *DT* 1:158.

34. *PWR* 4:551; Robinson, "The Dance of the Comedians," 71.

35. *Love's Labour's Lost*, act 5, scene 2.

36. *NYT*, January 7, 1928.

37. Telegram from McNitt, WRM; *PWR* 4:518.

38. *NYT*, January 14, 1928; *DT* 1:170.

39. *TDW*, February 5, 1928; *WA* 3:128.

40. Letter on The Willard stationery, WRM; *PWR* 4:519–20.

41. Letter on White House stationery, WRM; *PWR* 4:523.

42. *PWR* 4:528–29.

43. *NYT*, January 17, 1928; *DT* 1:171.

44. *CA* 93; Robinson, *American Original*, 194.

45. Yagoda, *Will Rogers*, 246.
46. *SEP,* January 28, 1928; *HTBF* 68.
47. *CA* 93. Quotation attributed to William Allen White, owner of the *Emporia Gazette.*
48. *Life,* May 31, 1928; *HCTR* 8.
49. Unidentified newspaper clipping, Scrapbook 17, WRM.
50. *HCTR* 12.
51. *HCTR* 94.
52. *CA* 93–94.
53. *CA* 106.
54. *CA* 94.
55. *CA* 105.
56. Ketchum, *Will Rogers*, 247.
57. Unidentified clipping, WRM. Quote from Right Reverend Francis Gilfillan.
58. *New York Evening Telegraph,* November 10, 1928.
59. Miller, *New World Coming,* 352.
60. Kyvig, *The United States,* 149.
61. *NYT,* April 19, 1927; *DT* 1:78–79.
62. Daniels, *The Time between the Wars.*
63. Robinson, *American Original,* 160.
64. Yagoda, *Will Rogers*, 293, attributed to Jonah J. Goldstein.
65. *NYT,* March 8, 1928; *DT* 1:187.
66. Yagoda, *Will Rogers*, 32.
67. *RB* 18, April 27, 1930.
68. *NYT,* March 8, 1928; *DT* 1:187.
69. *TDW,* December 23, 1928; *WA* 3:233.
70. MacNeill, "Reminiscences," 116.
71. *NYT,* October 16, 1928; *PWR* 5:81n.
72. *TDW,* November 4, 1928; *WA* 3:217–18.
73. Unidentified newspaper clipping, Scrapbook 21, WRM.
74. Bernard M. Baruch (1870–1965). Financier and public adviser. Born Camden, South Carolina. Graduated College of the City of New York. Held several jobs until accumulated enough money to buy seat on New York Stock Exchange. Millionaire at thirty. During World War I, member Advisory Commission to the Council of National Defense. Accompanied Wilson to Versailles peace conference. Member of "Brain Trust" in New Deal. Urged stockpiling of rubber and tin, anticipating U.S. entering World War II. Financial adviser during WWII, proposing pay-as-you-go tax plan, rent ceilings, stockpiling strategic resources, and synthetic rubber. (*DAB*)
75. *PWR* 5:11–12.

76. Robinson, *American Original,* 200.

77. *NYT,* November 22, 1928; *DT* 1:278.

78. *NYT,* January 28, 1935; *DT* 4:243.

79. Letter from Roosevelt dated November 23, 1928, WRM; *PWR* 5:88.

80. Letter from Roosevelt dated December 2, 1928, WRM; *PWR* 5:94–95.

81. *NYT,* July 8, 1929; *DT* 2:47.

CHAPTER EIGHT

1. *NYT,* August 12, 1923; *WA* 1:108.

2. *Nashville Banner,* November 5, 1925.

3. *NYT,* November 28, 1927; *DT* 1:153.

4. Miller, *New World Coming,* 10.

5. Kyvig, *The United States,* 181–82.

6. Miller, *New World Coming,* 211.

7. Sterling and Sterling, *Rogers: Reflections,* 141.

8. Kyvig, *The United States,* 116–17.

9. *SEP,* June 2, 1928; *ML* 71.

10. Kyvig, *The United States,* 145.

11. Ketchum, *Will Rogers,* 181; Brown, *Imagemaker,* 118.

12. Sterling and Sterling, *Rogers: Reflections,* 161.

13. *NYT,* April 25, 1930; *DT* 2:160.

14. *NYT,* June 19, 1934; *DT* 4:185.

15. *NYT,* March 21, 1931; *DT* 3:7.

16. *NYT,* September 1, 1932; *DT* 3:204.

17. *NYT,* February 3, 1934; *DT* 4:135.

18. *NYT,* October 19, 1931; *DT* 3:87.

19. *LAT,* March 12, 1932; *DT* 3:141.

20. *NYT,* December 31, 1927; *DT* 1:165.

21. *NYT,* September 21, 1924; *WA* 1:295.

22. *TDW,* September 20, 1925; *WA* 2:81–82.

23. Sterling and Sterling, *Rogers: A Photo-Biography,* 17.

24. Betty Rogers, *Will Rogers,* 274.

25. *Oolagah Chief,* June 3, 1897, clipping files, WRM.

26. Alvan Tufts Fuller (1878–1958). Businessman, politician. Born Boston. Engaged in bicycle business. Founder of Packard Motor Car Company of Boston. Massachusetts House of Representatives. U.S. House of Representatives, 1917–1921. Lieutenant governor of Massachusetts, 1921–1925. Governor, 1925–1929.

27. Kyvig, *The United States,* 150.

28. *TDW,* May 22, 1927; *WA* 3:31–32.

29. Miller, *New World Coming,* 59.

30. Waters, "Will Rogers: The Not Always Humorous Columnist," 58.

31. *NYT,* May 25, 1933; *DT* 4:33.

32. *NYT,* March 14, 1935; *DT* 4:287.

33. Baruch, *Baruch,* 223.

34. Letter from Baruch, June 6, 1931, correspondence file, WRM; *PWR* 5:255–56.

35. *Time,* June 28, 1943.

36. Baruch, *Baruch,* 178.

37. *TDW,* September 19, 1926; *WA* 2:242–43.

38. *NYT,* August 13, 1926; *DT* 1:4.

39. *New York Telegram,* November 26, 1928; *NYT,* November 23, 1928.

40. *Time,* June 28, 1943.

41. Baruch, *Baruch,* 228.

42. Sterling and Sterling, *Rogers in Hollywood.*

43. Baruch, *Baruch,* 223–24; *PWR* 5:257.

44. Baruch, *Baruch,* 223–24.

45. *PWR* 5:257.

46. Kyvig, *The United States,* 82.

47. Ketchum, *Will Rogers,* 254.

48. Unidentified clipping, Scrapbook 9, WRM.

49. Sterling and Sterling, *Rogers: A Photo-Biography,* 178.

50. *NYT,* September 18, 1929; *DT* 2:74.

51. Ketchum, *Will Rogers,* 262–63.

52. Lecture tour notes, November 10, 1926, Abilene, Texas, WRM.

53. Rogers, *Will Rogers at the Ziegfeld Follies,* xviii.

54. Jenkins, "Representative Clowns," 121.

55. *David Harum,* WRM; Yagoda, *Will Rogers,* 311.

56. Thomson, *A Biographical Dictionary of Film,* 487; Yagoda, *Will Rogers,* 311.

57. Betty Rogers, *Will Rogers,* 194.

58. *NYT,* October 22, 1929.

59. Betty Rogers, *Will Rogers,* 201–2.

60. *DT* 2:86–88.

61. *OCT,* February 3, 1931.

62. Sterling and Sterling, *Rogers: A Photo-Biography,* 178–79.

63. *NYT,* October 25, 1929; *DT* 2:89.

64. *NYT,* October 26, 1929; *DT* 2:89–90.

65. *PWR* 5:167–68n4.

66. *NYT,* November 1, 1929; *DT* 2:92.

67. *TDW,* December 1, 1929; *WA* 4:91.

68. *TDW,* November 23, 1924; *WA* 1:326.

69. *NYT,* June 28, 1930; *DT* 2:183.

70. Miller, *New World Coming,* 152.

71. *NYT,* September 27, 1928; *DT* 1:251–52.

72. Baruch, *Baruch,* 222.

73. Baruch, *Baruch,* 227.

74. Baruch, *Baruch,* 223–24.

75. *NYT,* September 16, 1929; *DT* 2:74.

76. *NYT,* September 16, 1929; *DT* 2:74.

77. *NYT,* May 9, 1929; *DT* 2:25.

78. Hodgson, *The Colonel,* 186.

79. *TDW,* April 13, 1930; *WA* 4:134.

80. *NYT,* January 29, 1930; *DT* 2:127.

81. *NYT,* December 23, 1929; *DT* 1:110.

82. *RB* 3, April 6, 1930.

83. Telegram, Ochs to Rogers, January 20, 1930, *NYT* archives; Yagoda, *Will Rogers,* 288–89.

84. *NYT,* January 30, 1931; *DT* 2:128.

85. *TDW,* February 8, 1925; *WA* 1:363.

86. *NYT,* January 30, 1930; *DT* 2:127.

87. *NYT,* January 25, 1930, 3–4; Ketchum, *Will Rogers,* 278.

88. George Bernard Shaw (1856–1950). British playwright. Born Dublin. Spurned formal education. Moved to London in 1876, became leading music and theatre critic. Began literary career as novelist. Earlier plays attacked social hypocrisy. *The Doctor's Dilemma* (1906), a comedy directed at the medical profession, *Candida* (1898), a satire about social attitudes on sex relations, and *Pygmalion* (1912), a witty study of phonetics and treatment of class distinction, were greatest stage successes. (*EWB*)

89. *NYT,* January 25, 1930.

90. Shaw, *John Bull's Other Island* (1907), act 2.

91. *TDW,* November 9, 1930; *WA* 4:203.

92. *NYT,* March 25, 1933; *DT* 4:8.

93. Shaw, *Misalliance* (1909).

94. *NYT,* October 24, 1930; *DT* 2:228.

95. Shaw, *Major Barbara* (1907).

96. *TDW,* October 30, 1932; *WA* 5:197.

97. *NYT,* February 11, 1930; *DT* 2:133.

98. *NYT,* June 8, 1924; *WA* 1:246.

99. *Claremore Weekly Press,* February 20, 1930.

100. *NYT,* March 5, 1930; *DT* 2:142.

101. *NYT,* April 28, 1930; *DT* 2:161.

102. *NYT,* November 15, 1930; *DT* 2:236.

103. *RB* 3–6, April 6, 1930.

104. Helen Adams Keller (1880–1968). Author, lecturer. Born Tuscumbia, Alabama. When nineteen months old, contracted undiagnosed disease, leaving her blind and deaf. In 1887, Annie Sullivan began teaching her to communicate through sign language. In 1904, graduated from Radcliffe, first deaf-blind person to earn bachelor's degree. Outspoken crusader for people with disabilities, women's suffrage, birth control, workers' rights, socialism, and pacifism. 1920, helped found ACLU. Awarded Presidential Medal of Freedom by Lyndon Johnson, 1964. (*DAB*)

105. *WA* 6:181.

106. *Midstream,* Will Rogers Ranch library.

107. Letter from Keller, April 1, 1930, WRM; *PWR* 5:158–59.

108. Letter from Rogers to Keller, May 25, 1930, WRM; *PWR* 5:179–80.

CHAPTER NINE

1. *NYT,* February 9, 1931; *DT* 2:269.

2. *SEP,* February 27, 1932; *ML* 96.

3. Kyvig, *The United States,* 183–85, 190.

4. *RB* 66, October 18, 1931.

5. *NYT,* January 7, 1931; *DT* 2:254

6. Sterling and Sterling, *Rogers: Reflections,* 178.

7. Kyvig, *The United States,* 190.

8. *TDW,* January 18, 1931; *WA* 4:224.

9. *NYT,* November 20, 1930; *DT* 2:238.

10. *Cleveland Plain Dealer,* November 23, 1930.

11. *NYT,* August 17, 1931; *DT* 3:66.

12. *TDW,* January 18, 1931; *WA* 4:225–26.

13. *NYT,* March 17, 1931; *DT* 3:5. The withholding of federal income taxes would take place during World War II.

14. *NYT,* November 13, 1931; *DT* 3:96.

15. *NYT,* April 29, 1932; *DT* 3:158.

16. *NYT,* July 21, 1933; *DT* 4:56–57.

17. *Beverly Hills Citizen,* October 22, 1931; *RB* 67.

18. *RB,* November 14, 1932, in support of the Christmas drive for the American Red Cross.

19. *RB* 14, April 20, 1930.

20. Correspondence file, WRM.

21. *RB* 10–14, April 20, 1930.

22. Kyvig, *The United States*, 193.

23. Sterling and Sterling, *Rogers: Reflections*, 159–60.

24. Unidentified clipping, Scrapbook 21, WRM.

25. *NYT*, June 14–15, 17, 1930; *PWR* 5:176.

26. Rollins, *Will Rogers*, 170.

27. *OCT*, February 3, 1931; *PWR* 5:224.

28. Brown, *Imagemaker*, 18; from Hoover speech on NBC Broadcast, November 19, 1935.

29. *American Magazine*, October 1930, 110.

30. *NYT*, July 8, 1931; *DT* 3:50.

31. Schlesinger, *The Age of Roosevelt*, 242.

32. *NYT*, February 22, 1932; *DT* 3:132, 134.

33. Rollins, *Will Rogers*, 248–49; *NYT*, October 19, 1931.

34. *RB* 67, October 18, 1931.

35. *RB* 66, October 18, 1931.

36. Telegram from Stuart M. Crocker, WRM; *PWR* 5:264–65.

37. Tennen, "Will Rogers," 70.

38. Betty Rogers, *Will Rogers*, 184.

39. Tennen, "Will Rogers," 67–68.

40. Tennen, "Will Rogers," 70.

41. *NYT*, February 6, 1931; *DT* 2:268.

42. *OCT*, February 3, 1931.

43. *RB* 66, October 18, 1931.

44. *NYT*, January 21, 1931; *DT* 2:260.

45. *NYT*, July 16, 1932; *DT* 3:186.

46. *NYT*, October 16, 1930; *DT* 2:225.

47. *NYT*, February 16, 1934; *DT* 4:139.

48. *NYT*, March 28, 1933; *DT* 4:10.

49. *NYT*, January 13, 1931.

50. Ketchum, *Will Rogers*, 285; *DT* 2:258.

51. *NYT*, January 17, 1931; *DT* 2:258.

52. *NYT*, January 8, 1931; *DT* 2:255.

53. Frank Monroe Hawks (1897–1938). American aviator. Born Marshalltown, Iowa. Attended University of California. WWI, enlisted in army, completed flight school, instructor pilot in Texas. During postwar, barnstormed country, performed at aerial exhibitions, including taking twenty-three-year-old Amelia Earhart on her first flight in 1920. Billed as "fastest airman in the world," setting 214 point-to-point air-speed records in the United States and Europe. Died in 1938 flying an experimental Gwinn Aircar in East Aurora, New York. (Walter A.

Musciano, "Frank Hawks: The Story of the Legendary Speed Flying King," *Aviation History*, November 2005)

54. *TDW*, March 1, 1931; *WA* 4:241.

55. William "Alfalfa Bill" Murray (1869–1956). Lawyer, politician. Born Collinsville, Texas. Practiced law in Indian Territory. Delegate to Oklahoma statehood convention, serving as president. First speaker of Oklahoma House of Representatives. U.S. representative from Oklahoma. In 1924, led agricultural colony in Bolivia. Elected governor of Oklahoma in 1930. Defied impeachment, relied on Oklahoma National Guard to enforce state laws through martial law, charging military with duties ranging from policing ticket sales at university football games to safeguarding oil wells. By 1935, had called out Guard forty-seven times.

56. *NYT*, February 3, 1931; *DT* 2:241.

57. *OCT*, February 3, 1931.

58. *PWR* 5:243.

59. *CA* 119; Ketchum, *Will Rogers*, 286.

60. *NYT*, February 27, 1931; *DT* 2:250.

61. *PWR* 5:250–51nn1–3.

62. *NYT*, April 9, 1931; *DT* 3:14.

63. Rollins, *Will Rogers*, 248; *NYT*, April 13, 1931.

64. *PWR* 5:250.

65. *NYT*, April 23, 1931.

66. *NYT*, April 28, 1931.

67. Correspondence file, WRM; *PWR* 5:252.

68. *DT* 3:23; *PWR* 5:254nn1–3.

69. *PWR* 5:254.

70. Brown, *Imagemaker*, 143–44.

71. *PWR* 5:277.

72. *Jackson Times* (Kentucky), July 3, 1931.

73. *Columbus Dispatch*, June 23, 1931.

74. Robinson, *American Original*, 236.

75. *Home Friend* magazine, May 1932, Scrapbook 9, WRM.

76. Brinkley, *Wheels for the World*, 362.

77. *NYT*, October 31, 1931.

78. *New York Herald-Tribune*, November 2, 1931.

79. *PWR* 5:273n1.

80. Betty Rogers, *Will Rogers*, 269.

Chapter Ten

1. *NYT*, September 21, 1931; *DT* 3:71.
2. Buhite, *Patrick J. Hurley*; Lohbeck, *Patrick J. Hurley*.
3. Lohbeck, *Patrick J. Hurley*, 31. Patrick Jay Hurley (1883–1963). Lawyer, diplomat. Born Choctaw Nation, Indian Territory. Practiced law in Oklahoma. Assistant secretary of war, 1929, promoted to secretary after death of James W. Good. World War II, brigadier general. Personal representative of President Roosevelt, flew to Soviet Union, first foreigner to visit Eastern Front. Visited Near East, Middle East, China, and Afghanistan. Minister to New Zealand, 1942. Ambassador to China, 1944. Lost three attempts for U.S. Senate from New Mexico, 1946, 1948, 1952. (*DAB*)
4. *TDW*, December 14, 1924; *WA* 1:336.
5. *TDW*, November 28, 1926; *WA* 2:278.
6. *NYT*, December 6, 1931; *DT* 3:108.
7. *TDW*, November 1, 1931; *WA* 5:84–85; Lohbeck, *Patrick J. Hurley*, 92.
8. *SEP*, April 30, 1932; *ML* 172.
9. Hurley letter to Rogers, November 18, 1931; *PWR* 5:279.
10. Abend, *My Life in China*, 149.
11. *SEP*, February 27, 1932; *ML* 108.
12. *PWR* 5:279n8.
13. Hurley letter to Rogers, November 18, 1931; *PWR* 5:280, 281n1.
14. Ketchum, *Will Rogers*, 345.
15. Riedel, "Conversations," 6.
16. Christian George Riedel (1887–1957). Born Goodwin, South Dakota. Owned apiaries in Canada. Entrepreneur in real estate, avocados, mahogany, gold mining in Southern California. Claimed to have brought the first banana trees to California. Emigrated to Austria shortly before death. (Riedel family papers)
17. Riedel, "Conversations," 4.
18. Riedel, "Conversations," 26.
19. Riedel, "Conversations," 47.
20. *NYT*, March 19, 1927; *DT* 1:69.
21. *NYT*, November 23, 1931; *DT* 3:99.
22. *SEP*, February 27, 1932; *ML* 107.
23. Riedel, "Conversations," 12.
24. *TDW*, January 31, 1932; *WA* 5:113.
25. *TDW*, December 25, 1932; *WA* 5:215.
26. *TDW*, December 25, 1932; *WA* 5:215.
27. *TDW*, December 11, 1932; *WA* 5:210.
28. *SEP*, March 5, 1932; *ML* 110.

29. Riedel, "Conversations," 27.

30. Riedel, "Conversations," 27–28.

31. Riedel, "Conversations," 28–29.

32. Riedel, "Conversations," 39.

33. Riedel, "Conversations," 21–22.

34. *TDW,* January 31, 1932; *WA* 5:115.

35. Riedel, "Conversations," 8–9.

36. Riedel, "Conversations," 5, 34, 58.

37. Riedel, "Conversations," 34–35.

38. *TDW,* January 31, 1932; *WA* 5:114–15.

39. Riedel, "Conversations," 26.

40. *NYT,* December 7, 1931; *DT* 3:104.

41. *SEP,* March 5, 1932; *ML* 109–23.

42. *ML* 120.

43. *SEP,* March 5, 1932; *ML* 120.

44. *NYT,* December 5, 1931; *DT* 3:104.

45. *TDW,* August 5, 1934; *WA* 6:141.

46. *TDW,* February 7, 1932; *WA* 5:117.

47. Abend, *My Life in China,* 163.

48. Snow, *Far Eastern Front,* 105.

49. Powell, *My Twenty-five Years in China,* 189.

50. *TDW,* September 9, 1934; *WA* 6:152.

51. *NYT,* December 16, 1931; *DT* 3:108.

52. Powell, *My Twenty-five Years in China,* 189.

53. *SEP,* March 12, 1932; *ML* 124.

54. *NYT,* December 15, 1931; *DT* 3:108.

55. Abend, *My Life in China,* 169.

56. *SEP,* March 19, 1932; *ML* 140–41.

57. *NYT,* December 22, 1931; *DT* 3:110.

58. *NYT,* December 26, 1931; *DT* 3:111–12.

59. Abend, *My Life in China,* 150–51.

60. *SEP,* April 30, 1932; *ML* 161.

61. *SEP,* April 30, 1932; *ML* 166–67.

62. *NYT,* December 28, 1931; *DT* 3:112.

63. Rogers's copies of *Far Eastern Review* and *China Digest,* WRM.

64. *NYT,* December 31, 1931; *DT* 3:113.

65. *TDW,* April 10, 1927; *WA* 3:16.

66. *TDW,* July 5, 1925; *WA* 2:50.

67. *TDW,* April 10, 1927; *WA* 3:16–17.

68. *TDW,* October 9, 1932; *WA* 5:212.

69. *SEP*, April 30, 1932; *ML* 173.

70. *SEP*, April 2, 1932; *ML* 160.

71. *SEP*, April 30, 1932; *ML* 172–73.

72. *NYT*, January 5, 1932; *DT* 3:115; *PWR* 5:283–85.

73. *NYT*, January 19, 1932; *DT* 3:119.

74. Collins, "Will Rogers," 58.

75. *NYT*, February 4, 1932; *DT* 3:126.

76. *NYT*, February 9, 1932; *DT* 3:127.

77. Warren, *Herbert Hoover and the Great Depression*, 331.

78. *NYA*, February 12, 1932; Hurley papers, University of Oklahoma Libraries.

79. *CA* 91.

CHAPTER ELEVEN

1. Typewritten notes, WRM; *PWR* 5:355. His use of "Mickey Mouse" to describe something gimmicky or false may be one of earliest recorded examples of adjectival application of the cartoon character's name.

2. *NYT*, October 28, 1927; *DT* 1:143.

3. *CA* 127.

4. Letter from Charles Curtis, June 24, 1932, WRM; *PWR* 5:341.

5. *NYT*, May 3, 1932; *DT* 3:159.

6. Letter from Roosevelt, April 3, 1931, WRM; *PWR* 5:249.

7. Jenkins, "Representative Clowns," 112.

8. Letter from Rogers, WRM; *PWR* 5:258–59.

9. Telegram to Roosevelt, May 23, 1932, WRM; *PWR* 5:330–31.

10. Letter from Roosevelt, June 1, 1932, WRM; *PWR* 5:332.

11. Amon G. Carter (1879–1955). Newspaper magnate, oil entrepreneur, civic booster. Born in log cabin in Crafton, Texas. Quit school at eleven. Worked in newspaper advertising, founded *Fort Worth Star-Telegram*. Created WBAP, first radio station in Fort Worth, in 1922, followed by Texas's first television station, WBAP-TV. Used national stage to drum up business for Fort Worth region, including Convair plant (now Lockheed-Martin), General Motors assembly plant, and Bell Helicopter. Persuaded Southern Air Transport (now American Airlines) to move headquarters from Dallas to Fort Worth, pressured several oil companies to keep their headquarters in Fort Worth. Convinced Texas state legislature to create Texas Tech University. Personified Texas cowboy image as inveterate storyteller, gambler, and drinker, generous with his millions, and quick to draw his six-shooters. (Amon Carter Museum)

12. Telegram from Carter, WRM; *PWR* 5:340.

13. Neal, *Happy Days Are Here Again*, 6.

14. *CA* 133.
15. *Chicago American*, June 29, 1932.
16. Robinson, *American Original*, 232.
17. Neal, *Happy Days Are Here Again*, 268.
18. *CA* 144.
19. Neal, *Happy Days Are Here Again*, 6.
20. Morris, *Rage for Fame*.
21. *NYT*, March 3, 1932; *DT* 3:137.
22. Henry Ford (1863–1947). Founder, Ford Motor Company. Inventor of Model T automobile that revolutionized American transportation and industry. Introduced modern assembly lines used in mass production. One of richest men in world. Intense commitment to lowering costs resulted in many technical and business innovations, including franchising network that put dealership in every city. Bequeathed vast wealth to Ford Foundation. (*EWB*)
23. *NYT*, February 18, 1932; *DT* 3:131.
24. *RB* 44; Watts, *The People's Tycoon*, 341.
25. *NYT*, March 25, 1923; *WA* 1:44.
26. *RB* 46–47, June 1, 1930.
27. *NYT*, October 28, 1923; *WA* 1:142.
28. Watts, *The People's Tycoon*, 396.
29. Brinkley, *Wheels for the World*, xxii.
30. *CA* 7.
31. *NYT*, March 3, 1932; *DT* 3:138.
32. *NYT*, March 4, 1932; *DT* 3:138.
33. *NYT*, March 12, 1932; *DT* 3:141.
34. Letter from Anne Lindbergh, WRM; *PWR* 5:505.
35. *NYT*, May 14, 1932; *DT* 3:166.
36. Weaver, "Bonus March"; Warren, *Herbert Hoover and the Great Depression*.
37. Mencken, *A Carnival of Buncombe*, 51–52.
38. *NYT*, December 30, 1923; *WA* 1:175.
39. *NYT*, June 7, 1932.
40. *NYT*, December 30, 1923; *WA* 1:172.
41. *Congressional Record*, vol. 65, pt. 1, January 7, 1924, p. 672.
42. *NYT*, July 30, 1932; *DT* 3:191.
43. *NYT*, July 30, 1932; *DT* 3:191–92.
44. *TDW*, August 21, 1932; *WA* 5:178.
45. *NYT*, July 25, 1932; *DT* 3:189.
46. *NYT*, July 25, 1932; *DT* 3:189.
47. Robinson, *American Original*, 214–15.
48. Handwritten notes, Western Union letterhead, WRM; *PWR* 5:351–52.

49. *NYT*, July 25, 1932; *DT* 3:189.

50. *NYT*, July 20, 1932; *DT* 3:187.

51. Handwritten notes, WRM; *PWR* 5:327.

52. *NYT*, October 11, 1932; *DT* 3:220.

53. *NYT*, October 12, 1932; *DT* 3:122.

54. *NYT*, October 18, 1932; *DT* 3:224.

55. *NYT*, November 6, 1932.

56. *LAT*, September 25, 1932.

57. Typewritten speech notes, WRM.

58. Letter from Chandler, WRM; *PWR* 5:356–57.

59. *NYT*, November 2, 1932; *DT* 3:230.

60. *NYT*, October 31, 1932; *DT* 3:229.

61. *NYT*, October 13, 1931; *DT* 3:85.

62. Letter from Borah, October 16, 1931, WRM.

63. *NYT*, November 28, 1932.

64. *NYT*, November 30, December 1, 1932; *PWR* 5:374.

65. *NYT*, December 8, 1932; *DT* 3:247.

66. Letter from Hurley dated December 29, 1932, WRM.

67. *LAT*, February 2, 1933; *DT* 3:271.

68. Yagoda, *Will Rogers*, 289.

69. *NYT*, December 8, 1931; *DT* 3:104, 106.

70. Telegram, WRM; *PWR* 5:384–85.

71. *TDW*, December 18, 1932; *DT* 5:213.

72. *TDW*, December 18, 1932; *DT* 5:213.

Chapter Twelve

1. Telegram on Western Union letterhead, WRM; *PWR* 5:367–69.

2. *NYT*, March 5, 1933; *DT* 4:1.

3. Kyvig, *The United States*, 196.

4. *NYT*, March 6, 1933; *DT* 4:1.

5. Letter from Evangeline Booth, WRM; *PWR* 5:392.

6. *PWR* 5:396.

7. Ketchum, *Will Rogers*, 340.

8. *NYT*, May 7, 1933.

9. *RB* 74, April 30, 1933.

10. *RB* 73, April 30, 1933.

11. *RB* 77, April 30, 1933.

12. *NYT*, March 15, 1933; *DT* 4:4.

13. Typewritten speech notes, WRM.

14. *NYT*, May 4, 1933; *DT* 4:25.
15. Rollins, *Will Rogers*, 210; *PWR* 5:398, 400.
16. *PWR* 5:402. A typewritten note on the bottom of Rogers's NBC text notes that the radio network received a call from the White House immediately after Rogers's broadcast requesting a transcript. The text was read over the phone to a White House stenographer. There is no evidence that Rogers and Roosevelt orchestrated their talks.
17. *NYT*, May 9–10, 1933; *DT* 4:27.
18. Rollins, *Will Rogers*, 222–23. Remarks from *Good Gulf* show, October 7, 1934.
19. Typewritten transcript of radio broadcast, May 14, 1933, WRM; *PWR* 5:405–8.
20. Carter Glass (1858–1946). Newspaper publisher, politician. Born Lynchburg, Virginia. Member, state senate, 1899–1903. Elected to U.S. House of Representatives, 1902–1918. Secretary of treasury, 1918–1920. U.S. Senate, 1920 until his death. Declined appointment by Franklin Roosevelt to become secretary of the treasury. (*DAB*)
21. *NYT*, May 20, 1933; *DT* 4:31.
22. Typewritten transcript of radio broadcast, WRM.
23. Typewritten transcript of radio broadcast, WRM; *PWR* 5:430.
24. Rollins, *Will Rogers*, 212.
25. *NYT*, April 8, 1933; *DT* 4:14.
26. *NYT*, May 20, 1932; *DT* 3:168.
27. Prohibition correspondence file, WRM.
28. Prohibition correspondence file, WRM.
29. Kyvig, *The United States*, 197.
30. *NYT*, March 30, 1933; *DT* 4:11.
31. Kyvig, *The United States*, 73.
32. *RB* 126, April 31, 1935.
33. Sterling and Sterling, *Rogers: Reflections*, 236; Kyvig, *The United States*, 131.
34. *TDW*, November 18, 1934; *WA* 6:172.
35. *PWR* 5:575n1.
36. *NYT*, July 13, 1934; *DT* 4:195–96.
37. *NYT*, July 14, 1934; *DT* 4:196.
38. *NYT*, August 8, 1933; *DT* 4:64.
39. Macfarlane, *Bing Crosby*; Rollins, *Will Rogers*, 98–99.
40. Typewritten "Blue Eagle" speech, WRM.
41. *NYT*, March 14, 1935; *DT* 4:287.
42. Correspondence file, WRM; *PWR* 5:584–85.
43. *DO*, March 31, 1935; *WA* 6:208.
44. *NYT*, July 14, 1933; *DT* 4:52–53.
45. *NYT*, August 29, 1933; *DT* 1:72.

46. *NYT*, August 23, 1933; *DT* 4:61.

47. *NYT*, May 23, 1933; *DT* 4:32.

48. *NYT*, September 21, 1933; *DT* 4:81.

49. *RB* 129–34, April 28, 1935.

50. *RB* 157, May 26, 1935.

51. Roach, "Lariat in the Sun," 31.

52. Letter from Garner dated December 14, 1934, WRM; *PWR* 5:535.

53. Letter from Baruch dated October 27, 1933, WRM; *PWR* 5:427.

54. *NYT*, October 18, 1933; *DT* 4:92.

55. *NYT*, December 23, 1933; *DT* 4:104–5. Bryan made his famous "Cross of Gold" speech in 1896, which called for free coinage of silver and led to his presidential nomination.

56. *PWR* 5:468.

57. Neal Gabler, *Walt Disney.*

58. Robinson, *American Original,* 164.

59. Ketchum, *Will Rogers,* 261.

60. Swindell, *Spencer Tracy,* 148.

61. MacNeill, "Reminiscences," 118–19.

62. *PWR* 5:254; telegram to Walter M. Harrison, May 18, 1931, WRM. Oklahoma City University considered granting Rogers a doctor of humanities degree.

63. Sterling and Sterling, *Rogers: Reflections,* 3.

64. *PWR* 4:216–17.

65. Ketchum, *Will Rogers,* 315.

66. Ketchum, *Will Rogers,* 303.

67. Betty Rogers, *Will Rogers,* 23.

68. Betty Rogers, *Will Rogers,* 175–76.

69. Ketchum, *Will Rogers,* 313.

70. *NYT*, October 22, 1933.

71. *NYT*, February 12, 1934; *DT* 4:137.

72. Transcript of radio broadcast, February 25, 1934, WRM; *PWR* 5:471.

73. Schlesinger, *Age of Roosevelt,* 452–55; *PWR* 5:477.

74. *NYT*, February 21, 1934; *DT* 4:141.

75. Transcript of radio broadcast, February 25, 1934, WRM; *PWR* 5:471.

76. Transcript of radio broadcast, February 25, 1934, WRM; *PWR* 5:471.

77. *PWR* 5:476–77n16.

78. Transcript of radio broadcast, February 25, 1934, WRM; *PWR* 5:471.

79. Transcript of radio broadcast, February 25, 1934, WRM; *PWR* 5:475n1.

80. Transcript of radio broadcast, February 25, 1934, WRM; *PWR* 5:471.

81. *PWR* 5:475n4.

82. Transcript of radio broadcast, February 25, 1934, WRM; *PWR* 5:471.

CHAPTER THIRTEEN

1. *NYT*, July 23, 1934; *DT* 4:200.

2. *NYT*, August 13, 1934; *DT* 4:205.

3. *NYT*, July 28, 1934; *DT* 4:201.

4. *NYT*, August 2, 1934; *DT* 4:203.

5. *NYT*, August 17, 1934; *DT* 4:208.

6. *TDW*, September 4, 1932; *WA* 5:181.

7. *NYT*, August 20, 1934; *DT* 4:208–9.

8. *NYT*, August 24, 1934; *DT* 4:210.

9. *NYT*, August 24, 1934; *DT* 4:210.

10. *NYT*, August 25, 1934; *DT* 4:210.

11. *NYT*, September 3, 1934; *DT* 4:213.

12. *NYT*, September 12, 1934; *DT* 4:216.

13. *NYT*, September 15, 1934; *DT* 4:217.

14. *NYT*, September 22, 1934; *DT* 4:219.

15. *RB* 229, March 31, 1935.

16. *NYT*, September 11, 1934; *DT* 4:216.

17. Typewritten speech notes, on Athenee Palace Hotel stationery, Bucharest, WRM; *PWR* 5:500–503.

18. *NYT*, August 11, 1933; *DT* 4:65.

19. *NYT*, January 23, 1934; *DT* 4:130.

20. Rollins, *Will Rogers*, 213–18.

21. *NYT*, May 23, 1934; *DT* 4:176.

22. *NYT*, June 6, 1931; *DT* 3:34–35. Presidential pensions were authorized in 1958.

23. *NYT*, October 14, 1933; *DT* 4:91.

24. *TDW*, August 19, 1934; *WA* 6:145–46.

25. *TDW*, December 28, 1924; *WA* 1:316.

26. *NYT*, September 25, 1933; *DT* 4:82.

27. *TDW*, August 19, 1934; *WA* 6:145–46.

28. *NYT*, March 27, 1933; *DT* 4:8.

29. Sterling and Sterling, *Rogers: Reflections*, 238.

30. *NYT*, October 19, 1934; *DT* 4:231.

31. Letter F. C. Sykes to Will Rogers, October 31, 1934, correspondence file, WRM.

32. Transcript of radio broadcast, January 21, 1934, WRM; *PWR* 5:459–60.

33. Letter from Charles D. Washington, January 21, 1934, WRM; *PWR* 5:459–60.

34. Telegram, on Western Union stationery, WRM; *PWR* 5:461–62.

35. Transcript of radio broadcast, January 28, 1934; March 4, 1934, WRM; *PWR* 5:461–62.

36. *NYT*, November 11, 1923; *WA* 1:148–49.

37. *TDW,* November 29, 1925; *WA* 2:115.

38. *NYT,* August 24, 1924; *WA* 1:279.

39. *NYT,* June 19, 1929; *DT* 2:36.

40. *TDW,* August 23, 1925; *WA* 2:72.

41. Telegram from Louis Howe, WRM; *PWR* 5:496.

42. Upton Beall Sinclair, Jr. (1878–1968). Journalist, Pulitzer Prize–winning author. Born Baltimore. Attended City College of New York at age fourteen, writing novels and magazine articles to pay tuition. In 1904, spent seven weeks undercover in Chicago's meatpacking plants to research fictional muckraker, *The Jungle.* Book caused public uproar and passage of federal Pure Food and Drug Act and Meat Inspection Act. Founded utopian colony in New Jersey. After move to California, ran unsuccessfully as socialist for U.S. House of Representatives (1920), U.S. Senate (1922), and governor (1934). Wrote over ninety books in various genres. (*DAB*)

43. Transcript of radio broadcast, October 14, 1934, WRM; *PWR* 5:510.

44. *TDW,* July 15, 1934; *WA* 6:135.

45. Transcript of radio broadcast, WRM.

46. Letter from Franklin Roosevelt, October 8, 1934; *PWR* 5:508.

47. Schlesinger, *Age of Roosevelt,* 256.

48. *NYT,* January 22, 1935; *DT* 4:241.

49. *NYT,* February 19, 1935.

50. Radio broadcast transcript, WRM; *PWR* 5:234–35; Rollins, *Will Rogers,* 234–35.

51. *NYT,* July 25, 1935.

52. Typewritten speech notes, WRM.

53. Typewritten speech notes, WRM.

54. Jenkins, "Representative Clowns," 81.

55. *TDW,* January 1, 1933; *WA* 5:220.

56. White, *Kingfish,* ix.

57. *NYT,* January 14, 1933; *DT* 3:238.

58. *NYT,* January 29, 1935; *DT* 4:269.

59. *NYT,* February 18, 1933; *DT* 3:277.

60. *Hollywood Citizen News,* January 29, 1935.

61. *NYT,* January 30, 1935; *DT* 4:270.

62. Transcript of radio broadcast, January 27, 1935, WRM.

63. *NYT,* January 17, 1935; *DT* 4:265.

64. *Time,* February 11, 1935.

65. Hull, *The Memoirs of Cordell Hull,* 1:389.

66. Burns, *Roosevelt,* 251; Leuchtenberg, *Franklin D. Roosevelt,* 216; *NYT,* January 30, 1935; *PWR* 5:565.

67. *American Freeman,* Gerard, Kansas, clipping files, WRM.

68. Transcript of radio broadcast, February 3, 1935, WRM; *PWR* 5:569.

69. Telegram from Hearst, January 29, 1935, WRM; *PWR* 5:565–66.

70. *TDW,* October 10, 1934.

71. Helen Richey (1909–1947). Pioneering female aviator, first American woman hired by commercial airline. Born McKeesport, Pennsylvania. Learned to fly at age twenty. In 1932, partnered with Frances Marsalis to set endurance record, staying airborne for nearly ten days with midair refueling. In 1934, hired by Central Airlines as pilot, eventually forced out by all-male pilots union. Flew with the British Air Transport Auxiliary, World War II. (Women in Aviation Resource Center)

72. Alfalfa Club, exclusive Washington DC organization existing only to hold annual banquet in January. Membership, about two hundred, composed of politicians and influential businessmen, including U.S. presidents. Name refers to plant's willingness to do anything for a drink. Activities include playful nomination of presidential candidate. Founded in 1913 to celebrate birthday of Robert E. Lee, did not admit blacks until 1970s and women until 1994.

73. Typewritten speech notes for Alfalfa Club, January 19, 1935, WRM.

74. Letter from Helen Keller, January 17, 1935, WRM.

75. Letter from Roosevelt, ca. January 16, 1935, WRM.

76. Herrmann, *Helen Keller,* 272–73, 368.

77. *TDW,* September 10, 1933; *WA* 6:52.

78. Sterling and Sterling, *Rogers: A Photo-Biography,* 212.

79. Socolofsky, *Arthur Capper,* 216–17.

80. Soviet visa, correspondence file, WRM.

81. Ketchum, *Will Rogers,* 369; *PWR* 5:603–4.

82. *NYT,* August 7, 1935; *DT* 4:342.

83. *NYT,* August 8, 1935; *DT* 4:344.

POSTSCRIPT

1. Memo from Director of Air Commerce Eugene L. Vidal to secretary of commerce, file 835, box 373, National Archives, Washington DC; *Time,* August 26, 1935.

2. *NYT,* August 23, 1935.

3. *PWR* 5:613–15.

4. Robinson, *American Original,* 4.

5. *TDW,* December 18, 1932; *WA* 5:214.

6. Jenkins, "Representative Clowns," 129.

7. Brown, *Imagemaker,* 18; from Hoover speech on NBC, November 19, 1935.

8. Brown, *Imagemaker,* 18; from Hoover speech on NBC, November 19, 1935.

9. A search of War Department intelligence files in the National Archives revealed no mentions of Rogers as a documented source of intelligence.
10. Riedel, "Conversations," 1–2.
11. Riedel, "Conversations," 73.

References

Abend, Hallett. (1943). *My Life in China, 1926–1941*. New York: Harcourt, Brace and Co.

Allen, Frederick Lewis. (1931). *Only Yesterday: An Informal History of the 1920s.* New York: Harper & Row.

Barry, John M. (1997). *Rising Tide: The Great Mississippi Flood of 1927 and How It Changed America.* New York: Simon & Schuster.

Baruch, Bernard M. (1960). *Baruch: The Public Years.* New York: Holt, Rinehart and Winston.

Bates, J. Leonard. (1963). *The Origins of Teapot Dome: Progressives, Parties, and Petroleum, 1909–1921.* Urbana: University of Illinois Press.

Behr, Edward. (1996). *Prohibition: Thirteen Years That Changed America.* New York: Arcade.

Brinkley, Douglas. (2003). *Wheels for the World: Henry Ford, His Company, and a Century of Progress, 1903–2003.* New York: Viking.

Brown, William R. (1970). *Imagemaker: Will Rogers and the American Dream.* Columbia: University of Missouri Press.

Buhite, Russell D. (1973). *Patrick J. Hurley and American Foreign Policy.* Ithaca, NY: Cornell University Press.

Burns, James MacGregor. (1956). *Roosevelt: The Lion and the Fox.* New York: Harcourt and Brace.

Collins, Reba Neighbor. (1967). "Will Rogers, Writer and Journalist." PhD diss., Oklahoma State University.

Combs, James E., and Dan Nimmo. (1996). *The Comedy of Democracy.* Westport, CT: Praeger.

Croy, Homer. (1953). *Our Will Rogers.* New York: Duell, Sloane, and Pearce.

————. (1961). "Will Rogers: Methodist Philosopher." *Together,* September.

Daniels, Jonathan. (1966). *The Time between the Wars: Armistice to Pearl Harbor.* Garden City, NY: Doubleday.

Davis, Burke. (1967). *The Billy Mitchell Affair.* New York: Random House.

Day, Donald. (1962). *Will Rogers: A Biography.* New York: David McKay Co.

Diner, Hasia. (1975). "Teapot Dome, 1924." In *Congress Investigates: A Documented History, 1792–1974,* ed. Arthur M. Schlesinger, Jr., and Roger Bruns. New York: Chelsea House.

Ervin, Spencer. (1935, 1974). *Henry Ford vs. Truman H. Newberry: The Famous Senate Election Contest.* New York: Arno Press.

Gabler, Neal. (2006). *Walt Disney: The Triumph of the American Imagination.* New York: Knopf.

Hays, Will H. (1955). *The Memoirs of Will H. Hays.* Garden City, NY: Doubleday.

Herrmann, Dorothy. (1998). *Helen Keller: A Life.* New York: Knopf.

Hodgson, Godfrey. (1990). *The Colonel: The Life and Wars of Henry Stimson, 1867–1950.* New York: Knopf.

Hull, Cordell. (1948). *The Memoirs of Cordell Hull.* 2 vols. New York: Macmillan.

Jenkins, Ronald Scott. (1984). "Representative Clowns: Comedy and Democracy in America." PhD diss., Harvard University.

Keith, Harold. (1937). *Will Rogers: A Boy's Life.* New York: Thomas Y. Crowell.

Ketchum, Richard M. (1973). *Will Rogers: His Life and Times.* New York: American Heritage Publishing.

Klapp, Orrin E. (January 1954). "The Clever Hero." *Journal of American Folklore* 67, no. 263:21–34.

Kyvig, David E. (2002). *The United States, 1920–1939: Decades of Promise and Pain.* Westport, CT: Greenwood Press.

Lacey, Robert. (1986). *Ford: The Men and the Machine.* Boston: Little, Brown.

Langhorne, Elizabeth. (1974). *Nancy Astor and Her Friends.* New York: Praeger.

Larson, Edward J. (2006). *Summer for the Gods: The Scopes Trial and America's Continuing Debate over Science and Religion.* New York: Basic Books.

Leuchtenburg, William Edward. (1967). *Franklin D. Roosevelt: A Profile.* New York: Hill and Wang.

Lohbeck, Don. (1956). *Patrick J. Hurley.* Chicago: Henry Regnery Co.

Macfarlane, Malcolm. (2001). *Bing Crosby: Day by Day.* Lanham, MD: Scarecrow Press.

MacNeill, Ben Dixon. (1936). "Reminiscences." In *Folks Say of Will Rogers: A Memorial Anecdotage,* ed. William H. Payne and Jake G. Lyons. New York: G. P. Putnam's Sons.

May, Lary. (2000). *The Big Tomorrow: Hollywood and the Politics of the American Way*. Chicago: University of Chicago Press.

McElvaine, Robert S. (1984, 1993). *The Great Depression: America, 1929–1941*. New York: Three Rivers Press.

Mencken, H. L. (1956). *A Carnival of Buncombe: Writings on Politics*. Baltimore: Johns Hopkins University Press.

Miller, Nathan. (2003). *New World Coming: The 1920s and the Making of Modern America*. New York: Scribner.

Milsten, David. (1936). *An Appreciation of Will Rogers*. San Antonio: Naylor Co.

Morris, Sylvia Jukes. (1997). *Rage for Fame: The Ascent of Clare Boothe Luce*. New York: Random House.

Murray, Robert K. (1976). *The 103rd Ballot: Democrats and the Disaster in Madison Square Garden*. New York: Harper & Row.

Neal, Steve. (2004). *Happy Days Are Here Again: The 1932 Democratic Convention, the Emergence of FDR—and How America Was Changed Forever*. New York: William Morrow.

Noggle, Burl. (1962). *Teapot Dome: Oil and Politics in the 1920s*. Baton Rouge: Louisiana State University Press.

O'Brien, P. J. (1935). *Will Rogers: Ambassador of Good Will, Prince of Wit and Wisdom*. Chicago: John C. Winston Co..

Powell, John B. (1945). *My Twenty-five Years in China*. New York: Macmillan.

Riedel, George. (n.d.). "Conversations with Will Rogers: 9 Intimate Days at Sea." Unpublished typewritten manuscript, Will Rogers Memorial, Claremore, OK.

Roach, Samuel Frederick. (1972). "Lariat in the Sun: The Story of Will Rogers." PhD diss., University of Oklahoma.

Robinson, Peter M. (2006). "The Dance of the Comedians: The People, the President, and the Performance of Political Standup Comedy in America." PhD diss., Miami University.

Robinson, Ray. (1996). *American Original: A Life of Will Rogers*. New York: Oxford University Press.

Rogers, Betty. (1943). *Will Rogers: The Story of His Life Told by His Wife*. Garden City, NY: Garden City Publishing.

Rogers, Will. (1917). "The Extemporaneous Line." *Theatre*, July.

———. (1924). *The Illiterate Digest*. Ed. Joseph A. Stout, Jr. Stillwater: Oklahoma State University Press, 1974.

———. (1926). *Letters of a Self-Made Diplomat to His President*. Ed. Joseph A. Stout, Jr., et al. Stillwater: Oklahoma State University Press, 1977.

———. (1927). *There's Not a Bathing Suit in Russia and Other Bare Facts*. Ed. Joseph A. Stout, Jr. Stillwater: Oklahoma State University Press, 1973.

———. (1929). "The Grand Champion." *American Magazine* 108, no. 6 (December): 34–37.

———. (1929). *Ether and Me or "Just Relax."* Rev. ed. Ed. Joseph A. Stout, Jr. Stillwater: Oklahoma State University Press, 1973.

———. (1949). *The Autobiography of Will Rogers.* Boston: Houghton Mifflin.

———. (1975). *Rogers-Isms: The Cowboy Philosopher on Prohibition.* Ed. Joesph A. Stout, Jr. Stillwater: Oklahoma State University Press.

———. (1975). *The Cowboy Philosopher on the Peace Conference.* Ed. Joseph A. Stout, Jr. Stillwater: Oklahoma State University Press.

———. (1976a). *Convention Articles of Will Rogers.* Ed. James A. Stout, Jr., and Peter C. Rollins. Stillwater: Oklahoma State University Press.

———. (1976b). *The Will Rogers Scrapbook.* Ed. Bryan B. Sterling. New York: Bonanza Books.

———. (1979). *The Best of Will Rogers.* Ed. Bryan B. Sterling. New York: Crown Books.

———. (1980). *Will Rogers' Weekly Articles.* 6 vols. Ed. James M. Smallwood and Steven K. Gragert. Stillwater: Oklahoma State University Press.

———. (1982). *More Letters of a Self-Made Diplomat.* Ed. Steven K. Gragert. Stillwater: Oklahoma State University Press.

———. (1978). *Will Rogers' Daily Telegrams.* Vol. 1, *The Coolidge Years: 1926–1929.* Ed. James M. Smallwood and Steven K. Gragert. Stillwater: Oklahoma State University Press.

———. (1978). *Will Rogers' Daily Telegrams.* Vol. 2, *The Hoover Years: 1929–1931.* Ed. James M. Smallwood and Steven K. Gragert. Stillwater: Oklahoma State University Press.

———. (1979). *Will Rogers' Daily Telegrams.* Vol. 3, *The Hoover Years: 1931–1933.* Ed. James M. Smallwood and Steven K. Gragert. Stillwater: Oklahoma State University Press.

———. (1979). *Will Rogers' Daily Telegrams.* Vol. 4, *The Roosevelt Years: 1933–1935.* Ed. James M. Smallwood and Steven K. Gragert. Stillwater: Oklahoma State University Press.

———. (1982). *"He Chews to Run": Will Rogers' Life Magazine Articles, 1928.* Ed. Steven K. Gragert. Stillwater: Oklahoma State University Press.

———. (1983). *The Radio Broadcasts of Will Rogers.* Ed. Steven K. Gragert. Stillwater: Oklahoma State University Press.

———. (1983). *"How to Be Funny" and Other Writings of Will Rogers.* Ed. Steven K. Gragert. Stillwater: Oklahoma State University Press.

———. (1992). *Will Rogers at the Ziegfeld Follies.* Ed. Arthur Frank Wertheim. Norman: University of Oklahoma Press.

———. (1996). *The Papers of Will Rogers.* Vol. 1, *The Early Years: November 1879–April 1904.* Ed. Arthur Frank Wertheim and Barbara Bair. Norman: University of Oklahoma Press.

———. (2000). *The Papers of Will Rogers.* Vol. 2, *Wild West and Vaudeville: April*

1904–September 1908. Ed. Arthur Frank Wertheim and Barbara Bair. Norman: University of Oklahoma Press.

———. (2001). *The Papers of Will Rogers*. Vol. 3, *From Vaudeville to Broadway: September 1908–August 1915*. Ed. Arthur Frank Wertheim and Barbara Bair. Norman: University of Oklahoma Press.

———. (2005). *The Papers of Will Rogers*. Vol. 4, *From the Broadway Stage to the National Stage: September 1915–July 1928*. Ed. Steven K. Gragert and M. Jane Johansson. Norman: University of Oklahoma Press.

———. (2006). *The Papers of Will Rogers*. Vol. 5, *The Final Years, August 1928–August 1935*. Ed. Steven K. Gragert and M. Jane Johansson. Norman: University of Oklahoma Press.

Rollins, Peter C. (1984). *Will Rogers: A Bio-Bibliography*. Westport, CT: Greenwood Press.

Russell, Francis. (1968). *The Shadow of Blooming Grove: Warren G. Harding in His Times*. New York: McGraw-Hill.

Schlesinger, Arthur M., Jr. (1957). *The Age of Roosevelt: The Crisis of the Old Order, 1919–1933*. Boston: Houghton Mifflin.

Simpich, Frederick. (1927). "The Great Mississippi Flood of 1927." *National Geographic*, September, 243–89.

Slayton, Robert A. (2001). *Empire Statesman: The Rise and Redemption of Al Smith*. New York: Free Press.

Snow, Edgar. (1933). *Far Eastern Front*. New York: H. Smith & R. Haas.

Socolofsky, Homer E. (1962). *Arthur Capper: Publisher, Politician, and Philanthropist*. Lawrence: University of Kansas Press.

Sterling, Bryan B., and Frances N. Sterling. (1982). *Will Rogers: Reflections and Observations*. New York: Crown.

———. (1984). *Will Rogers in Hollywood*. New York: Crown.

———. (1999). *Will Rogers: A Photo-Biography*. Dallas: Taylor.

Stratton, David B. (1998). *Tempest over Teapot Dome*. Norman: University of Oklahoma Press.

Swindell, Larry. (1969). *Spencer Tracy: A Biography*. New York: World Publishing Company.

Tebbel, John. (1948). *George Horace Lorimer and the Saturday Evening Post*. Garden City, NY: Doubleday.

Tennen, Steve. (1972). "Will Rogers: An American Performer as an Effective Social Conscience." MA thesis, Brooklyn College.

Thomson, David. (1976). *A Biographical Dictionary of Film*. New York: William Morrow.

Thurber, James. (1958). "State of the Nation's Humor." *New York Times Magazine*, December 7, 26.

Warren, Harris G. (1959). *Herbert Hoover and the Great Depression*. New York: Oxford University Press.

Waters, Marilyn. (1986). "Will Rogers: The Not Always Humorous Columnist." *Media History* 6, no. 1:54–61.

Watts, Steven. (2005). The People's Tycoon: Henry Ford and the American Century. New York: Knopf.

Weaver, John D. (1963). "Bonus March." *American Heritage* 14 (June): 4.

White, Richard D., Jr. (2006). *Kingfish: The Reign of Huey P. Long*. New York: Random House.

Whitney, Richard Merrill. (1924). *Reds in America*. New York: Beckwith Press.

Yagoda, Ben. (1993). *Will Rogers: A Biography*. New York: Knopf.

INDEX

ABOUT THE AUTHOR

RICHARD D. WHITE, JR., a former senior officer in the U.S. Coast Guard and icebreaker captain, received his Ph.D. from Penn State University. The author of *Roosevelt the Reformer: Theodore Roosevelt as Civil Service Commissioner 1889–1895* and *Kingfish: The Reign of Huey P. Long*, he is a professor of public administration and an associate dean at Louisiana State University. He lives in Baton Rouge, Louisiana.